KEYS TO EFFECTIVE LEARNING
DEVELOPING POWERFUL HABITS OF MIND

CAROL CARTER

JOYCE BISHOP

SARAH LYMAN KRAVITS

Custom Edition for Prince George's Community College

Taken from:
Keys to Effective Learning: Developing Powerful Habits of Mind, Fourth Edition
by Carol Carter, Joyce Bishop, and Sarah Lyman Kravits

Taken from:

Keys to Effective Learning: Developing Powerful Habits of Mind, Fourth Edition
by Carol Carter, Joyce Bishop, and Sarah Lyman Kravits
Copyright © 2005, 2002, 2000, 1998 by Pearson Education, Inc.
Published by Prentice Hall
Upper Saddle River, New Jersey 07458

This special edition published in cooperation with Pearson Custom Publishing.

All trademarks, service marks, registered trademarks, and registered service marks are the property of their respective owners and are used herein for identification purposes only.

Printed in the United States of America

10 9 8 7 6 5 4 3 2 1

ISBN 0-536-47468-0

2007420030

KH

Please visit our web site at *www.pearsoncustom.com*

PEARSON CUSTOM PUBLISHING
501 Boylston Street, Suite 900, Boston, MA 02116
A Pearson Education Company

Prince George's Community College

301 Largo Road, Largo, Maryland 20774-2199

Campus Map

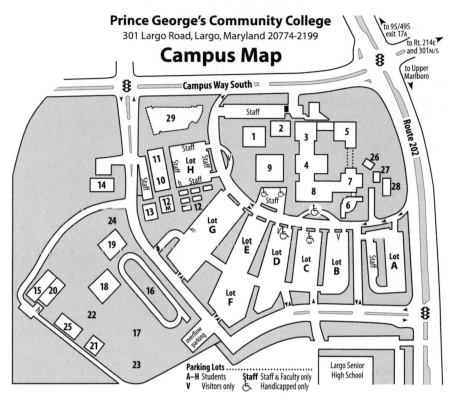

Parking Lots ....
A–H Students   **Staff** Staff & Faculty only
V   Visitors only   ♿ Handicapped only

Directory

1. **Kent Hall**
   Administration
   Continuing Education Offices
2. **Accokeek Hall (Library)**
3. **Bladen Hall**
   Admissions & Records
   Advising/Transfer Services
   Cashier
   Counseling
   Enrollment Services
   Financial Aid Office (FAO)
   Disability Support Services (DDS)
   Health Education Center
       Nurse
   Student Development Resource
       Center (SDRC)
   Recruitment
   Registration—Credit
   Registration—Noncredit Continuing
       Education
   Veterans Services
   Vocational Support Services (VSS)
4. **Bladen Hall**
   Campus Police Substation
   College Lab Services
       Computer Labs

Student Assessment Services
    Testing Center
Tutoring & Writing Centers
5. **Largo Student Center**
   Bookstore
   Campus Dining
   College Life Services
   Community Rooms A, B, C
   Rennie Forum
6. **Chesapeake Hall**
7. **Lanham Hall**
   International Education Center
8. **Marlboro Hall**
   ALANA
   Career/Job Services
   Marlboro Gallery
9. **Queen Anne Fine Arts**
   Hallam Theatre
10. **Novak Field House**
11. **Robert I. Bickford**
    Natatorium
    Pool
    Racquetball Courts
    Weight Room
12. **Temporary Bldgs. #6–17**

12m. **Continuing Education Bldg.**
13. **Steel Bldg.**
14. **Childtime Children's Center**
15. **Facilities Management Bldg.**
    Campus Police
16. **Track/Soccer Field**
17. **Golf Range**
18. **Tennis Courts**
19. **Racquetball Courts**
20. **Auto Bay**
21. **Warehouse**
22. **Baseball Diamond**
23. **Softball Diamond**
24. **Picnic Grove**
25. **Temporaries #1 and 2**
26. **Temporary Bldg. TS**
27. **Temporary Bldg. TO**
28. **Temporary Bldg. TZ**
    Language Studies Lab
29. **New High Technology Center**
    (Expected opening, fall 2007)

**Distance
Learning**

@ Prince George's
Community College

http://www.pgcconline.com

Blackboard Login Instructions

Blackboard is a web-based program that serves as the college's online classroom. You will use Blackboard to communicate with your instructor, to see your course materials, to submit assignments and to discuss course ideas with your classmates.

To login to your Blackboard course, please follow these steps:

∞ Go to the Prince George's Community College Blackboard Web site which is located at http://pgcconline.blackboard.com. *NOTE:* There is no "www" in the Blackboard address.

∞ ALL STUDENTS must login to Blackboard using their myPGCC account.

∞ **If you do not have a myPGCC account,**
   o Go to http://my.pgcc.edu to create a myPGCC account and receive the username and password you need to login to Blackboard.

∞ **If you already have a myPGCC account,**
   o Go to http://my.pgcc.edu to reset your myPGCC password if you created a myPGCC account prior to spring 2005. You must change your password to access Blackboard.

∞ Once you have your myPGCC account information, type it in the Blackboard login box at the http://pgcconline.blackboard.com.

∞ If your login is successful, you will see the Blackboard **"Welcome"** screen. In the box labeled **"My Courses"**, you will see the course or a list of courses in which you are enrolled. Click on the course name to enter your Blackboard course.

Immediately change your Blackboard email address.
To ensure that your instructor can contact you by email, it's VERY important to change your email address as soon as you login to Blackboard for the first time. Here are the steps for changing your Blackboard email address:
1. From YOUR Blackboard Welcome page (you will see **WELCOME**, ___! In bold letters at the top of this page), click on **Personal Information** in the Tools Box on the left side.
2. Click on **Edit Personal Information**.
3. Change your email address to your preferred email address (the one you check the most often).
4. Click the **Submit button** in the lower right corner to save the changes you've made.

Need help?

∞ Questions about myPGCC? View the myPGCC FAQs at http://my.pgcc.edu
∞ Need technical assistance? Visit the Distance Learning Website at http://www.pgcconline.com
∞ Missed the Campus Orientation? View the online orientation at http://www.pgcconline.com/onlineorientation.html
∞ Other questions? E-mail distancelearn@pgcc.edu

PRINCE GEORGE'S
COMMUNITY COLLEGE

Recommended Work/Credit Hours Guidelines

Scheduling Tips

If you are working part time or full time, you should be careful not to register for more courses than you can handle. Time spent in class is only part of the commitment required. You should also consider your work schedule, commuting time to and from school, homework, etc. As a rule, each student should plan to spend an additional two hours of study for each hour spent in class.

IF YOU TAKE	YOU WILL NEED:	WHICH EQUALS:
1 credit/CEUs	2 hours of study time	3 total hours per week
2 credits/CEUs	4 hours of study time	6 total hours per week
3 credits/CEUs	6 hours of study time	9 total hours per week
4 credits/CEUs	8 hours of study time	12 total hours per week
5 credits/CEUs	10 hours of study time	15 total hours per week
6 credits/CEUs	12 hours of study time	18 total hours per week
7 credits/CEUs	14 hours of study time	21 total hours per week
8 credits/CEUs	16 hours of study time	24 total hours per week
9 credits/CEUs	18 hours of study time	27 total hours per week
10 credits/CEUs	20 hours of study time	30 total hours per week
11 credits/CEUs	22 hours of study time	33 total hours per week
12 credits/CEUs	24 hours of study time	40 total hours per week

A General Guide

IF YOU WORK:	WE ADVISE NO MORE THAN:	WHICH EQUALS:
40 or more hours	4 credits/CEUs	1–2 classes
30–35 hours	6 credits/CEUs	2 classes
20–30 hours	6-9 credits/CEUs	2–3 classes
10–20 hours	9-12 credits/CEUs	3–4 classes
Under 10 hours	12–18 credits/CEUs	4 or more classes

I am employed: _____ full-time _____ part-time _____ on-call _____ unemployed

I plan to take _____ credits this semester. (12 credits or CEUs = full time status)

Our mission is to help students know and believe in themselves, successfully retain and use what they learn, and take advantage of resources and opportunities. With these abilities, we are confident that all students can achieve their goals, become lifelong learners, build fruitful and satisfying relationships with others, and experience the challenges and rewards that make life meaningful.

Brief Contents

Contents

Part 1
GETTING READY TO LEARN   1

CHAPTER 1

Welcome to College: Opening Doors   2

CHAPTER 2

Self-Awareness: Knowing How You Learn and What You Value   28

CHAPTER 3

Goal Setting and Time Management: Mapping Your Course   56

CHAPTER 4

Critical and Creative Thinking: Becoming an Active Learner   88

Part II
TARGETING SUCCESS IN SCHOOL   131

Part III
CREATING LIFE SUCCESS   333

NOTE: Every effort has been made to provide accurate and current Internet information in this book. However, the Internet and information posted on it are constantly changing, so it is inevitable that some of the Internet addresses listed in this textbook will change.

My mother didn't have a chance to go to college, and because of this she felt that she wasn't able to pursue her interests at the level she would have liked. Her experience taught me that I would need an education to accomplish what I wanted to do in life.

When I was in college, I was focused on learning and I enjoyed being surrounded by people who were genuinely interested in so many things that I had never thought about before. However, I'm not sure I was able to balance my life as well as I might have. Studying took an overwhelming amount of time when I was in college, and I never managed to participate in other things that would have enhanced my experience. That's how something as simple as knowing how to set goals and manage your time can make a big difference in how well you're able to take advantage of what college has to offer.

If my college had offered a study skills class where I could have read a book like *Keys to Effective Learning*, I would have benefited in at least two ways. One, I would have learned important day-to-day success skills—every student can become more successful with advice on topics like how to take notes, knowing your learning style, setting goals, and managing time. Two, I would have gained more insight into myself and my path. Right now I'm a biology researcher, and although I find it interesting, I have come to realize that I need more of a creative outlet and a more direct sense of making the world a better place. If I had read the chapter on self-awareness, it would have helped me gain insight on multiple intelligences that I happened to overlook, like my artistic side.

One of the most crucial messages of *Keys to Effective Learning* is to live your life intentionally—to first of all have foresight and then take the time to choose a goal, create a plan, and follow through with it. If you take advantage of the insight offered here, you will have the tools that you need to achieve your most ideal goals. If I had developed more awareness of my goals, values, and learning style, I think I would have made different choices. I consider my involvement in this book a first step in that direction.

When you read *Keys to Effective Learning*, you will find that school, career, and life success are interrelated. If you follow your heart and commit to making the time to do what you love, not just in class but outside as well, then success in your career will follow. I consider it a privilege to have been involved in this book, and I plan on passing my new knowledge on to my four younger siblings. I am sure that the skills that I have learned will benefit me greatly as I strive to grow my career and create the life I want to live.

Athena Dodd

GRADUATE EDITOR, REED COLLEGE
Athena.Dodd@Colorado.edu

In today's world a college education is a necessity if you want to be successful. One of the reasons I took the initiative to attend college is that I've seen so many of my family members with incredible potential but no credentials to take them to that next step. Also, as a student–athlete, I am attending college in part to set myself apart and to get away from the stereotypes surrounding athletes. Being able to attain a high GPA while participating in a sport at college seemed to be something that not too many teachers or coaches expected, so I see that as a challenge to myself to stand out.

I am a double major in business management and marketing. One of my biggest challenges in college is to adjust to having to do homework on my own time in order to prepare for tests. In high school I was used to having homework assignments that were geared toward helping me prepare for the test, whereas in college it is a different story. Working with *Keys to Effective Learning*, I have found tools and strategies to help me on this issue and many others. The exercises help me to analyze and get to know myself better; the Habits of Mind help me to see how I can use the material in the real world as opposed to just learning it for a test and then forgetting it the next day. Putting material to use while it is fresh in your mind will maximize the effectiveness of your learning.

As a senior, I realize now that it's never too soon to start preparing yourself for the real world. Consider adding a minor or additional major that expands your horizons. Talk to professors and turn them into your friends—they were, or still are, in your major field, and they might be willing to help you come graduation time. Also, go to class—the more your professors see your face, the more willing they will be to help you. By helping you to make these ideas part of your college experience, *Keys to Effective Learning* will help you face the real world with confidence when you graduate.

As you read this book, you will gradually come into the state of mind that you need in order to succeed in college. You will have to think about life decisions—majors and other goals—that you may not be too sure about. You will analyze yourself while preparing for what's ahead. You will cover all of the main topics that a student is going to encounter in the first year of college life. *Keys to Effective Learning* gets straight to the point—this book will help you to make the most of your time and follow your passion in college and beyond.

Lee Patterson

STUDENT EDITOR, THE UNIVERSITY OF ARIZONA
Stickhp_1430@yahoo.com

Students and professors have consistently praised the thorough coverage of study skills and strategies in *Keys to Effective Learning*. In this edition, we have built upon these strengths to cover three main ways for students to achieve their best as learners.

1. Managing yourself effectively
2. Putting knowledge into action
3. Taking initiative on your own behalf

Build Habits of Mind: Tools for Self-Management

Developed by educator Arthur Costa, who was intrigued by how successful students work through problems, the **Habits of Mind** are problem-solving attitudes and approaches that are transferable to all kinds of problems. Each chapter features a different Habit and shows you how to use it to enhance and actively apply the chapter material. When you complete the text, you will have twelve positive Habits that will help you to manage yourself successfully, enabling you to become a better problem solver and more successful learner.

Turn Knowledge into Action: Active Learning Exercises

We frequently learn information in the moment—and then, after the test or the course is over, we might forget it quickly if not forever. The best learning is the learning that you keep with you so that you can *use* it. The exercises in this book will help you solidify what you learn by putting your knowledge to work:

- *Take Action.* New to this edition, Take Action exercises provide the opportunity to use what you just learned to explore diverse topics such as your college's academic integrity policy and financial aid deadlines and your personal test-taking strategies. Three Take Action exercises appear in every chapter.
- *Critical Thinking: Applying Learning to Life.* You will apply critical thinking to chapter topics. Developing a habit of critical thinking will bring you success in all of your academic courses.

- *Teamwork: Collaborative Solutions.* You will interact and learn in a group setting, building your teamwork and leadership skills in the process.
- *Personal Improvement Plan.* You select the chapter strategies that mean something to you and design a detailed plan for using one of them to improve your skills.

Taking Initiative on Your Own Behalf: Resources and People

You are your own best advocate. As a freshman, you will need to recruit the resources of people who can help you. The following features help you to make and use these vital connections:

- *Quick Start to College "Prependix."* College success depends, in part, on making a rapid adjustment to a new environment. Quick Start will introduce you to information and requirements you will need to know, and resources you will need to access, in your first weeks of school.
- *Survival Checklist.* On a pullout card in the front of the book, you will find a Survival Checklist on which to write all the important course information you will need this semester—including course names and locations, how to contact the instructors, required texts, and syllabi. Carrying this card with you makes this information available anytime you need it.

Your Future–Your Choice

Choosing to commit to this course, this book, your instructor, and most of all yourself will strengthen your mind and skills for college and beyond. Your perseverance makes all the difference for your future. Your success is in your hands.

Students and instructors. Many of our best suggestions have come from you. Send your questions, comments, and ideas about *Keys to Effective Learning* to Carol Carter at caroljcarter@lifebound.com. We look forward to hearing from you, and we are grateful for the opportunity to work with you.

Features to Help You Succeed

- *Study Skills Material.* Chapters on reading and studying (5), listening and memory (6), note taking (7), test taking (8), and writing and researching (10) provide practical skill-building strategies useful in every one of your college courses. Since math and science are so important to success in the 21st century, a chapter on quantitative learning (9) presents basic problem-solving approaches and helps you conquer math anxiety, especially in testing situations.
- *Learning Styles.* When you know how you learn, you can choose learning strategies that maximize your unique skills. In Chapter 2 you will develop a picture of your learning styles through two

complementary assessments. In each of the chapters that follow, a Multiple Intelligences grid provides helpful strategies, linked to individual intelligences, for learning that chapter's material.

- *Creative and Critical Thinking Focus.* Thinking creatively and critically will boost comprehension and problem-solving abilities. Chapter 4 inspires your creativity and critical-thinking skills, and subsequent chapters connect study skills material to critical thinking.

- *Profiles in Success.* To inspire motivation, this text profiles courageous role models. The *Rising to the Challenge* profiles in each chapter feature a real-life story of a person who overcame difficult circumstances in the pursuit of education and fulfillment. The *Success Breakthrough* profiles at the end of each part feature stories of famous people who have achieved despite intense challenges.

- *Reflect & Respond Journal Questions.* Look for the *Reflect & Respond* box to appear three times in every chapter, at various points within the chapter text. Each journal question provides a different opportunity to reflect on chapter material and respond in writing using the "Reflect & Respond" module on the Companion Website.

- *Thinking It Through Checklist.* Checking off the ideas you can relate to encourages you to begin to connect your current knowledge and attitudes with what you will read in the chapter.

- *End-of-Part Exercises: Becoming a Better Test Taker.* This feature tests you on material from the chapters in each part, using multiple-choice, fill-in-the-blank, and essay questions. The objective questions help you make connections among material from different chapters, and the essay questions encourage you to develop new ideas.

New to This Edition

- Quick Start to College "Prependix"
- Expanded discussion of academic integrity (Chapter 1)
- Expanded discussion of values (Chapter 2)
- Expanded discussion of choosing a major (Chapter 3)
- Revised critical-thinking chapter with an enhanced focus on creative thinking (Chapter 4)
- Study-skills segments updated and refocused on the most useful strategies (Chapters 5 through 10)
- An independent chapter on note taking (Chapter 7)
- A variety of test questions in different disciplines (Chapter 8)
- A revised, improved chapter on writing and research, including new Internet research strategies (Chapter 10)
- Added material on plagiarism (Chapter 10)
- Multiple Intelligence grids
- Take Action exercises
- Reflect & Respond journal questions
- Personal Improvement Plan exercises
- Becoming a Better Test Taker questions

ACKNOWLEDGMENTS

The revision of *Keys to Effective Learning* involved many people to whom we owe a debt of gratitude. We could not have made the major improvements in our text without the help of the following people:

- Our graduate student editors, Athena Dodd and Lee Patterson, and student reviewers. Special thanks to Athena for her detailed work on chapters, reviews, and personal profiles.

- Our reviewers: Erskine P. Ausbrooks III, Dyersburg State Community College; Linda Blair, Pellissippi State Technical Community College; Rhonda Carroll, Pulaski Technical College; Katherine Erdman, South Dakota State University; Jo Ella Fields, Oklahoma State University, Oklahoma City; Carlesa Ramere Finney, Anne Arundel Community College; Vesna Hampel, University of Minnesota, Twin Cities; Gary G. John, Richland College; Deborah Kimbrough-Lowe, Nassau Community College; Heidi Koring, Lynchburg College; Kathie Morris, Edison Community College; Linda Qualia, Colin County Community College; Laura Reynolds, Fayetteville Technical Community College; Mary Rider, Grossmont College; Maria D. Salinas, Del Mar College; Lisa Taylor-Galizia, Carteret Community College; Karen N. Valencia, South Texas Community College; Peggy Walton, Howard Community College; Mary Walz-Chojnacki, University of Wisconsin-Milwaukee; Patricia Wright, Lenoir Community College; and Leesa Young, Asheville Buncombe Technical Community College.

- Previous edition reviewers: Glenda Belote, Florida International University; John Bennett, Jr., University of Connecticut; Ann Bingham-Newman, California State University–LA; Mary Bixby, University of Missouri–Columbia; Barbara Blandford, Education Enhancement Center at Lawrenceville, NJ; Jerry Bouchie, St. Cloud State University; Mona Casady, SW Missouri State University; Janet Cutshall, Sussex County Community College; Marie Davis-Heim, Mississippi Gulf Coast Community College; Valerie DeAngelis, Miami-Dade Community College; Rita Delude, NH Community Technical College; Judy Elsley, Weber State University in Utah; Kathie Erdman, South Dakota State University; Sue Halter, Delgado Community College in Louisiana; Suzy Hampton, University of Montana; Maureen Hurley, University of Missouri–Kansas City; Karen Iversen, Heald Colleges; Kathryn K. Kelly, St. Cloud State University; Nancy Kosmicke, Mesa State College in Colorado, Frank T. Lyman, Jr., University of Maryland; Jo McEwan, Fayetteville Technical Community College; Barnette Miller Moore, Indian River Community College in Florida; Rebecca Munro, Gonzaga University in Washington; Virginia Phares, DeVry of Atlanta; Brenda Prinzavalli, Beloit College in Wisconsin; Laura Reynolds, Fayetteville

Technical Community College; Tina Royal, Fayetteville Technical Community College; Jacqueline Simon, Education Enhancement Center at Lawrenceville, NJ; Carolyn Smith, University of Southern Indiana; Joan Stottlemyer, Carroll College in Montana; Thomas Tyson, SUNY Stony Brook; Mary Walkz-Chojnacki, University of Wisconsin at Milwaukee; Rose Wassman, DeAnza College in California; Michelle G. Wolf, Florida Southern College.

- Art Costa, for his insights that led to the development of the Habits of Mind and for his generosity in permitting us to use the Habits as a cornerstone of the fourth edition. Also Art's editor Nancy Modrak at ASCD for her endorsement of this collaboration.

- Editorial consultant Rich Bucher, professor of sociology at Baltimore City Community College, for his advice and consultation on diversity.

- Dr. Frank T. Lyman for his generous permission to use and adapt his Thinktrix system.

- Those who contributed stories for the Rising to the Challenge features: Dr. Baruj Benacerraf, Joyce Bishop, Richard Branson, Chip Case, Carly Eckart, Kevin Leman, Gustavo Minaya, Uriel Portillo, Tiffany Robertson, Michael Sanders, and Scott Stoffel.

- Erica Thode for her work on symposium events; and Kate Lareau, Sue Bierman, Kathleen Cole, Jackie Fitzgerald, Jordan Austin, and Cynthia Nordberg for invaluable assistance.

- Those who worked on the Instructor's Manual for this text: Linda Blair, Pellissippi State Technical Community College; Karyn Schulz, CCBC Dundalk; Heidi Koring, Lynchburg College; and Mary Rider, Grossmont College.

- Sande Johnson, Senior Acquisitions Editor, and Cecilia Johnson for their hard work and insight throughout the course of the revision.

- Vice President and Executive Publisher Jeff Johnston; President of Career, Health, Education, and Technology division Robin Baliszewski; and President and CEO of Pearson Technology Group Gary June, for their interest, commitment, and leadership with the Student Success list.

- Our production team, especially Gay Pauley, JoEllen Gohr, Pam Bennett, and Carlisle Communications.

- Our marketing gurus—especially Marketing Manager Eric Murray and Director of Marketing Ann Davis—as well as the Prentice Hall representatives and the management team led by David Gillespie.

- Our families and friends, for their support and encouragement.

- Special thanks to Judy Block, whose research, writing work, and editing suggestions on the text as a whole were essential and invaluable.

Finally, thanks to the students and instructors who have shared their ideas, especially our current adopters, too many to name, whose candid feedback continues to fuel our improvements. Joyce Bishop, in particular, would like to thank the thousands of students who have allowed her, as their professor, the privilege of sharing part of their journey through college. Thanks to all our readers for giving us the chance to travel with you on your educational journey.

About the Authors

Carol Carter is founder of Lifebound: Seminars, Coaching and Resources for high school and college students. She has written *Majoring in the Rest of Your Life: Career Secrets for College Students* and *Majoring in High School*. She has also co-authored *Keys to Preparing for College, Keys to College Studying, The Career Tool Kit, Keys to Career Success, Keys to Study Skills, Keys to Thinking and Learning,* and *Keys to Success.* Carol has taught classes for high school and college students and has conducted workshops for students and faculty around the country. She has also taught classes for welfare-to-work programs, for Native Americans, and for those making the transition from correctional facilities. She is the host of the Keys to Lifelong Learning Telecourse, a 26-episode telecourse to help students at a distance prepare for college, career, and life success. In addition to working with students of all ages, Carol thrives on foreign travel and culture; she has been fortunate enough to have been a guest in more than 40 foreign countries. Please visit her website and write her at www.lifebound.com.

Joyce Bishop holds a Ph.D. in psychology and has taught for more than 20 years, receiving a number of honors, including Teacher of the Year for 1995 and 2000. For five years she has been voted "favorite teacher" by the student body and Honor Society at Golden West College, Huntington Beach, CA, where she has taught since 1987 and is a tenured professor. She has worked with a federal grant to establish Learning Communities and Workplace Learning in her district, and has developed workshops and trained faculty in cooperative learning, active learning, Multiple Intelligences, workplace relevancy, learning styles, authentic assessment, team building, and the development of learning communities. She currently teaches online and multimedia classes and trains other faculty to teach online in her district and region of 21 colleges. She also co-authored *Keys to College Studying, Keys to Success, Keys to Thinking and Learning,* and *Keys to Study Skills.* Joyce is the lead academic of the Keys to Lifelong Learning Telecourse, distributed by Dallas Telelearning.

Sarah Lyman Kravits comes from a family of educators and has long cultivated an interest in educational development. She co-authored *Keys to College Studying, The Career Tool Kit, Keys to Success, Keys to Thinking and Learning*, and *Keys to Study Skills* and has served as Program Director for LifeSkills, Inc., a nonprofit organization that aims to further the career and personal development of high school students. In that capacity she helped to formulate both curricular and organizational elements of the program, working closely with instructors as well as members of the business community. She has also given faculty workshops in critical thinking, based on the Thinktrix critical-thinking system. Sarah holds a B.A. in English and drama from the University of Virginia, where she was a Jefferson Scholar, and an M.F.A. from Catholic University.

Instructor's Manual

Contains an abundance of useful materials to assist you in teaching student orientation or student success courses. Organized according to the objectives and lessons of each chapter, the IM includes class activities, Test Item File questions, pre- and post-class evaluations, lecture guides, and excerpts from specialists on a variety of topics, including Habits of Mind, multiple intelligences, learning communities, and the Web.

PowerPoint Transparencies

PowerPoint Transparencies relate directly to the course lecture material and help focus students on key objectives. Included are slides that enhance the text discussion of thinking, psychology of adjustment, leadership, diversity in the business world, and more. *(Available on www.prenhall.com/success under "Faculty Lounge.")*

Faculty Development Video Series*

1. Stress Management and Communication in a Diverse World (0–13–099578–9)
2. Critical Thinking in Today's Curriculum (0–13–099432–4)
3. Teaching Training Video (0–13–917205–X)

Student Key Advice Video* (0–13–233206–X)

Brief segments showcasing motivational tips and advice by first-year through fourth-year college students and professionals in a variety of areas.

Study Skills Video* (0–13–096095–0)

Features professional instruction on study skills and note taking, critical thinking, and school-to-work tips.

*Free to qualifying adopters

Student Success Reference Library

Valued at $100 each, this series of 13 videos features nationally known experts from across the curriculum. As an adopter of *Keys to Effective Learning,* you are eligible for one complete video sct—containing the Life Skills Video Pack, the Study Skills Video Pack, and the Career Skills Video Pack—per every 100 students enrolled in your course. Contact your local Prentice Hall representative to order.

Life Skills Video Pack (0–13–127079–6)

1. Learning Styles and Self-Awareness
2. Critical and Creative Thinking
3. Relating to Others
4. Personal Wellness

Study Skills Video Pack (0–13–127080-X)

1. Reading Effectively
2. Listening and Memory
3. Note Taking and Research
4. Writing Effectively
5. Effective Test Taking
6. Goal Setting and Time Management

Career Skills Video Pack (0–13–118529–2)

1. Skills for the 21st Century—Technology
2. Skills for the 21st Century—Math and Science
3. Managing Career and Money

ABC News Video Library (0–13–031901–5)

This unique video library contains brief (5–30 minutes long) segments from award-winning ABC News programs, such as *20/20* and *World News Tonight*. This innovative resource provides a connection between student success and the real world. Subjects include:

1. Hate & the Internet: Racism & Free Speech (21:31)
2. Cedrick's Journey: Inner City Students Become "Undercover Honor Students" (21:20)
3. American Media in Black & White: Children, Race & TV (21:37)
4. Violence Against Women (3:44)
5. The Latin Kings: Can They Be Trusted? Gang Reform (21:35)
6. Before It's Too Late: Predictors of Violence (27:37)
7. Failing Grades: Learning, Teaching & Success (10:00)
8. Eat, Drink & Be Wary: Why Alcohol Affects Women Differently Than Men (11:44)

9. A Sea of Alcohol: Fraternities & Hazing (13:42)

10. Jimmy Carter & Colin Powell Want You: Volunteerism (21:53)

11. Social Promotion in Public Schools (6:09)

12. Technology Revolution (4:43)

13. The Rules: Sexual Harassment (21:31)

14. Making Sense (4:52)

15. Caring for the Elderly or Disabled Relative at Home (4:57)

16. Emotional IQ (12:50)

Total running time approximately 200 minutes.

Prentice Hall Supersite—Faculty Lounge*

www.prenhall.com/success

Redesigned website offers a variety of resources for faculty under the Faculty Lounge area, including sample syllabi, supplement information, PowerPoint® slides, available speakers, conference schedules, and relevant articles.

Responding to Hate at School*

This supplement for teachers, produced by the Southern Poverty Law Center, provides a number of in-class activities and homework assignments to turn the tide of hate and prejudice to tolerance and open-mindedness among students.

RESPONDING to HATE at SCHOOL
A GUIDE for TEACHERS, COUNSELORS and ADMINISTRATORS
PUBLISHED by TEACHING TOLERANCE

* Free to qualifying adopters

Keys to Servicing Program

FREE Consultation/Class Development

Authors Dr. Joyce Bishop, Carol Carter, and Sarah Lyman Kravits are available to assist you with syllabus preparation, teaching on-line students, coaching students, and any other class development goals you and your staff have. If you need tips on how to integrate the Prentice Hall package, use the Companion Website, or implement any other part of the book or package, let us know.

To arrange for a consultation, contact your local Prentice Hall representative or contact the authors directly at (303)542–1811 or **caroljcarter@lifebound.com**.

In-Services at Your School

Seminars. For qualified adopters, our authors or trainers will come to your campus for a seminar with your staff. We will work closely with you to determine goals and objectives, and to overcome challenges your faculty may face when teaching first-year students. This is a collaborative process designed specifically with the needs of your faculty and students in mind.

Symposia. Prentice Hall also offers regional symposia and other events to help service the need for training and development. Workshop topics focus on techniques and tools that will promote effective teaching and learning. Please see your local representative for details. Conference schedule also appears on the Faculty Lounge section of the website (www.prenhall.com/success/FacultyRes/index.html). See the facing page for a list of suggested program topics.

Faculty Training in Denver, *SEMI-ANNUALLY*

In December and July each year, the authors give a two-day faculty training. This workshop offers an opportunity to learn in-depth strategy and methods for motivating and connecting with your staff and students. The authors also accept submissions if you are interested in facilitating one of the sessions. You can download all current information each semester from the Lifebound website at www.lifebound.com. Click on Faculty Training Course for registration and details.

The fee of $295 is waived for users of *Keys* products.

Specialty PowerPoint Presentations, *KEYS TO TEACHING SERIES*

(0–13–118800–3)

The authors have developed a series of PowerPoint resources available to adopters license-free while the book is in use at your school. Each school will be provided with a master copy from which others can be made as long as the text is in use.

Facilitator Workshop/ Professional Development

We will create a day of presentations based on your needs as a staff. If you would like to see workshops on topics not listed here, contact your representative; we will be glad to customize a workshop according to your request.

Motivating At-Risk Students

Connecting college to future life goals

Setting Goals and Expectations for Students

Gauging and evaluating student success

Developing a Positive Teacher-Student Relationship

How to have authority and still be personable and approachable

Climbing Out of the Box

Using different teaching techniques to enliven the classroom experience

Dealing with Diverse Populations

How to encourage students from all ages, stages, and backgrounds

Teaching Responsibility, Ethics, Values, and Citizenship

Creating tomorrow's leaders and doers

Collaborative Learning and Critical Thinking

Connecting both strategies for students in class

Using Popular Culture to Teach Student Success

Helping students understand themselves and the issues of their world through music, movies, magazines, and media

Multiple Intelligences

Based on Howard Gardner's research, this workshop emphasizes several assessments to help students understand their learning strengths and weaknesses

What Employers Look for in the People They Hire

Using education and personal abilities to prepare for success out of college

Have You Thought About Customizing This Book?
Pearson Custom (Database Program)

WWW.PEARSONCUSTOM.COM/DATABASE/FRESHMAN.HTML

The Custom Program allows you to choose chapters from any text in the *Keys to Success* series and create your own custom books. You decide the order of the chapters and include handouts or a chapter of your own material to make the custom book more applicable to your school and students.

FEATURES:

- **Customized Cover**—Your book will have a four-color cover and title page with your name, school, department, and course name.
- **Customized Pagination**—Table of Contents, chapters, exercises, and questions renumbered to reflect your custom organization, plus sequential pagination throughout the text.
- **Flexibility**—You can revise and update your book every semester to suit your changing course needs.
- **Instructional Support**—You will receive desk copies of your custom book and have access to all of the instructor's materials that accompany the traditional textbook. Your book will also have a full glossary.
- **Cost Savings**—Your students pay only for material they use.
- **Quick Turnaround**—You can have your custom text published in only 4–6 weeks from the time we receive your order from the bookstore.
- **Tear-out Pages**—Pages are perforated just like the text.
- **The book pages are black and white** and include all photos and charts from the Prentice Hall book.
- **Choose chapters from:**

  Keys to Success   *Keys to Career Success*
  Keys to Effective Learning   *Keys Reader*

Pricing and Ordering Information

- $2.50 for each chapter.
- Minimum length is 5 chapters ($12.50).
- Add $10 per page for professor's own material.
- Charges for outside readings requiring permissions will be added to the final book price.
- Minimum new order is 25 copies—minimum reorder is 10 copies, with reprints available in 7–10 days.

- Book ready in 4–6 weeks.
- Book can be shrink-wrapped with other Pearson textbooks for a 10% discount.
- For more information call 1–800–777–6872 or e-mail: dbase.pub@pearsoncustom.com

Student Success Supersite

www.prenhall.com/success

The Student Success Supersite contains a wealth of information for students interested in exploring different majors, career questions, resources for improving study strategies, concerns about financial planning, and more. This site is a free service to enhance the materials purchased for your class.

Prentice Hall Student Planner* (Newly Revised) (0–13–117386–3)

This tool includes a daily and a monthly planner, an address book, course and class planners, grade calculators, and other organizing materials. This planner is designed to help students organize and manage their time more effectively.

Student Reflection Journal* (Newly Revised) (0–13–113130–3)

Through this vehicle, students are encouraged to track their progress and share their insights, thoughts, and concerns.

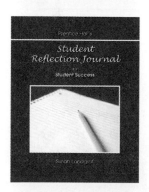

Ten Ways to Fight Hate* (0–13–028146–8)

This supplement, produced by the Southern Poverty Law Center, helps students to deal proactively with hate and prejudice within themselves and others.

* Available free when packaged with a text.

CD-ROM Shrink-Wrap Options

Strategies for Success CD-ROM: An Interactive Approach (0–13–061807–1) $5

With an emphasis on active learning, this interactive CD-ROM guides students through 18 of the most essential topics for student success (see the list below). Each topic includes these features:

- Pre- and post-assessment
- Video segments with reflective questions
- Meaningful text that explains the topic
- Thought-provoking activities that extend the content

Topics:	Creative Thinking	Relating to Others
Where Are You Now?	Listening Effectively	Research
Time Management/ Goal Setting	Reading Effectively	Managing Your Career
	Managing Your Money	Writing
Personal Wellness	Note Taking	Skills for the 21st Century:
Critical Thinking	Effective Test Taking	Technology, Math, Science

Career Visions CD-ROM (0–13–092276–5) $5

Career Visions is a set of modules that matches skills and interests with occupations. Students will learn more about occupations that interest them. As a student works through this innovative software program, it automatically builds a career plan for him or her.

- *Exploring Work:* Enables students to visit over 650 different occupations and discover connections between their personality traits and various jobs.
- *Workomatic:* Helps students identify occupations that match their goals and abilities.
- *Career Skills:* Allows students to select 35 work-related skills and find occupational matches.

Prentice Hall Self-Assessment Library (0–13–144713–0) $5

- Easy to use
- Provides instant feedback on more than 45 assessments
- Helps students learn more about themselves and how they relate to others
- The three categories ("What about me?" "Working with others," and "Life in organizations") will provide students with insights they will need to be successful in the business world.

These CD-ROMs, individually valued at over $50, are available for the prices listed above when shrink-wrapped with Keys to Effective Learning.

Text Companion Website

www.prenhall.com/carter

KEYS TO EFFECTIVE LEARNING
Fourth Edition

Carol Carter, Joyce Bishop, and Sarah Lyman Kravits

This site provides students using *Keys to Effective Learning,* Fourth Edition, by Carol Carter, Joyce Bishop, and Sarah Lyman Kravits, with a wealth of resources. Here students can review chapter content by viewing the **Objectives** for each chapter. Students can also test their knowledge by taking **Multiple Choice**, **True-False**, and **Essay** self-quizzes.

A list of **Web Destinations** for each chapter, coupled with a link to the Pearson Education **Learning Network**, provide students with vast web resources to aid in their understanding and application of content. In addition, users will find **Message Board** and **Chat Room** features that allow them to communicate with students and professors nationwide about pertinent topics and issues. Finally, for professors, there is a **Syllabus Manager** feature that allows them to create and modify an online syllabus for their courses.

Select a chapter:
4: Critical and Creative Thinking: Becoming

Keys to Effective Learning, Fourth Edition, offers a truly integrated technology solution, a text-specific Companion Website, and options to take the course completely online.

The Companion Website has instant scoring for multiple-choice quizzes. Answers to essay questions can be sent via email to the professor. Links to related sites and additional articles are also available in each chapter.

Link each chapter of *Keys to Effective Learning* to the rich resources found on the Internet! Whether you will test your students' knowledge through chapter-specific self-grading quizzes or have your students explore issues, these easy-to-use resources provide a fun and dynamic environment for learning.

Chapter 4: Critical and Creative Thinking: Becoming an Active Learner
Objectives

In this chapter, you will explore answers to the following questions:

- What is critical thinking?
- How does critical thinking help you solve problems and make decisions?
- How do you construct and evaluate arguments?
- How do you think logically?
- Why should you explore perspectives?
- Why plan strategically?
- How can you develop your creativity?
- What is media literacy?

Add Additional Value for Your Students!

Penguin Putnam Partnership

The following books are available at a 65% discount when used in conjunction with *Keys to Effective Learning*.

Who Moved My Cheese? by Spencer Johnson
0–13–111760–2 ($7 net)

Beat Procrastination and Make the Grade by Dr. Linda Sapadin
0–13–111756–4 ($4.25 net)

Once Upon a Time When We Were Colored by Clifton Taulbert
0–13–111759–9 ($4 net)

Lives on the Boundary by Mike Rose
0–13–111761–0 ($4.75 net)

Successful Intelligence by Robert Sternberg
0–13–111763–7 ($5 net)

The Color of Water by James McBride
0–13–111762–9 ($5 net)

Amusing Ourselves to Death by Neil Postman
0–13–111757–2 ($5 net)

Eight Habits of the Heart by Clifton Taulbert
0–13–142123–9 ($3.85 net)

The Lakota Way by Joseph M. Marshall
0–13–114346–8 ($4.90 net)

To add other books to the Penguin list, contact editor Sande Johnson (sande_johnson@prenhall.com).

The Essential Managers Series

This pocketbook series offers short booklets (less than 100 pages) of practical techniques to show you how to increase production and job satisfaction, empower individuals, and reward achievement. Each booklet includes exercises and questionnaires that encourage self-assessment and analysis to improve work skills.

Making Presentations by Tim Hindle 0–13–114687–4

Reducing Stress by Tim Hindle 0–13–114689–0

Dealing with Difficult People by Christina Osborne 0–13–114690–4

Increasing Confidence by Philippa Davies 0–13–114691–2

Balancing Work and Life by Robert Holden & Ben Renshaw 0–13–114693–9

Achieving Excellence by Robert Heller 0–13–114692–0

Booklets are available for $2 each.

Learning and Study Strategies Inventory (LASSI), Second Edition (0–13–114959–8)

To succeed in college, students need effective cognitive and learning strategies, meaningful goals, self-generated motivation, and a systematic approach to studying. LASSI is a reliable and valid self-report measure of ten scales assessing students' preparation in these areas:

- Attitude
- Motivation
- Time Management
- Anxiety
- Concentration
- Information Processing
- Selecting Main Ideas
- Study Aids
- Self-Testing
- Test Strategies

THE LASSI:

- gives normed diagnostic information about a student's strengths and weaknesses in college preparedness.
- can improve student retention by providing a basis for group or individual interventions.
- promotes students' responsibility for their performance.

It is recommended to use one LASSI at the beginning of the course and one at the end for optimal results. (*80 items. Available online or paper and pencil. Packaged with book for a discount.* Single copy paper, 0–13–114959–8; Single copy online, 0–13–028712–1; pre- & post-online, 0–13–029160–9.)

Inventory of Classroom Style and Skills (INCLASS) (0–13–089860–0)

INCLASS is a self-assessment instrument designed to help students, teachers, advisors, and counselors explore the underlying behaviors that influence a student's success in the classroom. It is diagnostic and prescriptive, and can be used to develop instructional and other interventions for students likely to have behavior patterns that might interfere with learning. It examines a student's proficiency in several competencies that directly relate to how that student approaches studying, homework, test taking, class projects, attendance, time management, and class participation. Areas assessed include:

- Interest in lifelong learning
- Commitment to quality
- Responsibility for work
- Persistence
- Working in teams
- Solving problems

(*40 items. Available online or paper and pencil. Packaged with book for a discount.*)

PEEK: Perceptions, Expectations, Emotions, and Knowledge About College (0–13–028712–1)

There are many differences between high school and college, and research has shown that students' expectations and perceptions of these changes can be a major factor in determining their success at negotiating the college environment. The PEEK is a brief 30-item self-report measure that assesses students' expectations in three different clusters: their personal, academic, and social environment. The WEB PEEK enables administrators to learn about their students before they ever arrive on campus. *(30 items. Online only.)*

The Retention Management System

Motivated by a commitment to improving student retention and overall success, Prentice Hall and Noel-Levitz are delighted to announce our newly formed alliance.

A Proactive Approach to Student Success and Retention

The Retention Management System™ (RMS) by Noel-Levitz is a comprehensive early-alert and intervention program, designed to enable institutions to:

1. Assess students' individual academic and personal needs.
2. Recognize students' specific strengths and coping mechanisms so that successful intervention techniques in areas of need can be implemented.
3. Identify students who are at risk for academic and/or personal difficulties and who may even drop out.
4. Understand students' attitudes and motivational patterns so that intervention is more successful.
5. Enable advisors to have effective and rewarding personal contact with students early in the first term.

System Components

Perhaps the most distinctive feature of the RMS Advisor/Counselor Report™ is the Summary of Academic Motivation. The summary information (which is not listed on the student report) includes an assessment of a student's:

- Dropout proneness
- Predicted academic difficulty
- Educational stress
- Receptivity to institutional help

Seven specific recommendations for each student are listed in the RMS Advisor/Counselor Report, ranging from suggestions to "get help with writing skills," to "discuss emotional tensions with a counselor." The strength of each recommendation is indicated by its priority score in parentheses.

In addition, 19 motivational scales (including openness, family emotional support, desire to finish college, intellectual interests, study habits, career planning, self-reliance) are reported in two ways: as a visual profile and in a percentile rank. The 19 scales are organized under five main categories:

1. Academic motivation
2. Social motivation
3. General coping skills
4. Receptivity to support services
5. Initial impression

The RMS Summary and Planning Report™ is a tool for campuswide planning. The analysis includes all of the means and standard deviations of the students who participated, presented in three statistical summaries. In addition, separate lists of students—provided according to need—can be used for programmatic intervention. This report is provided for each batch of 10 or more answer sheets that are submitted by the designated RMS coordinator on campus.

What Is the Relationship Between the RMS and Prentice Hall Materials?

An RMS Coordinator's Manual and Advisor's Guide will be sent to you when you order the RMS shrink-wrapped with selected texts from Prentice Hall. Notify the editor, Sande Johnson, of your interest in these materials (sande_johnson@prenhall.com).

How to Order

- Work with your Prentice Hall representative to order your textbook shrink-wrapped with the Retention Management System.
- Noel-Levitz sends you the Coordinator's Manual, Advisor's Guide, and Scoring Request Form as soon as they learn of your purchase. Noel-Levitz also assigns an RMS Institution code to your college.
- The answer sheets are collected and coordinated for shipment to Noel-Levitz by the designated RMS coordinator. Online scoring is more immediate.

College Student Inventory 0–13–031563-X ($5)
College Student Inventory Form A w/score sheet 0–13–072258–8 ($5)
College Student Inventory Form B w/score sheet 0–13–079193–8 ($5)
College Student Inventory Form A or B online access card 0–13–098158–3 ($5)

QUICK START TO COLLEGE

A GUIDE TO KNOWING WHAT TO DO, HOW TO DO IT, AND WHERE TO GET HELP

Welcome to college! Ahead of you are opportunities to learn more than you can imagine. Over the next years, you will explore the world of ideas, acquire information, and develop skills that will last a lifetime.

With these wonderful opportunities comes the challenge of adjusting to the realities of college. It may help you to know that nearly every college student—no matter what age or level of experience—feels overwhelmed as college begins.

Quick Start to College is designed to help you feel in control as you begin the most important educational journey of your life. *As you read, consult your college handbook and/or website to learn about the specific resources, policies, and practices of your college.* The Take Action exercises, interspersed throughout *Quick Start*, will also help you focus on your school.

As you encounter instructors, advisors, administrators, support personnel, and fellow students during your college career, remember that along with them you are a full participant in the educational process. You can create a future filled with opportunity. Take the first steps toward that future by:

- Envisioning what you want to accomplish and then making it happen
- Taking an active role in your courses from the first day of class
- Being in charge of your learning, which involves setting goals, managing your time, completing assignments on schedule, and seeking help, if necessary
- Striving to do your best and making a commitment to quality
- Being an advocate for yourself as you relate to others
- Taking care of your mind, body, and relationships

- Getting involved in activities that you like and that will help you develop your talents
- Deciding what you want to study—what you are passionate about
- Pursuing meaningful academic goals (honors or awards, involvement in academic organizations, internships or other work experiences that support your academic path)

One of the first steps in taking responsibility for your own success is learning what your college expects of you and what you have a right to expect in return as a consumer of higher education.

What Your College Expects of You

Before classes start, it is a good idea to define the set of expectations that accompany your new role as a college student. These expectations may be different from anything you encountered in high school or in other educational settings. By learning about what is expected of you in school, you will minimize surprises that may be obstacles later on.

Specific expectations involve understanding curriculum and graduation requirements, registering for classes, pursuing academic excellence, following school procedures, getting involved in extracurricular activities, and mastering the college's computer system. Do your best to understand all these areas and, if you need it, ask for help—from instructors, administrators, advisors, mentors, experienced classmates, and family members.

Understand Curriculum and Graduation Requirements

Every college has requirements for a degree that are stated in the catalog or website. Among the requirements you may encounter are:

- Number of credits needed to graduate, including credits required in major and minor fields
- Curriculum requirements, including specific course requirements
- Departmental major requirements, including the cumulative average needed for acceptance as a major in the department

Strive to remain in good academic standing throughout your college career. Among the degrees granted by two-year and four-year colleges are Bachelor of Arts, Bachelor of Science, Associate of Arts, Associate of Science, and Associate of Applied Science.

Choose and Register for Classes

Every time you register, you make important choices, because your selections define what you will learn and who will teach you. Course registration can be both exciting and challenging, especially the first time. Scan the college catalog and website and consider these factors as you make your selections:

- Core/general requirements for graduation
- Your major or minor or courses in departments you are considering
- Electives that sound interesting, even if they are out of your field

TAKE ACTION
Explore Your Curriculum and Graduation Requirements

Use your college catalog and website to explore your course requirements, and then complete the following:

- What are your course requirements for graduation?

  _____

  _____

  _____

- What are the requirements to major in a department that interests you? List, on a separate page if necessary, the courses in the order they must be taken.

  _____

  _____

  _____

- What grade point average must you maintain in order to remain in good standing at your college and to major in your area of interest? Identify two study-related activities you will start in the next month to help ensure that you will achieve that GPA.

  _____

  _____

  _____

In most schools, you can choose to attend a class without earning academic credit by *auditing* the class. The main reason students choose to audit is to explore different areas without worrying about a grade, although tuition charges are generally the same.

Once you decide on courses, but before you register, create a schedule that shows daily class times. If the first class meets at 8:00 A.M., ask yourself if you will be at your best at that early hour. Create one or more backup schedules in case one or more of the courses you want fills up before you register. Show your ideas to your advisor for comments and approval.

Actual course registration varies from school to school. Registration may take place through your school's computer network, via an automated phone system, or in the school gym or student union. When you register, you may be asked to pay tuition and other fees. If you are receiving financial aid, make sure that checks from all aid sources have arrived at the college before registration.

Pursue Academic Excellence

Pursuing academic excellence means doing your very best in every course. You can accomplish this through a series of small but important steps that cumulatively create success:

- read all assigned text material ahead of time
- attend every class with a positive attitude
- arrive on time
- complete assignments on schedule
- listen attentively and participate in discussions
- value honest scholarship
- study for exams
- seek help if you need it

In return for your efforts, you will learn a great deal and you will receive a course grade that reflects your knowledge.

Colleges often require you to learn material on your own. For example, your instructors may expect you to learn important concepts independently and to read material that is never covered in class. If you think about it, these expectations are reasonable, since your courses meet for only a few hours a week—independent work is necessary to cover key topics. Think of these requirements as opportunities to demonstrate—to yourself and your instructors—your maturity and resourcefulness.

When you receive grades, remember that they are reflections of your work, not your self-worth. A D or an F does not diminish you as a person, but rather tells you that your efforts or work products are below what the instructor expects. Similarly, an A does not inflate your value as a person, but recognizes the high quality of your academic performance.

Most schools use grading systems with numerical grades or equivalent letter grades (see Figure QS.1). Generally, the highest course grade is an A, or 4.0, and the lowest is an F, or 0.0. In every course, you earn a certain number of college credits, called semester hours. For example, Accounting 101 may be worth three hours, and Physical Education may be worth one hour. These numbers generally refer to the number of hours the course meets per week. When you multiply each numerical course grade by the number of hours the course is worth, take the average of all these numbers, and divide by the total number of semester hours you are taking, you obtain your grade point average, or GPA.

Learn the minimum GPA needed to remain in good standing and to be accepted and continue in your major. At some schools, for example, courses with grades below 2.0 may not be

FIGURE QS.1   Letter grades and equivalent numerical grades per semester hour.

Letter Grade	A	A–	B+	B	B–	C+	C	C–	D+	D	F
Numerical Grade	4.0	3.7	3.3	3.0	2.7	2.3	2.0	1.7	1.3	1.0	0.0

FIGURE **QS.2**	Calculating your GPA.		
COURSE	**SEMESTER HOURS**	**GRADE**	**GRADE POINTS**
Chemistry 1	4	C	4 credits × 2 points = 8
Freshman Writing	3	B+	3 credits × 3.3 points = 9.9
Spanish I	3	B–	3 credits × 2.7 points = 8.1
Introduction to Statistics	3	C+	3 credits × 2.3 points = 6.9
Social Justice	2	A–	2 credits × 3.7 points = 7.4

Total semester hours: 15
Total grade points for semester: 40.3

GPA for semester (total grade points divided by semester hours): 40.3 divided by 15 = 2.68
Letter equivalent grade: C+/B–

counted toward your major requirement. Figure QS.2 shows you how to calculate your GPA.

Inherent in the pursuit of academic excellence is honest, ethical behavior. Your school's academic integrity policy defines the behavioral standards that are expected of you in your studies and in your relationships with faculty, administrators, and fellow students. The values that are the foundation of academic integrity are examined in Chapter 1, and Chapter 10 focuses on the serious offense of plagiarism.

Follow School Procedures

Your college has established rules and regulations, which it asks all students to follow. You'll find these procedures spelled out in the college handbook and on the website. Among the most common procedures you will encounter are:

Adding or dropping a class. This should be done within the first few days of the semester if you find that a course is not right for you or that there are better choices. Late-semester unexcused withdrawals (i.e., almost any withdrawal after a predetermined date) receive a failing grade. However, course withdrawals that are approved for medical problems, a death in the family, or other special circumstances have no impact on your grade point average.

Taking an incomplete. If you can't finish your work due to circumstances beyond your control—an illness or injury, for example—many colleges allow you to take a grade of Incomplete. The school will require approval from your instructor and your commitment to make up the work later.

Transferring schools or moving from a two-year to a four-year college. If you are unhappy at a college and want a change, check out the degree requirements of the new college and complete an application. If you are a student at a community college and intend to transfer to a four-year school, be sure to take the courses required for admission to that school. In addition, be sure all your courses are transferable, which means they will be counted toward your degree at the four-year school. At most community colleges, advisors are available to help students through this process.

Taking a leave of absence. There are many reasons students take a leave of absence for a semester or a year and then return. You may want time away from academics to think through your long-term goals, or you may be needed for a family emergency. If you are in good standing at your college, leave is generally granted. In contrast, students with academic or disciplinary problems who take a leave may have to reapply for admission when their leave is complete.

Get Involved

A wealth of opportunities outside the classroom awaits students who seek them. Extracurricular activities enable you to develop your interpersonal intelligence—to meet people who share your interests and to develop teamwork and leadership skills. They also give you the chance to develop skills that may be important in your career. In addition, being connected to friends and a supportive network of people is one of the main reasons people stay in school.

Some freshmen take on more activities than they can comfortably handle. Pace yourself the first year. You can always add more activities later. As you seek the right balance, consider this:

TAKE ACTION

Find Out About Clubs and Organizations

Use your college catalog and website to identify clubs and organizations that interest you and to complete the following:

- Identify two subject-oriented organizations that are available in your specialized academic interest areas (e.g., the Accounting Club, the Computer Science Club):

  _____

  _____

- All colleges have student councils and governing groups. Name two you might be interested in joining (e.g., the Student Government Association, the Greek Life Committee):

  _____

  _____

- Identify three other special-interest groups you might be interested in joining (e.g., Black Students Union, Habitat for Humanity, Veterans' Association):

  _____

  _____

  _____

- Name three ways in which joining an extracurricular group might benefit you as you begin college. Keep in mind that some benefits have little to do with what the group is about. For example, as a member of a jazz quintet you may develop public-speaking skills when you introduce musical selections to audiences:

  _____

  _____

  _____

Studies have shown that students who join organizations tend to persist in their educational goals more than those who don't branch out.[1]

Master Your College's Computer System

A large part of the communication and work that you do in college involves the computer. Here are just some examples:

- Registering for classes
- Accessing a course syllabus and required-readings list
- E-mailing instructors for assignment clarification; receiving e-mail responses
- Tapping into library databases and the Internet for research
- Completing assignments and writing papers
- Submitting papers via e-mail to instructors
- Creating spreadsheets for math and science
- E-mailing classmates to schedule group/team meetings
- Receiving school-wide announcements via the college computer network
- Taking interactive quizzes

In most colleges, it is no longer possible to manage without a computer—your own, one borrowed from school, or one available in computer labs. Most dorm rooms are now wired for computers, which gives students access to the campus network. Here are some suggestions for using your computer effectively:

- *Get trained.* Start by getting help to connect to your college network. Then, take training classes to master word processing, data and spreadsheets, and the Internet. If you encounter technical problems, talk to technicians in the computer lab.
- *Use computers to find information.* If you have specific questions about your school, check the college website. You may find the information or the e-mail address of a contact person.
- *Be a safe and cautious user.* Computers sometimes fail. To safeguard your work, create regular backups by saving your work periodically onto the hard drive or a diskette, CD, or Zip disk. In addition, use an antivirus program.
- *Use computers for appropriate tasks.* During study time, try to stay away from Internet surfing and computer games. Set time limits at other times to keep your academic focus.
- *Protect yourself from trouble.* It's in your best interest not to reveal personal information, including financial data, to strangers you meet on the Internet.

A Special Word About E-mail

You may be required to communicate with your instructor, submit assignments, and even take exams via e-mail. Following are suggestions for improving your communication:

- *Use your college's e-mail system.* Register for an e-mail account at your school as soon as possible. You'll need this connection to receive school-wide e-mails and possibly to access the college library.
- *Use effective writing techniques.* To make the best impression—especially when communicating with an instructor—take the time to find the right words. Organize your thoughts and use proper spelling, punctuation, and grammar. To make your e-mails easy to read, get to the point in the first paragraph, use short paragraphs, use headings to divide long e-mails into digestible sections, and use lists. Always proofread before hitting "send."
- *Be careful of miscommunication.* Try to be diplomatic and pleasant, and think before you respond to upsetting messages. If you write back too quickly, you may be sorry later.
- *Rein in social e-mailing.* Prioritize your e-mailing. Respond to the most important and time-sensitive messages first. Save personal e-mail for when you have down time.

No matter what school or extracurricular activity you are involved in, you will be surrounded by people who are eager to help you succeed.

Connecting with People and Support Services

Instructors, administrators, advisors, and a range of support staff are available to help you. This overview will help you identify and connect to the people and services around you. As you read, keep in mind that the names of offices and personnel titles may vary, and remember that some colleges do not offer every resource.

Teaching and Learning Take Center Stage

The primary mission of most colleges and universities is teaching—communicating to students the knowledge and thinking skills they need to succeed in school and beyond. Responding as an active, engaged learner is your role and responsibility as a student.

In every course, you'll meet one—or sometimes several—instructors. Although the term "instructor" is used in this text, teachers have official titles that show their rank within your college. Instructors with the highest status are full professors. Moving down from there are associate professors, assistant professors, lecturers, instructors, and assistant instructors, more commonly known as teaching assistants or TAs. (Titles may vary from school to school.) Adjuncts may teach several courses, but are not official staff members.

Administrators Provide Support

The administrative staff enables your college—and the student body—to function. The duties of several of the vice presidents and deans you will encounter are described in Figure QS.3. Large universities may be divided into schools with separate administrative structures and staffs—for example, a School of Business or a School of Social Work. Each school normally has its own dean, and each department within

---

FIGURE QS.3   Administrative structure.

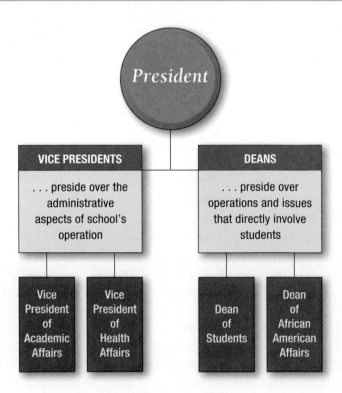

the school has a chairperson—an instructor who heads the department.

One of the most important administrative offices for students is the Office of the Dean of Student Affairs, which, in many colleges, is the center for student services. Staff members can answer your questions or direct you to others who can help.

Administrative Offices Dealing with Tuition Issues and Registration

Among the first administrative offices you will encounter are those involved with tuition payments, financial aid, and registration.

- The *bursar's office* (also called the office of finance, the accounting office, and cashiering services) issues bills for tuition and room and board and collects payments from students and financial aid sources.
- The *financial aid office* helps students apply for financial aid and understand the eligibility requirements of different federal, state, and private programs.
- The *registrar's office* handles course registration, sends grades at the end of the semester, and compiles your official transcript, which is a comprehensive record of your courses and grades. Graduate schools require a copy of your official transcript before considering you for admission, as do many employers before considering you for a job.

Student-Centered Services

A host of services helps students adjust to and succeed in college and deal with problems that arise. Here are some services you are likely to find.

Academic enhancement centers, including reading, writing, math, and study-skills centers. These centers offer consultations and tutoring to help students improve skills at all levels.

Academic computer center. Most schools have sophisticated computer facilities that are open every day, usually staffed by technicians who can assist with computer-related problems. Many facilities also offer training workshops.

Student housing or commuter affairs office. Residential colleges provide on-campus housing for undergraduate students, with many schools requiring lower classmen to live on campus. The housing office handles room and roommate placement, establishes behavioral standards, and deals with special needs (e.g., an allergic student's need for a room air conditioner) and problems. Schools with commuting students may have transportation and parking programs.

Health services. Health services generally include sick care, prescriptions for common medicines, routine diagnostic tests, vaccinations, and first aid. All clinics are affiliated with nearby hospitals for emergency care. In addition, psychological counseling is sometimes offered through health services, or you may find it at a separate facility or via the college website. Although services are available, you have to take the first steps to seek them out. Many colleges require proof of health insurance at the time of registration.

Career services. This office helps students find part-time and full-time jobs, as well as summer jobs and internships. Career offices have reference files on specific careers and employers. They also help students learn to write resumes and cover letters and search the Internet for opportunities. Career offices often invite employers to interview students on campus and hold career fairs to introduce companies and organizations. Summer internships and jobs are snapped up quickly, so check the office early and often to improve your chances.

Services for students with disabilities. Colleges must provide students with disabilities full access to facilities and programs. For students with documented disabilities, federal law requires that assistance be provided in the form of appropriate accommodations and aids. These range from interpreters for the hearing impaired to ramps for students in wheelchairs. If you have a disability, visit this office to learn what is offered. Remember, also, that this office is your advocate if you encounter problems. For specifics on learning disabilities, see Chapter 2.

Veteran affairs. The Office of Veteran Affairs provides veterans with various services, including academic and personal counseling and current benefit status, which may affect tuition waivers.

While affording college isn't easy, certain financial-aid resources can help ease the burden. Every school has a system in place to help you understand and apply for financial-aid opportunities. The following overview will help you explore these opportunities.

Understanding and Applying for Financial Aid

Financing your education—alone or with the help of your family—involves acquiring financial knowledge and making financial decisions. Visit your school's financial aid office in person or on the Internet, research the available options and decide what works best, and then apply early. The types of aid available are student loans, grants, and scholarships.

Student loans. As the recipient of a student loan, you are responsible for paying back the amount you borrow, plus interest, according to a predetermined payment schedule. The amount you borrow is known as the *loan principal,* and *interest* is the fee that you pay for the privilege of using money that belongs to someone else. Loan payments usually begin after graduation, after a grace period of between six months and a year, and generally last no more than 10 years.

The federal government administers or oversees most student loans. To receive aid from any federal program, you must be a citizen or eligible non-citizen and be enrolled in a program that meets government requirements. Individual states may differ in their aid programs, so check with the financial aid office for details. Table QS.1 describes the main student loan programs to which you can apply.

TABLE QS.1	Federal student loan programs.

LOAN	DESCRIPTION
Perkins	Low, fixed rate of interest. Available to those with exceptional financial need (determined by a government formula). Issued by schools from their allotment of federal funds. Grace period of up to nine months after graduation before repayment, in monthly installments, must begin.
Stafford	Available to students enrolled at least half-time. Exceptional need not required, although students who prove need can qualify for a subsidized Stafford loan (the government pays interest until repayment begins). Two types of Staffords: the direct loan comes from federal funds, and the FFEL (Federal Family Education Loan) comes from a bank or credit union. Repayment begins six months after the student graduates, leaves school, or drops below half-time enrollment.
PLUS	Available to students enrolled at least half-time and claimed as dependents by their parents. Parents must undergo a credit check to be eligible, or may be sponsored through a relative or friend who passes the check. Loan comes from government or a bank or credit union. Sponsor must begin repayment 60 days after receiving the last loan payment.

Grants and scholarships. Unlike student loans, neither grants nor scholarships require repayment. Grants, funded by federal, state, or local governments as well as private organizations, are awarded to students who show financial need. Table QS.2 describes federal grant programs. In contrast, scholarships are given for various abilities and talents. They may reward academic achievement, exceptional abilities in sports or the arts, citizenship, or leadership. Scholarships are sponsored by federal agencies and private organizations.

Researching financial aid. Start digging at your financial aid office and visit your library, bookstore, and the Internet. In addition, guides to funding sources catalog thousands of opportunities.

Additional information about federal grants and loans is available in the current version (updated yearly) of *The Student Guide to Financial Aid*. This publication can be found at your school's financial aid office, or you can request it by mail or phone (800–433–3243). The publication is also available on-line at **www.ed.gov/ prog_info/SFA/StudentGuide/**.

You can find the Free Application for Federal Student Aid (FAFSA) form at your library, at the Federal Student Aid Information Center, through your college's financial aid office or website, or via the U. S. Department of Education's website at **www.ed.gov/finaid.html**.

If you are receiving aid from your college, follow all the rules and regulations, including meeting application deadlines and remaining in academic good standing. In most cases, you will be required to reapply for aid every year. Even if you did not receive a grant or scholarship as a freshman, you may be eligible as a sophomore, junior, or senior. These opportunities are often based on grades and campus leadership, and they may be given by individual college departments.

You are beginning the journey of your college education and lifelong learning. The work you do in this course and in the remaining pages of *Keys to Effective Learning* will help you achieve your goals in your studies and in your personal life and career. As you move forward, think about the words Josh Billings, a 19th-century American writer, said over 100 years ago: *"Everyone who does the best he can do is a hero."* From this day forward, be your own personal hero.

TABLE QS.2   Federal grant programs.

GRANT	DESCRIPTION
Pell	Need-based; the government evaluates your reported financial information and determines eligibility from that "score" (called an expected family contribution or EFC). Available to undergraduates who have earned no other degrees. Amount varies according to education cost and EFC. Adding other aid sources is allowed.
Federal Supplemental Educational Opportunity (FSEOG)	Need-based; administered by the financial aid administrator at participating schools. Each participating school receives a limited amount of federal funds for FSEOGs and sets its own application deadlines.
Work–study	Need-based; encourages community service work or work related to your course of study. Pays by the hour, at least the federal minimum wage. Jobs may be on-campus (usually for your school) or off (often with a nonprofit organization or a public agency).

TAKE ACTION

You'll find detailed information about the financial aid application process in your college catalog, on the college website, and in federal publications and websites mentioned in Quick Start. Use these resources to complete the following:

- List the deadlines to submit FAFSA applications during the next year:

Term/Semester	FAFSA Filing Date
Fall 200_	_____
Spring 200_	_____
Summer 200_	_____

- Endowed scholarships may be available through your college. Find out about two scholarships for which you are eligible and describe them here:

1. _____

_____

2. _____

_____

Make a commitment to take three actions in the coming year to apply for these scholarships. Describe these actions in the space below.

1. _____
2. _____
3. _____

SUGGESTED READINGS

Gottesman, Greg, Daniel Baer, et al. *College Survival: A Crash Course for Students by Students,* Fifth edition. New York: Macmillan, 1999.

Light, Richard J. *Making the Most of College: Students Speak Their Minds.* Cambridge, MA: Harvard University Press, 2001.

Rozakis, Laurie. *The Complete Idiot's Guide to College Survival.* New York: Alpha Books, 2001.

INTERNET RESOURCES

www.prenhall.com/success
Prentice Hall Student Success Supersite (information about student life, student-to-student bulletin boards, personal stories, opinion polls, and more).

ENDNOTES

1. Alexander W. Astin, *Preventing Students from Dropping Out.* San Francisco: Jossey-Bass, 1976.

THINKING IT THROUGH

Check those statements that apply to you right now:

- ☐ I think that the most typical college student is an 18-year-old right out of high school.

- ☐ Sometimes school feels like a detour that's keeping me from moving ahead in my life.

- ☐ One moment I'm determined to succeed, and then my motivation takes a dive.

- ☐ I think that having high or low self-esteem can make or break my future success.

- ☐ I have a hard time bouncing back from a failure.

- ☐ Every once in a while I try to step back and look at the big picture of my life.

Welcome to College

OPENING DOORS

Persisting.

"Effective problem solvers stick to a task until it is completed. **They don't give up easily**. They are able to analyze a problem and develop a system, structure, or strategy to attack it." — ART COSTA

Persisting will help you hang on to your educational goals through the highs and lows of your college experience. If you persist through the obstacles, you will open doors to school and life success.

In this chapter you explore answers to the following questions:

- How will college prepare you for life?

- How can you get motivated?

- Who at school can help you make the most of your education?

- What is the connection between college and lifelong learning?

- What are the Habits of Mind and how can they help you succeed?

WELCOME—or welcome back—to your education. You are embarking on a new phase of life that may bring all kinds of questions and concerns. This chapter will give you a preview of how college will prepare you for life. You will explore specific strategies that will help motivate you. Finally, you will see how the skills you build in college can help you become a lifelong learner—and why that means greater success for you.

How will college prepare you for life?

Welcome to the Road to Successful Learning!

In choosing to pursue an education, you are building your power to create a better world. Whatever your reasons for attending college, what you do today—in a writing classroom, a study session, a conference with an instructor, or other educational setting—will help you navigate what lies ahead. Education both promotes your personal success and builds your ability to work with others.

Education Promotes Success

If you take advantage of all your college has to offer, you will develop the skills and talents you need to succeed in your career and life.

Education prepares you for career success. This happens in two ways. First, education expands your career choices by teaching you, through your courses and the people you meet, more about potential careers and jobs than you ever imagined. Second, your day-to-day course work gives you the hands-on skills you need to achieve the career goals you choose. Education makes you a more *literate* person—able to use written and mathematical skills to learn and to improve your life.

Education improves your employability and earning potential. Although education doesn't automatically guarantee a high-level, well-paying job, it greatly increases the probability you will find one (see Figure 1.1 and Figure 1.2 for details). Having a college degree makes an impression on potential employers and makes you eligible for higher-salaried positions. In basic terms, there is a significant wage gap between high school and college graduates, and you want to be on the winning side of it.

Education broadens your worldview. As it introduces you to new ways of learning, doing, being, and thinking, education increases your understanding of diversity and your appreciation of areas that affect and enrich human lives, such as music, art, literature, science, politics, and economics.

Education helps you develop flexibility. Today's world is marked by rapid workplace change, ever-increasing loads of information, and booming technology growth. The flexibility you build while in college will help you navigate that world successfully. You can embrace change by taking risks, being self-directed, and keeping an open mind about what lies in store.

reflect

People attend college for technical training, for the sake of learning, for increased earning power, and for many more reasons. What are some other reasons people go to college? Think about your own reasons. Why are you here? How do you feel about your reasons for being here? Out of all the reasons to be in college, which seem to you to be the "best" and why?

Companion Website

& respond

Median annual income of persons with income 25 years old and over, by gender and highest level of education, 1999.

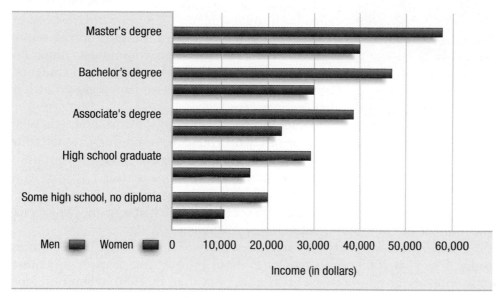

Source: U. S. Department of Commerce, Bureau of the Census, *Current Population Reports*, Series P-60, "Money Income in the United States: 1999."

Unemployment rates of persons 25 years old and over, by highest level of education, 2000.

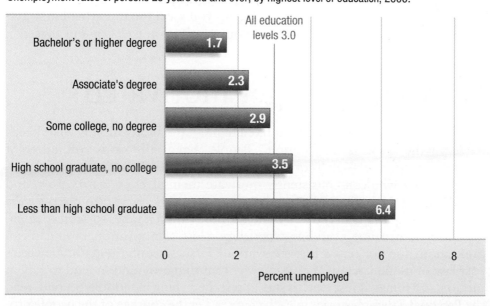

Source: U. S. Department of Labor, Bureau of Labor Statistics, Office of Employment and Unemployment Statistics, Current Population Survey, 2000.

Being able to team up with all kinds of people is one important key to school and life success.

Education Helps You Build Teamwork Skills

The needs of an increasingly diverse student body have molded a new educational experience. So-called traditional students—18 years old, just out of high school, and living in on-campus dorms—now often share classrooms with commuters, older returning students, and other less traditional students. Figure 1.3 shows how the student population has changed in recent years.

Think of your accomplishments and you will find that rarely do you achieve anything alone. Your success at school and at work depends on your ability to cooperate in a team setting. Teams gain strength from the diversity of their members, because the greater the diversity of a team, the greater the number of choices or solutions when problem solving.

Furthermore, diversity is part of the reality of living in the United States today. The year 2000 census reports that one in four Americans is a member of a minority group—a much greater number than in 1980, when only one in five reported minority status. The nation's diversity is expected to grow.

What does this mean for you? Being able to team up with all kinds of people is key to your success in school as well as in a world where you will almost certainly be working in a diverse environment. Throughout this book, you will find references to diverse people in different life circumstances (Chapter 11 provides more detail about communicating across lines of difference). During college, working with study partners and study groups will enhance your learning and promote your understanding of other perspectives. As you begin your classes this semester, start now to get to know your classmates and set up study arrangements. Chapter 5 has more on how to study with others successfully.

You are responsible for examining your unique challenges and seeking out the educational opportunities that help you meet them. Particular strategies can help you build and maintain your motivation to learn and succeed.

How can you get motivated?

Success is a process, not a fixed mark—and **motivation** is what keeps the process in motion. People have all kinds of different *motivators*—goals or ideas that move them forward. Successful people are those who can consistently motivate themselves to learn, grow, and work toward goals. College provides an opportunity for you to discover the goals most important to you and build the motivation it takes to achieve them.

From time to time, everyone experiences a loss of motivation. How can you build motivation or renew lost motivation? First, start on the path. Newton's first law of motion, a law of physics, says that things in motion tend to stay in motion and things at rest tend to stay at rest. Be a thing in motion. Second, read the Personal Triumph stories in each chapter. Let the courage of the people profiled inspire you to believe that you can leap your own hurdles successfully. Finally, explore the motivation-boosting strategies beginning on page 8.

Motivation
A force that moves a person to action; often inspired by an idea, a fact, an event, a goal.

Minority student enrollment is growing.

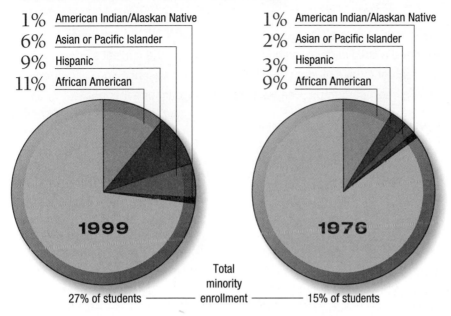

1% American Indian/Alaskan Native
6% Asian or Pacific Islander
9% Hispanic
11% African American

1% American Indian/Alaskan Native
2% Asian or Pacific Islander
3% Hispanic
9% African American

1999   **1976**

27% of students —— Total minority enrollment —— 15% of students

Students are older and have varied responsibilities.

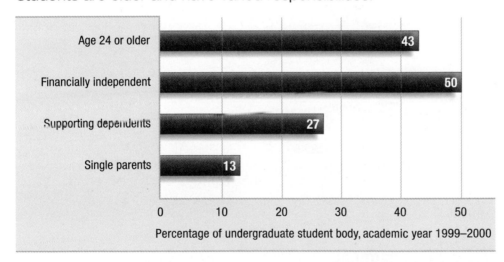

Age 24 or older 43
Financially independent 50
Supporting dependents 27
Single parents 13

Percentage of undergraduate student body, academic year 1999–2000

Students are following less traditional educational paths.

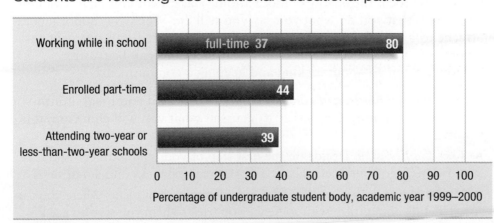

Working while in school full-time 37 80
Enrolled part-time 44
Attending two-year or less-than-two-year schools 39

Percentage of undergraduate student body, academic year 1999–2000

Sources: U. S. Department of Education, National Center for Education Statistics; 1999–2000 National Postsecondary Student Aid Study (NPSAS: 2000); and Digest of Education Statistics 2001, NCES 2002–130, Table 170.

TAKE ACTION

Define Yourself as a Student

Colleges design resources to suit the needs of their students. To know how to seek out the resources that will help you succeed in college, you need a solid understanding of how you fit into the current student body. Think about the description you have read of today's student population, and then describe your particular circumstances, opinions, and needs in a short paragraph. Use these questions to inspire thought:

- How do you describe yourself—your gender, age, culture, ethnicity, lifestyle, and so forth?

- Is this your first time in college or are you a returning student?

- How long are you planning to be in college? How do you need to schedule your course work (time of day, full- or part-time, etc.)?

- How do you describe your family?

- What is your work situation, if you work?

- What is your living situation?

To describe my self is that I think I'm in good age to start college, and I'm happy because in college are few people that are spanish.

Make a Commitment

Commitment
1) A pledge or promise to do something, or
2) dedication to a long-term course of action.

How do you focus the energy of motivation? Make a **commitment**. Commitment means that you do what you say you will do. When you honor a commitment to an academic goal, a career dream, or a self-improvement task, you prove to yourself and others that your intentions can be trusted.

How do you go about making and keeping a commitment?

- *State your commitment concretely.* Set a clear goal and break it into manageable pieces. Emphasize to yourself what you will gain from this commitment.

- *Take the first step.* Decide on the first step of your commitment and take it today. Then continue a day at a time, breaking tasks into small steps.

- *Stay aware of each commitment.* Keep a list of commitments where you can see it. Talk about them with someone you trust to help you stay on track.

- *Reward yourself as you move ahead.* Rewards help you feel good about what you've accomplished so far and can help keep you going. Treat yourself to dinner with a friend, a new CD, a movie night.

Making commitments helps you keep a steady focus on your most important goals. It gives you a sense of accomplishment as you experience gradual growth and progress.

> *"A journey of a thousand miles begins with a single step."*

LAO TZU

Develop Positive Habits

People have all kinds of **habits;** some you may consider "bad" and others "good." Bad habits stall motivation and prevent you from reaching important goals. Good habits are those that bring the kind of positive effects that keep motivation high.

Look at the positive and negative effects of your habits to decide which you want to keep and which you need to change or improve. Take the following steps to evaluate a habit and, if necessary, make a change (if the habit has more negative effects than positive ones).

1. *Define and evaluate the habit.* Name your habit and look at the negative and positive effects. If there are more negatives than positives, it is most likely a habit worth changing.

2. *Decide to keep or change the habit.* Until you are convinced that you will receive a benefit, efforts to change will not get you far. Commit to a change if you see too many negative effects.

3. *Start today—and keep it up.* Each day is a day you can benefit from a new lifestyle. Be consistent for at least three weeks so that you become accustomed to the new habit.

4. *Reward positive steps.* Choose a reward that encourages you to stay on target. If you earn a good grade, for example, treat yourself to one night out instead of slacking off on studying the following week.

Habit

A preference for a particular action that you do a certain way, and often on a regular basis or at certain times.

Finally, don't get too discouraged if the process seems difficult. Rarely does someone make the decision to change and do so without a setback or two. Take it one step at a time; when you lose steam, reflect on what you stand to gain. With persistence and positive thinking, you can reach your goal.

Be Responsible

In college, you are responsible for making decisions that keep you in motion and avoiding choices that stall you in your tracks. You are your own manager. Taking responsibility is all about living up to your obligations. Through action, you prove that you are responsible—"response-able"—able to respond.

Taking responsibility is taking action—and doing it reliably. In college, responsible people can be trusted to live up to obligations like these:

- Attending class and participating in activities and discussions
- Completing reading and assignments on time
- Communicating with instructors and fellow students

These actions may sound mundane. However, these building blocks of responsibility will get you where you want to go. Here's why:

- *Everyday responsibilities get you in the action habit.* As with any other habit, the more you do something, the more it becomes second nature. The more often you complete and turn in assignments on time, for example, the more likely you are to stay on top of your job tasks down the road when you are on a tight deadline.
- *The small accomplishments add up.* When you show up to class, pay attention, contribute, and work hard, you send a message. An instructor who observes these behaviors is more likely to trust and respect you. People who trust you may give you increasing power and opportunities for growth.
- *Fulfilling day-to-day responsibilities gives you freedom.* The more responsible you are, the more those around you will give you the freedom to handle situations and problems on your own.

initiative
The power to begin or to follow through energetically with a plan or task; determination.

Responsibility also means showing **initiative.** Initiative means that you make a move on your own instead of waiting for people, rules, requirements, or circumstances to push you. You show initiative when you make an appointment with an instructor to discuss a paper, find a better way to do a task at work, vote, or start an exercise program. Once you take that first step, it is often easier to keep your momentum going and continue to act responsibly.

Finally, responsibility will help you keep on top of important life issues that affect your school success. For example, managing your finances requires responsible behavior such as paying bills on time, searching for financial aid when necessary, and seeking work when you need extra income. (You will find information on financial aid in Quick Start and additional material on money management in Chapter 12.)

Face Your Fears

Everyone experiences fear. Anything unknown—new people, experiences, challenges, situations—can be frightening. The challenges you encounter as you work toward your goals demand a willingness to face your fears and push your limits. The following steps will help you work through fear with courage:

1. *Acknowledge fears.* The act of naming your fear begins to lessen its hold on you. Be specific.
2. *Examine fears.* Sometimes one fear hides a larger one. If you fear a test, determine whether you fear the test itself or the fact that if you pass it, you will have to take a tougher class next.

"He has not learned the lesson of life who does not every day surmount a fear."

RALPH WALDO EMERSON

3. *Develop a plan.* Evaluate what will help you overcome your fear. For example, if Shakespeare intimidates you, consider asking your instructor for advice or watching a Shakespeare movie.

4. *Move ahead with your plan.* Courage is the key to moving ahead. Take the steps that help you to confront and move beyond your fears.

As you work through your fears, talk about them with people you trust. Everyone has fears, and when people share strategies, everyone benefits.

TAKE ACTION

Face Your Fears[1]

Face one school-related fear that you have as you begin this semester. Break the task into manageable units and do one step at a time. First, describe your fear—and be specific.

In the begining of this semester my fear was to not be prepare for the class

Now, list three small activities that get you closer to working through that fear: If you don't want to start a major project, for example, you can read a book on the subject, brainstorm what you already know about it, or write one page about it.

1. *I follow the introccion.*
2. *First day a read the book*
3. _____

Commit yourself to one step that you will take within the next two days. State it here. Include the time and date you will begin and how much time you will spend.

1:00 pm   9-4-07 spent two hours

What reward will you give yourself for having taken that step?

I would reward with a Vacation and with a congratulation

After taking the step, describe how it felt. Did it make a difference in your motivation?

yes, because I took it easily

Affirm that you have taken that first step and are on the way to success by signing your name here and writing the date.

Name   *yesica Rivera*   Date   *8-30-07*

Build Self-Esteem

self-esteem
A belief in your value as a person.

When people believe in their value and capabilities, their high level of **self-esteem** fuels their motivation to succeed. Belief, though, is only half the game. The other half is the action and effort that help you feel that you have earned your self-esteem. Rick Pitino discusses self-esteem in his book *Success Is a Choice:* "Self-esteem is directly linked to deserving success. If you have established a great work ethic and have begun the discipline that is inherent with that, you will automatically begin to feel better about yourself. It's all interrelated. You must deserve victory to feel good about yourself."[2]

Building and maintaining a high level of self-esteem, therefore, involve both *thinking positively* and *taking action*. Together, they help you generate the belief in yourself that keeps you motivated.

Think Positively

Positive self-talk
Supportive and positive thoughts and ideas that a person communicates to himself or herself.

Attitudes influence your choices and affect how you perceive and relate to others. A positive attitude can open your mind to learning experiences and inspire you to action. One way to create a positive attitude is through **positive self-talk.** These hints will help:

- *Stop negative talk in its tracks.* If you catch yourself thinking, "I can never write a decent paper," stop and say to yourself, "I can write better than that and next time I will." Then think about some specific steps you can take to improve.

- *Pay yourself a compliment.* Note your successes. Be specific: "I have really improved my spelling and proofreading."

- *Replace words of obligation with words of personal intent.*

  I should   *becomes*   I choose to
  I'll try   *becomes*   I will

Words of intent give you power and control because they imply a personal decision to act.

Take Action

Although thinking positively sets the tone for success, it cannot get you there by itself. You have to take action. Without action, positive thoughts become empty statements or even lies.

Consider, for example, a student in a freshman composition class. This student thinks every possible positive thought: "I know how to write well. I can get a B in this class. I will succeed in school." And so on. Then, during the semester, she misses about one-third of the class meetings, turns in some of her papers late, and completely forgets a couple of assignments. At the end of the course, when she barely passes the class, she wonders how things went so wrong when she had such a positive attitude.

This student did not succeed because she did not earn her belief in herself through action and effort. By the end of a semester like this, positive thoughts look like lies. "If I can get a B, why did I get a D? If I am such a great student, why did I barely make it through this course?" Eventually, with no action to support them, the positive thoughts disappear.

Following are some ways to get moving in a positive direction:

- *Build your own code of discipline.* Develop general guidelines to follow, based on your top priorities. Construct each day's goals and actions so that they help you achieve your larger objectives.
- *Make action plans and follow through.* Figure out how you plan to take action for any situation, so that, for example, "I am a great student" is backed up by specific actions to ensure success.
- *Acknowledge every step.* Even the smallest action is worth your attention because every action reinforces a positive thought and builds self-esteem.

Believing in yourself helps you make good choices. When your self-esteem is strong, you are more likely to choose actions that you can be proud of. You are also more likely to seek help when you need it.

Who at school can help you make the most of your education?

Attending college is one of the best decisions you've made. However, deadlines, academic and social pressures, and simply being in new surroundings can make the experience stressful at times. (Chapter 12 will talk more about stress management.) Understanding that help is available is the first step in helping yourself. Step 2 is actually *seeking* help from those who can give it. This requires knowing where to go and what assistance you can reasonably expect.

When you have questions, do some sleuthing on your own to track down answers. In many cases, your college catalog, handbook, and website will have the information you need. When they don't, or when you need some personal attention and an exchange of ideas, your instructors, teaching assistants, advisors, mentors, and tutors can help you.

Instructors and Teaching Assistants

The people who teach your courses—instructors and teaching assistants—are your most available human resources at college. You see them from one to five times per week and interact with them more directly than with any other authority on campus. They see your work and, if your class size is small, they hear your ideas and consequently may get to know you quite well.

What kind of help might you seek from an instructor or teaching assistant?

- Clarification on material presented in class
- Help on homework
- Information about how to prepare for a test
- Consultation on a paper you are working on

- Details about why you received a particular grade on a test or assignment
- Advice about the department—courses, majoring, and so forth
- Information about career areas linked to the subject area

You may get along with some instructors better than with others, and you may respond better to some teaching styles than to others. However, instructors are potential resources and necessary allies in your education. When you need help, try to seek out your instructor, no matter how you feel about him or her. You may find that, in person, you get a different response than what you experience in the classroom.

When you want to speak personally with an instructor for longer than a minute or two, choose your time carefully. Before or after class is usually not the best time for anything more than a quick question—instructors may be thinking about their lecture, fielding other students' questions, or heading off to the next class. When you need your instructor's full attention, there are three ways to communicate effectively: make an appointment during office hours, send e-mail, or leave voice-mail messages.

Office hours. Instructors keep regular office hours during which students can schedule personal conferences. Generally, these are posted during the first class, on instructors' office doors, and on instructors' or departmental web pages. Always make an appointment for a conference; if you show up unannounced, your instructor may be busy. Face-to-face conferences are ideal for working through ideas and problems (for example, deciding on a term paper topic) or asking for advice (for example, looking for guidance on choosing courses in the department).

E-mail. Use e-mail to clarify assignments and assignment deadlines, to ask specific questions about lectures or readings, and to clarify what will be covered on a test. Try not to wait until the last minute to ask test-related questions; your instructor may not have time to respond. Instructors' e-mail addresses are generally posted on the first day of class and may also be found in your student handbook or syllabus (a detailed description of what you will learn in the course). Links may also be available on the college website.

Voice mail. If something comes up at the last minute, you can leave a message in your instructor's office voice mailbox. Make your message short, but specific. Tell the instructor your reason for calling ("This is Rick Jones from your ten o'clock Intro to Psychology class. I'm supposed to present my project today, but I'm sick in bed with a fever"), and avoid general messages ("This is Rick Jones from your ten o'clock class. Please call me at 555-5555"). Avoid calling instructors at home unless they give specific permission to do so.

If you are taking a large lecture course, you may have a primary instructor plus a teaching assistant (TA) who meets with a small group of students on a regular basis. You may want to approach your TA with course-related questions and problems before approaching the instructor. Because TAs deal with fewer students, they may have more time to devote to specific issues.

Academic Advisors

In most colleges, every student is assigned an advisor who is the student's personal liaison with the college. (At some schools, students receive help at an advising center.) Your advisor will help you choose courses every semester, plan your overall academic program, and understand college regulations, including graduation requirements. He or she will point out possible consequences of your decisions ("If you put off taking Biology this semester, you're facing two lab courses next semester"), help you shape your educational goals, and monitor your academic progress. Your advisor also knows about tutoring and personal counseling programs and may write recommendations when you are searching for a job.

While you are responsible for fully understanding graduation requirements—including credit requirements—and choosing the courses you need, your advisor is there to help you with these critical decisions. You will most likely be required to meet with your advisor once each semester; however, you can schedule additional meetings if and when you need them.

Mentors

If you are fortunate, you will find a mentor during college—a trusted counselor or guide who takes a special interest in helping you reach your goals. Mentoring relationships demand time and energy on both sides. A mentor can give you a private audience for questions and problems, advice tailored to your needs, support, guidance, and trust. A mentor cares about you enough to be devoted to your development. In return, you owe it to a mentor to be open to his or her ideas and, respectfully, to take advice into consideration. You and your mentor can learn from each other, receive positive energy from your relationship, and grow together.

Your mentor might be your advisor, an instructor in your major or minor field, or an academic support instructor. You may also be drawn to someone outside school—for example, a longtime friend whose judgment and experience you admire or a supervisor at work. Some schools have faculty or peer mentoring programs to match students with people who can help them. Check your student handbook or website or ask your faculty advisor if this is offered at your school.

Tutors

Tutors can give you valuable and detailed help on specific academic subjects. Most campuses have private tutoring available, and many schools offer free peer tutoring. If you feel you could benefit from the kind of one-on-one work a tutor can give, ask your instructor or your academic advisor to recommend a tutor. You may also be able to find tutors through academic centers, if your school has them, such as a writing center or computer center.

reflect

Writer Henry David Thoreau said: "If you have built castles in the air, your work need not be lost. That is where they should be. Now put the foundation under them." Think about this quote as you begin your college career: What are your "castles"—your dreams for school and for life? Why is "in the air" where they "should be"? What kind of "foundation" or support do you think you need in order to make them happen? How do you think your college education can provide that foundation?

& respond

What is the connection between college and lifelong learning?

n his book *Techno Trends—24 Technologies That Will Revolutionize Our Lives*, futurist Daniel Burns describes a tomorrow that is linked to continuing education: "The future belongs to those who are capable of being retrained again and again," he says. "Think of it as periodically upgrading your human assets throughout your career. . . . Humans are infinitely upgradeable, but it does require an investment" in lifelong learning.[3] College is the ideal training ground for learning skills that will serve you throughout your life.

College Prepares You to Learn from Failure and Celebrate Success

College brings new challenges, and with them come situations in which you may fail. Failure is an opportunity to realize what you didn't know so that you can learn and improve; in fact, what you learn from a failure will most likely guide you more effectively than many other things you learn. If you can accept failure as part of life, forgive yourself, and learn from it, you will be able to pick yourself up and keep improving.

Learning from Failure

Learning from your failures and mistakes involves careful thinking. One useful course of action is first to look at what happened, then make any improvements that you can, and finally decide how to change your action or approach in the future. For example, imagine that after a long night of studying for a test, you forgot that you had a deadline for a five-page paper the next day.

Look at what happened. Your exhaustion and concern about the test caused you to forget to check your planner to see what else was on your plate. Now you may face a lower grade on your paper if you turn it in late, plus you may be inclined to rush it and quickly turn in a paper that isn't as good as it could be.

Make any possible improvements on the situation. You could visit your instructor during office hours, or send an e-mail, to explain the situation and ask if you can have a brief extension on the paper.

Integrity
Adherence to a code of moral values, incorruptibility, honesty.

Make changes for the future. You can set a goal to note deadlines in a bright color and to check your planner more often. You can also try arranging your study schedule so that you will be less exhausted.

Keep in mind that your value as a human being does not diminish when you make a mistake. Expect that you always will do the best that you can, knowing that just getting through another day as a student, employee, or parent is a success.

Celebrating Success

Success is being who you want to be and doing what you want to do. In addition, although you may not feel successful until you reach an important goal, success is a process. Each step along the way to improvement and growth, no matter how small, is a success worth acknowledging.

Here are some ways to celebrate successes big and small:

- *Appreciate yourself.* Take time to congratulate yourself for a job well done—whether it is a good grade, a job offer, or a personal victory over substance abuse.

- *Build your confidence for future challenges.* Let this experience help you to solidify your confidence. Show yourself and others that you are capable of building on and continuing your success.

- *Stay sensitive to others.* Some people around you may not have been as successful. Remember that you have been in their place and they in yours. Enjoy what you have and support others as they need it.

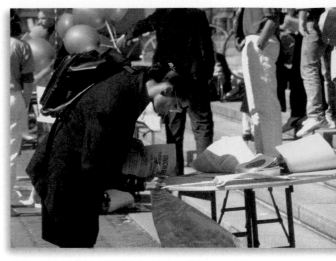

Take advantage of available opportunities, such as extracurricular activities and internships, throughout your college career.

TAKE ACTION

Learn from a Mistake

Describe an academic situation—a poor grade on a test, a difficult relationship with an instructor, an assignment that was never completed—where you made a mistake. What happened?

The most poor grades. that I get was in math I always have a poor grade in high school

What were the consequences of the mistake?

The consequence of this mistake was that I never increase the grade.

What did you do to improve the situation—or, if you took no action, what could you have done?

I probbely talk more with the introcture to work more on the subject.

How might you act differently next time, and why?

I will act more contisly about the subject.

Both failure and success will be a bottomless source of learning as you move through college and beyond. The better coping skills you build now, the more you will benefit in the future.

College Helps You Become a Person of Integrity

Integrity is at the heart of your actions as a member of your academic community. Having integrity implies that you adhere to a code of moral values, prizing honesty and fairness in all aspects of life. *Academic integrity,* specifically, refers to integrity in academic situations: classes, assignments, tests, papers, projects, and relationships with students and faculty.

When you register for college, you agree, either implicitly or explicitly, to a code of academic conduct consisting of positive actions as well as actions to avoid. Your school's code of honor, or academic integrity policy, should be printed in your student handbook. Following this code—doing what is asked of you honestly and in a manner that promotes learning—ensures a quality education based on ethics and hard work. Furthermore, it helps you develop a habit of integrity that will make you a desirable and trustworthy employee, friend, and family member.

The Center for Academic Integrity, part of the Kenan Institute for Ethics at Duke University, defines academic integrity as a commitment to five fundamental values: honesty, trust, fairness, respect, and responsibility.[4] These values form the basis of acceptable behaviors for students and instructors.

- *Honesty.* The most fundamental value in college is honesty. Honesty defines the pursuit of knowledge and implies a search for truth in your class work, papers and lab reports, and teamwork.
- *Trust.* Mutual trust—between instructor and student, as well as among students—forms the basis for the free exchange of ideas that is fundamental to learning. Trust means that you are known as being true to your word.
- *Fairness.* Instructors must create a fair academic environment in which students are judged against clear standards and in which procedures are well defined.

RISING
TO THE CHALLENGE

Tiffany Robertson
Student at Colorado College,
Colorado Springs, Colorado

Sometimes the pressures of college can make you forget to take care of yourself. When this happened to Tiffany Robertson, she suffered depression. Through professional help and stress-relief strategies, Tiffany recovered and has been able to excel in her studies.

At Colorado College, students take one intensive class at a time. My second class was an introductory psychology class—one of the hardest at the school, although I didn't realize it at the time. For three and a half weeks, I had to attend class six hours a day with daily lab write-ups and article summaries, read at least 70 pages a night, write papers in standardized format, lead debates, and study for twice-a-week tests. On top of all that, I had to find time to train a rat for experiments. I was still new to college, so I thought that college classes were always this hard.

I had excelled in high school, but mostly through putting pressure on myself and putting myself down. In college there was not enough time in the day to do all of the work for this class, never mind eating, showering, or making friends—so I stopped sleeping. I couldn't sleep anyway since I was stressed over my grade and certain that I wasn't college material. I believed one of my teachers who said that insomnia could kill you. I was so sick from worry that I had a major depressive episode. I cried for a month straight, convinced I would never return to college.

Finally, I went on antidepressants. They helped me to sleep and calm down. My doctor reassured me that I wasn't abnormal. After a month of treatment, the new semester was about to start, so I had to make a decision about whether to return to school. I was sure I would flunk out and I never wanted to relive the despair I had experienced, but talking with a good friend made me willing to try school again.

The first thing I learned was to let go of my fear of failure and think positively. I saw that I would lose nothing by trying again, and that I would still be okay if I failed. Basically, I realized that it was normal to struggle with the pressures that I had been feeling, and that I just needed some help. Second, I realized that I needed to put myself first! If I needed 10 hours of sleep a night to function properly, then I would do it. If I needed to exercise for 30 minutes each day to be happy and alert, then I made time for it. Sometimes this meant not doing all of my homework. Giving myself a break was much healthier than worrying myself to death.

Some practical changes helped me actualize these new priorities. I started using earplugs so that I could study or sleep anytime. To relieve myself from deadline pressure, I made a commitment never to procrastinate. By studying and starting papers early, I could handle unexpected issues. I discovered which activities I enjoyed and volunteered to do them. I found out what subjects I liked. Since I'm a natural at learning foreign languages, I took a Spanish class. Homework took a lot less time to finish! I realized that I wasn't bad at psychology, I am just better at remembering things that I am interested in.

Since I stopped stressing about grades and started doing more of what I like, such as volunteering and spending time with friends, my grades have been great. I enjoyed what I was doing so much that I was awarded a Spanish scholarship that I didn't even apply for! Instead of letting one class make me feel stupid and unworthy, I stuck it out for the year, and I'm glad.

Take a Moment to Consider . . .

- *A subject you really like that you haven't prioritized in your course schedule.*

- *Something you could do right now to "put yourself first."*

- *Respect.* In a respectful academic environment, both students and instructors accept and honor a wide range of opinions, even if the opinions are contrary to their own core beliefs.

- *Responsibility.* You are responsible for your own choices in school and in striving for the best education. Personal responsibility implies a commitment to choices that reflect fairness and honesty.

These five values illustrate that academic integrity goes beyond promising not to cheat on tests. Being honest, for example, means following other school rules and policies, such as those governing when, where, and how you can use cell phones and personal computers. Being fair may mean not helping another student when it is inappropriate; being responsible may mean reaching out to another student when you can and when it's right.

Having academic integrity has important positive effects on the following:

Your behavior patterns. When you condition yourself to play fair now, you set a pattern that follows you on the job and in your personal relationships.

Your knowledge level. If you cheat on a test, you might pass the test—and the course—but what will you remember after you receive your grade? The point of college is to acquire knowledge and skills that you will use in more advanced courses and after you graduate. Retaining knowledge leads to success in higher-level course work and to obtaining—and retaining—jobs.

Your interaction with others. When you act with academic integrity, you show respect for the work of others. In turn, you earn trust and respect from them, which may lead to friendships and opportunities.

Your self-esteem. Remember that self-esteem is tied to action. The more you act in respectful and honorable ways, the better you feel about yourself, and the more you are able to achieve.

Above all, you are responsible for your own integrity. You can choose actions that build your confidence, ability, knowledge, and reputation. Make choices that serve you well. With

reflect

In your school's student handbook or on the school website, read the academic integrity policy and any related rules. Describe your reaction to them: Do they seem reasonable? Why do you think colleges have academic integrity policies? Do you think these policies promote academic integrity and prevent cheating?

& respond

a strong sense of integrity, you are able to learn throughout your life.

College Provides an Opportunity to Reflect on Yourself and Your Life

Making the commitment to work toward a college education means thinking about yourself on a big-picture level. What do you do well? What do you want out of life? What can you improve? College gives you the chance to evaluate where you are and to make some concrete decisions about how to get where you want to be.

This course, and this textbook, provide an ideal opportunity to kick off this exploration. Throughout the semester, the topics you cover will lead you to a deeper understanding of who you are and what you want out of life.

- *Part I, Getting Ready to Learn,* encourages you to examine your reasons for being in college, your learning styles and values, your goals, how you manage time, and how you think creatively and critically.
- *Part II, Targeting Success in School,* promotes exploration of what you do well and what you can improve in your study skills—reading, studying, listening, remembering, note taking, test taking, math and science learning, writing, and researching.
- *Part III, Creating Life Success,* improves your understanding of how you communicate with and relate to others in the world, your personal wellness, your career goals, and how you manage your finances.

As you move through your work in this course, try to remember your goal of greater self-knowledge. From time to time, step back and think about how the topic you are covering can help you understand something important about yourself. When a topic seems boring or frustrating, try to connect it back to yourself—think, "How is this important to me? How will it help me achieve my most important goals?" The more you see how material will help you, the more comprehensive and long-lasting your learning will be.

One additional element of this text is designed to help you maximize your success and learn for life: the Habits of Mind.

What are the Habits of Mind and how can they help you succeed?

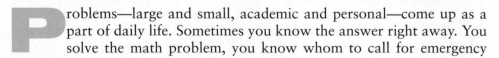

Problems—large and small, academic and personal—come up as a part of daily life. Sometimes you know the answer right away. You solve the math problem, you know whom to call for emergency child care, you have a backup when you don't get the course you want. Often, though, problems are not so clear-cut. What do you do?

In situations where you do not know how to respond to a problem right off the bat, your ability to *behave intelligently*—that is, to think through and act on the situation in ways that bring about the most favorable results—will give you the best chance at success. The essential ingredient of intelligent behavior is "not only having information, but also knowing how to act on it,"[5] reports Art Costa, Ed.D., an Emeritus Professor of Education at California State University, Sacramento, and Co-director of the Institute for Intelligent Behavior in El Dorado Hills, California. Costa studied how students respond to problems, looking specifically at what they did when working with what they did not yet know. Based on observation and on his evaluation of research, he determined that when students demonstrated particular behavior patterns, they tended to solve problems. He calls these behaviors the Habits of Mind.

"By 'habit of mind,' I mean a disposition toward behaving intelligently when confronted with problems," says Costa. "When we draw upon these resources [the Habits], the results are more powerful, of higher quality, and of greater significance."[6] The Habits of Mind are as follows:

1. Persisting
2. Managing impulsivity
3. Listening to others with understanding and empathy
4. Thinking flexibly
5. Thinking about our thinking (metacognition)
6. Striving for accuracy and precision
7. Questioning and posing problems
8. Applying past knowledge to new situations
9. Thinking and communicating with clarity and precision
10. Gathering data through all senses
11. Creating, imagining, and innovating
12. Responding with wonderment and awe
13. Taking responsible risks
14. Finding humor
15. Thinking interdependently
16. Learning continuously

Although they are not the only ways in which people respond intelligently to the unknown, the Habits of Mind are a collection of key behaviors that promote success and growth. Each chapter in *Keys to Effective Learning* will feature one Habit. The descriptions of the Habits, appearing at the ends of the chapters, will show how each Habit can help you actively use the chapter material to process your problems and achieve your goals. The Personal Improvement Plan exercise will also incorporate that chapter's Habit.

As you know from your reading earlier in the chapter, a habit is a preference for an action that you do in a certain way and often on a regular basis. Ultimately, your goal is to make the Habits true *habits* of yours—to enjoy the positive effects that come from using them regularly and in ways that suit you best. Costa describes five characteristics demonstrated by those who have made habits of the Habits of Mind:

1. *Inclination:* They tend to use behavior patterns that work.
2. *Value:* They value the behaviors that work rather than other, less useful ones.
3. *Sensitivity:* They notice when it is possible, and appropriate, to use certain behaviors.
4. *Capability:* They have the basic skills and ability to carry out the behaviors.
5. *Commitment:* They make a continual effort to evaluate how they did and to improve upon their performance.[7]

As you learn the Habits, you will become better able to identify which will be most useful in a situation and to decide how to implement them. Most of the time you will use more than one Habit for a situation—for example, when brainstorming a problem with a study group, you may think interdependently, listen to others with understanding, and communicate clearly. The more you make the Habits your own, the more effectively and consistently you will approach the problems that will inevitably come your way.

I will persist.

Persisting doesn't mean just trying again when the first try doesn't work. Someone using this Habit of Mind will evaluate a situation to see what might help, stop if one idea isn't working, think about why it didn't work and what might work better, and try something different. You might call this "intelligent trying." Here is an example: When trying to use a key that doesn't fit into a door, you wouldn't keep trying the same key—you would stop, look at the rest of your keys, decide which should work, and then try that one. Another important part of persisting is being able to sustain your focus on a problem long enough to resolve it.

As you begin college and throughout your experience, persisting will be essential to your success. It's easy to get pumped up at the beginning—but the road can get long when you hit a tough exam, a long research project, an instructor with whom you don't get along, or a subject you feel you just can't master. If you give up entirely or rush to finish tasks because you are tired of how long they are taking, you will miss out on the rewards that come from persisting. Keep going, think as you go, and you will achieve your goals.

TEAM BUILDING
COLLABORATIVE SOLUTIONS

Motivators

Gather in a group of three to five students. Each person should take out a blank sheet of paper. Together, brainstorm some typical school motivation issues—situations or things that dampen motivation for students—and have each person write a different issue at the top of his or her paper. Remember that issues don't have to be school-related to affect motivation in school—for example, a problem at home can dampen your desire to focus on academics.

When everyone has an issue written down, each person should pass his or her page to the person to the left. Take a minute to think; then write, on the page you receive, one idea about how to overcome the particular motivation issue. Again, when everyone is finished, pass the pages to the left. Continue until your original page comes back to you.

If there is time, you may want to talk over some of the solutions. What seems like it may work, and why? Might different solutions work for different people? You may also want to make copies of the pages so that each group member has a copy of each solution page.

personal IMPROVEMENT plan

I commit to three specific motivation strategies to keep me moving on the path toward college success.
From this chapter, I choose three strategies that I think will help me.

Strategy 1: improve writing

Strategy 2: reading

Strategy 3: spent more time on work

I choose one strategy to focus on (circle this strategy above) and I will:

- describe my goal—what I want to gain by using this strategy.

  is so I would be prepare in the subject.

- describe in detail how I plan to use the strategy.

  be spent more time each day

- describe how I will measure my progress toward the goal this semester.

  by measure each work of my improve to follow my goal

Activate the Habit of Mind

HABITS OF MIND — MIND

Here's how I will *persist* to achieve this goal.

never to give up

SUGGESTED READINGS

Baker, Sunny and Kim Baker. *College After 30: It's Never Too Late to Get the Degree You Need!* Holbrook, MA: Bob Adams, 1992.

Evers, Frederick T., James Cameron Rush, and Iris Berdow. *The Bases of Competence: Skills for Lifelong Learning and Employability.* San Francisco: Jossey-Bass, 1998.

Jeffers, Susan. *Feel the Fear and Do It Anyway.* New York: Fawcett Columbine, 1992.

Shields, Charles J. *Back in School: A Guide for Adult Learners.* Hawthorne, NJ: Career Press, 1994.

Weinberg, Carol. *The Complete Handbook for College Women: Making the Most of Your College Experience.* New York: New York University Press, 1994.

INTERNET RESOURCES

Student Center: www.studentcenter.org

Student.Com: College Life Online: www.student.com

Prentice Hall Student Success Supersite:Student Union: www.prenhall.com/success/StudentUn/index.html

Success Stories: www.prenhall.com/success/Stories/index.html

Habits of Mind Website: www.habits-of-mind.net

ENDNOTES

1. Rita Lenken Hawkins, Baltimore City Community College, 1997.

2. Rick Pitino, *Success Is a Choice.* New York: Broadway Books, 1997, p. 40.

3. Cited in Colin Rise and Malcolm J. Nicholl, *Accelerated Learning for the 21st Century.* New York: Dell, 1997, pp. 5–6.

4. Center for Academic Integrity, Kenan Institute for Ethics, Duke University. A Report from the Center for Academic Integrity, October 1999. Downloaded March 19, 2001 from www.academicintegrity.org.

5. Costa, Arthur L. "Habits of Mind." In *Developing Minds: A Resource Book for Teaching Thinking*, Arthur L. Costa, ed. Alexandria, VA: ASCD, 2001, p. 80.

6. Ibid.

7. Ibid.

Check those statements that apply to you right now:

- ☐ I'm not sure what "learning style" means.

- ☐ I feel out of touch in some of my classes.

- ☐ I do better in a class when I can relate to the instructor's style.

- ☐ I want to know more about what study techniques work best for me.

- ☐ I know what classes I do best in but I'm not sure why.

- ☐ I have a strong sense of my personal values.

- ☐ I'm unsure of how to improve my weak areas.

Self-Awareness

KNOWING HOW YOU LEARN AND WHAT YOU VALUE

IN THIS CHAPTER

In this chapter you explore answers to the following questions:

- What are learning styles?

- How can you discover how you learn?

- Why is it important to know how you learn?

- What defines your values?

- How can you identify and manage learning disabilities?

Gathering data through all senses.

"Intelligent people know that **all information gets into the brain through the sensory pathways**. . . . Those whose sensory pathways are open [and] alert absorb more information from the environment."   —ART COSTA

*When you **take in information using all of your senses** and observe how you respond to that information, you build self-awareness. With that awareness of how you respond to all kinds of information, you can understand how you learn and decide what you value.*

As you begin your academic journey, you will be looking for tools and aids to help you on your way. Self-awareness is one important key to making the most of your education. This chapter will help you build that awareness, giving you tools to become an even more effective learner. First, through two different learning-style assessments, you will explore how you learn. Next, you will examine the advantages of knowing your learning styles and read about what to do if

your challenges fall into the category of learning disability. Finally, you will think carefully about your values, defining what means the most to you and considering the role values play in your educational choices. With increased awareness of how you learn and what you value, you will move ahead on your path to success.

What is a learning style?

Your experiences in the courses ahead may range from fulfillment and high grades to disconnection and low grades or withdrawals. Reasons for this wide range include varying levels of interest and effort, outside stresses, and personal reactions to instructors. How well you know and use your **learning styles** is another crucial factor. Understanding how you learn will help you choose strategies that will bring you success in college and life.

Two Aspects of Learning Styles

Learning style
A particular way in which the mind receives and processes information.

Students process information in different ways and have varied styles of interaction with others. Say, for example, that a group of students is taking a freshman composition class that is broken up into study groups during two out of three class meetings. Students who are comfortable working with words or who enjoy study groups may do well in the course. Students who are more mathematical than verbal, or who prefer to work alone, might not do as well. The learning-style factor results in different levels of success with the course.

How you learn can be seen as having two equally important aspects:

- Learning preferences—what abilities and areas of learning interest you and come most easily to you
- Personality traits—how you interact with information and with others

These two aspects are important partners in defining how you learn and how you succeed. Imagine that a freshman composition instructor teaches a group discussion–based course to a class of students with strong verbal learning preferences. After finals, she is surprised to find a wide array of grades. A possible reason: Not everyone functions well in small group discussions.

Likewise, suppose another instructor chances on a course section composed entirely of students who love the experience-based, hands-on style of his biology course. He assumes that everyone will pass with flying colors. They don't, however—because, of course, not everyone has a natural learning preference in the sciences, no matter how much a student might like the style of interacting with the course material.

Getting Perspective on Learning Style

What you find out about your learning styles through the assessments in this chapter can help you manage yourself effectively. Your thinking skills—your ability to evaluate information—enable you to see yourself as a whole, including strengths and weaknesses. Your job is to analyze the information you gain from the assessments and use what you have learned as a guide on the path to self-improvement.

Approach any assessment as a tool with which you can expand your idea of yourself. There are no "right" answers, no "best" set of scores. Think of it in the same way you would a new set of eyeglasses for a person with somewhat blurred vision. The glasses will not create new paths and possibilities, but will help the person see more clearly the ones that already exist.

You continually learn, change, and grow throughout your life. Any evaluation is simply a snapshot, a look at who you are in a given moment. Your answers can, and will, change as you change and as circumstances change. They provide an opportunity for you to look at the present moment by asking questions: Who am I right now? How does this compare to who I want to be?

Using Assessments for Understanding

Understanding your preferred learning styles helps to prevent you from boxing yourself into categories that limit your life. Instead of saying, "I'm no good in math," someone who is not a natural in math can make the subject easier by tapping into learning style–related strategies. For example, a learner who responds to visuals can learn better by drawing diagrams of math problems; a learner who benefits from discussing material with others can improve comprehension by talking out problems with a study partner.

Most people have one or two dominant learning styles. In addition, you may change which abilities you emphasize, depending on the situation. For example, a student with a highly developed visual sense might find it easy to take notes in think link style (see Chapter 7 for an explanation of different note-taking styles). However, if an instructor writes an outline on the board as a guide to a detailed topic, the same student might work with the outline. The better you know yourself, the better you are able to assess and adapt to any situation.

Facing Challenges Realistically

Any assessment reveals areas of challenge as well as ability. Rather than dwelling on limitations (which often results in a negative self-image) or ignoring them (which often leads to unproductive choices), use what you know from the assessment to face your limitations and work to improve them.

"To be what we are, and to become what we are capable of becoming, is the only end of life."

ROBERT LOUIS STEVENSON

TAKE ACTION

Explore What Makes a Successful Learner

Speak with two different people at school whom you respect—an instructor, an academic advisor, an upper-classman, a fellow freshman. Ask questions that will help you arrive at a description of a successful learner; for example, "What are three characteristics of a student who is successful in class?" "What strategies were most helpful to you when you were a freshman?" Make notes as you talk. Write here to whom you will speak and state the questions you plan to ask:

Person: _____

Your questions: _____

_____

_____

_____

Person: _____

_____

Your questions: _____

_____

_____

From your conversations, describe your image of a successful learner.

_____

_____

_____

_____

In any area of challenge, look at where you are and set goals that help you reach where you want to be. If a class is difficult, examine what improvements to make in order to succeed. If a project involves tasks that give you trouble, face your limitations head-on and ask for help. Exploring what you gain from working on a limitation helps you build the motivation you need to move ahead.

How can you discover how you learn?

This chapter presents two assessments that help you discover your learning styles and personality traits. The first assessment focuses on learning preferences and is called *Multiple Pathways to Learning*. It is based on the Multiple Intelligences Theory developed by Howard Gardner.

The second assessment is based on the Myers–Briggs Type Inventory® (MBTI). The assessment is called *Personality Spectrum* and helps you evaluate how you react to people and situations.

Multiple Intelligences

There is a saying, "It is not how smart you are, but how you are smart." In 1983, Howard Gardner, a Harvard University professor, changed the way people perceive intelligence and learning with his theory of Multiple Intelligences. This theory holds that there are at least eight distinct **intelligences** possessed by all people, and that every person has developed some intelligences more fully than others. According to the Multiple Intelligences Theory, when you find a task or subject easy, you are probably using a more fully developed intelligence; when you have more trouble, you may be using a less developed intelligence.[1]

Intelligence
As defined by H. Gardner, an ability to solve problems or fashion products that are useful in a particular cultural setting or community.

Gardner believes that the way you learn is a unique blend of intelligences, resulting from your distinctive abilities, challenges, experiences, and training. In addition, particular levels of ability in the intelligences may develop or recede based on changes in your life. Gardner thinks that the traditional view of intelligence, based on mathematical, logical, and verbal measurements, doesn't accurately reflect the entire spectrum of human ability:

> I believe that we should . . . look . . . at more naturalistic sources of information about how peoples around the world develop skills important to their way of life. Think, for example, of sailors in the South Seas, who find their way around hundreds, or even thousands, of islands by looking at the constellations of stars in the sky, feeling the way a boat passes over the water, and noticing a few scattered landmarks. A word for intelligence in a society of these sailors would probably refer to that kind of navigational ability.[2]

Table 2.1 offers brief descriptions of the focus of each of the intelligences. You can find information on related skills and study techniques on page 37. The Multiple Pathways to Learning assessment helps you determine the levels to which your intelligences are developed.

Personality Spectrum

Personality assessments indicate how you respond to both internal and external situations—in other words, how you react to information, thoughts, and feelings, as well as to people and events. The Myers–Briggs Type Inventory is one of the most widely used personality inventories. Katharine Briggs and her daughter, Isabel Briggs Myers, together designed the MBTI. Later, David Keirsey and Marilyn Bates combined the 16 Myers–Briggs types into four

A sound engineer most likely has highly developed musical and logical–mathematical intelligences.

TABLE 2.1	Multiple intelligences.

INTELLIGENCE	DESCRIPTION
Verbal–Linguistic	Ability to communicate through language (listening, reading, writing, speaking)
Logical–Mathematical	Ability to understand logical reasoning and problem solving (math, science, patterns, sequences)
Bodily–Kinesthetic	Ability to use the physical body skillfully and to take in knowledge through bodily sensation (coordination, working with hands)
Visual–Spatial	Ability to understand spatial relationships and to perceive and create images (visual art, graphic design, charts and maps)
Interpersonal	Ability to relate to others, noticing their moods, motivations, and feelings (social activity, cooperative learning, teamwork)
Intrapersonal	Ability to understand one's own behavior and feelings (self-awareness, independence, time spent alone)
Musical	Ability to comprehend and create meaningful sound and recognize patterns (music, sensitivity to sound and patterns)
Naturalistic	Ability to understand features of the environment (interest in nature, environmental balance, ecosystem, stress relief brought by natural environments)

temperaments and developed an assessment called the Keirsey Sorter based on those temperaments.

Derived in part from the Myers–Briggs and Keirsey theories, the Personality Spectrum assessment adapts and simplifies their material into four personality types—Thinker, Organizer, Giver, and Adventurer—and was developed by Dr. Joyce Bishop. The Personality Spectrum gives you a personality perspective on how you can maximize your functioning. For each personality type, you'll see techniques that improve performance, learning strategies, and ways of relating to others. Page 39 gives you more details about each type.

Scoring the Assessments

The assessments begin on page 36. As you complete them, try to answer the questions objectively—in other words, answer the questions to best indicate who you are, not who you want to be (or who your parents or instructors want you to be). Then, enter your scores on page 40. Don't be concerned if some of your scores are low—that is true for almost everyone.

Following each assessment is information about the typical traits of, and appropriate study strategies for, each intelligence or spectrum dimension. You have abilities in all areas, though some are more de-

reflect

Before you take the assessments in this chapter, take a moment to think about how you perceive yourself as a student. Describe what you consider your strengths and challenges, courses or topics that draw you in or turn you off, and classroom settings that seem to work well or not so well for you.

& respond

veloped than others. Therefore, you may encounter useful suggestions under any of the headings. During this course, try many new study techniques and keep what works for you.

Remember, also, that knowing your learning styles is not only about guiding your life toward your strongest abilities; it is also about using other strategies when you face challenges. When what is required of you involves tasks and academic areas that you find difficult, use the strategies for your weaker areas, or try to apply strategies from your strengths to the difficult material. For example, a visual learner having trouble in math could either try some logical–mathematical strategies or apply visual strategies to the math material.

IMPORTANT NOTE   *about scoring . . .*

The two assessments are scored *differently.* For *Multiple Pathways to Learning,* each intelligence has a set of numbered statements, and you consider each numbered statement on its own, giving it the number you feel best suits your response to it. You will, therefore, have any combination of numbers for each intelligence, from all 4s to all 1s or anywhere in between.

For *Personality Spectrum,* you rank order the four statements that complete each statement, giving a 4 to the one most like you, a 3 to the next most, a 2 to the next, and a 1 to the one least like you. You will, therefore, have a 4, 3, 2, and 1 for each of the eight numbered questions.

Why is it important to know how you learn?

The knowledge you gain by taking the assessments in this chapter can guide you to smart choices that will bring success in your studies, the classroom, and the workplace.

Study Benefits

Knowing how you learn helps you choose techniques that suit your needs. One aspect of this benefit is the ability to maximize what you do best. Say you respond well to information presented in a linear, logical way. You can use this knowledge to choose to develop an orderly, linear system of reviewing your notes. You can use lists both as a study aid and as a way to order your priorities.

The other aspect is the ability to tackle strategically situations and topics that you don't take to as readily. A student who does *not* respond well to linear information, for example, has two choices when faced with a course focused on logical, well-structured material. One choice is to apply techniques from that student's strengths to the material—in this case, if the student is a strong interpersonal learner, he might spend a lot of time with a study group. The other choice is to use the study techniques geared toward logical learners in an attempt to build logical skills.

The charts on pages 37 and 39 offer a variety of strategies for each of the Multiple Intelligences and Personality Spectrum dimensions. When you face

MULTIPLE PATHWAYS TO LEARNING

Developed by Joyce Bishop, Ph.D., and based upon Howard Gardner's *Frames of Mind: The Theory of Multiple Intelligences.*[3]

Directions: Rate each statement as follows. Write the number of your response (1–4) on the line next to the statement and total each set of six questions.

1 rarely 2 sometimes 3 usually 4 always

1. __2__ I enjoy physical activities.
2. __1__ I am uncomfortable sitting still.
3. __4__ I prefer to learn through doing.
4. __3__ When sitting I move my legs or hands.
5. __4__ I enjoy working with my hands.
6. __3__ I like to pace when I'm thinking or studying.

__17__ TOTAL FOR BODILY–KINESTHETIC

7. __1__ I enjoy telling stories.
8. __4__ I like to write.
9. __3__ I like to read.
10. __2__ I express myself clearly.
11. __2__ I am good at negotiating.
12. __3__ I like to discuss topics that interest me.

__16__ TOTAL FOR VERBAL–LINGUISTIC

13. __2__ I use maps easily.
14. __1__ I draw pictures/diagrams when explaining ideas.
15. __1__ I can assemble items easily from diagrams.
16. __2__ I enjoy drawing or photography.
17. __2__ I do not like to read long paragraphs.
18. __2__ I prefer a drawn map over written directions.

__10__ TOTAL FOR VISUAL–SPATIAL

19. __2__ I like math in school.
20. __4__ I like science.
21. __3__ I problem solve well.
22. __2__ I question how things work.
23. __4__ I enjoy planning or designing something new.
24. __2__ I am able to fix things.

__15__ TOTAL FOR LOGICAL–MATHEMATICAL

25. __3__ I listen to music.
26. __1__ I move my fingers or feet when I hear music.
27. __2__ I have good rhythm.
28. __1__ I like to sing along with music.
29. __1__ People have said I have musical talent.
30. __1__ I like to express my ideas through music.

__9__ TOTAL FOR MUSICAL

31. __2__ I need quiet time to think.
32. __4__ I think about issues before I want to talk.
33. __3__ I am interested in self-improvement.
34. __3__ I understand my thoughts and feelings.
35. __4__ I know what I want out of life.
36. __2__ I prefer to work on projects alone.

__19__ TOTAL FOR INTRAPERSONAL

37. __3__ I like doing a project with other people.
38. __1__ People come to me to help settle conflicts.
39. __2__ I like to spend time with friends.
40. __3__ I am good at understanding people.
41. __4__ I am good at making people feel comfortable.
42. __4__ I enjoy helping others.

__18__ TOTAL FOR INTERPERSONAL

43. __3__ I enjoy nature whenever possible.
44. __2__ I think about having a career involving nature.
45. __4__ I enjoy studying plants, animals, or oceans.
46. __2__ I avoid being indoors except when I sleep.
47. __1__ As a child I played with bugs and leaves.
48. __3__ When I feel stressed I want to be out in nature.

__15__ TOTAL FOR NATURALISTIC

MULTIPLE INTELLIGENCES

SKILLS	STUDY TECHNIQUES

VERBAL–LINGUISTIC

- Analyzing own use of language
- Remembering terms
- Explaining, teaching, learning, using humor
- Understanding syntax and meaning of words
- Convincing someone to do something

VERBAL–LINGUISTIC

- Read text and highlight no more than 10%
- Rewrite notes
- Outline chapters
- Teach someone else
- Recite information or write scripts/debates

MUSICAL–RHYTHMIC

- Sensing tonal qualities
- Creating or enjoying melodies and rhythms
- Being sensitive to sounds and rhythms
- Using "schemas" to hear music
- Understanding the structure of music

MUSICAL–RHYTHMIC

- Create rhythms out of words
- Beat out rhythms with hand or stick
- Play instrumental music/write raps
- Put new material to songs you already know
- Take music breaks

LOGICAL–MATHEMATICAL

- Recognizing abstract patterns
- Reasoning inductively and deductively
- Discerning relationships and connections
- Performing complex calculations
- Reasoning scientifically

LOGICAL–MATHEMATICAL

- Organize material logically
- Explain material sequentially to someone
- Develop systems and find patterns
- Write outlines and develop charts and graphs
- Analyze information

VISUAL–SPATIAL

- Perceiving and forming objects accurately
- Recognizing relationships between objects
- Representing something graphically
- Manipulating images
- Finding one's way in space

VISUAL–SPATIAL

- Develop graphic organizers for new material
- Draw mind maps
- Develop charts and graphs
- Use color in notes to organize
- Visualize material

BODILY–KINESTHETIC

- Connecting mind and body
- Controlling movement
- Improving body functions
- Expanding body awareness to all senses
- Coordinating body movement

BODILY–KINESTHETIC

- Move or rap while you learn
- Pace and recite
- Move fingers under words while reading
- Create "living sculptures"
- Act out scripts of material, design games

INTRAPERSONAL

- Evaluating own thinking
- Being aware of and expressing feelings
- Understanding self in relationship to others
- Thinking and reasoning on higher levels

INTRAPERSONAL

- Reflect on personal meaning of information
- Visualize information/keep a journal
- Study in quiet settings
- Imagine experiments

INTERPERSONAL

- Seeing things from others' perspectives
- Cooperating within a group
- Communicating verbally and nonverbally
- Creating and maintaining relationships

INTERPERSONAL

- Study in a group
- Discuss information
- Use flash cards with others
- Teach someone else

NATURALIST

- Understanding nature at a deep level
- Appreciating the delicate balance in nature

NATURALIST

- Connect with nature whenever possible
- Form study groups of people with like interests

PERSONALITY SPECTRUM

Adapted by Dr. Joyce Bishop from David Lazear, Pathways of Learning, 1994.

STEP 1. Rank order all four responses to each question from most like you (4) to least like you (1). Use the circles next to the responses to indicate your rankings.

4	**3**	**2**	**1**
most like me	*more like me*	*less like me*	*least like me*

1. I like instructors who
   a. ③ tell me exactly what is expected of me.
   b. ② make learning active and exciting.
   c. ④ maintain a safe and supportive classroom.
   d. ③ challenge me to think at higher levels.

2. I learn best when the material is
   a. ④ well organized.
   b. ① something I can do hands-on.
   c. ② about understanding and improving the human condition.
   d. ③ intellectually challenging.

3. A high priority in my life is to
   a. ③ keep my commitments.
   b. ② experience as much of life as possible.
   c. ① make a difference in the lives of others.
   d. ④ understand how things work.

4. Other people think of me as
   a. ③ dependable and loyal.
   b. ② dynamic and creative.
   c. ④ caring and honest.
   d. ② intelligent and inventive.

5. When I experience stress I would most likely
   a. ④ do something to help me feel more in control of my life.
   b. ② do something physical and daring.
   c. ① talk with a friend.
   d. ③ go off by myself and think about my situation.

6. I would probably not be close friends with someone who is
   a. ② irresponsible.
   b. ③ unwilling to try new things.
   c. ① selfish and unkind to others.
   d. ① an illogical thinker.

7. My vacations could be described as
   a. ④ traditional.
   b. ② adventuresome.
   c. ③ pleasing to others.
   d. ① a new learning experience.

8. One word that best describes me is
   a. ④ sensible.
   b. ④ spontaneous.
   c. ⑤ giving.
   d. ① analytical.

STEP 2. Add up the total points for each letter.

TOTAL for a. ㉕ Organizer   TOTAL for c. ⑰ Giver

TOTAL for b. ⑲ Adventurer   TOTAL for d. ⑳ Thinker

STEP 3. Plot these numbers on the brain diagram on page 40.

PERSONALITY SPECTRUM

SKILLS

THINKER

- Solving problems
- Developing models and systems
- Analytical and abstract thinking
- Exploring ideas and potentials
- Ingenuity
- Going beyond established boundaries
- Global thinking—seeking universal truth

ORGANIZER

- Responsibility, reliability
- Operating successfully within social structures
- Sense of history, culture, and dignity
- Neatness and organization
- Loyalty
- Orientation to detail
- Comprehensive follow-through on tasks
- Efficiency

GIVER

- Honesty, authenticity
- Successful, close relationships
- Making a difference in the world
- Cultivating your own potential and that of others
- Negotiation; promoting peace
- Communicating with others
- Openness
- Helping others

ADVENTURER

- High ability in a variety of fields
- Courage and daring
- Approaching problem solving in a hands-on fashion
- Living in the present
- Spontaneity and action
- Negotiating
- Nontraditional style
- Flexibility
- Zest for life

STUDY TECHNIQUES

THINKER

- Find time to reflect independently on new information
- Learn through problem solving
- Design new ways of approaching issues
- Convert material into logical charts and graphs
- Try to minimize repetitive tasks
- Look for opportunities where you have the freedom to work independently

ORGANIZER

- Try to have tasks defined in clear, concrete terms so that you know what is required
- Look for a well structured, stable environment
- Request feedback
- Use a planner to schedule tasks and dates
- Organize material by rewriting and organizing class or text notes, making flash cards, or carefully highlighting

GIVER

- Study with others
- Teach material to others
- Seek out tasks, groups, and subjects that involve helping people
- Find ways to express thoughts and feelings clearly and honestly
- Put energy into your most important relationships

ADVENTURER

- Look for environments that encourage nontraditional approaches
- Find hands-on ways to learn
- Seek people whom you find stimulating
- Use or develop games and puzzles to help memorize terms
- Fight boredom by asking if you can do something extra or perform a task in a more active way

Scoring Sheet for Assessments

Personality Spectrum: Place a dot on the appropriate number line in the brain diagram for each of your four scores from p. 38; connect the dots; then shade each section using a different color. Write your scores in the four circles just outside the diagram. See information regarding scores below.

Multiple Pathways to Learning: In the vertical bars below the brain diagram, indicate your scores from p. 36 by shading from the bottom going up until you reach the number corresponding to your score for that intelligence. See information regarding scores below.

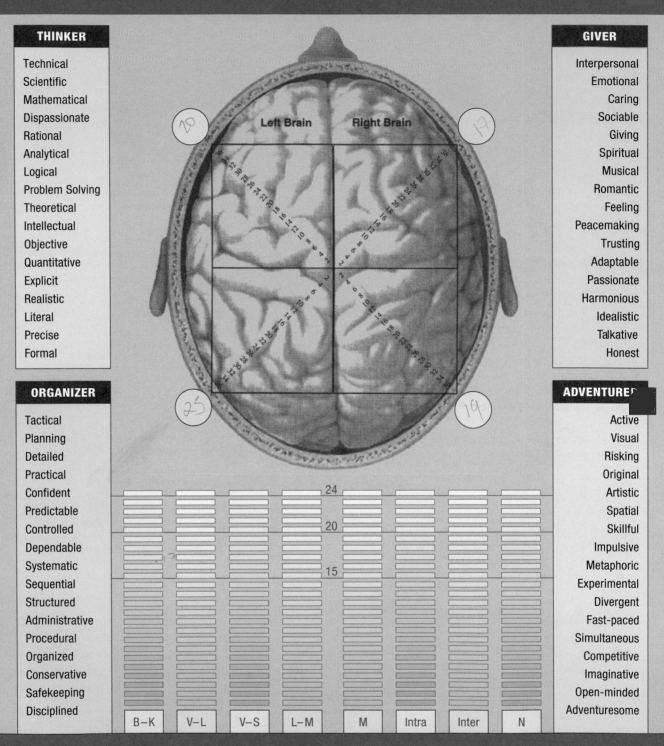

THINKER

Technical
Scientific
Mathematical
Dispassionate
Rational
Analytical
Logical
Problem Solving
Theoretical
Intellectual
Objective
Quantitative
Explicit
Realistic
Literal
Precise
Formal

GIVER

Interpersonal
Emotional
Caring
Sociable
Giving
Spiritual
Musical
Romantic
Feeling
Peacemaking
Trusting
Adaptable
Passionate
Harmonious
Idealistic
Talkative
Honest

ORGANIZER

Tactical
Planning
Detailed
Practical
Confident
Predictable
Controlled
Dependable
Systematic
Sequential
Structured
Administrative
Procedural
Organized
Conservative
Safekeeping
Disciplined

ADVENTURER

Active
Visual
Risking
Original
Artistic
Spatial
Skillful
Impulsive
Metaphoric
Experimental
Divergent
Fast-paced
Simultaneous
Competitive
Imaginative
Open-minded
Adventuresome

Left Brain   Right Brain

Bar labels: B–K | V–L | V–S | L–M | M | Intra | Inter | N

For the Personality Spectrum, 26–36 indicates a strong tendency in that dimension, 14–25 a moderate tendency, and below 14 a minimal tendency.

For Multiple Pathways to Learning, 21–24 indicates a high level of development in that particular type of intelligence, 15–20 a moderate level, and below 15 an underdeveloped intelligence.

Source for brain diagram: Understanding Psychology, 3/e, by Morris, © 1996. Adapted by permission of Prentice-Hall, Inc., Upper Saddle River, NJ.

TAKE ACTION

Explore Your Personality Spectrum

What did you discover is your most dominant Personality Spectrum dimension?

Organizer becouse my personality is describe in this strategies

Which of your current courses is most likely to tap into this dimension?

Duroof becouse I will need to have all of this strategies higher.

Look at the study strategies associated with this dimension on page 39. Name one that you feel will help you maximize your success in this course and briefly describe one way you will use it.

Thinker is the first thing that I will need to success.

Name your weakest Personality Spectrum dimension: *Giver*

Which of your current courses is likely to demand the greatest skill in this area?

Giver because I don't need to come down.

Look at the study strategies associated with this dimension on page 39. Name one that you feel will help you maximize your success in this course and briefly describe one way you will use it.

Organice because I will need to organize my life, when I go on.

decisions about how to approach material and courses, refer to these charts for ideas. Develop your own strategies as you grow more acquainted with your learning styles. This text also helps you apply your learning styles knowledge with Multiple Intelligence Strategies grids—each of the following chapters has a grid that shows how to improve your mastery of different skill areas through strategies specific to each of the Multiple Intelligences.

Classroom Benefits

Knowing your learning styles can help you make the most of the teaching styles of your instructors (an instructor's dominant teaching style often reflects his or her learning styles). Your particular learning style may work well with the way some instructors teach and be a mismatch with other instructors. Occasionally, you may be able to choose an instructor who teaches in a way that maximizes how you learn. Class schedules, however, usually don't make such choices possible.

After several class meetings, you should be able to assess the instructor's teaching styles (it's common for instructors to have more than one). Table 2.2 sets forth some common styles. If your styles don't match up well with those of your instructor, you have a number of options.

TABLE 2.2	Teaching styles reflect instructor learning styles.
Lecture	Instructor speaks to the class for the entire period, little to no class interaction.
Group discussion	Instructor presents material but encourages class discussion throughout.
Small groups	Instructor presents material and then breaks class into small groups for discussion or project work.
Visual focus	Instructor uses visual elements such as diagrams, photographs, drawings, transparencies.
Verbal focus	Instructor relies primarily on words, either spoken or written on the board or overhead projector.
Logical presentation	Instructor organizes material in a logical sequence, such as by time or importance.
Random presentation	Instructor tackles topics in no particular order, jumps around a lot, or digresses.

Bring extra focus to your weaker areas. Working on your weaker points helps you break new ground in your learning. For example, if you're a verbal person in a math- and logic-oriented class, increase your focus and concentration during class so that you get as much as you can from the presentation. Then spend extra study time on the material, ask others from your class to help you, and search for additional supplemental materials and exercises to reinforce your knowledge.

Ask your instructor for additional help. For example, a visual person might ask an instructor to recommend visuals that help to illustrate the points made in class. Take advantage of your instructor's office hours to talk one-on-one about what's giving you trouble—especially in a large lecture, your instructor won't know what's going on with you unless you speak up.

"Convert" class material during study time. For example, an interpersonal learner takes a class with an instructor who presents big-picture information in lecture format. This student might organize study groups and talk through concepts with other group members while filling in the factual gaps. Likewise, a visual student might rewrite notes in different colors to add a visual element—for example, using one color for central ideas, another for supporting examples.

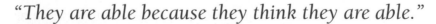

"They are able because they think they are able."

VIRGIL

Instructors are as unique as students, and no instructor can fulfill the particular needs of a whole classroom of individuals. You often have to shift elements of your habitual learning approach to mesh with how your instructor presents material. Being flexible in this way benefits you throughout life. Just as you can't hand-pick your instructors, in the workplace you are rarely, if ever, able to choose your boss or change his or her styles.

Workplace Benefits

While you are working in school as well as in your future career, knowing how you learn brings you the following key benefits on the job:

- *Better performance.* Your learning styles are essentially the same as your working styles. If you know how you learn, you can look for a career, position, and environment that suit you best. You can perform at the top of your ability if you work at a job in which you feel competent and happy. (Chapter 12 relates the Personality Spectrum to career and workplace choices in more detail.)

- *Better teamwork.* Teamwork is a primary feature of the modern workplace. The better your awareness of your abilities and personality traits, the better you are able to communicate with others and identify what tasks you can best perform in a team situation.

- *Better self-awareness.* Knowing how you learn helps you to maximize strengths and work on difficult areas. When you know you are particularly strong in an area or type of task, you can try to focus on it in your work. When a task requires a skill that is tough for you, you can either take special care with it or suggest someone else whose style may be better suited to it.

Although almost everyone has some measure of difficulty in some aspect of learning, people with diagnosed learning differences have conditions that make certain kinds of learning difficult. Specific strategies and focused assistance can help learning-disabled students manage their conditions and excel in school.

reflect

What have the personal assessments in this chapter taught you about your strengths? Choose what you consider your greatest strength and discuss how you plan to use it to your advantage this semester. What areas of weakness did the assessments highlight? Choose a weakness that has given you difficulty in school and brainstorm ways to compensate for it this semester.

& respond

How can you identify and manage learning disabilities?

Some learning disabilities cause reading problems, some create difficulties in math, and still others make it difficult for students to process the language they hear. The following will help you understand learning disabilities and, should you be diagnosed with one, help you to manage your disability successfully.

Identifying a Learning Disability

The National Center for Learning Disabilities (NCLD) has published these important facts that will help you define and identify learning disability.[4]

- *A learning disability is a neurological disorder that interferes with one's ability to store, process, and produce information.* Learning disabilities can affect reading, writing, speaking, math abilities, areas of development, and/or social skills.

- *Learning disabilities do not include mental retardation, autism, or behavioral disorders.* Generally, learning-disabled people are of average or above-average intelligence. The disability creates a "gap" that prevents them from performing according to their abilities.

- *Learning disabilities do not include impaired vision, hearing loss, or other physical disabilities.* The learning issue is separate from other physical issues that may be present.

- *Learning disabilities are life long.* You cannot be cured of a learning disability. However, you can use specific strategies to manage and even overcome areas of weakness.

- *Learning disabilities often run in families.* Although exact causes are not certain, researchers have found that heredity seems to play a significant role.

- *Learning disabilities must be diagnosed by professionals in order for the person with the disability to receive federally funded aid.* A professional will use a mix of interview, observation, and assessment tools to arrive at a diagnosis.

How can you determine if you should be evaluated for a learning disability? The NCLD recommends you watch out for persistent problems with any of the following:[5]

- reading, or reading comprehension
- math calculations, language, and concepts
- social skills, or interpreting social cues
- following a schedule, being on time, meeting deadlines
- reading or following maps
- balancing a checkbook
- following directions, especially on multistep tasks
- writing, sentence structure, spelling, and organizing written work

If you would like to be evaluated, contact your school learning center or student health center for a referral to a licensed professional. An important note: Contrary to popular belief, ADD (Attention Deficit Disorder) and ADHD (Attention Deficit Hyperactivity Disorder) are not classified as learning disabilities. They do, however, often cause problems with learning, and a student may have ADD or ADHD in addition to particular learning disabilities.[6]

Although only a small percentage of the student population has a diagnosable learning disability, these students are as capable of success as any other student and deserve support. If you are diagnosed with a learning disability, read on to explore ways to get the assistance you need.

Managing a Learning Disability

If you have a learning disability, you may label as failure anything that does not live up to the examples set by students around you. You can beat this attitude, though, with focused strategies. Table 2.3 shows some useful strategies for some learning disabilities and related conditions.

DISABILITY/CONDITION	WHAT ARE THE SIGNS?	WHAT HELPS?
Developmental writing disorders (dysgraphia)	Difficulties in composing complete sentences, organizing a writing assignment, or translating thoughts coherently to the page	Take extra time with your work. Use visual organizers to map out your thoughts before you write. Include a delay between drafting and revising an assignment. Use spell check and grammar check. Have your work evaluated by a peer editor or tutor.
Dyscalculia (developmental arithmetic disorders)	Difficulties in recognizing numbers and symbols, memorizing facts, aligning numbers, understanding abstract concepts such as fractions, and applying math to life skills (managing time, gauging distance, handling money, etc.)	Estimate answers before you start work on problems. Work in groups. Draw or graph problems if you are a strong visual learner. Ask someone to help you reword a problem. Work with math in everyday situations.
Dyslexia and related reading disorders	Problems with reading (including spelling, word sequencing, and comprehension) and processing (translating written language to thought or thought to written language)	Find a tutor who can give you a multisensory experience of reading—through hearing, writing, and speaking as well as through sight. Approach reading by learning the sounds of letters and letter combinations systematically.
Speech and language disorders	Problems with producing speech sounds, using spoken language to communicate, and/or understanding what others say	Seek a therapist who knows how to address your particular disorder. Write or type when this will allow you to communicate more clearly than speaking.
ADD/ADHD	Disorders involving consistent and problematic inattention, hyperactivity, and/or impulsivity	Structure will help; establish time structures, rules, and routines for academic, work, and personal situations. Ask instructors to clarify instructions when they aren't clear enough for you. List problematic behaviors and set rewards for yourself when you avoid them. Medication is sometimes prescribed based on a medical evaluation.
LD-related organizational issues	Difficulties in scheduling and in organizing personal, academic, and work-related materials	Structure and routine are key; establish regular modes of behavior, for example, spending ten minutes with your date book every morning. Find a "buddy" who can check in on you and keep you on track.
LD-related social issues	Problems in recognizing facial or vocal cues from others, controlling verbal and physical impulsivity, and respecting others' personal space	With a trusted friend, family member, or professional counselor or therapist, practice appropriate behavior. Look at past situations and evaluate the effects of your behavior.

Source: LD Online: Learning Disabilities Information and Resources, www.ldonline.org/ accessed 5/02/03. © 2001 WETA.

You will also benefit from becoming an advocate for your rights and by redefining failure and success in terms of your own accomplishments. Consider the following strategies.

Be informed about your disability. The more you know, the better able you will be to find help. Use the library to find books on learning disability. Search the Internet—you can find NCLD at www.ncld.org or LD Online at www.ldonline.org (other helpful disorder-specific websites are listed at the end of the chapter). You can also call NCLD toll-free at 1-888-575-7373. If you are diagnosed, you will receive an Individualized Education Program (IEP) that details your disability and recommended strategies. Make sure you understand what's in your IEP.

Seek assistance from your school. If you are officially diagnosed with a learning disability, you are legally entitled to particular aid. Armed with your test results and IEP, speak with your advisor about how you can secure specific accommodations that will help you learn. Among the services mandated by law for learning-disabled students are:

- extended time on tests
- note-taking assistance (for example, having a fellow student take notes for you)
- assistive technology devices (tape recorders or laptop computers)
- modified assignments
- alternative assessments and test formats

Other services that may help learning-disabled students include tutoring, study skills assistance, and counseling. Know, and ask for, what works best for you.

Be a dedicated student. Perhaps more than for other students, your focus and dedication will help you get where you want to go. Be on time and attend as many class meetings as you can. Read the assignments before class. Sit up front. Review your notes as soon after class as you can. Plan to spend extra time on assignments. Ask instructors for help.

Build a positive attitude. See your accomplishments in light of where you were before

RISING
TO THE CHALLENGE

Dr. Joyce Bishop
Professor of Psychology,
Golden West College,
Huntington Beach, California

Dr. Bishop, the creator of the assessments in this chapter, has a passion for learning styles that was inspired by her ordeal as a college student with a learning disability. As it did with her, knowing your learning styles can help you surmount the obstacles that come your way.

I have learning problems understanding words I hear, which made listening to lectures in college very hard. No one would know I had this difficulty because I learned how to compensate for it. In fact, I didn't even know it until years later. This learning disability is called *auditory discrimination*.

College was very confusing for me. I did well in some classes and felt totally lost in others. The hardest were the lecture-based classes. When I wasn't familiar with the information or the words, I couldn't make sense of what I was hearing.

If I read the material ahead of time, I could make visual pictures in my mind that would help me absorb the material. I could also look up words and research concepts I didn't understand. Then the lectures made more sense.

I read lips and facial expressions well, so I did well in small classes where I could consistently see the teacher's face. The disadvantage for me in small classes was the noise. Because I heard voices around me as much as I heard the speaker, I had trouble blocking the extra noise. To make my lecture classes easier to understand, I would drag a tape recorder to class so that I could play back the lecture a number of times later. I found, however, that it didn't really help when I re-listened to the tapes. After that, I bargained with my classmates to borrow their notes in exchange for typing their term papers. Typing is bodily–kinesthetic and helped me to internalize what I was learning.

The only reason I got by in college was that I am strong in logical–mathematical intelligence. School is primarily taught in the verbal–linguistic and logical–mathematical learning styles. I am also a strong visual learner. Science classes were easiest for me because they are more visual. I switched from sociology to biology my freshman year; it was easier for me to remember the visual biology material as opposed to the more verbal liberal arts classes. Without my commitment to my education and my will to succeed, I probably would not have graduated.

Twelve years after graduating, I pursued my master's in public health. Part of why I waited so long was that I needed to heal from the trauma of my own learning process. My graduate classes were much more hands-on, but there was still a great deal of reading. One day my eye doctor expressed concern about the stress my school work was causing my eyes and suggested that I get tested for a learning problem. He sent me to a center that usually tests small children for learning disabilities. The person giving the test said words and I was to spell out the words with blocks. I couldn't get some of the words right. I would consistently confuse or mistake words with close sounds. They determined that I processed language on a fourth-grade level, a condition that has not changed in my adult life.

"How far did you go through school?" asked the therapist conducting the test.

"How far do you think I went?" I asked.

After thinking for a moment, she answered, "The tenth grade." I shared that I was just completing my master's degree. Her eyes got big and she said: "You work really hard in school, don't you?"

At that moment my head flooded with memories of report cards saying "doesn't pay attention in class" and "isn't working up to potential." I started to cry. An explanation for what had brought years of pain and struggle had finally come to the surface.

Now that I know what the problem is, I use strategies that allow me to deal with the way I learn. This is why I am so passionate about the power of learning styles. We all have our strengths and weaknesses; the way we work to manage those weaknesses while maximizing our strengths makes all the difference.

Take a Moment to Consider . . .

- *What previously confusing comments from teachers might be explained through a greater understanding of your learning styles.*

- *How important hard work might be to your success, especially in a subject that challenges you.*

and how far you have come. Keep a list of your successes and refer to it often to reinforce positive feeling. Rely on people in your life who support you and see you as a capable person. Focus on what you do well, not just on what causes you difficulty. Know that the help you receive at school is deserved—it will give you the best possible chance to learn and grow.

You will learn most effectively and comfortably if you make choices that match your unique combination of learning styles. Learning style, however, is not the only personal factor involved in your choices. Your path should also reflect your personal value system. Understanding what you value will help to guide you to the subjects, activities, and people most meaningful to you.

What defines your values?

Your personal **values** are the beliefs that form the basis for your actions and life choices. As a group, they constitute your *value system*. For example, your values may include strong family relationships, education, and worthwhile employment. Together, the values that form your value system set guidelines for how you live.

You demonstrate your value system in the priorities you set, how you relate to friends and family, your educational and career choices, and even the material things with which you surround yourself. Think about what your choices say about you. Going all-out to be on time to appointments and classes, for example, shows that you value punctuality. Finding a way to pay for and attend school shows that you value education.

Sources of Values

We construct a value system over time, using information from many different sources, including the following:

- parents, guardians, siblings, and other relatives

- friends and peers
- personal experience
- religious beliefs, teachings, and figures
- instructors, supervisors, mentors, and others
- ideas from books, newspapers, magazines, television, the Internet, and other media
- workplace and school

Values
Principles or qualities that one considers important.

A particular value may come from one or more sources. For example, a student may value education (primary source: parents) and sports (primary sources: friends and media). Being influenced by the values of others is natural; the challenge is to make sure your choices are right for you.

Identifying and Evaluating Values

Thinking in depth about your values involves careful questioning. Consider what is important to you in the categories of personal choices, family, community, and education. When you have identified potential values, examine them through the following questions:

- Did I choose this value freely?
- Did I have multiple options for the choice?
- Did I consider my options carefully?

TAKE ACTION

Link Educational Choices to Your Values

Values are often reflected in students' educational choices—where to study, what to study, what activities to pursue, and so on. Choose three personal values that affect your approach to your education.

1. _Family_
2. _Experience_
3. _money_

Students in any academic discipline can hold particular values, of course. However, some disciplines reinforce certain values more than others—for example, a student who values helping others may gravitate toward education, medicine, or social work. For each value you listed above, name an area of study that you think would complement your efforts to live according to that value.

1. _Writing_
2. _listen_
3. _reading_
4. _work, learning_

- Have I made a public commitment to this choice?
- Do I carry out this value on a regular basis?[7]

Answering yes to these questions means that you have positively identified a personal value.

As you learn and experience new things, your opinion of what is important may change. Periodic evaluation will help you maintain a value system that propels you in the direction that is right for you. Think through the following when evaluating your values:

Effects of your value choices. Although some values may seem positive on the surface, they may have a negative impact. For example, you might consider it important to keep up with the latest technologies, but continually buying computer components, software, and cell phones might jeopardize your finances. Look closely at how any value affects your life.

Integrity of the value. Friends or family may encourage you to strive for what they value. You may share their values, of course—but if you don't, you may have a hard time sticking to them. Making decisions that make sense for your life requires maintaining values that feel right to you.

As you learn and experience new things, your opinion of what is important may change.

Personal change. Life changes and new experiences may alter what you consider important. For example, a student who experiences a health crisis may begin to value health above all else, shifting his course choices and extracurricular activities to reflect this change. Your responsibility is to make value choices based on what is right for you and, in some cases, for those involved in your life.

"Great minds have purposes; others have wishes."

WASHINGTON IRVING

How Values Affect Your Educational Experience

Understanding what you value has a use that goes beyond increasing your general self-awareness. Your values, well considered as you map out your path in college, can lead you to the choices that are the most fulfilling and beneficial for you.

- *Achieving educational goals.* Once you know what you value, you can define meaningful school goals by tailoring them to those values. (Chapter 3 will go into more detail about goal setting.) For example, a student who values preserving the environment may focus on environmental sciences or engineering when deciding on a major.

- *Relating to the world around you.* Understanding what you value helps you choose relationships with people (e.g., friends or instructors) and organizations (e.g., schools or extracurricular groups) according to how

reflect

Think about this idea: *You reveal your values in how you choose to spend your money and time.* Where does the bulk of your time and money go? What does this say about you? Does this conclusion differ from your idea of what your values are or should be?

& respond

their values compare with yours. A student who values the arts might get involved in a drama or photography club; another who values knowledge of different cultures may cultivate relationships with instructors from diverse backgrounds.

- *Building a personal foundation.* Having a strong set of values gives you a foundation to return to when you have a life-changing experience or encounter difficulty in achieving a goal. A student who needs to put school on hold for a while because of a family crisis might find strength in the value of family, since the break from school will afford more family time.

As you move through your educational experience, keep your values front and center in your mind. Having a solid understanding of what you value will help you choose the best possible educational path for yourself and to follow it with conviction.

I gather data through all senses.

The senses are your pathway to the world. The only way to gather information about something is through some combination of hearing it, seeing it, smelling it, tasting it, and feeling it. This information is the "raw material" on which all learning is built. For this reason, processing the information gathered through the senses is one of the foundations of learning.

Learning more about yourself means staying aware of the information that comes your way as you act. When you open your sensory pathways as you participate in experiences, you become better able to discover what you enjoy or learn easily as well as what you have trouble with or dislike. These discoveries will help to lead you to the academic focus and life choices that are right for you.

REMEMBER!
the important points ○○○

What are learning styles?

Learning styles are particular ways in which the mind receives and processes information. Each person has a unique set of learning styles with some highly developed areas and some underdeveloped areas of ability. How you learn can be divided into two parts: learning preferences (abilities and areas of interest) and personality traits (how you interact with people and information). Having a realistic perspective on learning styles includes approaching assessments as a guide rather than a label, knowing that learning styles will change as you change, and working to improve areas of challenge.

How can you discover how you learn?

The Pathways to Learning inventory, based on Howard Gardner's Multiple Intelligences Theory (which holds that people have varying degrees of development within eight different intelligences), helps you understand your natural abilities. The Personality Spectrum, based on the Myers–Briggs assessment, helps you evaluate how you react to people and situations. Together, these two assessments can give you a comprehensive snapshot of yourself as a learner.

Why is it important to know how you learn?

Knowing how you learn has at least three kinds of benefits. In your studies, it helps you choose techniques that maximize what you do best as well as find strategies that help you improve when you have trouble. In the classroom, it can help you make the most of the teaching styles of your instructors by helping you understand how well your styles mesh with those of your instructors. In the workplace, because how you learn is essentially how you work, it helps you improve performance, improve teamwork, and become more self-aware.

How can you identify and manage learning disabilities?

Going beyond basic weakness in an area of ability, a learning disability is a neurological disorder that interferes with one's ability to store, process, and produce information. Generally, learning-disabled people are of average or above-average intelligence. The disability prevents them from realizing their potential. Learning disabilities may involve problems with reading, math, organization, social interaction, and writing. If you have a diagnosed learning disability, you are eligible to receive federally funded aid. You can help yourself by being informed about your disability and by actively seeking assistance.

What defines your values?

Values are principles or qualities that you consider right, important, or good. Your values are the beliefs that guide your choices in life. Sources of values include parents, friends, religious beliefs, mentors, and others. When choosing and examining values, be careful to evaluate values according to your own needs, reevaluate values periodically as you experience change, and avoid living according to other people's values if they are not right for you. Examining your values helps you understand yourself, relate to the world around you, and build a personal foundation.

Name   Date

CRITICAL THINKING
APPLYING LEARNING TO LIFE

Your Values

Begin to explore your values by rating the following values on a scale from 1 to 4, 1 being least important to you and 4 being most important. If you have values that you don't see in the chart, list and rate them in the blank spaces at the bottom.

VALUE	RATING	VALUE	RATING
Knowing yourself	1	Mental health	4
Physical health	4	Fitness/exercise	4
Spending time with family	4	Close friendships	4
Helping others	4	Education	4
Being well paid	1	Being employed	4
Being liked by others	4	Free time/vacations	1
Enjoying entertainment	1	Time to yourself	4
Spiritual/religious life	4	Reading	4
Keeping up with news	1	Staying organized	4
Financial stability	4	Intimate relationships	1
Creative/artistic pursuits	1	Self-improvement	4
Lifelong learning	4	Facing your fears	4
			</TB></UNTBL>

Looking at what you have rated most highly, write your three overall top values here.

1. Helping others
2. Education
3. Physical Health

Choose one and evaluate it using the questions from pages 48 and 49.

    Did you choose this value freely? If not, whose choice is it and why have you not rejected it?

    yes.

Did you have multiple options for the choice? If so, name a couple of options you considered.

_Phisical health_____, _lifelong learning_
spending time with family, staying organized.

Did you consider your options carefully? If not, why not?

Yes, because I think first to responde
the questions.

Have you made a public commitment to the choice? If so, describe how.

_NO_

Do you carry out this value on a regular basis? If so, what actions demonstrate this?

"Yes, because my personality is describe
in some of those values.

Based on this evaluation, do you still feel that this value is right for you? Why or why not?

Yes because I go back on my life
and I think of this values on life

TEAM BUILDING
COLLABORATIVE SOLUTIONS

The Power of Personality Types

Divide into groups according to the four types of the Personality Spectrum—Thinker-dominant students in one group, Organizer-dominant students in another, Giver-dominant students in a third, and Adventurer-dominant students in the fourth. If you have scored the same in more than one of these types, join the group that is smaller. With your group, brainstorm four lists for your type:

1. the **strengths** of this type

2. the **challenges** it brings

3. the **stressors** (things or situations that cause stress) for this type

4. **career** areas that tend to suit this type

Next, problem solve together: Brainstorm strategies for dealing with your intelligence's challenges and stressors. If there is time, each group can present this information to the entire class to enable everyone to have a better understanding and acceptance of one another's intelligences.

personal IMPROVEMENT *plan*

I commit to three specific learning styles–related strategies to improve my study skills.

From this chapter, I choose three strategies that I think will help me.

Strategy 1: Study

Strategy 2: keep up with works

Strategy 3: be prepare to work.

I choose one strategy to focus on (circle this strategy above) and I will:

- describe my goal—what I want to gain by using this strategy.

So I can follow my goal by studing and be prepare for life.

- describe in detail how I plan to use the strategy.

I plan to use this strategies so would be prepare every day for class.

- describe how I will measure my progress toward the goal this semester.

by think each ending day to measy my progress.

Activate the Habit of Mind

HABITS OF MIND · HABITS OF MIND · HABITS OF MIND · HABITS OF MIND

MIND

Here's how I will *gather data through the senses* to achieve this goal.

SUGGESTED READINGS

Barger, Nancy J., Linda K. Kirby, and Jean M. Kummerow. *Work Types: Understand Your Work Personality— How It Helps You and Holds You Back, and What You Can Do to Understand It*. New York: Warner Books, 1997.

Cobb, Joyanne. *Learning How to Learn: A Guide for Getting into College with a Learning Disability, Staying In, and Staying Sane*. Washington, DC: Child Welfare League of America, 2001.

Gardner, Howard. *Intelligence Reframed: Multiple Intelligences for the 21st Century*. New York: Basic Books, 2000.

Keirsey, David. *Please Understand Me II: Temperament, Character, Intelligence*. Del Mar, CA: Prometheus Nemesis Book Company, 1998.

Lewis, Erica-Lee and Eric L. Lewis. *Help Yourself: Handbook for College-Bound Students with Learning Disabilities*. New York: Princeton Review, 1996.

Pearman, Roger R. and Sarah C. Albritton. *I'm Not Crazy, I'm Just Not You: The Real Meaning of the 16 Personality Types*. Palo Alto, CA: Consulting Psychologists Press, 1997.

INTERNET RESOURCES

Keirsey Sorter and other Myers–Briggs information: www.keirsey.com

Prentice Hall Student Success Supersite Exploring Multiple Intelligences: www.multi-intell.com

National Center for Learning Disabilities: www.ncld.org

Attention Deficit Disorder (ADD)

Attention Deficit Disorder Association: www.add.org

Attention Deficit Hyperactivity Disorder (ADHD)

Children and Adults with Attention Deficit/Hyperactivity Disorder: www.chadd.org

ADHD News.com: www.adhdnews.com

National Institute of Mental Health: www.nimh.nih.gov/publicat/adhd.cfm

Dyscalculia

Dyscalculia.org: www.dyscalculia.org

Learning Disabilities Online: www.ldonline.org/ld_indepth/math_skills/ math-skills.html

Dysgraphia

Learning Disabilities Online: www.ldonline.org/ld_indepth/writing/dysgraphia.html

International Dyslexia Association—Inland Empire Branch: www.dyslexia-ca.org/dysgraphia.htm

Dyslexia

International Dyslexia Association: www.interdys.org

Davis Dyslexia Association International: www.dyslexia.com

Dyslexia Teacher: www.dyslexia-teacher.com

Dyspraxia

Dyspraxia Foundation: www.dyspraxiafoundation.org.uk

Taylored Marketing: www.tayloredmktg.com/dyspraxia

ENDNOTES

1. Howard Gardner, *Multiple Intelligences: The Theory in Practice*. New York: Harper-Collins, 1993, pp. 5–49.

2. Ibid, p. 7.

3. Developed by Joyce Bishop, Ph.D., Psychology faculty, Golden West College, Huntington Beach, CA. Based on Howard Gardner, *Frames of Mind: The Theory of Multiple Intelligences*. New York: Harper-Collins, 1993.

4. National Center for Learning Disabilities. "LD at a Glance" [on-line]. Available: www.ncld.org/LDInfoZone/InfoZone_FactSheet_LD.cfm (May 2003).

5. National Center for Learning Disabilities. "Adult Learning Disabilities: A Learning Disability Isn't Something You Outgrow. It's Something You Learn to Master" (pamphlet). New York: National Center for Learning Disabilities.

6. National Center for Learning Disabilities. "LD Advocates Guide" [on-line]. Available: www.ld.org/Advocacy/tutorial_talking_about.cfm (May 2003).

7. Wilson, Chris. "Unique Value Systems" [on-line]. Available at www.cyberparent.com/men/valuesystem.htm (February 2003).

THINKING IT THROUGH

Check those statements that apply to you right now:

- ☐ I set goals but don't always feel that I achieve them.

- ☑ I feel that my priorities have changed since I entered college.

- ☐ I have a date book but I don't use it all that much.

- ☐ I feel frequently overwhelmed by all that I have to do.

- ☐ I tend to procrastinate.

- ☐ I have a pretty good idea of what majors interest me.

Goal Setting and Time Management

MAPPING YOUR COURSE

Managing impulsivity.

"Effective problem solvers **think before they act**. They intentionally form a vision of a product, a plan of action, a goal, or a destination before they begin."

—ART COSTA

Every time management or goal-setting strategy can be put under the umbrella of "thinking before you act." If you avoid quick and impulsive decisions, you will be able to make the best use of your time and forge the most effective paths toward your goals.

IN THIS CHAPTER

In this chapter you explore answers to the following questions:

- How do you set and achieve goals?

- How can you manage your time?

- Why is procrastination a problem?

- How can goal setting and time management help you choose a major?

Setting goals and managing time are essential and interdependent skills. Goals, to be achieved successfully, must be carefully placed in a time frame. Time, to be used effectively, must be scheduled in segments linked to tasks that pave the way to important goals. Working as a team, these skills can help you realize the life you dream of.

This chapter begins with an explanation of how to take specific steps toward your most important goals. The section on time shows how scheduling helps you to translate goals into daily, weekly, monthly, and yearly steps. You will explore how procrastination can derail your dreams and how to avoid it. Finally, you will learn how to apply your goal-setting and time management skills to an important long-term goal: Declaring and fulfilling a major.

How do you set and achieve goals?

A **goal** can be something as concrete as buying a health insurance plan or as abstract as working to control your temper. When you set goals and work to achieve them, you define how you want to live and what you want to achieve. You set goals in all areas of your life—academic, personal, and career.

Like learning a new physical task, setting and working toward goals takes a lot of practice and repeated efforts. Paul Timm, an expert in self-management, believes that focus is a key ingredient in setting and achieving goals: "Focus adds power to our actions. If somebody threw a bucket of water on you, you'd get wet. . . . But if water was shot at you through a high-pressure nozzle, you might get injured. The only difference is focus."[1] Focus your goal-setting energy by examining your personal mission, placing your goals in long-term and short-term time frames, evaluating goals in terms of your values, and setting priorities.

Goal
An end toward which effort is directed; an aim or intention.

Identify Your Personal Mission

Life moves fast, and you may not often step back and look at where you are, where you've been, and where you want to be. One helpful way to determine your big-picture direction is to write a personal mission statement. Dr. Stephen Covey, author of *The Seven Habits of Highly Effective People*, defines a mission statement as a philosophy outlining what you want to be (character), what you want to do (contributions and achievements), and the principles by which you live (your values). Dr. Covey describes the personal mission statement as "a personal constitution, the basis for making major, life-directing decisions, the basis for making daily decisions in the midst of the circumstances and emotions that affect our lives."[2]

As an example, here is a mission statement written by Carol Carter, one of the authors of *Keys to Effective Learning*.

> My mission is to use my talents and abilities to help people of all ages, stages, backgrounds, and economic levels achieve their human potential through fully developing their minds and their talents. I also aim to balance work with people in my life, understanding that my family and friends are a priority above all else.

How can you start formulating a mission statement? Try using Covey's three aspects of personal mission as a guide. Think through the following:

- *Character.* What aspects of character do you think are most valuable? When you consider the people you admire most, which of their qualities stand out?
- *Contributions and achievements.* What do you want to accomplish in your life? Where do you want to make a difference?
- *Values.* How do the values you established in your work in Chapter 2 inform your life goals? What in your mission could help you live according to what you value most highly? For example, if you value community involvement, your mission may reflect a life goal of political involvement, which may translate into an interim goal of running for class office at college.

Once you establish the components of your mission, your goal is to unite them into a whole as your mission statement. One option is to aim for a one-sentence mission that leaves out details but identifies the most important overarching themes that you want to focus on in life. Carol's one-sentence mission statement is as follows:

Cultivate peace, joy, love, talent, and compassion within the hearts of every person so that they can truly love and appreciate themselves, their neighbors, those who are different from them, and every creature on Earth.

What you want out of life changes as you move from one phase to the next—from single person to spouse, from student to working citizen. There-fore, your personal mission should remain flexible and open to revision. If you frame your mission statement carefully so that it truly reflects your goals, it can be your guide in everything you do. Use the *Take Action* box on the following page to draft your mission statement.

"Obstacles are what people see when they take their eyes off the goal."

NEW YORK SUBWAY BULLETIN BOARD

Establish Goals

If developing a personal mission statement establishes the big picture, estab-lishing individual goals allows you to bring areas of that picture into the fore-ground. Planning your progress, step by step, helps you maintain your efforts over the extended time period often needed to accomplish a goal. There are two categories: long-term goals and short-term goals.

Setting Long-Term Goals

Establish first the goals that have the largest scope, the *long-term goals* that you aim to attain over a lengthy period of time, up to a few years or more. As

TAKE ACTION

Explore Your Personal Mission

As a way of exploring what you most want out of life, consider the following questions and brainstorm some answers on a separate piece of paper.

1. You are at your retirement dinner. You have had an esteemed career in whatever you ended up doing in your life. Your best friend stands up and talks about the 10 aspects of your character that have taken you to the top. What do you think they are?

2. You are preparing for a late-in-life job change. Updating your resume, you need to list your contributions and achievements. What would you like them to be?

3. You have been told that you have one year to live. What do you decide are the most important ways to spend your time? Describe what, where, with whom, and any other details you can think of.

Thinking about your answers, draft a personal mission statement here. It can be one sentence or a bit longer. Let this be a first stab at something you will revise and refine over time, as you learn more about yourself throughout the semester.

I Personal mission that I have is to finish a carreer so I can help my parents, so they can't work more, I can be successful too.

---

a student, you have set a goal to attend school and earn a degree or certificate. Getting an education is a significant goal that often takes years to reach.

Some long-term goals are lifelong, such as a goal continually to learn more about yourself and the world around you. Others have a more definite end, such as a goal to complete a course successfully. For example, you may have a long-term goal of developing your computer and Internet skills while in school. Here is Carol Carter's long-term goal statement:

> To accomplish my mission through writing books, creating an Internet website, giving seminars, and developing programs that create opportunities for students to learn and develop. To create a personal, professional, and family environment that allows me to manifest my abilities and duly tend to each of my responsibilities.

Long-term goals can be other than lifelong goals. Consider what you want to accomplish in a year's time. Continuing the computer example, you may aim to learn two computer programs in the coming year. Carol's current year-long goals include the following:

1. Develop books, Internet-based material, and programs to provide internships, scholarships, and other quality initiatives for students.

2. Allow time in my personal life to eat well, exercise five days a week, and spend quality time with family and friends. Allow time daily for quiet reflection and spiritual devotion.

To determine your long-term goals, think about who you are and what you want out of life. In the same way that Carol's goals are tailored to her personality and interests, your goals should reflect your uniqueness. Consider learning style, too, and what that says about you.

Be sure to keep your values in mind when setting goals. Recall the section on values in Chapter 2. Your most meaningful goals will be based on what is most important to you. Therefore, your goals should express your values and translate them into action, as in the following examples:

- *Values:* Health and fitness, helping others

  Goal: To become a physical therapist
- *Values:* Independence, financial success

  Goal: To get a degree in business and start a company

In addition, basing goals on values increases your motivation. The more your goals focus on what is most important to you, the greater your drive to reach them.

Setting Short-Term Goals

When you divide your long-term goals into smaller, manageable goals that you hope to accomplish within a relatively short time, you are setting *short-term goals*. Short-term goals narrow your focus, helping you to maintain your progress toward your long-term goals. To stay on track toward the goal of learning two computer programs, you may want to accomplish these short-term goals in the next six months:

- I will write an assigned paper using MS Word.
- I will set up a tutoring session with a computer TA.

These same goals can be broken down into even smaller parts, such as the following one-month goals:

- I will do an MS Word on-screen tutorial.
- I will spend an hour a week this month exploring on a computer at the computer center.

In addition to monthly goals, you may have short-term goals that extend for a week, a day, or even a couple of hours in a given day. Short-term goals connected to the long-term goal of improving Internet skills may include the following:

- By the end of today: Find out what the major search directories are.
- One week from now: Read an Internet guide book to learn how to use search directories effectively.
- Two weeks from now: Experiment with search directories to see which ones will be most useful to me.
- Three weeks from now: Research my topic using the two search directories that have the most helpful information.

FIGURE 3.1   Goals reinforce one another.

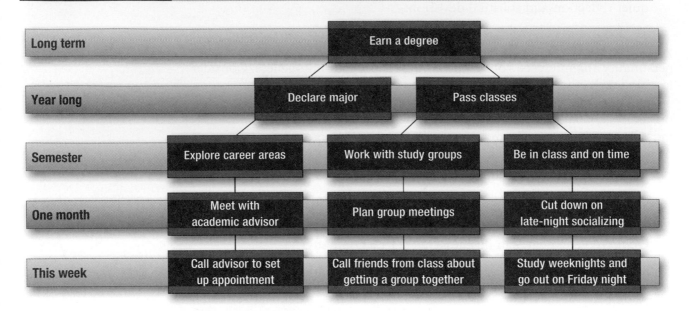

As you consider your long- and short-term goals, notice how all of your goals are linked to one another. As Figure 3.1 shows, your long-term goals establish a context for the short-term goals. In turn, your short-term goals make the long-term goals seem clearer and more reachable. Try to pay special attention to intermediate goals—the one-month, one-semester–type goals on the way to a year-long goal, for example—when you are forging ahead toward a long-term goal. Why? Because motivation tends to peak at the beginning of a goal process, when you are gearing up, and at the end, when you have almost fulfilled the goal. If you work extra hard to stay motivated in the middle, you will have a more successful journey and a better result at the end.

Achieving goals becomes easier when you are realistic about what is possible. Setting priorities helps you make that distinction.

reflect

Name an important goal you achieved this year. How did you do it? How did the achieve-ment make you feel? By contrast, name a goal that you have not been able to attain. What obstacles have you encountered? What feelings have resulted and how have those helped or hindered your efforts?

& respond

Priority
An action or intention that takes precedence in time, attention, or position.

Prioritize Goals

Everyone has the same 24 hours in a day. When you set a **priority**, you decide on the best way to use those hours by identifying which goals are most important at any given moment. Consider these different factors when you prioritize:

- *Your values.* What do you value most highly? What goals would best reflect your values? Thinking about your values and personal mission will help you establish your more large-scale priorities—for example, graduating with a particular honor or GPA, developing a strong network of personal contacts. These priorities then inform the shorter-term goals you set.

- *Your relationships with others.* If you are a parent, your children's needs are probably a priority. If you are in a committed relationship, your partner is most likely a priority. For example, you may try to arrange your school day so that you and your children and/or partner are home together as often as possible.

- *Your time.* On any given day, you may or may not have enough time to do all that you want to do. Depending on how much time that day's goals take, you may establish priorities based on what you can fit in.

Setting priorities involves thinking about more than just educational goals. Career and personal goals compete for your time as well. When deciding how to arrange your priorities, consider the following important factors:

Career Goals

- The job you want after you graduate—duties and level of responsibility (e.g., manager, supervisor, independent contractor, business owner), hours, coworkers, salary, commuting distance, industry, company size, location.

- Career areas that reflect your strongest and most important values.

- Financial goals—how much money you are aiming for to pay your bills, live comfortably, and save for the future.

Personal Goals

- Yourself—who you are and who you want to be (character, personality, health-fitness, values, and conduct).

- Family—whether you want to stay single, be married, be a parent, or increase a family you've already started, and what kind of relationship you want with family members.

- Lifestyle—where and with whom you want to live, in what kind of home, how you want to participate in your community, and what you want to do in your leisure time.

It's important to put academic goals in the context of your goals in all life areas because goals are interconnected. You may want to graduate on a particular date, but not meeting a personal health goal may result in a problem that gets in the way. You might want to major in a particular subject, but thinking over your career goals may show you that your values and skills don't match up well with that subject. Keeping everything in mind helps you make better choices for yourself.

Personal goals may include completing a race or fulfilling a commitment to volunteer.

Choosing what to make a priority involves making decisions based on numerous factors (you will learn more about decision making in Chapter 4). Try to make decisions based on your own priorities and not those of others. What may be top priority to someone else may not mean that much to you, and vice versa.

Setting priorities helps you achieve your goals within specific time frames. Being able to achieve your goals is directly linked to effective time management. In fact, the main goal of time management is to facilitate the achievement of your goals.

How can you manage your time?

Time is a valuable and precious resource. If you make wise choices about how you use it, you will be better able to manage your responsibilities and stay on target toward your goals. Throughout your life, your ability to manage your time will vary with your stress level, how busy you are, and other factors. Do your best, and keep working at it using the strategies that follow.

What you have learned about yourself as a learner in Chapter 2 will serve as an introduction to yourself as a time manager. Think about your styles' characteristics and what they mean for time management. For example, students with strong logical–mathematical intelligence and Thinker types tend to organize activities within a framework of time. By contrast, Adventurer types and less logical learners may neglect details such as how much time they have to complete a task, but may have a greater understanding of the total goal, assignment, or concept. Once you recognize your styles and have knowledge of other styles' strategies, you can incorporate the strategies that work best for you into your way of managing time and tasks.

Time management involves building a schedule, taking responsibility for how you spend your time, and being flexible.

Build a Schedule

Just as a road map helps you travel from place to place, a schedule is a time-and-activity map that helps you get from the beginning of the day (or week, or month) to the end as smoothly as possible. Schedules help you gain control of your life in two ways: They allocate segments of time for the fulfillment of your daily, weekly, monthly, and longer-term goals, and they serve as a concrete reminder of tasks, events, due dates, responsibilities, and deadlines.

Keep a Planner

Gather the tools of the trade: a pen or pencil and a planner (sometimes called a date book). A planner is indispensable for keeping track of your time. Paul Timm says, "Most time management experts agree that rule number one in a thoughtful planning process is: Use some form of a planner where you can write things down."[3]

MULTIPLE PATHWAYS TO LEARNING

MULTIPLE INTELLIGENCE STRATEGIES *for* Scheduling

These strategies help you find effective ways to handle your many responsibilities through time management.

INTELLIGENCE	SUGGESTED STRATEGIES	WHAT WORKS FOR YOU? WRITE NEW IDEAS HERE
Verbal–Linguistic	■ Carry a small calendar and to-do list. Try carrying a small cassette recorder and dictate important scheduling. ■ Write out your main weekly priorities. Looking at what is stressful and what inspires confidence, make adjustments.	
Logical–Mathematical	■ Schedule time each day to organize and plan your tasks. Develop a logical system for indicating priority. ■ Compute how many hours a week you spend studying, working, having fun, and doing extracurricular activities. Evaluate the balance and make any necessary changes.	
Bodily–Kinesthetic	■ Schedule classes so that you have time in between to exercise or to take a long walk from one class to the next. ■ Create a schedule for the month. Take an exercise break. Come back and write your goals for this week and today.	
Visual–Spatial	■ Create your daily schedule and to-do lists using think links or other visual organizers. ■ Use wall calendars or charts to map out goals for the week and month, using different colors for different tasks/goals.	
Interpersonal	■ Involve someone in your goal achievement—make a commitment to someone to complete a step toward a goal. ■ Discuss monthly goals with friends. Ask them to evaluate whether they are too ambitious or not ambitious enough.	
Intrapersonal	■ Schedule quiet time each day to reflect on your priorities and upcoming tasks. ■ Each week, sit alone and write down that week's scheduling challenges. Brainstorm three productive ways you can deal with these challenges.	
Musical	■ Make time in your schedule for music—listen to CDs, go to a concert, play an instrument.	
Naturalistic	■ Try to schedule some time outside each day. ■ Sit outside where you feel relaxed. In this state of mind, plan out your schedule for the next week and month.	

There are two major types of planners. The day-at-a-glance version devotes a page to each day. The week-at-a-glance book gives you a view of the week's plans but has less room to write per day. If you write detailed daily plans, you might like the day-at-a-glance version. If you prefer to remind yourself of plans ahead of time, try the book that shows a week's schedule all at once. Some planners contain sections for monthly and yearly goals.

Another option is an electronic planner or personal digital assistant (PDA), which can hold a large amount of information. You can use it to schedule your days and weeks, make to-do lists, perform mathematical calculations, and create and store an address book. You can enter information with an on-screen or attachable keyboard or handwrite with a stylus. You can also transfer information to and from a desktop computer.

Electronic planners are powerful, convenient, and often fun. However, they cost more than the paper versions and their small size and popularity means they are easy to lose through oversight or theft. Evaluate your options and decide what works for you. The bottom line is how likely you are to use what you select. A dime-store notebook and a top-of-the-line PDA will work equally well for their owners if used conscientiously.

Schedule Daily and Weekly Goals That Support Long-Term Goals

After you evaluate what you need to accomplish in the coming year, semester, month, week, and day to reach your long-term goals, use your schedule to record those steps. Write down the short-term goals that will enable you to stay on track. Here is how a student might map out a goal over a year's time:

This year:	Complete enough courses to maintain class standing.
This semester:	Complete my biology class with a B average or higher.
This month:	Set up biology study group schedule to coincide with quizzes.
This week:	Meet with study group; go over material for Friday's quiz.
Today:	Go over Chapter 3 in biology text.

To manage your time so that you stay on top of your goals, you need to focus first on scheduling the most immediate, smaller goals—what you do on a daily and weekly basis. Scheduling daily and weekly goals, or tasks, that tie in to your long-term goals lends the following benefits:

- increased meaning for your daily activities
- a greater chance of achieving long-term goals
- a sense of order and progress

The week is often the easiest unit of time to consider at one shot. Weekly goal setting and planning allows you to keep track of day-to-day activities while giving you the larger perspective of what is coming up during the week. Take some time before each week starts to remind yourself of your long-term goals. Keeping long-term goals in mind helps you determine related short-term goals you can accomplish during the week to come.

Figure 3.2 shows parts of a daily schedule and a weekly schedule.

FIGURE 3.2   Note daily and weekly tasks.

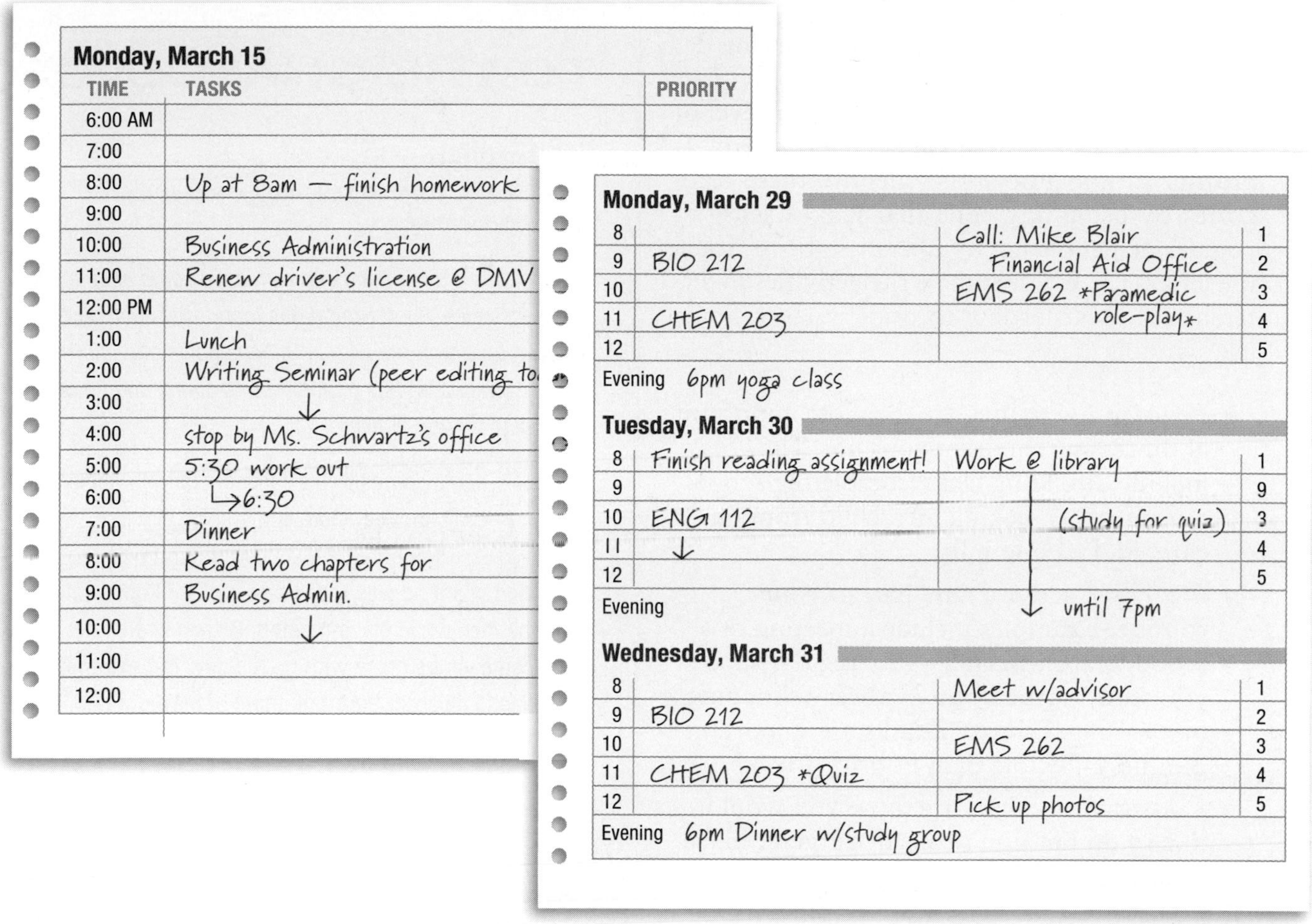

Monday, March 15

TIME	TASKS	PRIORITY
6:00 AM		
7:00		
8:00	Up at 8am — finish homework	
9:00		
10:00	Business Administration	
11:00	Renew driver's license @ DMV	
12:00 PM		
1:00	Lunch	
2:00	Writing Seminar (peer editing to	
3:00	↓	
4:00	stop by Ms. Schwartz's office	
5:00	5:30 work out	
6:00	↳6:30	
7:00	Dinner	
8:00	Read two chapters for	
9:00	Business Admin.	
10:00	↓	
11:00		
12:00		

Monday, March 29

8		Call: Mike Blair	1
9	BIO 212	Financial Aid Office	2
10		EMS 262 *Paramedic	3
11	CHEM 203	role-play*	4
12			5
Evening	6pm yoga class		

Tuesday, March 30

8	Finish reading assignment!	Work @ library	1
9			9
10	ENG 112	(study for quiz)	3
11	↓		4
12			5
Evening		↓ until 7pm	

Wednesday, March 31

8		Meet w/advisor	1
9	BIO 212		2
10		EMS 262	3
11	CHEM 203 *Quiz		4
12		Pick up photos	5
Evening	6pm Dinner w/study group		

TAKE ACTION

Map Out a Personal Goal

What is one important personal goal you have for this year?

try to Pass all of the class and try to work hard

Think about the short-term actions you will take to achieve this goal, remembering that short-term actions can take place over an extended period. What will you do to support this goal . . .

This semester? *Study the best I can*

This month? *Think about my goal, for motivation*

This week? *Understand each class and chapters of the books.*

Today? *go over of all the work that I have done.*

Indicate Priority Levels

On any given day, your goals have varying degrees of importance. Record your goals first, and then label them according to their level of importance using these categories: Priority 1, Priority 2, and Priority 3. Identify these categories by using any code that makes sense to you. Some people use numbers, as above. Some use letters (A, B, C). Some write activities in different colors according to priority level. Some use symbols (*, +, −).

- *Priority 1* activities are the most important and pressing things in your life. They may include attending class, completing school assignments, picking up a child from day care, and paying bills.
- *Priority 2* activities are part of your routine. Examples include a meeting of a school club, working out, a regular time you study at the library, grocery shopping, or cleaning. Priority 2 tasks are important but more flexible than Priority 1 tasks.
- *Priority 3* activities are those you would like to do but don't consider urgent, like a phone call or a night out. Many people don't enter Priority 3 tasks in their planners until they are sure they have time to get them done.

Prioritizing your activities is essential for two reasons. First, some activities are more important than others, and effective time management requires that you focus most of your energy on Priority 1 items. Second, looking at all of your priorities helps you plan when you can get things done. Often, it's not possible to get all of your Priority 1 activities done early in the day, especially if they involve scheduled classes or meetings. Prioritizing helps you set Priority 1 items and then schedule Priority 2 and 3 items around them as they fit.

Priority 3 tasks often get put off. One solution is to keep a list of Priority 3 tasks in a separate place in your planner. That way, when you have an unexpected block of free time, you can consult your list and see what you have time to accomplish.

RISING
TO THE CHALLENGE

Scott Stoffel
Graduate of Temple University, Philadelphia, Pennsylvania

Uncontrollable circumstances can leave some people with great obstacles. Scott Stoffel has found that such obstacles can be overcome with ambitious goals and enormous effort. Each person has a mountain to climb, and he is on the way to the top of his.

When it comes to his senses, Scott Stoffel is basically left with taste and smell.

His parents discovered Scott was practically blind when he was four years old and kept getting hit in the face while playing catch. Fifteen years later, music became vague noise with no melody. The extremely rare genetic disorder that took most of his sight and hearing has also decreased the sensitivity in his fingers and his limbs; his thumbs hardly work, and he limps with a cane.

"Life is a testing ground—everyone has adversity to deal with," Mr. Stoffel, 32, wrote in an e-mail interview. "The point is to see who has the grit to overcome and who doesn't. And since my challenges seemed so indomitable, maybe that was a compliment, like saying I had something special down deep that could help me win a hopeless battle."

This month, Mr. Stoffel graduated, magna cum laude, from Temple University in Philadelphia, having pursued his degree in electrical engineering and computer science largely through independent study, since he can neither see chalkboards nor hear lectures. His senior project, a palm-read Braille device, is designed to help people who are deaf and blind with dull fingers like his own communicate better.

"I will never again look at a person with disabilities and say, you know what, I don't think he can do it," said John Helferty, Mr. Stoffel's mentor and department chairman.

"When the hearing caved in, it was like my whole life just came to an end," Mr. Stoffel recalled. "If I went to a restaurant, I couldn't understand the waitress. If I turned on the TV, it was like watching a silent movie with a blurry picture."

So Mr. Stoffel quit his job selling computers in Chattanooga, Tenn., and hid out in his parents' basement in Connecticut for a few years, writing science fiction and designing computer games.

In 1994, he started rehabilitation at the Helen Keller National Center in Sands Point on Long Island, and later he took writing classes at nearby Hofstra University. In 1998, Mr. Stoffel switched to Temple, and to engineering, seeing technology as a potential savior for people with disabilities (and a lucrative profession for him).

He got migraines reading 15 hours a day, using large magnifying glasses or sitting with his face two inches from text projected onto a closed-circuit television screen. A sign language interpreter, her fingers in Mr. Stoffel's left palm, helped him with weekly meetings with professors, but he ended most semesters behind and worked through school breaks.

The palm-read Braille device is a 9-inch by 5-inch by 4-inch wooden box with six pins that pop up and down, controlled by a computer program to form Braille characters people can feel with body parts other than fingertips. It cost less than $400 to make.

Professor Helferty taught about half of Mr. Stoffel's courses himself, urged colleagues to accommodate him, and constructed the hardware for the Braille device, since his student could not.

"When I see somebody with his aspirations, his commitment and his drive, I have to step up to the plate too and say we're in this journey together," Mr. Helferty said. "You're climbing Mount Everest and I'm your Sherpa guide and I'm going to go every inch with you."

Now Mr. Stoffel—who lives in North Wales, Pa., with his wife, Sandra, a woman he met at Helen Keller who also has limited sight and hearing—is job searching, eager to have his $474 monthly disability payments cut off and start working on his debt.

"Planting the flag at the top of the mountain," Mr. Helferty said, "will be getting the job."

Take a Moment to Consider . . .

- *How this story gives you perspective on your own abilities and limitations.*

- *What goal for you is worth a great deal of effort and difficulty to attain.*

Keep Track of Events

Your planner also enables you to schedule events. Think of events in terms of how they tie in with your long-term goals, just as you would your other tasks. For example, being aware of quiz dates and due dates for assignments helps you reach your goal to achieve in school.

Note events in daily, weekly, monthly, or even yearly sections in your planner, where a quick look will remind you that they are approaching. Writing them down also helps you see where they fit in the context of your other activities. For example, if you have three tests and a presentation all in one week, you'll want to take time in the weeks before to prepare for them.

Following are some kinds of events worth noting in your planner:

- due dates for papers, projects, presentations, and tests
- the details of your academic schedule, including semester and holiday breaks
- important meetings, medical appointments, or due dates for bill payments
- birthdays, anniversaries, social events, holidays, and other special occasions
- milestones for steps toward a goal, such as due dates for sections of a project

Take Responsibility for How You Spend Your Time

No matter your circumstances, you are in charge of choosing how to manage them. Use the following strategies to plan your activities with your most important goals in mind:

Plan your schedule each week. Before each week starts, note events, goals, and priorities. Decide where to fit activities like studying and Priority 3 items. For example, if you have a test on Thursday, you can plan study sessions on the preceding days. If you have more free time on Tuesday and Friday than on other days, you can plan workouts or Priority 3 activities at those times.

Make and use to-do lists. Use a *to-do list* to record the things you want to accomplish. If you generate a daily or weekly to-do list on a separate piece of paper, you can look at all tasks and goals at once. This helps you consider time frames and priorities. You might want to prioritize your tasks and transfer them to appropriate places in your planner. You can tailor a to-do list to an important event such as exam week. This kind of specific to-do list can help you prioritize and accomplish an unusually large task load.

Make thinking about time a priority. Take a few minutes each day to plan. Although making a schedule takes time, it can mean hours of saved time later. Say you have two errands to run, both on the other side of town; if you don't plan ahead, you could end up driving across town twice in one day. Also, be sure to carry your planner with you and check it throughout the day.

Post monthly and yearly calendars at home. Keeping a calendar on the wall helps you stay aware of important events. Use a yearly or a monthly version (Figure 3.3 shows a monthly calendar), and keep it where you can refer to it often. If you live with family or friends, make the calendar a group

FIGURE 3.3   Keep track with a monthly calendar.

MARCH

SUNDAY	MONDAY	TUESDAY	WEDNESDAY	THURSDAY	FRIDAY	SATURDAY
	1 WORK	2 Turn in English paper topic	3 Dentist 2pm	4 WORK	5	6
7 Frank's birthday	8 Psych Test 9am WORK	9	10 6:30 pm Meeting @ Student Ctr.	11 WORK	12	13 Dinner @ Ryan's
14	15 English paper due WORK	16 Western Civ paper—Library research	17	18 Library 6 p.m.	19 Western Civ makeup class	20
21	22 WORK	23 2 p.m. meeting, psych group project	24 Start running program: 2 miles	25 WORK	26 Run 2 miles	27
28 Run 3 miles	29 WORK	30 Western Civ paper due	31 Run 2 miles			

project so that you stay aware of each other's plans. Knowing each other's schedules can also help you avoid problems such as two people needing the car at the same time.

"Even if you're on the right track, you'll get run over if you just sit there."

WILL ROGERS

Schedule down time. When you're wiped out, it's hard to accomplish much. A little **down time** will refresh you. Even half an hour a day helps. Fill the time with whatever relaxes you—reading, watching television, chatting on-line, playing a game or sport, walking, writing, or just doing nothing.

Be Flexible

No matter how well you plan your time, life changes can make you feel out of control. Coping with changes, whether minor (a room change for a class) or major (a medical emergency), can cause stress. As your stress level rises, your sense of control dwindles.

Although you cannot always choose your circumstances, you may have some control over how you handle them. Use the following ideas to cope with changes large and small.

Day-to-Day Changes

Small changes—a cancelled class, a meeting that runs late—can result in priority shifts that jumble your schedule. Think of change as part of life and you will be more effective in solving the dilemmas that come up. For changes that occur frequently, think through a backup plan ahead of time. For sudden changes, the best you can do is to keep an open mind about possibilities and to remember to call on your resources in a pinch.

Life Changes

Sometimes changes are more serious than a class schedule shift. Your car breaks down; you fail a class; a family member develops a medical problem. Such changes call for more extensive problem solving. They also require an ability to look at the big picture. Although a class change affects your schedule for a day, a medical problem may affect your schedule for much longer.

When life throws you a major curve ball, lay out your options. Explore all of the potential effects before making a decision (the problem-solving and decision-making skills in Chapter 4 will serve you well here). Finally, make full use of your school's resources. Your academic advisor, counselor, dean, financial aid advisor, and instructors may have ideas and assistance to offer you—but they can help only if you let them know what you need.

Down time
Quiet time set aside for relaxation and low-key activity.

No matter how well you manage time, you will have moments when it's hard to stay in control. Knowing how to identify and avoid procrastination and other time traps will help you get back on track.

Flexibility and effective prioritizing are essentials for students who juggle school and family responsibilities.

Procrastination
The act of putting off a task until another time.

Why is procrastination a problem?

"I'll do it tomorrow . . . next week . . . maybe right before finals . . . it won't be a big deal." When you just can't manage to get going on a task and you put it off until later, you are experiencing **procrastination**. It's human to procrastinate, and common for busy students; if taken to the extreme, however, it can develop into a habit that causes serious problems. This excerpt from the Study Skills Library at California Polytechnic State University at San Luis Obispo illustrates a typical procrastination situation and its results.

The procrastinator is often remarkably optimistic about his ability to complete a task on a tight deadline. . . . For example, he may estimate that a paper will take only five days to write; he has fifteen days; there is plenty of time; no need to start. Lulled by a false sense of security, time passes. At some point, he crosses over an imaginary starting time and suddenly realizes, "Oh no! I am not in control! There isn't enough time!"

At this point, considerable effort is directed towards completing the task, and work progresses. This sudden spurt of energy is the source of the erroneous feeling that "I only work well under pressure." Actually, at this point you are making progress only because you haven't any choice. . . . Progress is being made, but you have lost your freedom.

Barely completed in time, the paper may actually earn a fairly good grade; whereupon the student experiences mixed feelings: pride of accomplishment (sort of), scorn for the professor who cannot recognize substandard work, and guilt for getting an undeserved grade. But the net result is reinforcement: the procrastinator is rewarded positively for his poor behavior. ("Look what a decent grade I got after all!") As a result, the counterproductive behavior is repeated over and over again.[4]

Why do people procrastinate? Some significant reasons follow:

- *Perfectionism.* Jane B. Burka and Lenora M. Yuen, authors of *Procrastination: Why You Do It and What to Do About It,* say that habitual procrastinators are often perfectionists who use their ability to achieve as the only measure of their self-worth: "The performance becomes the only measure of the person . . . an outstanding performance means an outstanding person; a mediocre performance means a mediocre person."[5] Therefore, fearing failure and the resulting loss of self-esteem, the perfectionist procrastinator puts off trying at all.

- *Avoiding knowledge of your capabilities.* People also procrastinate in order to avoid the truth about what they can achieve. "As long as you procrastinate, you never have to confront the real limits of your ability, whatever those limits are,"[6] say Burka and Yuen. If you procrastinate and fail, you can blame the failure on waiting too long, not on any personal shortcoming.

- *Being unsure of the next step.* If you get stuck and don't know what to do, sometimes it seems easier to procrastinate than to make the leap to the next level of what you are working on. You may also be likely to procrastinate in this situation if you don't ordinarily like to reach out for help when you hit a roadblock.

- *Facing an overwhelming task.* Some projects are so big that you can't see the trees for the forest—and the forest looks like Muir Woods, a towering expanse of redwood trees. It's natural to want to run in the other direction and hope that it just goes away or at least seems easier in time.

- *Fear and poor self-esteem.* If a person fears failure, he may procrastinate in order to avoid having to face this fear. If a person has poor self-esteem, she may procrastinate because there doesn't seem to be any point in trying when she's convinced that she isn't worth the effort.

The Effects of Procrastination and How to Combat Them

Procrastinating might help you feel good, or at least relieved, in the short term. However, avoiding tasks almost always causes long-term problems. It leads to a buildup of responsibilities and less time to complete them, often resulting in work that is not up to par. In addition, procrastinators may hamper their ability to improve and prevent themselves from finding out how far their abilities can take them. Finally, procrastination takes a personal toll. The weight of the waiting tasks often causes stress, feelings of helplessness, and a sense of incapability.

You can avoid these negative effects if you fight procrastination. The following strategies will help you.

Look at the effects of procrastinating versus not procrastinating. What rewards lie ahead if you get it done? What are the effects if you continue to put it off? Which situation has better effects? Chances are you will benefit more from facing the task head-on.

Set reasonable goals. Plan your goals carefully, allowing enough time to complete them. Unreasonable goals can be so intimidating that you do nothing at all. "Pay off the credit card bill next month" could throw you. However, "Pay off the credit card bill in 10 months" might inspire you to take action.

Break the task into smaller parts. How can you approach the task step by step? If you can concentrate on achieving one small goal at a time, the task may become less of a burden. In addition, setting concrete time limits for each task may help you feel more in control.

reflect

Think about your procrastination habits. What kind of task tends to lead you to procrastinate?

What situations make you want to stall? Do you put off work in some academic subjects more than others? Reflect on the effects of procrastination. What happens to your work, your feelings, your self-perception, and others around you when you procrastinate?

& respond

Get started whether or not you "feel like it." Going from doing nothing to doing something is often the hardest part of avoiding procrastination. The motivation techniques from Chapter 1 might help you take the first step. Once you start, your actions may have a positive effect on your attitude, and you may find it easier to continue.

Ask for help. You don't have to go it alone. For example, if you avoid a project because you dislike the student with whom you have to work, talk to your instructor about adjusting tasks or group assignments. Once you identify what's holding you up, see who can help you face the task.

Don't expect perfection. No one is perfect. Most people learn by starting at the beginning and wading through plenty of mistakes and confusion. It's better to try your best than to do nothing at all.

Reward yourself. The reward that lies at the end of a long road to a goal may not always be enough to motivate you. Find ways to boost your mood when you accomplish a particular task along the way. Remind yourself—with a break, a movie, some kind of treat that you like—that you are making successful progress.

Note that particular strategies may be more suited to particular kinds of procrastination. If you explore the reasons behind your own procrastination and try different strategies, you will find the ones that work best for you.

Other Time Traps to Avoid

Procrastination isn't the only way to spend your time in less-than-productive ways. Keep an eye out for these situations too.

Saying yes when you don't have the time. First, think before you respond. Ask yourself what effects a new responsibility will have on your schedule. If it will cause you more trouble than it seems to be worth, say no graciously.

Studying at a bad time or in a distracting location. When you are tired or distracted, you may need extra time to understand your material fully. If you study when you are most alert, you can take in more information in less time.

"I have always thought that one man of tolerable abilities may work great changes, and accomplish great affairs among mankind, if he first forms a good plan."

BENJAMIN FRANKLIN

Not curbing your social time. You plan to make a quick telephone call, but the next thing you know you've been talking for an hour, losing sleep or study time. Don't cut out all socializing, but stay aware.

Taking on too many tasks and projects. You may feel overwhelmed by all that you want to accomplish in your life. See what tasks you can reasonably delegate to others. No one can take a test for you, but another day-care parent could pick up your child on a day when your time runs short.

Of course no one is going to be able to avoid all of these time traps all of the time. Do the best that you can. The first step is an awareness of your particular tendencies. Once you know how you tend to procrastinate and waste time, you can take steps to change your habits. Time is your ally—make the most of the time that you have.

How can goal setting and time management help you choose a major?

Sometime in the first half of your time in college, after you complete your general education courses, you will be asked to declare an academic **major**. Your major will largely determine the courses you take, what you learn, and with whom you interact. Your major may also have a significant influence on your future career.

Choosing a major is a perfect example of a long-term goal that you can achieve through short-term goal setting and effective time management. You will be wise to start the process now, even though you probably don't need to decide right away—and even if, as is true of many students, you don't yet know what you want to study. Think of choosing a major as a long-term goal made up of multiple steps (short-term goals) that include knowing your interests and abilities, exploring academic options, establishing your academic schedule, and looking into career areas.

Major

An academic subject area chosen as a field of specialization, requiring a specific course of study.

Short-Term Goal #1: Identify Interests and Abilities

The best majors for you are ones that involve your interests and abilities. Considering what you like and what you do well can lead you to a fulfilling area of study. In an insecure economy, of course, financial potential and job opportunities are important considerations. Why might focusing on your interests be just as, if not more, important?

- *You will perform better.* The more you like something, the harder you work at it—and the harder you work, the more you will improve and the more success you will have. Also, chances are that you have a natural talent in the subjects you love.

- *You will have a more positive attitude.* A positive attitude will contribute to your success no matter what your level of ability or experience.

- *You will have more energy.* When you're doing something you like, time seems to pass quickly. You will accomplish more when what you study energizes you.

Think about this quote from acclaimed jazz vo-
calist Ella Fitzgerald: "*Just don't give up trying*

to do what you really want to do.
Where there's love and inspiration; I
don't think you can go wrong." How
do you react to this in terms of choosing a major? How important are "love and inspiration"
to you as you explore majors?

& respond

Set a goal to answer questions like the following to pinpoint your areas of interest:

- What courses have I enjoyed the most? What
  might these courses have in common?
- What subjects are interesting to me when I
  read and study?
- What activities do I look forward to most?
- In what skills or academic areas do I perform
  best? Am I a "natural" in any area?
- What areas are most difficult for me? What do
  I struggle with?

Short-Term Goal #2:
Explore Academic Options

Once you have begun to explore your interests,
find out about the academic choices available at
your school. Plan to achieve these mini-goals in order to reach this short-
term goal:

- *Learn what's possible.* Read your college catalog to find out your
  school's rules regarding the declaration (and changing) of majors. Find
  answers to these general questions first:
  - When do I have to declare a major? (generally at the end of the sec-
    ond year for four-year programs; earlier for associates' or certificate
    programs)
  - What are my options in majoring? (double majors, minors, or inter-
    disciplinary majors)
  - What majors are offered at my school?

  If a major looks interesting, explore it further by answering the
  following questions:
  - What minimum GPA, if any, does the department require before ac-
    cepting me as a major?
  - What preparatory courses (prerequisites) are required?
  - What courses will I be required to take? How many credits do I
    need to graduate in the major?
  - What is the recommended or required order of courses?
  - Will I have to write a thesis to graduate in this major?
- *Work closely with your advisor.* Begin discussing your major early on
  with your advisor. Your advisor can help you evaluate what's available,
  and together you can find the best options.
- *Visit the department.* Ask the departmental secretary for information
  about majors offered by that department. Then ask about sitting in on
  several classes to get a firsthand introduction to the instructors and the
  work. Consider asking an instructor for an appointment to discuss the
  major.

- *Speak to people with experience in the major.* Ask students who are a year or two ahead of you in school to describe their experiences with the courses, the workload, and the professors.
- *Think "out of the box"—consider creative options for majoring.* One or more of the following possibilities may be open to you:
  - *Double majors.* If, for example, you are interested in majoring in English and Philosophy, ask your academic advisor if it is possible to meet the requirements for both departments.
  - *Interdisciplinary majors.* If your preferred major isn't in the catalog, consult your advisor. Some schools allow students to design majors with guidance from advisors and instructors.
  - *Minors.* A minor also involves a concentration of courses in a particular department, but has fewer requirements than a major. A sociology major, for example, can work toward a goal to become a social worker by minoring in a language or in psychology.
  - *Majors involving courses outside your school.* Some schools may have study abroad programs (students spend a semester or a year at an affiliated college in a different country) or opportunities to take courses at nearby schools. Such courses might apply to a major that interests you.

TAKE ACTION

Explore Majoring at Your School

Use your college catalog and website to answer these questions.

When are students required to declare a major? _____

What are the options for majoring (double majors, minors, interdisciplinary majors, and so on)?

__double majors, mines_____

_____

_____

What does a student have to do in order to change a major?

__First you must consult with your advisor_____

_____

Look at the list of majors available at your school. Name three that look interesting right now.

1. _____
2. _____
3. _____

Short-Term Goal #3: Establish Your Academic Schedule

Your time management skills play a crucial role in achieving your academic goals. Apply the following time management principles to the entire period of time you plan to be in college:

- *Look at your time frame.* How many years or semesters do you plan to study? Make a timeline on which to place deadlines for important goals such as major declaration.

- *Set timing for short-term goals.* Within your time frame, pinpoint when to accomplish the important short-term goals that lead you to graduation. When will you need to complete core requirements, declare a major, write a thesis? Although you won't necessarily want to plan out your entire college course load at the beginning of your first semester, planning a tentative **curriculum**—both within and outside your major—can help to clarify where you are heading.

- *Identify dates connected to your goal fulfillment.* Pay attention to academic dates—you will find an academic calendar in each year's college catalog. Such dates include registration dates, final date to declare a major, final date to drop a course, and so forth. Plan ahead so you don't miss a deadline.

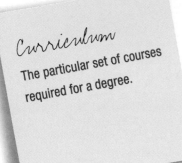

Curriculum
The particular set of courses required for a degree.

Short-Term Goal #4: Look into Career Areas

The point of declaring and pursuing a major is to help you reach a significant level of knowledge in one subject, often in preparation for a particular career area. Having some idea of your career interests will help you evaluate when you have narrowed the field to a few potential majors.

Many students select a major because it prepares them to find work in a particular field after they graduate. Other undergraduates are looking for intellectual growth and a field that interests them; they don't focus on a direct career link. Ultimately, only you can decide how important the career connection is to you. Use the following strategies to explore what's out there.

- *Use career resources.* Visit the career center to read current media, take an assessment, or explore the career areas that currently have good prospects. Talk to people who have jobs that interest you.

- *Explore the educational requirements of various careers.* Your choice of major may be more or less crucial depending on the career area. For example, pursuing a career in medicine almost always requires a major in some area of the biological sciences.

- *Try hands-on exploration.* Extracurricular activities and volunteering opportunities might give you particular insight into what works well for you. For example, a student interested in architecture may volunteer for a group that builds houses for the disadvantaged.

- *Keep your values in mind.* Ask yourself what careers support the principles that guide your life choices. How important to you are service to others, financial security, a broad-based education, time for family? Where do you stand on political and moral issues?

- *Follow your passion.* In many cases, family and financial circumstances lead students to choose a major that will take them directly to well-paying job opportunities. Prestige and money may be important—but they usually are not viable replacements for deep personal satisfaction. Consider making a choice that leads you toward the life you have dreamed of.

Throughout the Goal Process: Be Flexible

As with any time management challenge, flexibility is the key to success in the face of change. Changes in available courses and other academic factors may come into play. Many students change their minds as they consider majors, even declaring a major and then changing it one or more times before finding a good fit. You have the right to change your mind. Just act on any change of major right away—once you have considered it carefully—by informing your advisor, completing any required paperwork, and redesigning your schedule to reflect your new choices.

Working toward any major will help you develop your most important skill—knowing how to use your mind. More than anything, your future success will depend on your ability to contribute through clear, effective, and creative thinking.

I manage impulsivity.

Student life is, most often, a jumble of responsibilities and events. In the attempt to keep up with everything to do and everywhere to be, students often make impulsive decisions about how to spend their time or try to achieve a particular goal with almost no time available to do so. If you have ever abandoned your studying for a social event or forgotten about an assignment until the night before it was due, you understand how this can happen.

If you can manage your impulsivity—in basic terms, think about the consequences before you make a decision about how to spend your time or achieve a goal—you can boost your success.

First of all, mapping out a plan in advance will help you devote an appropriate amount of time to each element, bringing the most ideal results. Second, the act of thinking ahead will help you avoid situations that lead to impulsive decisions. Managing impulsivity means that you give yourself a chance to think—and therefore to succeed.

REMEMBER!
the important points ° ° °

1 **How do you set and achieve goals?**

A goal is a target toward which you direct your efforts. Goals can be long term or short term. A personal mission statement helps you define your most important long-term goals and adjust to changing life circumstances. Placing goals within time frames—a week, a month, a semester—can help you plan how to pursue them, especially when short-term goals act as steps toward a long-term goal. Prioritizing goals allows you to focus on what is most important at any given time.

2 **How can you manage your time?**

Effective time management will help you achieve your goals. Building a schedule is your main time management task. This involves using a planner, linking daily and weekly goals to long-term goals, prioritizing, and keeping track of events. When you take responsibility for how you spend your time, you are more able to take steps toward your goals. Taking responsibility involves planning each week's schedule, using to-do lists, thinking about time, using monthly and yearly calendars, and scheduling down time. Flexibility will help you handle schedule changes, whether they are minor day-to-day changes or major life shifts.

3 **Why is procrastination a problem?**

Procrastination, the habit of putting off tasks, can keep you from achieving your goals. Explore your reasons for procrastinating and take steps to overcome them. Strategies to fight procrastination include asking for help with tasks, weighing the positive and negative effects of procrastination, setting reasonable goals, breaking the task into parts, and avoiding perfectionism. Other time traps to avoid include taking on too many tasks and not curbing social time.

4 **How can goal setting and time management help you choose a major?**

Choosing a major is a long-term goal achievable through short-term goal steps and effective management of your time in school. First, identify your interests and abilities, considering what you like to do can lead you to a fulfilling major. Next, explore your school's academic options—what majors are available, when you must declare, required courses, and so on. Then establish your academic schedule; look at the time you plan to spend in college and use time management skills to place your major-related short-term goals and important dates within that time frame. Think too about career areas that interest you and find out which majors relate to, or are perhaps required for, those areas. Finally, be flexible throughout the process, open to change in your academic situation or in your interests and goals.

Name	Date

CRITICAL THINKING
APPLYING LEARNING TO LIFE

Discover How You Spend Your Time

In the table below, estimate the total time you think you spend per week on each listed activity. Then, add the hours. If your number is over 168 (the number of hours in a week), rethink your estimates and recalculate so that the total is equal to or below 168. Then, subtract your total from 168. Whatever is left over is your estimate of hours that you spend in unscheduled activities.

ACTIVITY	ESTIMATED TIME SPENT
Class	9:00 – 12:50
Work	10:00 – 5:00
Studying	2:00 – 3:30
Sleeping	9:00 – 6:00 am
Eating	12:00 – 12:30
Family time/child care	3:00 – 8:30
Commuting/traveling	0
Chores and personal business	0
Friends and important relationships	0
Telephone time	30 minutes
Leisure/entertainment	1:30 – 2:00
Spiritual life	0
Total	120

Now, spend a week recording exactly how you spend your time. The chart on pages 82 and 83 has blocks showing half-hour increments. As you go through the week, write in what you do each hour, indicating when you started and when you stopped (for the 12–6 A.M. slot at the bottom of the page, indicate the amount of time spent on any activity you write in). Don't forget activities such as sleeping, relaxing, and watching TV. Be honest—record your actual activities, not how you want to spend your time or think you should have spent your time. There are no wrong answers.

MONDAY		TUESDAY		WEDNESDAY		THURSDAY	
TIME	ACTIVITY	TIME	ACTIVITY	TIME	ACTIVITY	TIME	ACTIVITY
6:00 AM	mom work	6:00 AM	morning work	6:00 AM	Take mom to work	6:00 AM	morning work
6:30 AM		6:30 AM		6:30 AM		6:30 AM	
7:00 AM	School brothers	7:00 AM	Took my brothers & sister to school.	7:00 AM	Take my brothers & sister to school.	7:00 AM	Take brother & sister to school
7:30 AM		7:30 AM		7:30 AM		7:30 AM	
8:00 AM	babysiter	8:00 AM	babysitter	8:00 AM	babysitter	8:00 AM	babysitter
8:30 AM		8:30 AM		8:30 AM		8:30 AM	
9:00 AM	School	9:00 AM		9:00 AM	School	9:00 AM	
9:30 AM		9:30 AM		9:30 AM		9:30 AM	
10:00 AM		10:00 AM	Work	10:00 AM		10:00 AM	work
10:30 AM		10:30 AM		10:30 AM		10:30 AM	
11:00 AM		11:00 AM		11:00 AM		11:00 AM	
11:30 AM		11:30 AM		11:30 AM		11:30 AM	
12:00 PM		12:00 PM		12:00 PM		12:00 PM	
12:30 PM		12:30 PM		12:30 PM		12:30 PM	
1:00 PM	School	1:00 PM		1:00 PM	School	1:00 PM	
1:30 PM	babysitter	1:30 PM		1:30 PM	babysitter	1:30 PM	
2:00 PM	sister school	2:00 PM		2:00 PM	sister & brother school	2:00 PM	
2:30 PM	study	2:30 PM		2:30 PM	Study	2:30 PM	
3:00 PM		3:00 PM		3:00 PM		3:00 PM	
3:30 PM		3:30 PM		3:30 PM		3:30 PM	
4:00 PM		4:00 PM		4:00 PM		4:00 PM	
4:30 PM		4:30 PM		4:30 PM		4:30 PM	
5:00 PM	Study	5:00 PM		5:00 PM	Study	5:00 PM	
5:30 PM	spent time	5:30 PM	Do homework.	5:30 PM	spent time	5:30 PM	Do homework
6:00 PM	family	6:00 PM		6:00 PM	family	6:00 PM	
6:30 PM		6:30 PM		6:30 PM		6:30 PM	
7:00 PM		7:00 PM		7:00 PM		7:00 PM	
7:30 PM		7:30 PM	Chores	7:30 PM		7:30 PM	Chores
8:00 PM	Sleep	8:00 PM	Sleep	8:00 PM	Sleep	8:00 PM	sleep
8:30 PM		8:30 PM		8:30 PM		8:30 PM	
9:00 PM		9:00 PM		9:00 PM		9:00 PM	
9:30 PM		9:30 PM		9:30 PM		9:30 PM	
10:00 PM		10:00 PM		10:00 PM		10:00 PM	
10:30 PM		10:30 PM		10:30 PM		10:30 PM	
11:00 PM		11:00 PM		11:00 PM		11:00 PM	
11:30 PM		11:30 PM		11:30 PM		11:30 PM	
12–6 AM		12–6 AM		12–6 AM		12–6 AM	

TIME	FRIDAY ACTIVITY	TIME	SATURDAY ACTIVITY	TIME	SUNDAY ACTIVITY	NOTES
6:00 AM	Take mom to work	6:00 AM		6:00 AM		
6:30 AM		6:30 AM	home	6:30 AM		
7:00 AM	Take my brothers	7:00 AM		7:00 AM		
7:30 AM	& sister to school	7:30 AM		7:30 AM		
8:00 AM	babysitter	8:00 AM		8:00 AM		
8:30 AM		8:30 AM		8:30 AM		
9:00 AM	school	9:00 AM	study	9:00 AM		
9:30 AM		9:30 AM		9:30 AM		
10:00 AM		10:00 AM	shop	10:00 AM		
10:30 AM		10:30 AM		10:30 AM		
11:00 AM		11:00 AM		11:00 AM		
11:30 AM		11:30 AM		11:30 AM		
12:00 PM		12:00 PM		12:00 PM	study	
12:30 PM		12:30 PM		12:30 PM		
1:00 PM	school	1:00 PM	study	1:00 PM		
1:30 PM	babysitter	1:30 PM		1:30 PM		
2:00 PM	sister & brother school	2:00 PM		2:00 PM		
2:30 PM	study	2:30 PM		2:30 PM		
3:00 PM		3:00 PM	study	3:00 PM		
3:30 PM		3:30 PM		3:30 PM	study	
4:00 PM		4:00 PM	work	4:00 PM		
4:30 PM		4:30 PM		4:30 PM		
5:00 PM	study	5:00 PM		5:00 PM		
5:30 PM	spent	5:30 PM		5:30 PM		
6:00 PM	time with	6:00 PM		6:00 PM		
6:30 PM	family	6:30 PM		6:30 PM		
7:00 PM		7:00 PM		7:00 PM		
7:30 PM		7:30 PM		7:30 PM		
8:00 PM	sleep	8:00 PM		8:00 PM		
8:30 PM		8:30 PM		8:30 PM		
9:00 PM		9:00 PM		9:00 PM		
9:30 PM		9:30 PM		9:30 PM		
10:00 PM		10:00 PM		10:00 PM		
10:30 PM		10:30 PM	work	10:30 PM		
11:00 PM		11:00 PM		11:00 PM		
11:30 PM		11:30 PM		11:30 PM		
12–6 AM		12–6 AM		12–6 AM		

83

After a week, go through the chart and look at how many hours you actually spent on the activities for which you estimated your hours before. Tally the hours in the boxes in the following table using straight tally marks; round off to half hours and use a short tally mark for each half hour. In the third column, total the hours for each activity. Leave the "Ideal Time in Hours" column blank for now.

ACTIVITY	TIME TALLIED OVER ONE-WEEK PERIOD	TOTAL TIME IN HOURS	IDEAL TIME IN HOURS
Example: Class	JHT JHT JHT II	16.5	
Class	HHT I IIII	12.5	13
Work	HHT HHT HHHTI	32.5	
Studying	HHH HHHH HHH I	16	
Sleeping	HHT HHT HHT HHH	60	
Eating	HHT HHHTII	14.5	
Family time/child care	HHH HHT HHT	16	
Commuting/traveling	HHT	20.5	
Chores and personal business	HHT II	7 hours	
Friends and important relationships			
Telephone time	IIII	2 hours	
Leisure/entertainment	I	1 hour	
Spiritual life			
Other		179	

Add the totals in the third column to find your grand total. Compare your grand total to your estimated grand total; compare your actual activity hour totals to your estimated activity hour totals. What matches and what doesn't? Describe the most interesting similarities and differences.

_____

_____

_____

What is the one biggest surprise about how you spend your time?

_school and work_____

_____

_____

Name one change you would like to make in how you spend your time.

_Read more studying_____

_____

_____

Think about what kinds of changes might help you improve your ability to set and achieve goals. Ask yourself important questions about what you do daily, weekly, and monthly. On what activities do you think you should spend more or less time? Go back to the table on page 84 and fill in the "Ideal Time in Hours" column. Consider the difference between actual hours and ideal hours when you think about the changes you want to make in your life.

TEAM BUILDING
COLLABORATIVE SOLUTIONS

The Effects of Procrastination

In a group of three to five students, or as a class if your class is small, brainstorm situations in which you tend to procrastinate. Write down as many as you can. Next, if you have brainstormed as a class, break into groups of three to five. Each small group should choose one situation from the list.

Divide a blank piece of paper into two columns marked "Pros" and "Cons." Then, with your small group, think of and write down the pros (positive effects or good results) and cons (negative effects or drawbacks) in your chosen situation. Talk about these effects, thinking about both the short term and the long term. Consider, for example, how procrastinating in this situation may affect the quality of your work, motivation, productivity, ability to be on time, grades, or self-perception.

Finally, as a group, come up with an alternative to procrastination. What would you do differently in this situation? How can you achieve what you want?

If there is time, small groups can share their insights with the class.

personal IMPROVEMENT plan

I commit to three goal setting and/or time management strategies to improve my study skills.
From this chapter, I choose three strategies that I think will help me.

Strategy 1: _____

Strategy 2: _____

Strategy 3: _____

I choose one strategy to focus on (circle this strategy above) and I will:

- describe my goal—what I want to gain by using this strategy.

_____

_____

_____

- describe in detail how I plan to use the strategy.

_____

_____

_____

_____

- describe how I will measure my progress toward the goal this semester.

_____

_____

_____

_____

Activate the Habit of Mind

MIND HABITS OF MIND

Here's how I will *manage impulsivity* to achieve this goal.

_____

_____

_____

_____

SUGGESTED READINGS

College Board, ed. *The College Board Index of Majors and Graduate Degrees 2003: All New Twenty-Fifth Edition*. New York: College Entrance Examination Board, 2002.

Covey, Stephen. *The Seven Habits of Highly Effective People*. New York: Simon & Schuster, 1995.

Emmett, Rita. *The Procrastinator's Handbook: Mastering the Art of Doing It Now*. New York: Walker & Co., 2000.

Gleeson, Kerry. *The Personal Efficiency Program: How to Get Organized to Do More Work in Less Time, 2nd ed*. New York: John Wiley & Sons, 2000.

Harrington, Paul, et al. *The College Majors Handbook: The Actual Jobs, Earnings, and Trends for Graduates of 60 College Majors*. Indianapolis, IN: Jist Works, 1999.

Lakein, Alan. *How to Get Control of Your Time and Your Life*. New York: New American Library, 1996.

McGee-Cooper, Ann with Duane Trammell. *Time Management for Unmanageable People*. New York: Bantam Books, 1994.

Phifer, Paul. *College Majors and Careers: A Resource Guide for Effective Life Planning, 4th ed*. Chicago: Ferguson Publishing, 1999.

Phifer, Paul. *Great Careers in Two Years: The Associate Degree Option*. Chicago: Ferguson Publishing, 2003.

Sapadin, Linda and Jack Maguire. *Beat Procrastination and Make the Grade: The Six Styles of Procrastination and How Students Can Overcome Them*. New York: Penguin USA, 1999.

Timm, Paul R. *Successful Self-Management: A Psychologically Sound Approach to Personal Effectiveness*. Los Altos, CA: Crisp Publications, 1996.

INTERNET RESOURCES

Franklin Covey (mission builder) www.franklincovey.com

Mind Tools (section on time management): www.mindtools.com/page5.html

Prentice Hall Student Success Supersite Majors Exploration: www.prenhall.com/success/MajorExp/index.html

Top Achievement—goal setting and self-improvement resources: www.topachievement.com

ENDNOTES

1. Paul R. Timm, Ph.D., *Successful Self-Management: A Psychologically Sound Approach to Personal Effectiveness*. Los Altos, CA: Crisp Publications, Inc., 1987, pp. 22–41.

2. Stephen Covey, *The Seven Habits of Highly Effective People*. New York: Simon & Schuster, 1989, pp. 70–144, 309–318.

3. Timm, pp. 22–41.

4. William Sydnor, "Procrastination," from the California Polytechnic State University Study Skills Library [online]. Based on *Overcoming Procrastination* by Albert Ellis. Available: http://www.sas.calpoly.edu/asc/ssl/procrastination.html (May 2003). Used with permission.

5. Jane B. Burka, Ph.D. and Lenora M. Yuen, Ph.D., *Procrastination*. Reading, MA: Perseus Books, 1983, pp. 21–22.

6. Ibid.

THINKING IT THROUGH

Check those statements that apply to you right now:

- I'm not quite sure what "critical thinking" means.

- I am usually happy with how I've solved a problem.

- Plan for next year? I can hardly get past next week.

- I don't often question the validity of my opinions.

- I think my perspective is generally on target.

- I consider myself to be a creative person.

- The skill of creative thinking is more necessary for the arts than for other subject areas.

Critical and Creative Thinking

BECOMING AN ACTIVE LEARNER

Creating, imagining, innovating.

"All human beings have the capacity to **generate novel, original, clever, or ingenious products, solutions, and techniques**. Creative human beings develop that capacity . . . Creative people take risks and frequently push the boundaries of their perceived limits." —**ART COSTA**

Taking risks is an inherent part of being a creative and critical thinker. If you believe in yourself enough to go beyond what you think you are capable of, you will discover new ideas and build your brain power.

The biological basis of thinking is rooted in the quest for survival. Imagine a member of a hunting tribe in Tanzania or a solo camper in the Kootenai National Forest in Montana. When each person hears a noise in the brush, each brain springs into action: Is it a predator? Is it something I can eat or use? How will I respond, and what might happen as a result? In such cases, a life could depend on the act of questioning.

Your need to question is just as strong, even if you aren't often facing a life-threatening situation. Making day-to-day decisions, major or minor, means asking important questions

In this chapter you explore answers to the following questions:

- How can you spark your creative mind?

- What is critical thinking?

- What skills will help you become a better thinker?

- How can you effectively solve problems, make decisions, and plan strategically?

about ideas and information—the essence of critical and creative thinking. After first helping to jump-start your creativity, this chapter will show you how you think critically every day and how your mind works when you think. Once you have a basic understanding of thinking, you will learn effective ways to distinguish fact from opinion, examine perspectives, evaluate assumptions, solve problems, make decisions, and plan strategically.

How can you spark your creative mind?

Because you will often need to engage your creative abilities when thinking critically, start your exploration of thinking with the concept of creativity. Critical thinking and creative thinking are interrelated and often dependent upon each other. An open, creative mind will help you to generate the ideas and possibilities required in a successful critical-thinking process.

Creativity can be hard to define. How do you describe the "Eureka!" moment when a person experiences a creative insight? Some researchers define creativity as combining existing elements in an innovative way that creates a new purpose (for example, Dr. Alexander Fleming observed the interaction of a petri dish mold with bacteria and realized that the mold—penicillin—could function as a powerful antibacterial drug). Others see creativity as the art of generating novel ideas from taking a fresh look at how things are interrelated (noting the regular diet of ladybugs inspired organic farmers to bring ladybugs in to consume crop-destroying aphids).[1]

Thinking about what is creative may call to mind images such as a street drummer banging out a complex rhythm or the designs for the World Trade Center site in New York. Creativity, however, encompasses much more than art and music. Creativity gives rise to innovative ideas and products that bring changes both great and small. Consider the following examples of creative innovations that have had an impact:

- Art Fry and Spencer Silver invented the Post-it™ in 1980, enabling people to save paper and protect documents by using removable notes.
- Agricultural chemist George Washington Carver developed the revolutionary method of crop rotation—alternating soil-depleting crops with soil-enriching ones—allowing land to be used more efficiently.
- Grace Murray Hopper, a mathematician, worked in the 1940s on one of the first computers. She pioneered the effort to create computer languages that people who are not mathematicians could understand, and her efforts opened the world of computers to a wide audience.

- Jim Henson revolutionized children's television and the way children learn about the world through his invention of the Muppets and development of *Sesame Street*.

Creativity doesn't just happen on these world-shifting levels. You too are a creative thinker. Your everyday moments of creativity might include events similar to the following:

- Thinking of a new way to talk to an instructor about a problem
- Changing how you commute to school so that you can work while you are in transit
- Finding a unique way to approach a research paper topic that sets it apart from the other papers submitted by class members

Learning how to heighten your creativity will boost your ability to think productively and successfully. Begin by thinking of creativity in four separate ways:[2]

- The characteristics of the creative *person*
- The type of *environment* that fosters creativity
- The stages of the creative *process*
- The aspects of the creative *product* or *outcome*

As you work toward any creative outcome—a novel solution, idea, approach, tangible product, work of art, system, or program—focus on the other three elements to maximize your creative abilities.

reflect

Oliver Wendell Holmes, a famous 19th-century writer, doctor, and professor, once said: "A mind that is stretched to a new idea never returns to its original dimensions." What thoughts does this inspire? Can you think of an example of when your mind was stretched when you encountered, or came up with, a creative new idea? What kinds of risks might be involved when stretching to a new idea?

& respond

The Characteristics of the Creative Person

Creative thinkers combine ideas and information in ways that form new solutions, ideas, processes, or products. "The hallmark of creative people is their mental flexibility," says creativity expert Roger von Oech. "Like race-car drivers who shift in and out of different gears depending on where they are on the course, creative people are able to shift in and out of different types of thinking depending on the needs of the situation at hand."[3] Look at Figure 4.1 to see some primary characteristics of creative people. Underneath all these qualities lie a desire to learn, a drive to question, and a commitment to keep an open mind.

"The world of reality has its limits. The world of imagination is boundless."

JEAN-JACQUES ROUSSEAU

FIGURE 4.1   Characteristics of creative people.

CHARACTERISTIC	EXAMPLE
Willingness to take risks	Taking a difficult, high-level course
Tendency to break away from limitations	Entering a marathon race
Tendency to seek new challenges & experiences	Taking on an internship in a high-pressure workplace
Broad range of interests	Inventing new moves on the basketball court and playing guitar at an open-mike night
Ability to make new things out of available materials	Making curtains out of bedsheets
Tendency to question norms & assumptions	Adopting a child of different ethnic background than the family's
Willingness to deviate from popular opinion	Working for a small, relatively unknown political party
Curiosity and inquisitiveness	Wanting to know how a computer program works

Source: Adapted from T. Z. Tardif and R. J. Sternberg, "What Do We Know About Creativity?" in *The Nature of Creativity*, ed. R. J. Sternberg (London: Cambridge University Press, 1988).

Try some or all of the following strategies to boost your creative abilities.

Be curious. The more information and ideas you gather as you think, the more perspective you have to build a creative idea or solution. Collect information and ideas from reading materials, people, the radio, anywhere—and record them on tape or in writing. Branch out and cultivate new interests. Seek out new experiences and take in the ideas and perspectives that you encounter.[4]

Shift your perspective. At first, a problem may look like "The house isn't quiet when I study." If you take a wider look, you may discover hidden causes or effects of the problem, such as "I haven't chosen the best time of day to study" or "I haven't let my housemates know that I need quiet." Question your assumptions; ask people you trust for their perspectives; read in order to discover new ways of looking at situations.[5]

Don't get hooked on finding the one right answer. There can be lots of "right answers" to any question. The more possibilities you generate, the better your chance of finding the best one. Also, don't stop the process when you think you have the best answer—keep going until you are out of steam. You never know what may come up in those last gasps of creative energy.[6]

Break the rules sometimes. All kinds of creative breakthroughs have occurred because someone questioned a rule or an assumption. Women and members of minorities can vote and hold jobs because someone questioned a rule—a law—many years ago. Even the rules of logic don't always hold—

following strict logic may cause you to miss analogies or ignore your hunches. At one time in the not-so-distant past, for example, it made no logical sense that two people could talk to one another while in different cities—and now the telephone is a fact of life.[7]

Ask "what if" questions. Set up hypothetical environments in which new ideas can grow. "What if I knew I couldn't fail?" "What if I had unlimited money or time?" See what idea, however outrageous, comes from a "what if" question—and then think about how to make it happen. Faced with generations of conflict in the Middle East, the founders of Seeds of Peace created an organization to prepare Israeli and Palestinian teenagers with the leadership skills needed to coexist peacefully. What if, they asked, these teens met at a summer camp in Maine so that the next generation has greater understanding and respect than the last? And what if follow-up programs and reunions are put in place to cement summer friendships so that relationships change the politics of the Middle East?

Take risks and, when necessary, embrace failure. Even though failure is always a possibility, taking risks is the only way to make your highest goals reachable. Even Michael Jordan got cut from the basketball team as a high school sophomore in Wilmington, N.C. If you insist on playing it safe, you may miss out on the path—often paved with failures—leading to the best possible solution or situation.[8]

The Creative Environment

Just as any plant needs a specific setting in which to thrive, your mind needs a nurturing environment in which to maximize its creative abilities. The perfect creative environment will vary from person to person. Use these ideas to find yours.

Choose the best atmosphere. T. M. Amabile says that people are more creative and imaginative when they spend time around other creative folk.[9] Hang out with people whose thinking inspires you. Find locales that energize you. Play music that puts you in your desired mental state. Paint your study walls your favorite color. Experiment to find the atmosphere that most seems to free your mind.[10]

Give yourself time to "sit" with a question. Rushing can stifle your creative ability. When you allow time for thought to percolate, or you take breaks when figuring out a problem, you may increase your creative output. Change your environment, get some exercise, snooze; talk with a friend, work on something else. Some of the best ideas pop up when you have given your brain permission to go "off the job" for a while.[11]

Let yourself play. People often hit upon their most creative ideas when they are exercising or just relaxing. Often when your mind switches into play mode, it can more freely generate new thoughts. Mental play can allow you to find a brilliant discovery in what seems like a crazy idea. For example, the idea for Velcro™ came when an inventor examined how a burr sticks to clothing.[12]

Write it down. Many people think of ideas while exercising, driving, or in the shower; upon waking; or even while dreaming. When an idea occurs—a solution to a problem or a new thought—write it down as soon as possible. To make sure your creative environment includes a way to write ideas, try keeping a pen and paper by your bed, your PDA in your pocket, a marker attached to your notebook, or a notepad and pen in your car. Try keeping an idea list; many PDAs will allow you to sort ideas into categories (personal, school, work, and so on, or smaller categories such as individual classes or goals).

The Creative Process: Brainstorming

Like creativity itself, the "creative process"—the process by which an individual arrives at a creative product—takes many forms. *Brainstorming*—one specific version of the creative process—is an essential element of decision making and strategic planning. You are brainstorming when you approach a problem by letting your mind free-associate, coming up with as many possible ideas, examples, or solutions as you can. Brainstorming is also referred to as *divergent thinking:* You start with the issue or problem and then let your mind diverge, or go in many different directions, in search of ideas or solutions.

Following are some general guidelines for creative and successful brainstorming.[13]

Don't evaluate or criticize an idea right away. Write down your ideas so that you remember them. Evaluate them later, after you have had a chance to think about them. Try to avoid criticizing other people's ideas as well. People often become stifled when their ideas are evaluated during brainstorming.

Focus on quantity; don't worry about quality until later. Generate as many ideas or examples as you can without worrying about which one is "right." The more thoughts you generate, the better the chance that one may be useful. Brainstorming works well in groups. Group members can become inspired by, and make creative use of, one another's ideas.

Analogy
A comparison based on a resemblance between things otherwise unlike.

Use analogy. Think of similar situations and write down what you remember. What ideas or strategies have worked before? **Analogy** puts the mind to work recalling potentially helpful ideas and examples and helping you to generate new ones. For example, the Velcro discovery is a product of analogy: When imagining how two pieces of fabric could stick to each other, the inventor thought of the similar situation of a burr sticking to clothing.

As you read through the rest of the chapter, you will see that creative thinking is an essential component of critical thinking. Creative thinking plays a pivotal role in the critical-thinking processes that you will study— problem solving, decision making, and strategic planning. In each process, you think creatively when you brainstorm and evaluate potential solutions, decisions, ideas, or strategic paths.

TAKE ACTION

Gather Evidence of Your Creativity

Think about the past week, then make a list of 10 creative acts you performed—small, earth-shattering, or anything in between.

1. study more hours
2. spent more time with family
3. work, more hours.
4. organize my life.
5.
6.
7.
8.
9.
10.

What is critical thinking?

You may have heard the term "critical thinking" before. Although you might assume that the word *critical* implies something difficult and negative, as it is used here it actually means "indispensable" and "important." Critical thinking means finding that which is important. Questioning is at the heart of critical thinking because it allows you to go beyond the basic recall of information. When you think critically, you become an active examiner by asking questions.

You ask and answer critical-thinking questions every day, whether or not you realize it. For example, in deciding to pursue a college degree—a major life decision—you asked critical-thinking questions as you thought through the consequences of the choice. "What if I go full-time—what will that do to my schedule at work and at home?" "What if I don't go to school—how will that affect my ability to earn a good living in the short and long term?" Other examples of student critical-thinking moments are:

- Choosing the best term paper topic by looking at the list of topics, thinking about the available library and Internet sources, and taking your personal interest and instructor's approval into consideration
- Deciding between two different courses by reading course descriptions and talking to your advisor
- After listening to one point of view in a class discussion, offering a solidly supported opposing opinion

Questioning the status quo and coming up with alternatives is an act of critical thinking.

- Coming up with examples that back up the central idea of a paper you are writing

Why put in the effort to think critically? Critical thinking brings you countless advantages, including:

- *Study success through increased brain power.* Critical thinkers understand how their minds work—and they use their minds actively. The more you think consciously, using specific strategies and patterns, the more effectively you can think. The more effective a thinker you are, the more you boost your chances for success in any college course, no matter what the subject.

- *Being able to apply knowledge.* Critical thinking moves you beyond repeating back what you learn. For instance, it won't mean much for elementary education students to quote child development facts on an exam unless they can evaluate real children's needs in the classroom. Through critical thinking you put your learning to use and benefit from your hard work at school.

- *Being an innovator.* As a questioner, you do not necessarily accept the status quo or conventional wisdom. Rather, you look for new approaches and answers, which is at the heart of innovation. Innovators are valued as collaborators, at school and on the job.

The Path of Critical Thinking

Critical thinking consists of a path of actions performed in order. When you think critically, you:

1. Take in information
2. Examine the information through questioning
3. Draw conclusions based on the questions you ask
4. Use what you learn, through thinking processes such as problem solving, decision making, and strategic planning

Look at Figure 4.2 to see a visual representation of the critical-thinking path.

Take In Information

The information you receive and recall is your raw material. When you take in information accurately and without judgment, you have the best material with which to work as you think. Once you have clear, complete information, examine it through questioning.

Ask Questions

Questioning is the key to learning and to linking what you learn to other information. As you will see later in the chapter, critical thinkers ask many kinds

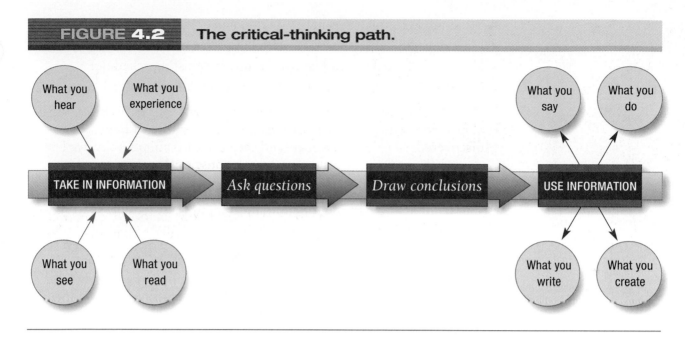

FIGURE 4.2 The critical-thinking path.

of questions about any given piece of information or situation, including: *How can I connect this to what I already know? What does this make me think of? Is it good or bad, true or false, and why? What effects does it have? What about this isn't clear? What is its source? How can I get more information?*

Critical thinkers also ask whether information can help them with a specific action—solving a problem, for example, or making a decision.

Draw Conclusions

You draw conclusions from considering the information, the questions you have asked, and the answers you have found. Move yourself toward conclusions by looking at the information and asking yourself: *So what? What comes to mind? What does this mean?*

Use Information

After taking in information, examining it by questioning, and drawing conclusions from the questions, critical thinkers put the information to work. Now comes the actual work of solving the problem, making the strategic plan, and so on. This last stage of the critical-thinking path is where new knowledge—ideas and creations—is born out of the mix of what you already know, what you have newly acquired, and the power of your mind.

Learning How Your Mind Works

Start to put critical thinking into real-world perspective by imagining a specific scenario. You have to fulfill a math requirement and are trying to decide between two courses—Algebra I and Developmental Math for Health Sciences. As you work toward a decision, you might ask questions like the following:

- Do these courses have any prerequisites—and if so, what are they?

- What are the similarities in the workloads?
- How does the subject matter for these two courses differ?
- How would the Algebra I course fit into my existing schedule?
- Would either of the courses fit a major that interests me? If so, how?
- How do I investigate the rumor that the Algebra I instructor is too tough?
- Which course is the best fit for me considering all that I have discovered?

When you ask important questions like these, your mind performs basic *actions*. Sometimes it uses one action by itself, but most often it uses two or more in combination. To identify and understand these actions is to have a fundamental understanding of thinking. These actions are the building blocks with which you construct the critical-thinking processes described later in the chapter.

Identify your mind's actions using a system originally derived by educators Frank Lyman, Arlene Mindus, and Charlene Lopez[14] and developed by numerous other instructors. Based on their studies of how people think, they named seven basic types of thought. These types, referred to here as actions, are not new to you, although some of their names may be. They represent the ways in which you think all the time.

Through exploring these actions, you go beyond just thinking in order to learn *how* you think. In a way, you are studying an instruction manual for your mind. Following are explanations of each of the mind actions, including examples (some from the questions you just read). The *Take Action* exercise—writing your own examples in the blank spaces—is interspersed through the explanations.

Icons representing each action help you visualize and remember them. As you work through other chapters in this book, you will see these icons marking where particular mind actions are taking place. These will help you to identify how your mind is working.

The Mind Actions

Recall. *Facts, sequence, and description.* This is the simplest mind action, representing the simplest level of thinking. When you **recall,** you name or describe previously learned ideas, facts, objects, or events, or put them into sequence.

The icon: Capital R stands for *recall* or *remembering*.

Examples:
- Identifying the prerequisites for Developmental Math for Health Sciences and Algebra I (you discover there are placement test requirements for both).
- Naming the steps of a geometry proof, in order.

Take Action. Recall two school-related events scheduled this month.

Parkdale High
Carrollton High

Similarity. *Analogy, likeness, comparison.* This action examines what is **similar** about one or more elements—situations, ideas, people, stories, events, or objects.

The icon: The Venn diagram illustrates the idea of similarity. The two circles represent the elements being compared, and the shaded area of intersection indicates that they have some degree of similarity.

Examples:

- Comparing the workloads of Algebra I and Developmental Math for Health Sciences (both require quizzes and a final exam, both have a weekly study group component).

- Comparing class notes with another student to see what facts and ideas you both consider important.

Take Action. State how your two favorite classes are similar.

They are similar because it includes numbers.

Difference. *Distinction, contrast.* This action examines what is **different** about one or more elements.

The icon: Here the Venn diagram is used again to show difference. The nonintersecting parts of the circles are shaded, indicating that the focus is on what is not in common.

Examples:

- Examining differences in the subject matter between Algebra I and Developmental Math for Health Sciences (DM for HS focuses more on statistics and basic math functions, while Algebra I covers algebra basics such as linear equations).

- Looking at differences between two of your instructors—one divides the class into discussion groups; the other keeps desks in place and always lectures.

Take Action. Explain how one of your favorite courses differs from a course you don't like as much.

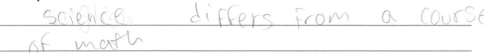

Science differs from a course of math

Cause and Effect. *Reasons, consequences, prediction.* Using this action, you look at what has **caused** a fact, situation, or event and what **effects** come from it. In other words, you look at why something happened and the consequence of its occurrence.

The icon: The arrows, pointing toward one another in a circular pattern, show how a cause leads to an effect.

Examples:

- Thinking through how taking the Algebra I course would affect your existing schedule (it means moving or changing another class you've already registered for because it comes right after that class and is located across campus).

- Seeing how staying up too late causes you to oversleep, which causes you to be late to class, which results in missing material, which causes you to feel confused about course topics.

Take Action.   Write what causes you to become motivated in a class.

introedures   explai's   clearly .

Example to Idea.   *Generalization, classification.* From one or more known **examples** (facts or events), you develop a general **idea** or ideas. Grouping facts or events into patterns may allow you to make a general statement about several of them at once. This mind action moves from the known to the previously unknown and from the specific to the general.

The icon: The arrow and "Ex" pointing to a lightbulb on their right indicate how an example or examples lead to the idea (the lightbulb lit up).

Examples:

- Exploring whether Algebra I or Developmental Math for Health Sciences fits a major. (You start with the examples: You like to work with people; health workers are currently in demand; math isn't your strongest academic area; you are interested in medicine. These examples lead you to the idea—Developmental Math for Health Sciences would probably be a better fit.)
- From several successful experiences in classes where the instructor uses visuals to illustrate ideas, you conclude that your learning style has a strong *visual* component.

Take Action.   Name activities you enjoy. Using them, derive an idea of a class you want to take.

do   special   excercess

Idea to Example.   *Analysis, substantiation, proof.* In a reverse of the previous action, you take a known **idea** or ideas and think of **examples** (events or facts) that support or prove that idea. This mind action moves from the general to the specific, the reverse of example to idea.

The icon: In a reverse of the previous icon, this one starts with the lightbulb and has an arrow pointing to "Ex." This indicates that you start with the idea and then move to the supporting examples.

Examples:

- Investigating the rumor that the Algebra I instructor is too tough on students. (Starting with the idea that the instructor is too tough on students, you talk to three different students who have taken the class.

Examples they give you lead you to believe that the instructor is indeed demanding.)

- You present an argument to your advisor regarding a change of major. (You start with the idea—you are a good candidate for a change of major—and support it with examples—you have worked in the field you want to change to, you have already fulfilled some of the requirements for the new major.)

Take Action.   Name an idea of a career path you would like to follow, and support this idea with examples of your interests and skills.

business administrative
sites

Evaluation. *Value, judgment, rating.* Here you **judge** whether something is useful or not useful, important or unimportant, good or bad, or right or wrong by identifying and weighing its positive and negative effects (pros and cons). Be sure to consider the specific situation at hand (a cold drink might be good on the beach in August but not so good in the snowdrifts in January). With the facts you have gathered, you determine the value of something in terms of the predicted effects on you and others. Cause-and-effect analysis almost always accompanies evaluation.

The icon: A set of scales out of balance indicates how you weigh positive and negative effects to arrive at an evaluation.

Examples:

- Looking at all that you have discovered—scheduling, relation to interests, difficulty, prerequisites, subject matter—about the potential effects of taking one of the two courses you are considering, you evaluate that Developmental Math for Health Sciences makes the most sense.

- Someone offers you a chance to cheat on a test. You evaluate the potential effects if you are caught. You also evaluate the long-term effects of not actually learning the material and of doing something ethically wrong. You decide that it isn't right or worthwhile to cheat.

Take Action. Evaluate your mode of transportation to school.

My mode of transportation is
in car and is a good transportion
to transfer fast

You may want to use a mnemonic device—a memory tool, as explained in Chapter 6—to remember the seven mind actions. You can make a sentence of words that each start with a mind action's first letter, such as "Really Smart Dogs Cook Eggs In Enchiladas."

Putting Mind Actions to Work

When you first learned to write, someone taught you how to create the shape of each letter or character. You slowly practiced each curve and line. Later you carefully put letters or characters together to form words. Now, much later, you write without thinking consciously about making proper letters. You focus primarily on how to express your ideas; your words appear on paper as you work toward that goal.

The process of learning and using mind actions is similar. If you take time now to think through the specific actions your mind uses when you think, they will eventually become second nature to you, a solid foundation for your thinking on which you can build productive skills. Because you have been using these actions for a long time, developing a working understanding of your mind will take you far less time than it took to learn to write.

You will rarely use the mind actions one at a time as they have been presented here. Usually you combine them and repeat them. Sometimes they overlap. When you combine them in working toward a goal (a problem to solve, a decision to make), you are performing a *thinking process*.

Begin to put the mind actions to use and to combat barriers to critical thinking as you gather the skills essential to every thinker.

What skills will help you become a better thinker?

When you are solving problems, making decisions, or simply evaluating information, successful results depend on your ability to think broadly and clearly. Three critical-thinking skills will pave your way: distinguishing fact from opinion, examining perspectives, and evaluating assumptions.

You can build thinking skills even in your leisure time. Strategic games like chess demand decision-making and problem-solving skills.

Distinguishing Fact from Opinion

A statement of fact is information presented as objectively real and verifiable ("It's raining outside right now"). In contrast, a statement of opinion is a belief, conclusion, or judgment and is inherently difficult, and sometimes impossible, to verify ("This is the worst rainstorm of the last 10 years"). Being able to distinguish fact from opinion enables you to evaluate the credibility of what you read, hear, and experience. The information in Table 4.1 will help you determine what is fact and what is opinion.

Keep in mind that just because a statement is factual does not mean that it is true. For example, "There are 25 hours in a day" is a false factual statement. Establishing truth requires investigation through questioning. Once you label a statement as a fact or opinion, ask questions like the following to explore its degree of truth:

- What facts or examples provide evidence of truth?

TABLE 4.1	Characteristics of fact and opinion.

OPINIONS INCLUDE STATEMENTS THAT . . .	FACTS INCLUDE STATEMENTS THAT . . .
. . . *show evaluation.* Any statement of value indicates an opinion. Words such as *bad, good, pointless,* and *beneficial* indicate value judgments. Example: "Jimmy Carter is the most successful negotiator to sit in the White House."	. . . *deal with actual people, places, objects, or events.* Example: "In 1978, Jimmy Carter's 13-day summit meeting with Egyptian President Anwar Sadat and Israeli Prime Minister Menachem Begin led to a peace treaty between the two countries."
. . . *use* **abstract** *words.* Words that are complicated to define, like *misery* or *success,* usually indicate a personal opinion. Example: "The charity event was a smashing success."	. . . *use concrete words or measurable statistics.* Example: "The charity event raised $5,862."
. . . *predict future events.* Excepting predictions of regularly occurring events such as tax day, statements that discuss future occurrences are often opinions. Example: "Mr. Barrett's course is going to set a new enrollment record this year."	. . . *describe current events in exact terms.* Example: "Mr. Barrett's course has 378 students enrolled this semester."
. . . *use emotional words.* Emotions are by nature unverifiable. Chances are that statements using such words as *delightful* or *miserable* express an opinion. Example: "That class is a miserable experience."	. . . *avoid emotional words and focus on the verifiable.* Example: "Citing dissatisfaction with the instruction, 7 out of the 25 students in that class have withdrawn in September."
. . . *use absolutes.* Absolute **qualifiers**, such as *all, none, never,* and *always,* often point to an opinion. Example: "All students need to have a job while in school."	. . . *avoid absolutes.* Example: "Some students need to have a job while in school."

Source: Adapted from Ben E. Johnson, *Stirring Up Thinking.* New York: Houghton Mifflin, 1998, pp. 268–270.

- Is there another fact that disproves this statement or information or that shows it to be an opinion?
- How reliable are the sources of information?
- What about this statement is similar to or different from other information I consider fact?
- Are these truly the causes and effects?

Distinguishing fact from opinion by asking important questions helps you to approach a variety of situations with an open mind. Supporting your opinions with indisputable facts increases your credibility; recognizing whether others support their opinions likewise helps you respond to them thoughtfully.

Examining Perspectives

Perspective is a point of view that forms the basis for and guides your thinking. Perspective is complex and unique to each individual. Consider the classic question: Do you generally see the glass as half full or half empty? Your

Abstract
Theoretical: disassociated from any specific instance.

Qualifier
A word, such as *always, never,* or *often,* that changes the meaning of another word or word group.

reflect

Describe your perspective on pursuing an education. (Hint: Consider how important it is to

Companion Website

you and why, what you consider the best way to become educated, how you think it can be used, and so on.) How did you develop this perspective—what are its sources? What influence does it have on how you think and how you live?

& respond

answer points to your tendency toward optimism or pessimism, which is a big-picture life perspective.

When your opinion clashes with someone else's this often reflects a difference in perspective. If a friend has a negative opinion of your choosing to live with a significant other, for example, that friend might have a different perspective on relationships, with accompanying different opinions and assumptions about how they should progress.

Opening your mind to other perspectives has distinct benefits. It helps you to evaluate and refine your own views and behavior; it teaches you something new; it opens lines of communication and promotes mutual respect. Use an evaluation system based on the critical-thinking path (Figure 4.2) to think more broadly about the world around you and enjoy these benefits.

Step 1: Take In New Information

The first step is to take in new perspectives and simply acknowledge that they exist without immediately judging, rejecting, or accepting them. Critical thinkers acknowledge differing perspectives, even those that negate their own. Author F. Scott Fitzgerald said: "The test of a first-rate intelligence is the ability to hold two opposed ideas in mind at the same time and still retain the ability to function."

Step 2: Evaluate the Perspective

Asking questions helps you maintain flexibility and openness.

- What is similar and different about this perspective and mine? What personal experiences may have created these different views?
- What examples, evidence, or reasons could be used to support or justify this perspective? Do some reasons provide good support even if I don't agree with those reasons?
- What might result, positively, or negatively, from this perspective?
- Whether I would adopt it or not, what can I learn from this perspective?

Step 3: Accept—and Perhaps Adopt

On the one hand, thinking through the new perspective may lead you to feel that you want to try it out or adopt it as your own. On the other hand, perhaps your evaluation leads you simply to recognize and appreciate the other perspective, even if it doesn't suit you. Each person is entitled to his or her perspective, no matter how foreign it may be to others.

"We do not live to think, but, on the contrary, we think in order that we may succeed in surviving."

JOSÉ ORTEGA Y GASSET

FIGURE 4.3   Questioning an assumption.

Identifying and Evaluating Assumptions

"A more expensive car is a better car." "Students get more work done in a library." These statements reveal *assumptions*—evaluations or generalizations influenced by values and based on observing cause and effect—that can often hide within seemingly truthful statements. Assumptions can close your mind to opportunities and even cause harm. Investigate each assumption as you would any statement of fact or opinion, questioning the truth of the supposed causes and effects. Figure 4.3 gives examples of questions you can ask to uncover and evaluate an assumption.

For example, the statement "The best schedule involves getting started early" reveals this assumption: "The morning is when people are most productive." Here's how you might question it:

- This assumption may be true for people who get going easily in the morning. Does it work for people who are at their best in the afternoon or evening?

- An early start has become society's standard. Therefore, we accept the assumption without thinking about people who work later shifts or take evening classes. Is this a fair assumption for this group?

- What effect does this have on those who are not "morning people"? Because it implies they will not be productive, it may dampen their confidence.

- This assumption does not indicate that some people can arrange school/work schedules in the afternoon or evening hours.

Be careful to question all assumptions, not just those that seem problematic from the start. Form your opinion after investigating the positive and negative effects of making the assumption.

media literacy
The ability to respond with critical thinking to the agencies of mass communication—television, film, journalism (magazines and newspapers), and the Internet.

Barriers to Critical Thinking

In addition to the energy and focus that critical thinking demands, particular barriers can make critical thinking difficult. Fortunately, the skills you have just explored will help you leap over these barriers. Here are some significant barriers and ways to overcome them.[15]

Personal beliefs. It is human to feel comfortable with your beliefs and consider them important and maybe even superior to others. However, this can prevent you from thinking critically about ideas that don't fit your beliefs. Considering new perspectives critically can help you avoid using your frame of reference as a measure for all other perspectives.

Resistance to change. People naturally resist change and view current ideas as right and good. However, this tendency blocks critical thinking. Consider Galileo, the astronomer who in 1632 wrote that the earth revolves around the sun rather than the opposite. He was personally threatened and his book banned until the early 1800s. However, he was right. Looking at what is fact and opinion and actively challenging assumptions will help you avoid sticking with ideas that are ultimately not correct or useful.

Wishful thinking. It's natural to assume to be true what you wish were true. However, this prevents the kind of critical thinking that could uncover the real truth. For example, a student who assumes that a study partner is trustworthy may suffer if the other student fails to deliver on a group project. Uncover and examine assumptions to combat this barrier.

Ethnocentricity. People band together in groups for support and survival. However, the strength of belief in what a group represents, even while it serves an important purpose, can lead to assumptions about other groups and people. Challenging assumptions and being open to new perspectives will help you avoid judging others by the standards of your group.

Reliance on authority. People often trust someone in a position of authority—an instructor, a doctor, a politician—simply based on that

RISING
TO THE CHALLENGE

Richard Branson
Founder of Virgin Records and Virgin Atlantic Airways

A learning disability can be the source of something positive. Successful businessman Richard Branson discovered that his unusual way of seeing things, a result of his dyslexia, could help him to envision and grow a world-renowned company or two.

A generation ago dyslexia was a problem with no name. Says Richard Branson: "At some point, I think I decided that being dyslexic was better than being stupid." Branson was spanked by his teachers for bad grades and a poor attitude. He dropped out of school at 16. Later, Branson developed one of Britain's top brands with Virgin Records and Virgin Atlantic Airways.

Dyslexia has nothing to do with IQ; many smart, accomplished people have it, or are thought to have had it, including Winston Churchill and Albert Einstein. Sally Shaywitz, a leading dyslexia neuroscientist at Yale, believes the disorder can carry surprising talents along with its well-known disadvantages. "Dyslexics are overrepresented in the top ranks of people who are unusually insightful, who bring a new perspective, who think out of the box," says Shaywitz. She is co-director of the Center for Learning and Attention at Yale, along with her husband, Dr. Bennett Shaywitz, a professor of pediatrics and neurology.

What exactly is dyslexia? The Everyman definition calls it a reading disorder in which people jumble letters, confusing *dog* with *god*, say, or *box* with *pox*. The exact cause is unclear; scientists believe it has to do with the way a developing brain is wired. Difficulty reading, spelling, and writing are typical symptoms. But dyslexia often comes with one or more other learning problems as well, including trouble with math, auditory processing, organizational skills, and memory. No two dyslexics are alike—each has his own set of weaknesses and strengths.

About 5% to 6% of American public school children have been diagnosed with a learning disability; 80% of the diagnoses are dyslexia-related. But some studies indicate that up to 20% of the population may have some degree of dyslexia.

On a recent trip to Boston, Richard Branson arrived in a spray of champagne to open a Virgin Megastore. He is a true business celebrity, having come straight from hosting a party in London celebrating the honorary knighthood of Rudy Giuliani (Sir Richard, too, is a knight) and going later that evening to address the blue-blood Chief Executives' Club of Boston.

Branson's success and his dyslexia seem contradictory. He never made it through high school. He has a wickedly unreliable memory; because his mind goes blank at the most inopportune times, he writes important things—like names—in black ink on the back of his hand. He won't use a computer. He's terrible at math. Until recently, he confesses, he was still confusing gross profit with net. He'd been faking it, but not too well. One of his board members finally pulled him aside to give him a mnemonic, or memory aid—mnemonics often come in handy for dyslexics. "Pretend you're fishing," the board member said. "Net is all the fish in your net at the end of the year. Gross is that plus everything that got away."

Branson approaches business completely differently from most. "I never, ever thought of myself as a businessman," he told the Boston CEOs. "I was interested in creating things I would be proud of." He started Virgin Atlantic because flying other airlines was so dreadful. He knew he could provide better service. There's an irony here, says Branson: "Look, if I'd been good at math, I probably never would have started an airline."

Take a Moment to Consider . . .

- *What the up side might be of an issue of yours that you consider very difficult.*

- *What's different about you that you think will set you apart in a positive way.*

position. However, an authority can be wrong just like anyone else. Evaluating statements from an authority based on what you know about fact and opinion will help you think critically instead of just accepting authoritative statements as truth.

Media Literacy

Distinguishing fact from opinion, examining perspectives, and evaluating assumptions are all crucial skills for **media literacy**.

Essential for a realistic understanding of the information that bombards you daily, media literacy means that instead of accepting anything you see, hear, or read as fact, you question the information critically. The Center for Media Literacy explains the following "Five Core Concepts of Media Literacy."[16]

1. *All media are constructions.* The creators of any media design it to have a particular effect on people. For example, an article promoting positive feelings about the president will focus on his strengths.

2. *Media use unique "languages."* Creators of media carefully choose wording, music, colors, timing, and other factors to produce a desired effect.

3. *Different audiences understand the same media message differently.* Individuals understand media in the context of their unique experiences. Someone who has climbed a mountain, for example, will experience a Mount Everest documentary differently than someone who has not.

4. *Media have commercial interests.* Creators of media are driven by the intent to sell you a product, service, or idea. Advertising is chosen to appeal to those most likely to be reading or seeing that particular kind of media (for example, ads for beer and cars appear often during sports events).

5. *Media have embedded values and points of view.* Any media product carries and displays the values of the people who created it. For example, the magazine *Runner's World* reflects the belief that knowing how to stay warm on a winter run is important.

TAKE ACTION

Use Thinking Skills to Evaluate a Statement

Evaluate the following statement: *"The Internet is the best place to find information about any topic."*

■ Is this statement fact or opinion? Why?

opinion because it say (best place)

■ What perspective is guiding this statement? Do you agree or disagree with the perspective? Why?

■ What assumption(s) underlie the statement? What effects might making these assumptions have?

Now work with a statement about college students or college life that you have heard. Write it here.

■ Is this statement fact or opinion? Why?

Fact because, it say's (work)

■ What perspective is guiding this statement? Do you agree or disagree with the perspective? Why?

■ What assumption(s) underlie the statement? What effects might making these assumptions have?

The purpose of being media literate is to approach what you see, hear, and read with thought and consideration. If you ask questions, look for evidence, recognize perspectives, and challenge assumptions, you will gain the maximum benefit from the media you encounter.

You are now ready to use what you know to explore three significant thinking processes—problem solving, decision making, and strategic planning.

How can you effectively solve problems, make decisions, and plan strategically?

You've primed your mind by exploring creativity, learning about mind actions, and learning to respond critically to fact and opinion, perspectives, and assumptions. Now you are ready to put it all to work in the thinking processes you will use most often—problem solving, decision making, and strategic planning. When you face a difficult situation, you may approach it as a problem to be solved, a question to be decided, or a strategic plan to be made. Figure 4.4 demonstrates the general path your thinking would take to solve a problem, make a decision, or make a plan. It has four main components:

1. Identifying the central problem, question, or goal
2. Analyzing the problem, question, or goal
3. Evaluating possible solutions, answers, or plans
4. Making a choice, followed by a final evaluation of results

Figures 4.5, 4.6, and 4.7 show the specific thinking path for solving a problem, making a decision, and planning strategically. These processes are closely related. Throughout each process, you will engage a combination of mind actions. The power in all three approaches is careful cause and effect analysis. When you follow these paths you will avoid false solutions and make fewer mistakes.

Keep in mind that you will not always need to work through each step. As you learn the processes, your mind will start to click through the steps. Also, you will become more adept at evaluating which problems, questions, or goals require serious consideration and which do not.

Problem Solving

Life constantly presents problems to be solved, ranging from common daily problems (the management of study time) to life-altering situations (a family emergency). Choosing a solution without thinking critically may have negative effects. If you move through the steps of a problem-solving process, however, you will maximize the number of possible solutions, exploring each one carefully.

"The best way to escape from a problem is to solve it."

ALAN SAPORTA

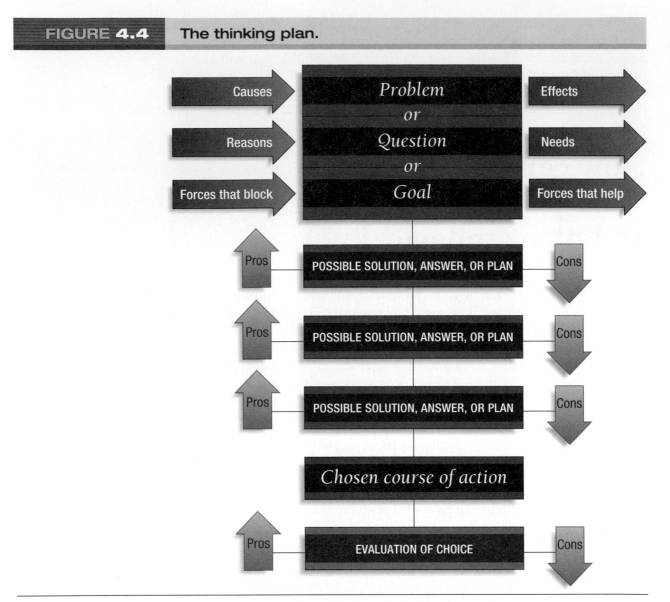

FIGURE 4.4   The thinking plan.

Source: Adapted from problem-solving heuristic, ©1983 George Eley and Frank Lyman, University of Maryland.

Step 1. Identify the problem accurately. What are the facts? *Recall* the details of the situation. Focus on the *causes* of the problem—this clarifies the problem and helps you see which solutions might work. Consider the Chinese saying: "Give a man a fish, and he will eat for a day. Teach a man to fish, and he will eat for a lifetime." If you state the problem as "The man is hungry," giving him a fish seems like a good solution. Unfortunately, the problem returns—because hunger is only an effect. Focusing on the probable cause redefines the problem and gives a clue to the solution: "The man does not know how to find food." Given that his lack of knowledge is the true cause, teaching him to fish truly solves the problem.

Step 2. Analyze the problem. Analyze, or break down into understandable pieces, the causes and effects that surround the problem. What *effects* of the situation concern you? What *causes* these effects? Which causes are most powerful or significant? Are there hidden causes?

FIGURE 4.5   **Walking through a problem . . . relating to an instructor.**

CAUSES OF PROBLEM

We have radically different views
   and personality types
I don't feel listened to in class or
   respected

STATE PROBLEM HERE:

I don't like my
instructor for a
particular course

EFFECTS OF PROBLEM

Dampened interest in the class
   material
No motivation to work on assignments
Grades are suffering

Use boxes below to list possible solutions:

POTENTIAL POSITIVE EFFECTS

List for each solution:
Don't have to deal with that
   instructor
Less stress

SOLUTION #1

Drop the course

POTENTIAL NEGATIVE EFFECTS

List for each solution:
Grade gets entered on my transcript
I'll have to take the course
   eventually; it's required for
   my major

Getting credit for the course
Feeling like I've honored a
   commitment

SOLUTION #2

Put up with it until the
end of the semester

Stress every time I'm there
Lowered motivation
Probably not such a good final grade

A chance to express myself
Could get good advice
An opportunity to ask direct questions
   of the instructor

SOLUTION #3

Schedule meetings with
advisor and instructor

Have to face instructor one-on-one
Might just make things worse

Now choose the solution you think is best—and try it.

ACTUAL POSITIVE EFFECTS

List for chosen solution:
Got some helpful advice from advisor
Talking in person with the
   instructor actually promoted a
   fairly honest discussion
I won't have to take the course again

CHOSEN SOLUTION

Schedule meetings with
both advisor and
instructor, and stick
with the course

ACTUAL NEGATIVE EFFECTS

List for chosen solution:
The discussion was difficult and
   sometimes tense
I still don't know how much
   learning I'll retain from this
   course

FINAL EVALUATION: Was it a good or bad choice?

The solution has improved things. I'll finish the course, and even though the instructor and I aren't the best of friends, we have a mutual understanding now. I feel more respected and more willing to put my time into the course.

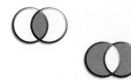

Step 3. Brainstorm possible solutions. Put your creative mind to work in this stage (see page 94 for details about brainstorming). Brainstorming helps you to think of examples of how you solved *similar* problems, consider what is *different* about this problem, and come up with new possible solutions. Remember that to get to the heart of a problem, you must base possible solutions on the most significant causes.

Step 4. Explore each solution. Why might your solution work or not work? Might a solution work partially or in a particular situation? *Evaluate* ahead of time the pros and cons (positive and negative effects) of each proposed solution. Create a chain of causes and effects in your head, as far into the future as you can, to see where this solution might lead.

Step 5. Choose and implement the solution you decide will have the most, or most important, positive effects. Decide how you will put your solution to work. Then, carry out your plan.

Step 6. Evaluate the solution that you acted on. What are the positive and negative *effects* of what you did? In terms of your needs and those of others, was it a useful solution or not? Could the solution benefit from any adjustments to be more useful? In evaluating, you are collecting data.

Step 7. Refine the solution. Problem solving is an ongoing process. You may have opportunities to apply the same solution again. *Evaluate* repeatedly, making changes that you decide could make the solution better (i.e., more closely related to the causes of the problem).

Using this process enables you to solve school, work, and personal problems in a thoughtful, comprehensive way. Figure 4.5 shows one example of how to use this plan to solve a problem.

Decision Making

Decisions are choices, and you face them every day. Making a decision requires thinking critically through the possible choices and evaluating which will work best for you and others. Before you begin the process, evaluate what kind of decision you have to make. Minor decisions, such as which books to bring to class, can be dealt with quickly. Major ones, such as what to major in or whether to quit your part-time job, require thoughtful evaluation, time, and perhaps the input of others you trust.

The following steps guide you through a process for making a decision. You will find a specific decision-making plan example in Figure 4.6.

Step 1. Identify a question. What has *caused* you to ask this question—what are your reasons for needing to make this decision? In other words, why is it important?

Step 2. Establish needs. What results, or *effects*, do you want from this decision? *Recall* the needs of everyone involved in the decision. Considering needs will help you formulate potential solutions.

FIGURE 4.6 Making a decision . . . whether to transfer.

REASONS OR CAUSES	STATE QUESTION HERE:	DESIRED EFFECTS OR NEEDS
I attend a small private college and want to become a physical therapist	Whether or not to transfer schools	I need a school with a full physical therapy program
My father has changed jobs and can no longer afford tuition and fees		My family needs to cut costs
		I may need to transfer credits

Use boxes below to list possible answers:

POTENTIAL POSITIVE EFFECTS	ANSWER #1	POTENTIAL NEGATIVE EFFECTS
List for each solution:	Continue at the current college.	*List for each solution:*
No need to adjust to a new place or new people		Need to finance most of my tuition and costs on my own
Ability to continue course work as planned		Difficult to find time for a job
		Might not qualify for aid

	ANSWER #2	
Opportunity to connect with some high school friends	Transfer to the state college	Need to earn some money or get financial aid
Cheaper tuition and room costs		Physical therapy program is small and not very strong
Credits will transfer		

	ANSWER #3	
Many physical therapy courses available	Transfer to the community college	No personal contacts there that I know of
School is close so I could live at home and save room costs		Less independence if I live at home
Reasonable tuition		No bachelor's degree available
Credits will transfer		

ACTUAL POSITIVE EFFECTS	CHOSEN ANSWER	ACTUAL NEGATIVE EFFECTS
List for chosen solution:	Go to community college for two years; then transfer to a four-year school to get a B.A. and complete physical therapy course work	*List for chosen solution:*
Money saved		Loss of some independence
Opportunity to spend time on studies rather than on working to earn tuition money		Less contact with friends
Availability of classes I need		

FINAL EVALUATION: Was it a good or bad choice?

I'm satisfied with the decision. It can be hard being at home at times, but my parents are adjusting to my independence and I'm trying to respect their concerns. With fewer social distractions, I'm really getting my work done. Plus the financial aspect of the decision is ideal.

Step 3. Name, investigate, and evaluate available answers. Engage your creativity as you brainstorm possibilities. Then, look at the facts surrounding each, evaluating the good and bad *effects* of each possibility. Weigh these effects in light of the needs you have established and *evaluate* which is the best answer.

Step 4. Decide on a plan and take action. Make a choice based on your evaluation, and act on it.

Step 5. Evaluate the result. Was it useful? Not useful? Some of both? Weigh the positive and negative *effects*.

Making important decisions can take time. Think through your decisions thoroughly, considering your own ideas as well as those of others you trust, but don't hesitate to act once you have your plan. You cannot benefit from your decision until you follow through on it.

Strategic Planning

If you've ever played a game of chess, participated in a martial arts match, or made a detailed plan of how to reach a particular goal, you have had experience with strategy. *Strategy* is a plan of action or method. Strategic planning means using critical-thinking skills to set and achieve long-term goals. It often involves delaying immediate gratification in favor of future gain.

When you plan strategically, you look at the next week, month, year, or 10 years and explore the future positive and negative effects that current choices and actions may have. As a student, for example, you have planned strategically by deciding that the effort of school is a legitimate price to pay for the skills and opportunities you will receive.

The most important questions for successful strategic planning begin with "how." How do you remember what you learn? How do you establish a relationship with a professor? How can you develop a productive idea in your biology lab? The process of strategic planning helps you find the best answers.

In situations that demand strategy, think critically by asking questions like these:

- If you aim for a certain goal, how can you achieve that goal?
- What are the potential effects, positive or negative, of different actions or choices?
- What is the sequence or order of these actions or choices?
- Which set of effects is most helpful or desirable to you and others?
- What can you learn from previous experiences that may inspire similar or different choices?
- How might you fail—what barriers stand in the way?
- How have others made plans for similar goals?

For any situation that would benefit from strategic planning, from preparing for a study session to thinking through your career options, the steps in the process outlined next will help you make choices that bring about

FIGURE 4.7   Planning strategically . . . to finance course work.

FORCES THAT BLOCK	STATE GOAL HERE:	FORCES THAT HELP
Lost financial aid due to slipping grades	Raise enough money to cover tuition next year	Earning power
Part-time job doesn't bring in much money	Deadline: June 1 Time available: 4 months	Schedule flexibility

Use boxes below to list possible plans:

POTENTIAL POSITIVE EFFECTS	PLAN #1	POTENTIAL NEGATIVE EFFECTS
List for each plan:	Find new source of financial aid	*List for each plan:*
Ability to stay on planned school schedule		Money might not be renewable like current grant
Ability to stay in school		Time and effort spent to find and qualify for new aid

	PLAN #2	
More money to pay for college	Find full-time, better-paying job	Less time for college
More on-the-job experience		May have to take classes part-time, graduate later

	PLAN #3	
More time to study	Take classes part-time next year	Extends how long I'll be in college
More ability to focus		Could make me ineligible for certain kinds of aid

Now choose the plan you think is best—and try it.

ACTUAL POSITIVE EFFECTS	CHOSEN PLAN	ACTUAL NEGATIVE EFFECTS
List for chosen plan:	Next year, take classes part-time and work full-time	*List for chosen plan:*
More money earned	**STEPS**	Had to put off planned graduation date
More study time and ability to focus resulted in better grades	1. Now: cut personal expenses to save money	Ineligible this semester for most aid, had to use my own money for tuition
	2. One month from now: inform family of new graduation date	
	3. Two months from now: Apply for full-time job	
	4. Three months from now: meet with advisor to plan out fall course work	

FINAL EVALUATION: Was it a good or bad choice?

It was tough but it worked out well. Even though I had to pay for classes myself, the full-time job and fewer classes allowed me to do that. Then, with better focus, I was able to raise my GPA back up. I hope this will help me requalify for aid so that I can eventually go back to being a full-time student.

MULTIPLE PATHWAYS TO LEARNING

MULTIPLE INTELLIGENCE STRATEGIES *for* Problem Solving

Apply techniques in both your stronger and weaker intelligences to become a more versatile critical thinker.

INTELLIGENCE	SUGGESTED STRATEGIES	WHAT WORKS FOR YOU? WRITE NEW IDEAS HERE
Verbal–Linguistic	■ When a problem bothers you, write it out. Challenge yourself to come up with at least 10 possible solutions. ■ Discuss new ideas or problems with other people. Write down any useful ideas they come up with.	
Logical–Mathematical	■ Outline all possible outcomes to various possible actions. ■ Analyze each possible solution to a problem. What effects might occur? What is the best choice and why?	
Bodily–Kinesthetic	■ Pace while you brainstorm—have a tape recorder running and record your ideas as they come up. ■ Think about solutions to a problem while you are running or doing any other type of exercise.	
Visual–Spatial	■ Use a problem-solving flow chart like the one in Figure 4.5 and complete all the areas. ■ Brainstorm ideas about and solutions to a problem by drawing a think link about the problem.	
Interpersonal	■ When you are stuck on a problem, ask one of your friends to discuss it with you. Consider any new ideas or solutions the friend may offer. ■ Discuss new creative ideas with one or more people and analyze the feedback.	
Intrapersonal	■ Take time alone to think through a problem. Freewrite your thoughts about the problem in a journal. ■ Sit quietly and think about your ability to evaluate solutions to a problem. Write three ways you can improve.	
Musical	■ When you are stuck on a problem, shut down your brain for a while and listen to music you love. Come back to the problem later to see if new ideas have surfaced.	
Naturalistic	■ Take a long walk in nature to inspire creative ideas or to think of solutions to a problem. ■ Think about your favorite place in nature before concentrating on brainstorming about a problem.	

the most positive effects. Stay flexible as you plan. You never know what may turn your plan upside down—flexibility will help you land on your feet with the most options available to you. Look at Figure 4.7 to see an example of strategic planning.

Step 1. Establish a goal. What do you want to achieve, and when? Why do you want to achieve it?

Step 2. Evaluate the goal. What forces block your ability to achieve the goal? What forces will help you move along toward it? Looking at how to use forces that help will give you ideas for plans.

Step 3. Brainstorm possible plans. What are some plans for how to get where you want to go? What steps—to take today, or 1 year, 5 years, 10 years, or 20 years from now—do these plans require? Engage your creative thinking here. Ask "What if" (What if I could design my own job?), imagine what would happen if you took a risk, sit with the question for a while, entertain outrageous ideas.

Step 4. Anticipate potential effects of each plan. What positive and negative effects may occur, both soon and in the long term? What approach may best help you to overcome blocking forces and achieve your goal? Talk to people who are where you want to be and ask them what you should anticipate.

Step 5. Put your plan into action. Act on the decision you have made. For strategic planning, this includes breaking the plan into steps that are scheduled in time.

Step 6. Evaluate continually. Because a long-term goal lies in the future, the evaluation period could be long. Check regularly to see whether your strategy is having the effects you predicted. If events are not going the way you planned, for any reason, reevaluate and make changes.

With what you learn by asking questions about the potential effects of your plans, you can create the best effects for you and others. Strategic planning has positive effects that include the following:

- *Staying current technologically.* Technological developments have increased the pace of workplace change. Thinking strategically about job opportunities may lead you to a broader range of courses or a major and career in a growing area, making it more likely that you will be in demand when you graduate.
- *Successful goal setting.* Thinking strategically improves your ability to work toward and achieve goals over time. For example, a student might have a goal of paying tuition; this student could plan a strategy of part-time

reflect

Name an area of your life in which you would like to be able to plan strategically for the long term. Discuss a specific plan you want to make, in as much detail as you can. Name the ways in which thinking ahead using this plan will benefit you.

Companion Website

& respond

jobs and cutting back on spending in order to achieve that goal. Strategy keeps you headed toward the target, able to surmount any obstacle you encounter.

■ *School and work success.* A student who wants to do well in a course needs to plan study sessions. A lawyer needs to anticipate how to respond to points raised in court. Strategic planning allows the planner to anticipate possibilities and to be prepared for them. It also helps you to see where you're going so that your resolve can help you to persevere.

I create, imagine, and innovate.

Being creative means putting energy into dreaming up ideas where there were none before. For example, suppose you are having trouble coming up with a good topic for an assigned essay. You start with what you know—the assigned reading materials. Thinking through the connections among the pieces of information, you imagine the possibilities and create new ideas. Then you innovate (i.e., introduce or begin something new) as you write—you implement the idea you think is best, introducing a new way of looking at your topic.

Imagination will power your abilities as a problem solver. The most successful problem solvers are those who use imagination to project themselves into situations to "see" how any given solution would pan out. As a problem solver, you can empower your imaginative vision through asking "what if I . . ." questions: "What if I took two sciences this semester?" "What if I worked part-time on campus?" "What if I designed my own major?" Use your imagination to think about what might happen in the future and you will make the best choices for yourself today.

REMEMBER!
the important points ○○○

How can you spark your creative mind?

Creative thinking is an important part of many critical-thinking processes. Creativity produces innovative ideas and products. Think of creativity as having four elements: the *characteristics* of the creative person, the type of *environment* that fosters creativity, the stages of the creative *process*, and the creative *product*. As you work toward a creative product, boost your creativity by activating your creative characteristics, providing the most effective environment for yourself, and using the creative process of brainstorming to generate ideas.

What is critical thinking?

Critical thinking, at its heart, is questioning. When you think critically you take in information, question it, draw conclusions, and then use what you have learned. The building blocks of critical thinking are seven mind actions: *recall, similarity, difference, cause and effect, example to idea, idea to example,* and *evaluation*. These mind actions, in various combinations, build the thinking processes that help you achieve your goals.

What skills will help you become a better thinker?

Distinguishing fact from opinion helps you separate the objectively verifiable from judgments and beliefs. Examining perspectives helps you to evaluate your own views and behavior, teaches you something new, opens lines of communication, and promotes mutual respect. Investigating assumptions—evaluations or generalizations influenced by values—helps you to keep an open mind and uncover faulty reasoning. All of these skills will help you combat barriers to critical thinking and know how to "read" the media with a critical eye.

How can you effectively solve problems, make decisions, and plan strategically?

These critical-thinking processes hinge on a plan that has a series of steps: identifying the problem, decision, or goal; analyzing it; brainstorming solutions, choices, or plans; exploring each; choosing and executing one; evaluating the choice; refining the choice. The problem-solving version of this plan focuses on evaluating possible solutions; the decision-making version focuses on evaluating possible decisions; the strategic-planning version focuses on evaluating possible paths to a goal. Strategic planning means making long-range plans toward goals. By taking the time to work through the various versions of this step-by-step plan, you will be able to solve problems effectively, make the best decisions for yourself, and plan strategically to achieve the goals that you want to reach in the near or far future.

Name _____ Date _____

CRITICAL THINKING
APPLYING LEARNING TO LIFE

Make an Important Decision

First, write here a decision you need to make. Choose an important decision that needs to be made soon.

to make better grades or not atten to school.

Step 1: Decide on a goal. Be specific: What goal, or desired effects, do you seek from this decision? For example, if your decision is a choice between two courses, effects you want might include credit toward a major and experience. Write down the desired effects here, prioritizing them from most important to least.

The goal is to have a better education.

Step 2: Establish needs. Who and what will be affected by your decision? If you are deciding how to finance your education and you have a family to support, for example, you must take into consideration their financial needs.

List here the people, things, or situations that may be affected by your decision and indicate how your decision will affect them.

My parents because I will need to be with them

Step 3: Name, investigate, and evaluate available options. Look at any options you can imagine. Consider options even if they seem impossible or unlikely; you can evaluate them later. Some decisions only have two options (to move to a new apartment or not; to get a new roommate or not); others have a wider selection of choices.

List two possible options for your decision. Evaluate the potential good and bad effects of each.

Option 1 ___Support_____

Positive effects _____

Negative effects _____

Option 2 _____

Positive effects _____

Negative effects _____

Have you or someone else ever made a decision similar to the one you are about to make? If so, what can you learn from that decision that may help you?

___Yes because if you don't___
___make a decision in your___
___life. you have that in your life.___

Step 4: Decide on a plan and take action. Taking your entire analysis into account, decide what to do. Write your decision here.

_____

_____

_____

_____

Next is perhaps the most important part of the process: Act on your decision.

Step 5: Evaluate the result. After you have acted on your decision, evaluate how everything turned out. Did you achieve the effects you wanted to achieve? What were the effects on you? On others? On the situation? To what extent were they positive, negative, or some of both?

List two effects here. Name each effect, circle whether it was positive or negative, and explain your evaluation.

Effect _____

Positive   *Negative*

Why? _____

Effect _____

Positive   *Negative*

Why? _____

_____

Final evaluation: Write one statement in reaction to the decision you made. Indicate whether you feel the decision was useful or not useful, and why. Indicate any adjustments that could have made the effects of your decision more positive.

_____

_____

_____

TEAM BUILDING
COLLABORATIVE SOLUTIONS

Group Problem Solving

As a class, brainstorm a list of problems in your lives. Include any problems you feel comfortable discussing with others. Such problems may involve academics, relationships, jobs, discrimination, parenting, housing, procrastination, and others. Divide into groups of two to four and choose or assign one problem for each group to work on. Use the blank problem-solving flowchart on the next page to fill in your work.

1. *Identify the problem.* As a group, state your problem specifically, without causes ("I'm not attending all of my classes" is better than "lack of motivation"). Then, explore and record the causes and effects that surround it.

2. *Brainstorm possible solutions.* Determine the most likely causes of the problem; from those causes, derive possible solutions. Record all the ideas that group members offer. After 10 minutes or so, each group member should choose one possible solution to explore independently.

3. *Explore each solution.* Each group member should (a) weigh the positive and negative effects, (b) consider similar problems, and (c) describe how the solution affects the causes of the problem. Evaluate your assigned solution. Will it work?

4. *Choose your top solution(s).* Come together again as a group. Take turns sharing your observations and recommendations, and then take a vote: Which solution is the best? You may have a tie or may want to combine two different solutions. Although it's not always possible to reach agreement, try to find the solution that works for most of the group.

5. *Evaluate the solution you decide is best.* When you decide on your top solution or solutions, discuss what would happen if you went through with it. What do you predict would be the positive and negative effects of this solution? Would it turn out to be a truly good solution for everyone?

FIGURE 4.8 Walking through a problem. . . .

CAUSES OF PROBLEM	STATE PROBLEM HERE:	EFFECTS OF PROBLEM
Study less	*I study less and not make importance to a subject*	*lower grade.*

Use boxes below to list possible solutions:

POTENTIAL POSITIVE EFFECTS	SOLUTION #1	POTENTIAL NEGATIVE EFFECTS
List for each solution:		List for each solution:

	SOLUTION #2	

	SOLUTION #3	

Now choose the solution you think is best—and try it.

ACTUAL POSITIVE EFFECTS	CHOSEN SOLUTION	ACTUAL NEGATIVE EFFECTS
List for chosen solution:		List for chosen solution:

FINAL EVALUATION: Was it a good or bad choice?

123

personal IMPROVEMENT plan

I commit to three specific creative or critical-thinking strategies to improve my thinking skills.
From this chapter, I choose three strategies that I think will help me.

Strategy 1: _____

Strategy 2: _____

Strategy 3: _____

I choose one strategy to focus on (circle this strategy above) and I will:

- describe my goal—what I want to gain by using this strategy.

  _____work hard_____

  _____

  _____

- describe in detail how I plan to use the strategy.

  _____work   and spent more_____

  _____time in study to success._____

  _____

  _____

- describe how I will measure my progress toward the goal this semester.

  _____

  _____

  _____

  _____

Activate the Habit of Mind

Here's how I will *create, imagine, and innovate* to achieve this goal.

_____I will put energy's into the_____

_____goal_____

_____

_____

SUGGESTED READINGS

Cameron, Julia with Mark Bryan. *The Artist's Way: A Spiritual Path to Higher Creativity*. New York: G. P. Putnam's Sons, 2002.

deBono, Edward. *Lateral Thinking: Creativity Step by Step*. New York: Perennial Library, 1990.

Noone, Donald J., Ph.D. *Creative Problem Solving*. New York: Barron's, 1998.

Sark. *Living Juicy: Daily Morsels for Your Creative Soul*. Berkeley, CA: Celestial Arts, 1994.

von Oech, Roger. *A Kick in the Seat of the Pants*. New York: Harper & Row Publishers, 1986.

von Oech, Roger. *A Whack on the Side of the Head*. New York: Warner Books, 1998.

INTERNET RESOURCES

Roger von Oech's Creative Think website: www.creativethink.com

Tim van Gelder's Critical Thinking on the Web: www.austhink.org/critical/

ENDNOTES

1. Charles Cave (August 1999). "Definitions of Creativity" [on-line]. Available: http://members.ozemail.com.au/~caveman/Creative/Basics/definitions.htm (April 2003).

2. R. L. Mooney, "A conceptual model for integrating four approaches to the identification of creative talent." In *Scientific Creativity: Its Recognition and Development*, C. W. Taylor & F. Barron (eds.). New York: Wiley, 1963, pp. 331–340.

3. Roger von Oech, *A Kick in the Seat of the Pants*. New York: Harper & Row Publishers, 1986, pp. 5–21.

4. J. R. Hayes, *Cognitive Psychology: Thinking and Creating* (Homewood, IL: Dorsey, 1978).

5. Ibid.

6. Roger von Oech, *A Whack on the Side of the Head*. New York: Warner Books, 1998, pp. 11–168.

7. Ibid.

8. Ibid.

9. T. M. Amabile, *The Social Psychology of Creativity* (New York: Springer-Verlag, 1983).

10. Hayes.

11. Ibid.

12. von Oech.

13. Dennis Coon, *Introduction to Psychology: Exploration and Application*, 6th edition. St. Paul: West Publishing Company, 1992, p. 295.

14. Frank T. Lyman Jr., Ph.D., "Think-Pair-Share, Thinktrix, Thinklinks, and Weird Facts: An Interactive System for Cooperative Thinking." In *Enhancing Thinking Through Cooperative Learning*, Neil Davidson and Toni Worsham, eds. New York: Teachers College Press, 1992, pp. 169–181.

15. Section on barriers adapted from Joel Rudinow and Vincent E. Barry, *Invitation to Critical Thinking*, 4th ed. Fort Worth, TX: Harcourt Brace College Publishers, 1999.

16. Center for Media Literacy, 1998.

Multiple Choice. *Circle or highlight the answer that seems to fit best.*

1. A *motivator* is
   A. the ability to achieve a goal.
   B. progress toward a goal.
   C. a decision to take action.
   D. a want or need that moves a person to action.

2. A *learning style* is
   A. the best way to learn when attending classes.
   B. a particular way of being intelligent.
   C. an affinity for a particular job choice or career area.
   D. a way in which the mind receives and processes information.

3. When choosing and evaluating your values, it is important to
   A. set goals according to what your friends and family value.
   B. keep your values steady over time.
   C. reevaluate values periodically as you experience change.
   D. set aside values that no one else seems to think are good for you.

4. It is important to link daily and weekly goals with long-term goals because
   A. the process will help you focus on the things that are most important to you.
   B. short-term goals have no meaning if they are not placed in a longer time frame.
   C. the process will help you eliminate frivolous activities.
   D. others expect you to know how everything you do relates to what you want to accomplish in life.

5. The activity that lies at the heart of critical thinking is
   A. solving problems.
   B. taking in information.
   C. reasoning.
   D. asking questions.

6. The problem-solving process is complete after you have
   A. identified the problem.
   B. brainstormed possible solutions.
   C. evaluated and refined how your chosen solution worked out.
   D. chosen and executed the solution you think is best.

Fill-in-the-Blank. *Complete the following sentences with the word(s) or phrase(s) that best reflect what you learned in the chapter. Choose from the items that follow each sentence.*

1. A student who commits to _____ _____ (academic excellence, academic success, academic integrity) behaves according to five values—honesty, trust, fairness, _____ (respect, motivation, commitment), and _____ (timeliness, equality, responsibility).

2. One way to look at learning style is to divide it into two equally important aspects: _____ and _____ (learning preferences/personality traits, verbal/visual, interests/abilities).

3. When you set _____ (long-term goals, short-term goals, priorities) you focus on the goals that are most important at that moment.

4. The best careers and majors for you are ones that take into consideration your _____ and _____ (references/contacts, learning style/abilities, interests/abilities).

5. A broad range of interests and a willingness to take risks are two common characteristics of _____ (creativity, critical thinking, cause and effect).

6. One particular _____ (booster, barrier, bridge) to critical thinking, _____ (resistance to change, personal beliefs, embedded values), refers to the tendency to see current ideas as right and good.

Essay Questions. *The following essay questions will help you organize and communicate your ideas in writing, just as you must do on an essay test. Before you begin answering a question, spend a few minutes planning (brainstorm possible approaches, write a thesis statement, jot down main thoughts in outline or think link form). To prepare yourself for actual test conditions, limit writing time to no more than 20 minutes per question.*

1. Discuss the Habits of Mind. What does the term "Habits of Mind" refer to, and how were they developed? What is their purpose? Include a discussion of how you feel the Habits of Mind could have an impact on your progress on the road to life success.

2. Define *values* and *value system*. How do values develop, and what effect do they have on personal choices? How are values connected to goal setting? Give an example from your life of how values have influenced a personal goal.

SUCCESS
BREAKTHROUGH

Jackie Chan
*Kung Fu Action Star, Comedian,
and Director*

*Born to a poor family in China, Jackie Chan
quit school at an early age and then spent a
decade training in the arts of the Chinese opera. The
acting, singing, dancing, acrobatics, and martial arts
skills he learned prepared him for his life's work as
the creator of kung fu comedy—a totally new movie
genre.*

Jackie Chan attributes his success not only to
perseverance, but also to a willingness to
reinvent himself, a trait he developed early in
his career. When he faced a bleak job market after
completing Chinese opera school in Hong Kong, Chan
had to change career tracks and support himself by
doing stunts. He proved to be a daring stuntman and
even worked in Bruce Lee movies.

Chan was dissatisfied with stunt work. Since
stuntmen were paid by the day rather than by the
stunt, they were at the mercy of the stunt coordinator,
who worked the crew hard in order to put leftover
budget money in his own pocket. Luckily, Chan's talent was soon recognized, and he was promoted to
stunt coordinator. He enjoyed this position because it
allowed him to follow his creative impulses in direct-
ing the action. The position was also his entrée into
acting.

Unfortunately, Chan's career as a movie actor did
not start off well. He was under pressure to emulate
Bruce Lee, but the stern acting style didn't suit him,
and he made a series of flops. After a couple of years,
he was considered box office poison in the Hong Kong
film industry and was assigned to work for another
studio. There, he was given greater creative control,
and he took the opportunity to try something that he
had wanted to do all along—comedy. His first martial
arts comedy was a blockbuster hit in Asia and became
even more popular than Bruce Lee's best films. Chan
made other successful films, and soon there were imi-
tations everywhere. Instead of following the standard
martial arts formula, he had transformed the Hong
Kong film industry by creating a totally new genre.

After a string of successful films, Chan set
his sights on Hollywood. It took him more than
10 years of hard work to achieve recognition
there. Language and cultural differences
complicated the task. When he first came to
the United States, he knew little English. He was
insulted when interviewers, ignorant of the fact that he
practiced the Chinese martial art of kung fu rather
than the Japanese martial art of karate, asked him to
show off his karate moves. Tired of feeling insulted,
and determined that his unique talents would win out,
he decided to stand up for himself: "I wasn't going to
jump through any more hoops for patronizing re-
porters or feel any shame for being Chinese," he said.
"I know who I am; I'm Jackie Chan. I may not have
perfect English, but tell me, how many talk show hosts
can speak Chinese?. . . I can guarantee that I know
more of their language than they know of mine!"

Chan finally broke into Hollywood by continually
pushing the envelope. Committed to performing all of
his stunts himself, he strives to make them bigger and
more difficult with each new film. The outtakes reel
that always appears at the end of his films has become a major draw for fans. He tries to surprise his
audiences by changing his formulas and going against
trends. This constant level of change is nothing new—
he has been doing it all along.

Take a Moment to Consider . . .

- *When you faced obstacles that you overcame by being true to yourself—even when your actions were
unpopular or different from the actions of others.*

- *How, if your plans did not work out as you had
hoped, you would reinvent yourself in order to
achieve success.*

Source: Information about Jackie Chan's life from *I Am Jackie Chan: My Life in Action*,
by Jackie Chan, with Jeff Yang. New York: Ballantine Books, 1998.

SUCCESS BREAKTHROUGH

Cesar Chavez
Farm Labor Organizer

Born to a poor family of farm workers, Cesar Chavez had experienced injustice all of his life. None of the workers dreamed it would be possible to confront the growers who abused them, but Cesar Chavez, through conviction and sacrifice, took a stand and spearheaded an extremely effective labor movement.

Born in 1927 near Yuma, Arizona, Cesar Chavez was a second-generation American. When he was young, his family lost their farm and moved to California to become migrant farm workers, harvesting whatever fruits and vegetables were in season and moving constantly from one temporary, cramped home to another. The young Chavez attended more than 30 different schools, all while working part-time in the fields. After he finished the eighth grade, he quit school and worked full-time to help support his family. Witnessing the pervasive exploitation of workers, he tried to speak up for fair pay and better working conditions, but growers ignored him. Initially, Chavez had no support from other workers because they feared losing their jobs and felt powerless against the growers.

After working for the Community Service Organization (CSO) for 10 years and rising through the ranks, Chavez became the national director of the organization at the age of 35. At this point he realized that organizing the workers into a labor union was the only way to make them powerful enough to stand up for their basic rights. His most significant obstacle was that the CSO position, his first steady job, provided important security for his family—he now had a wife and eight children to support. However, he was driven to find a solution.

I saw the trap most people get themselves into—tying themselves to a job for security. It was easier for us and our family to try to escape poverty than to change the conditions that keep so many work-ers poor. But we inherited the poverty from our fathers and our fathers from our grandfathers and our grandfathers from their fathers. We had to stop someplace! . . . So I resigned my job and set out to found a union. At first I was frightened, very frightened. But by the time I had missed the fourth paycheck and found things were still going, that the moon was still there and the sky and the flowers, I began to laugh. I really began to feel free. It was one of my biggest triumphs in terms of finding myself and of being able to discipline myself.

When Chavez left his job, he started the National Farm Workers Association (NFWA). Initially, he allowed himself only a low level of subsistence pay, so his wife had to work in the fields seven days a week to support the family. Chavez brought the youngest children with him as he traveled to California farming communities building membership for the new organization. In 1966 the NFWA merged with another workers' organization to become the United Farm Workers (UFW).

In the 1960s and 1970s Chavez organized the NFWA and UFW against grape and lettuce growers. He faced strong opposition from police and paid hit men: Chavez and other union members were repeatedly jailed, many strikers were beaten, and a few lost their lives. However, Chavez, who adhered to the principles of peaceful resistance preached by Mohandas K. Gandhi and Dr. Martin Luther King, Jr., remained committed to non-violence. Having carefully studied the failures of early organized resistance, he formulated a novel mixed tactic that included strikes, boycotts, marches, and hunger strikes. These actions would effectively publicize the efforts of the strikers, and the swell of support gradually led to major advances for farm workers. By the 1980s, tens of thousands of farm laborers worked under UFW contracts that brought them higher pay, family health coverage, pension benefits, and other contract protections. In following his convictions, Chavez succeeded beyond all expectations.

Take a Moment to Consider . . .

- *When you have taken—or should take—a risk in order to stand up for something that is important to you.*
- *What kind of patterns or traditions, in your life and family, you feel are harmful and should be changed.*

Source: From *Cesar Chavez: Autobiography of La Causa*, by Jacques E. Levy. New York: W. W. Norton & Co., 1975.

PART II
TARGETING SUCCESS IN SCHOOL

THINKING IT THROUGH

Check those statements that apply to you right now:

- ☑ I find myself struggling to get through many of my texts.

- ☐ I can read rapidly and understand and remember what I read.

- ☐ When I learn a new vocabulary word, I try to remember the definition and use the word in sentences. I am usually successful.

- ☑ When I study, I often have to read material over and over to grasp the meaning.

- ☐ When I learn something new, I try to think how it relates to what I already know.

- ☐ I often take a leadership role when studying with a group of classmates.

Reading and Studying

FOCUSING ON CONTENT

Applying past knowledge to new situations.

"Intelligent human beings **learn from experience**. When confronted with a new and perplexing problem, they . . . call upon their store of knowledge and experience for sources of data and for processes that will help them solve each new challenge." **—ART COSTA**

*As a reader, you bring the knowledge you have gained from all you have read and experienced in the past to the material you are now reading. By **applying past knowledge to new situations,** you are able to place what is new and different in the context of what you know and understand.*

In this chapter you explore the following questions:

- What will help you understand what you read?

- How can you set the stage for reading?

- How can SQ3R help you own what you read?

- How can you respond critically to what you read?

- How and why should you study with others?

In every college course, reading and studying are essential to learning. Becoming more proficient in these skills requires a step-by-step approach linked to specific techniques. This chapter will help you learn reading and studying strategies to increase your speed, efficiency, and depth of understanding. By the end of the chapter, every hour you spend with your books will become more valuable as you learn more and retain more of what you learn.

What will help you understand what you read?

Reading is a process that requires you, the reader, to *make meaning* from written words. When you make meaning, you connect yourself to the concepts being communicated. Your prior knowledge or familiarity with a subject, culture and home environment, life experiences, and even personal interpretation of words and phrases affect your understanding. Because these factors are different for every person, your reading experiences are uniquely your own.

Reading *comprehension* refers to your ability to understand what you read. True comprehension goes beyond just knowing facts and figures—a student can parrot back a pile of economics statistics on a test, for example, without understanding what they mean. Only when you thoroughly comprehend the information you read can you put it to effective use.

All reading strategies help you to achieve a greater understanding of what you read. Improving your reading comprehension is especially important in college because the reading assignments will be longer and more difficult and you will be asked to complete them independently. In addition, the reading you do in introductory-level courses is the foundation for the reading you will do in advanced courses. Therefore, mastering comprehension strategies early in college is even more important than you might expect.

Every section in this chapter will in some way help you maximize your comprehension. Following are some general comprehension boosters to keep in mind as you work through the chapter and as you tackle individual reading assignments.

reflect

Henry David Thoreau, a 19th-century American author, poet, and philosopher, made the following observation: "*How many a man has dated a new era in his life from the reading of a book.*" What do you think Thoreau meant by this statement? Discuss why this statement may be especially meaningful to you now as you begin college.

& respond

Context
Written or spoken knowledge that can help to illuminate the meaning of a word or passage.

Build knowledge through reading and studying. More than any other factor, what you already know before you read a passage influences your ability to understand and remember important ideas. Previous knowledge gives you a **context** for what you read.

Think positively. Instead of telling yourself that you cannot understand, think positively. Tell yourself: *I can learn this material. The reading requirements for this class are within my ability.*

Think critically. Ask yourself questions. Do you understand the sentence, paragraph, or chapter you just read? Are the ideas and supporting examples clear? Could you explain the material to someone else? Later in this chapter, you will learn strategies for responding critically to what you read.

Build vocabulary. Lifelong learners never stop learning new words. The more you know, the more material you can understand without stopping to check your dictionary.

Look for order and meaning in seemingly chaotic reading materials. The information in this chapter on the SQ3R reading technique and on critical reading will help you discover patterns and achieve a depth of understanding.

How can you set the stage for reading?

On any given day during your college career, you may be faced with reading assignments like these:

- A textbook chapter on the history of South African apartheid (world history)
- An original research study on the relationship between sleep deprivation and the development of memory problems (psychology)
- Chapters 4–6 in John Steinbeck's classic novel *The Grapes of Wrath* (American literature)
- A technical manual on the design of computer antivirus programs (computer science—software design)

This material is rigorous by anyone's standards. In fact, many students are surprised at how much reading there is in college, and that they are often expected to read and learn pages and pages of material that is never explicitly covered in class. To get through all this reading—and master its contents—you need a systematic approach. The following strategies help you set the stage for reading success.

If you have a reading disability, if English is not your primary language, or if you have limited reading skills, you may need additional support (see Chapter 2 for more on learning disabilities and support services). Most colleges provide services for students through a reading center or tutoring program. Remember: The ability to succeed is often linked to the ability to ask for help.

Take an Active Approach to Difficult Texts

Generally, the further you advance in your education, the more complex your required reading. You may encounter new concepts, words, and terms that seem like a foreign language. Assignments can also be difficult when the required reading is from *primary sources*—original documents rather than another writer's interpretation of these documents—or from academic journal articles and scientific studies that don't define basic terms or supply a wealth of examples. Primary sources include:

- historical documents
- works of literature (e.g., novels, poems, and plays)
- scientific studies, including lab reports and accounts of experiments
- journal articles

When studying, select the time and setting that are best for you, minimizing internal and external distractions.

The following strategies may help you approach difficult material actively and positively:

Approach your reading assignments with an open mind. Be careful not to prejudge them as impossible or boring before you even start.

Know that some texts require extra work and concentration. Set a goal to make your way through the material and learn. Do whatever it takes.

Define concepts that your material does not explain. Consult resources—instructors, students, reference materials—for help.

To help with your make-meaning-of-textbooks mission, you may want to create your own mini-library at home. Collect reference materials that you use often, such as a dictionary, a thesaurus, a writer's style handbook, and maybe an atlas or a computer manual. You may also benefit from owning reference materials in your particular areas of study. "If you find yourself going to the library to look up the same reference again and again, consider purchasing that book for your personal library," advises library expert Sherwood Harris.[1]

Choose the Right Setting

Finding a place and time that minimize distractions helps you achieve the focus and discipline that your reading requires. Here are some suggestions.

Select the right company (or lack thereof). If you prefer to read alone, establish a relatively interruption-proof place and time such as an out-of-the-way spot at the library or an after-class hour in an empty classroom. Even if you don't mind activity nearby, try to minimize distractions.

Select the right location. Many students study at a library desk. Others prefer an easy chair or even the floor. Choose a spot that's comfortable but not so cushy that you fall asleep. Make sure that you have adequate lighting and aren't too hot or cold.

"No barrier of the senses shuts me out from the sweet, gracious discourse of my book friends. They talk to me without embarrassment or awkwardness."

HELEN KELLER

Select the right time. Choose a time when you feel alert and focused. Try reading just before or after the class for which the reading is assigned, if you can. Eventually, you will associate preferred places and times with focused reading. Pay attention to your natural body rhythms to choose study times; your goal is to study when your energy is at a peak. For example, while night owls may be productive between 10 P.M. and 1 A.M., morning people will probably get little done during late-night sessions.

Deal with internal distractions.   Internal distractions—for example, personal worries, anticipation of an event, or even hunger—can get in the way of work. You may want to take a break and tend to the issue that worries you. Physical exercise may relax and refocus you. For some people, studying while listening to music quiets a busy mind. For others, silence may do the trick. If you're hungry, take a snack break and come back to your work.

Students with families have an added factor when deciding when, where, and how to read. Figure 5.1 explores some ways that parents or others caring for children may be able to maximize their study efforts.

Define Your Purpose for Reading

When you define your purpose, you ask yourself *why* you are reading something. Completing this sentence will help you clarify your purpose: "In reading this material, I intend to define/learn/answer/achieve . . . " You can then decide how much time and effort to expend.

Achieving your reading purpose requires adapting to different types of reading materials. Being a flexible reader—adjusting your reading strategies and pace—helps you to adapt successfully.

Your purpose for reading will determine your reading strategy. With purpose comes direction; with direction comes a strategy. Following are four reading purposes. You may have one or more for any "reading event."

Purpose 1: Read for understanding.   In college, studying means reading to comprehend *general ideas* and *specific facts or examples*. Facts and examples help to explain or support ideas, and ideas provide a framework for remembering facts and examples.

- *General ideas.* Reading for a general idea is rapid reading to gain an overview of the material. You search for general ideas by focusing on headings, subheadings, and summary statements.
- *Specific facts or examples.* At times, readers may focus on locating specific pieces of information—for example, the stages of intellectual development in children. Often, a reader may search for examples that support or explain general ideas—for example, the causes of economic recession.

Purpose 2: Read to evaluate critically.   Critical evaluation involves examining causes and effects, evaluating ideas, and asking questions that test the writer's argument and search for assumptions. Critical reading brings an understanding of the material that goes beyond basic information recall (see pages 152–156 for more on critical reading).

Purpose 3: Read for practical application.   When you read a computer manual or an instruction sheet for assembling a gas grill, your goal is to learn how to do something. Reading and action usually go hand in hand. Remembering the specifics requires a certain degree of general comprehension.

FIGURE 5.1   Managing children while studying.

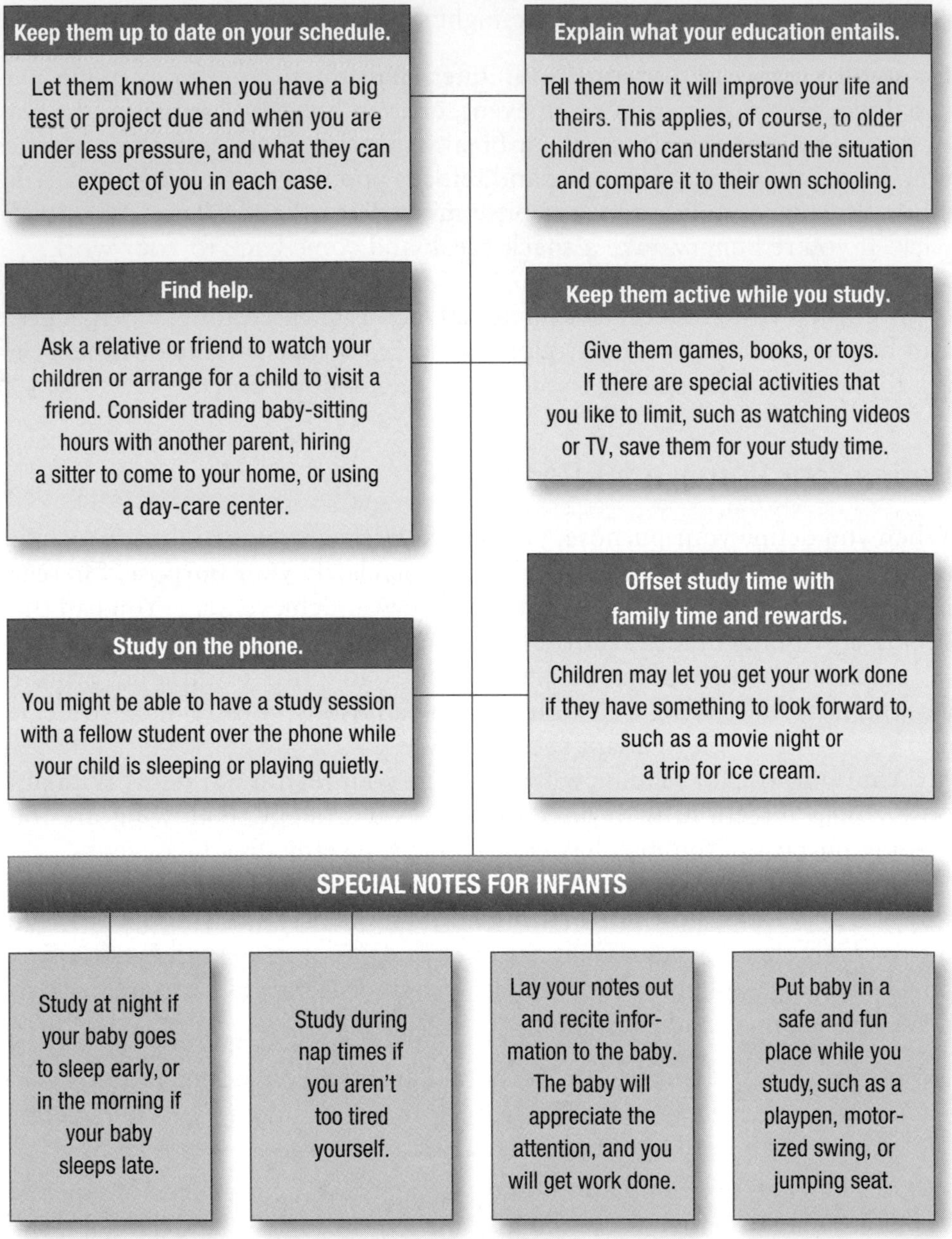

Keep them up to date on your schedule.

Let them know when you have a big test or project due and when you are under less pressure, and what they can expect of you in each case.

Explain what your education entails.

Tell them how it will improve your life and theirs. This applies, of course, to older children who can understand the situation and compare it to their own schooling.

Find help.

Ask a relative or friend to watch your children or arrange for a child to visit a friend. Consider trading baby-sitting hours with another parent, hiring a sitter to come to your home, or using a day-care center.

Keep them active while you study.

Give them games, books, or toys. If there are special activities that you like to limit, such as watching videos or TV, save them for your study time.

Study on the phone.

You might be able to have a study session with a fellow student over the phone while your child is sleeping or playing quietly.

Offset study time with family time and rewards.

Children may let you get your work done if they have something to look forward to, such as a movie night or a trip for ice cream.

SPECIAL NOTES FOR INFANTS

Study at night if your baby goes to sleep early, or in the morning if your baby sleeps late.

Study during nap times if you aren't too tired yourself.

Lay your notes out and recite information to the baby. The baby will appreciate the attention, and you will get work done.

Put baby in a safe and fun place while you study, such as a playpen, motorized swing, or jumping seat.

Purpose 4: Read for pleasure. Some materials you read for entertainment, such as *Sports Illustrated* magazine, the latest John Grisham courtroom thriller, or even a Jane Austen novel.

Match Strategies to Different Areas of Study

Different subjects present different reading challenges. This is due to essential differences between the subjects (a calculus text and a world religions text have little in common), and to reader learning style and preferences (most people are more comfortable with some subjects than with others).

MULTIPLE PATHWAYS TO LEARNING

MULTIPLE INTELLIGENCE STRATEGIES *for* Reading

Use selected reading techniques in Multiple Intelligence areas to strengthen your ability to read for meaning and retention.

INTELLIGENCE	SUGGESTED STRATEGIES	WHAT WORKS FOR YOU? WRITE NEW IDEAS HERE
Verbal–Linguistic	■ Mark up your text with marginal notes while you read. ■ When tackling a chapter, use every stage of SQ3R, taking advantage of each writing opportunity (writing Q stage questions, writing summaries, and so on).	
Logical–Mathematical	■ Read material in sequence. ■ Think about the logical connections between what you are reading and the world at large; consider similarities, differences, and cause-and-effect relationships.	
Bodily–Kinesthetic	■ Take physical breaks during reading sessions—walk, stretch, exercise. ■ Pace while reciting important ideas.	
Visual–Spatial	■ As you read, take particular note of photos, tables, figures, and other visual aids. ■ Make charts, diagrams, or think links illustrating difficult concepts you encounter in your reading.	
Interpersonal	■ With a friend, have a joint reading session. One should read a section silently and then summarize aloud the important concepts for the other. Reverse the order of summarizer and listener for each section. ■ Discuss reading material and clarify important concepts in a study group.	
Intrapersonal	■ Read in a solitary setting and allow time for reflection. ■ Think about how a particular reading assignment makes you feel, and evaluate your reaction by considering the material in light of what you already know.	
Musical	■ Play music while you read. ■ Recite important concepts in your reading to rhythms, or write a song to depict those concepts.	
Naturalistic	■ Read and study in a natural environment. ■ Before reading indoors, imagine your favorite place in nature in order to create a relaxed frame of mind.	

Although the information in this chapter will help with any academic subject, math and science often present unique challenges. You may benefit from using some of the following techniques in these areas.

Interact with the material critically as you go. Math and science texts move sequentially (later chapters build on concepts introduced in previous chapters) and are often problem-and-solution–based. Keep a pad of paper nearby and take notes of examples. Work steps out on your pad. Draw sketches to help visualize the material. Try not to move on until you understand the example and how it relates to the central ideas. Write down questions to ask your instructor or fellow students.

Note formulas. Make sure you understand the principle behind every **formula**—why it works—rather than just memorizing the formula itself. Read the assigned material to prepare for homework.

Use memory techniques. Science textbooks are often packed with vocabulary specific to that particular science. Put your memory skills to use when reading science texts—use mnemonic devices, test yourself with flash cards, and rehearse aloud or silently (see Chapter 6). Selective highlighting and writing summaries of your readings, in table format for example, also help.

Formula
A general fact, rule, or principle usually expressed in mathematical symbols.

Build Reading Speed

If you can increase your reading speed, you will save valuable time and effort—as long as you don't sacrifice comprehension. Greater comprehension is the primary goal and actually promotes faster reading.

The average American adult reads between 150 and 350 words per minute, and faster readers can be capable of speeds up to 1,000 words per minute.[2] However, the human eye can only move so fast; reading speeds in excess of 350 words per minute involve "skimming" and "scanning" (see page 144). The following suggestions will help increase your reading speed:

- Try to read groups of words rather than single words.
- Avoid pointing your finger to guide your reading; use an index card to move quickly down the page.
- When reading narrow columns, focus your eyes in the middle of the column. With practice, you'll be able to read the entire column width as you read down the page.
- Avoid *subvocalization*—speaking the words or moving your lips—when reading.

The key to building reading speed is practice and more practice, says reading expert Steve Moidel. To achieve your goal of reading between 500 and 1,000 words per minute, Moidel suggests that you start practicing at three times the rate you want to achieve, a rate that is much faster than you can comprehend.[3] For example, if your goal is 500 words per minute, speed up to 1,500 words per minute. Reading at such an accelerated rate pushes your eyes and mind to adjust to the faster pace. When you slow down to 500 words per minute—the pace at which you can read and comprehend—your reading rate will feel comfortable even though it is much faster than your original speed. You may even want to check into self-paced computer software that helps you improve reading speed.

Expand Your Vocabulary

A strong vocabulary increases reading speed and comprehension; when you understand the words in your reading material, you don't have to stop as often to think about what they mean.

The best way to build your vocabulary is to commit yourself to learning new and unfamiliar words as you encounter them. This involves certain steps.

Analyze Word Parts

Often, if you understand part of a word, you can figure out what the entire word means. This is true because many English words are made up of a combination of Greek and Latin prefixes, roots, and suffixes. *Prefixes* are word parts that are added to the beginning of a **root**. *Suffixes* are added to the end of the root.

Table 5.1 contains some of the prefixes, roots, and suffixes you will encounter as you read. Knowing these verbal building blocks dramatically increases your vocabulary. Figure 5.2 shows how one root can be the stem of many words.

Using prefixes, roots, and suffixes, you can piece together the meaning of new words. To use a simple example, the word *prologue* is made up of the prefix *pro* (before) and the root *logue* (to speak). Thus, *prologue* refers to words spoken or written before the main text.

Root

The central part or basis of a word, to which prefixes and suffixes can be added to produce different words.

Use Words in Context

Although a definition tells you what a word means, it may not include a context. Using a word in context after defining it helps to anchor the information so that you can remember it and continue to build on it. Here are some strategies for using context to solidify new vocabulary words.

- *Use new words in a sentence or two right away.* Do this immediately after reading their definitions while everything is still fresh in your mind.

- *Reread the sentence where you originally saw the word.* Go over it a few times to make sure that you understand how the word is used.

- *Use the word over the next few days whenever it may apply.* Try it while talking with friends, writing letters or notes, or in your own thoughts.

- *Consider where you may have seen or heard the word before.* When you learn a word, going back to sentences you previously didn't "get" may solidify your understanding. For example, most children learn the Pledge of Allegiance by rote without understanding what "allegiance" means. Later, when they learn the definition of "allegiance," the pledge provides a context that helps them better understand the word.

TABLE 5.1   Common prefixes, roots, and suffixes.

Prefix	Primary Meaning	Example
a-, ab-	from	abstain, avert
con-, cor-, com-	with, together	convene, correlate, compare
il-	not	illegal, illegible
sub-, sup-	under	subordinate, suppose

Root	Primary Meaning	Example
-chron-	time	synchronize
-ann-	year	biannual
-sper-	hope	desperate
-voc-	speak, talk	convocation

Suffix	Primary Meaning	Example
-able	able	recyclable
-meter	measure	thermometer
-ness	state of	carelessness
-y	inclined to	sleepy

FIGURE 5.2   Building words from a single root.

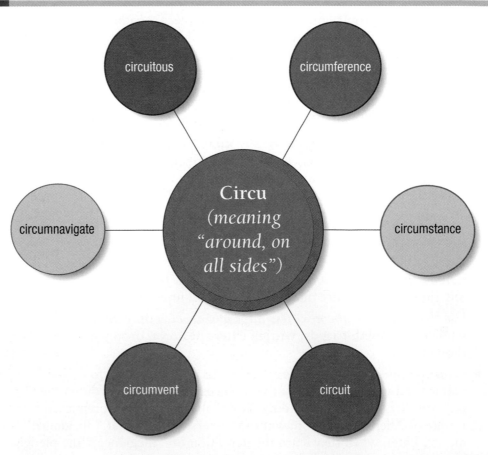

- *Seek knowledgeable advice.* If after looking up a word you still have trouble with its meaning, ask an instructor or a friend to help you figure it out.

Use a Dictionary

Dictionaries provide broad information such as word origin, pronunciation, part of speech, and multiple meanings. Buy a standard dictionary, keep it nearby, and consult it for help in understanding passages that contain unfamiliar words. Some textbooks also have a text-specific "dictionary" called a *glossary* that defines terms found in the text. Electronic dictionaries are also handy, although definitions are less complete. Dictionaries are also available on the Internet.

You may not always have time to use the following suggestions, but when you can, they will help you make the most of your dictionary.

- *Read every meaning of a word, not just the first.* Think critically about which meaning suits the context of the word in question, and choose the one that makes the most sense.
- *Substitute a word or phrase from the definition for the word.* Use the definition you have chosen. Imagine, for example, that you read the following sentence and do not know the word *indoctrinated*:

The cult indoctrinated its members to reject society's values.

In the dictionary, you find several definitions, including "brainwashed" and "instructed." You decide that the one closest to the correct meaning is "brainwashed." With this term, the sentence reads as follows:

The cult brainwashed its members to reject society's values.

So far, this chapter has focused on reading as a deliberate, purposeful process of constructing meaning. Recognizing obstacles and defining reading purposes lay the groundwork for effective studying—the process of mastering the concepts and skills contained in your texts.

How can *SQ3R* help you own what you read?

You can count on spending a great deal of time and effort completing reading assignments for your courses. It is far less certain, however, that you will understand and remember what you read in such a way that you create a foundation of knowledge and do well on tests. The SQ3R study method will help you accomplish these reading and studying goals as you progress into more complex and difficult texts.

SQ3R is a technique that will help you grasp ideas quickly, remember more, and review effectively for tests. SQ3R stands for *Survey, Question, Read,*

Recite, and Review—all steps in the studying process. Developed about 60 years ago by Francis Robinson, the technique is still used today because it works.[4]

Moving through the stages of SQ3R requires that you know how to skim and scan. **Skimming** involves the rapid reading of chapter elements, including introductions, conclusions, and summaries; the first and last lines of paragraphs; boldfaced or italicized terms; and pictures, charts, and diagrams. The goal of skimming is a quick construction of the main ideas. In contrast, **scanning** involves the careful search for specific facts and examples. You might use scanning during the review phase of SQ3R to locate particular information (such as a chemistry formula).

Approach SQ3R as a framework on which you build your house, not as a tower of stone. In other words, instead of following each step by rote, bring your personal learning styles and study preferences to the system. For example, you and another classmate may focus on elements in a different order when you survey, write different types of questions, or favor different sets of review strategies. Explore the strategies, evaluate what works, and then make the system your own. Note that although SQ3R will help you as you study almost every subject, it is not appropriate for literature.

Skimming

Rapid, superficial reading of material that involves glancing through to determine central ideas and main elements.

Scanning

Reading material in an investigative way, searching for specific information.

Survey

Surveying refers to the process of previewing, or pre-reading, a book before you actually study it. Compare it to looking at a map before you drive somewhere—taking a few minutes to look at your surroundings and where you intend to go will save you a lot of time and trouble once you are on the road.

Most textbooks include devices that give students an overview of the whole text as well as of the contents of individual chapters. When you survey, pay attention to the following elements.

The front matter. Before you even get to page 1, most textbooks have a table of contents, a preface, and other materials. The table of contents gives you an overview with clues about coverage, topic order, and features. The preface, in particular, can point out the book's unique approach. For example, the preface for the American history text *Out of Many* states that it highlights "the experiences of diverse communities of Americans in the unfolding story of our country."[5] This tells you that cultural diversity is a central theme.

reflect

How does reading assigned textbook material enrich your classroom experience? What aspects of your favorite text this semester make it a helpful learning tool for you? After reading about text survey techniques, how do you intend to change your approach to all your text reading?

Companion Website

& respond

The chapter elements. Generally, each chapter has devices that help you make meaning out of the material. Among these are:

- The chapter title, which establishes the topic and perhaps author perspective
- The chapter introduction, outline, list of objectives, or list of key topics

- Within the chapter, headings, tables and figures, quotes, marginal notes, and photographs that help you perceive structure and important concepts
- Special chapter features, often presented in boxes set off from the main text, that point you to ideas connected to themes that run through the text
- Particular styles or arrangements of type (**boldface**, *italics*, <u>underline</u>, larger fonts, bullet points, boxed text) that call your attention to new words or important concepts

At the end of each chapter, a summary may help you tie concepts together. Review questions and exercises help you review and think critically about the material. Skimming these *before* reading the chapter gives you clues about what's important.

The back matter. Here some texts include a glossary. You may also find an *index* to help you locate individual topics and a *bibliography* that lists additional reading on particular topics covered in the text.

Figure 5.3 shows the many devices that books employ. Think about how many of these devices you already use, and which you can start using now to boost your comprehension.

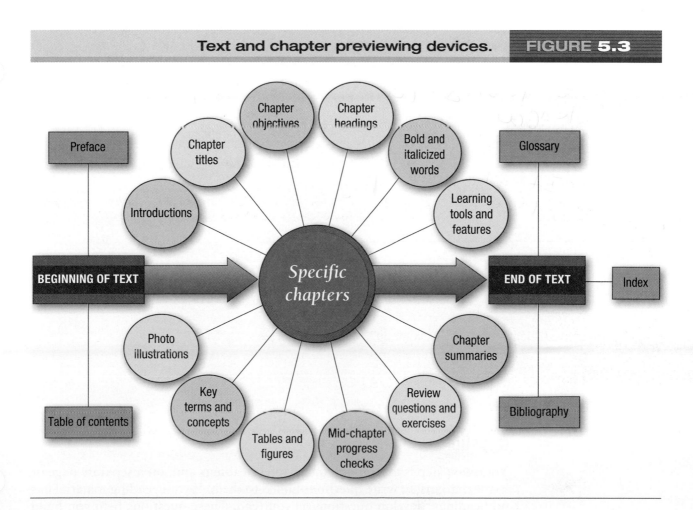

Text and chapter previewing devices.   FIGURE 5.3

TAKE ACTION

Surveying gives you an overview that sets the stage for your studying. To practice this technique, follow these steps with one of your current textbooks:

- Read the front matter, including the table of contents and preface.

  What does this material tell you about the theme of the text? About its unique approach and point of view?

  It tells me the introduction on a chapter

  Are there any unexpected topics listed in the table of contents? Are there topics that you expected to see but are missing?

  No there is not unexpected topics.

- Now look at a typical text chapter.

  Can you identify the devices that help make the concepts more clear and organized?

  to found words that you dont know

  After skimming the chapter, what do you know about the material? What elements helped you skim quickly?

  It helped me to skim any word that I don't undersand.

- Finally, look at the back matter.

  What back-matter elements can you identify?

  Which of these elements do you think will be helpful when you begin studying?

Question

Your next step is to examine the chapter headings and, on a separate page or in the margins, to write *questions* linked to them. If your reading material has no headings, develop questions as you read. These questions help you build comprehension and relate new ideas to what you already know. You can take questions from the textbook or from your lecture notes, or come up with them when you survey, based on the ideas you think are most important.

The table below shows how this works. The column on the left contains primary- and secondary-level headings from a section of *Out of Many*. The column on the right rephrases these headings in question form.

There is no "correct" set of questions. Given the same headings, you could create different questions. Your goal is to engage the critical-thinking mind actions discussed in Chapter 4.

The Meaning of Freedom	What did freedom mean for both slaves and citizens in the United States?
Moving About	Where did African Americans go after they were freed from slavery?
The African American Family	How did freedom change the structure of the African American family?
African American Churches and Schools	What effect did freedom have on the formation of African American churches and schools?
Land and Labor After Slavery	How was land farmed and maintained after slaves were freed?
The Origins of African American Politics	How did the end of slavery bring about the beginning of African American political life?

Read

Your questions give you a starting point for *reading*, the first R in SQ3R. Learning from textbooks requires that you read *actively*. Active reading means engaging with the material through questioning, writing, note taking, and other activities. As you can see in Figure 5.4, the activities of SQ3R promote active reading. Following are some specific strategies that will keep you active when you read.

Focus on your Q-stage questions. Read the material with the purpose of answering each question. As you come on ideas and examples that relate to your question, write them down or note them in the text.

Look for important concepts. As you read, record key words, phrases, and concepts in your notebook. Some students divide the notebook page into two columns, writing questions on the left and answers on the right. This method is called the Cornell note-taking system (see Chapter 7).

Mark up your textbook. Being able to make notations will help you to make sense of the material; for this reason, owning your textbooks is an enormous advantage. You may want to write notes in the margins, circle key ideas, or highlight key points. Figure 5.5 shows how this is done on a marketing textbook section that introduces the concept of markets. Some people prefer to underline, although underlining adds more ink to the lines of text and may overwhelm your eyes. Bracketing an entire key passage is a good alternative to underlining.

Selective highlighting may help you pinpoint material to review before an exam, although excessive highlighting may actually interfere with comprehension. Here are some tips on how to strike a balance.

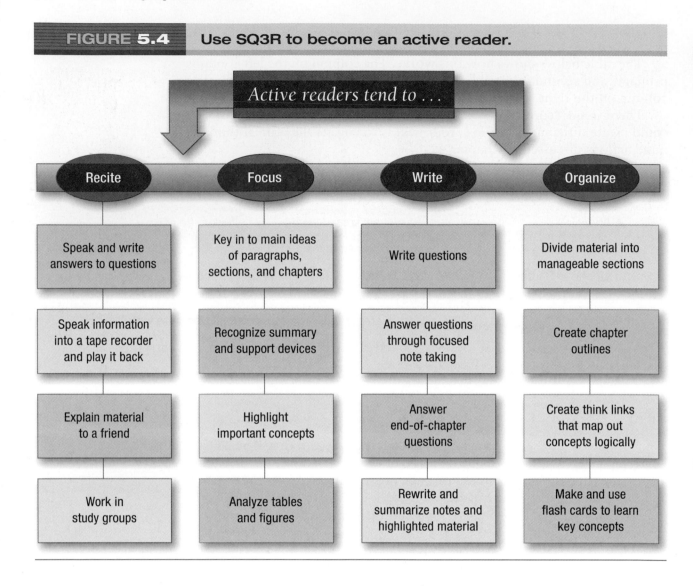

FIGURE 5.4   Use SQ3R to become an active reader.

Active readers tend to . . .

Recite	Focus	Write	Organize
Speak and write answers to questions	Key in to main ideas of paragraphs, sections, and chapters	Write questions	Divide material into manageable sections
Speak information into a tape recorder and play it back	Recognize summary and support devices	Answer questions through focused note taking	Create chapter outlines
Explain material to a friend	Highlight important concepts	Answer end-of-chapter questions	Create think links that map out concepts logically
Work in study groups	Analyze tables and figures	Rewrite and summarize notes and highlighted material	Make and use flash cards to learn key concepts

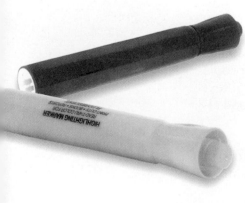

- *Mark the text* after *you read the material once through*. If you do it on the first reading, you may mark less important passages.
- *Highlight key terms and concepts.* Mark the examples that explain and support important ideas.
- *Avoid overmarking.* A phrase or two in any paragraph is usually enough. Set off long passages with brackets rather than marking every line.
  - *Don't mistake highlighting for learning.* You will not learn what you highlight unless you interact with it through careful review—questioning, writing, and reciting.

Divide your reading into digestible segments. If you find you are losing the thread of the ideas, you may want to try smaller segments or take a break and come back to it later. Try to avoid reading according to the clock—such as, "I'll read for 30 minutes and then quit"—or you may short-circuit your understanding by stopping in the middle of a key explanation.

FIGURE 5.5   Effective highlighting and marginal notes aid memory.

Markets

The term *market* has acquired many meanings over the years. In its original meaning, a market is a physical place where buyers and sellers gather to exchange goods and services. Medieval towns had market squares where sellers brought their goods and buyers shopped for goods. In today's cities, buying and selling occur in shopping areas rather than markets. To an economist, a market describes all the buyers and sellers who transact over some good or service. Thus, the soft-drink market consists of sellers such as Coca-Cola and PepsiCo, and of all the consumers who buy soft drinks. To a marketer, a market is the set of all actual and potential buyers of a product or service.

[margin note: Definition of a market]

Organizations that sell to consumer and business markets recognize that they cannot appeal to all buyers in those markets, or at least not to all buyers in the same way. Buyers are too numerous, too widely scattered, and too varied in their needs and buying practices. And different companies vary widely in their abilities to serve different segments of the market. Rather than trying to compete in an entire market, sometimes against superior competitors, each company must identify the parts of the market that it can serve best.

[margin note: Companies can't appeal to everyone]

Sellers have not always practiced this philisophy. Their thinking has passed through three stages:

[margin note: One-size-fits-all approach]
- *Mass marketing.* In mass marketing, the seller mass produces, mass distributes, and mass promotes one product to all buyers. At one time, Coca-Cola produced only one drink for the whole market, hoping it would appeal to everyone. The argument for mass marketing is that it should lead to the lowest costs and prices and create the largest potential market.

[margin note: Offer variety to buyers]
- *Product-variety marketing.* Here, the seller produces two or more products that have different features, styles, quality, sizes, and so on. Later, Coca-Cola produced several soft drinks packaged in different sizes and containers that were designed to offer variety to buyers rather than to appeal to different market segments. The argument for product-variety marketing is that consumers have different tastes that change over time. Consumers seek variety and change.

[margin note: A tailored approach to specific market segments]
- *Target marketing.* Here, the seller identifies market segments, selects one or more of them, and develops products and marketing mixes tailored to each. For example, Coca-Cola now produces soft drinks for the sugared-cola segment (Coca-Cola Classic and Cherry Coke), the diet segment (Diet Coke and Tab), the no-caffeine segment (Caffeine-Free Coke), and the noncola segment (Minute Maid sodas).

[margin note: Current approach is usually TARGET MARKETING]

Today's companies are moving away from mass marketing and product-variety marketing toward target marketing. Target marketing can better help sellers find their marketing opportunities. Sellers can develop the right product for each target market and adjust their prices, distribution channels, and advertising to reach the target market efficiently. Instead of scattering their marketing efforts (the "shotgun" approach), they can focus on the buyers who have greater purchase interest (the "rifle" approach).

87

Source: Marketing: An Introduction, 4/E by Kotler/Armstrong, © 1997. Reprinted with permission of Pearson Education, Inc., Upper Saddle River, NJ.

Finding the Main Idea

One crucial skill in textbook reading is finding the main, or central, idea of a piece of writing (e.g., a book, a chapter, an article, a paragraph). The *main idea* refers to the thoughts that are at the heart of the writing, the idea that creates its essential meaning. Comprehension depends on your ability to recognize main ideas and to link the author's other thoughts to them.

Where do you find the main idea? As an example, consider a paragraph. The main idea may be:

- In a *topic sentence* at the very beginning of the paragraph, stating the topic of the paragraph and what about that topic the author wants to communicate, followed by sentences adding support.

- At the end of the paragraph, following supporting details that lead up to it.

- Buried in the middle of the paragraph, sandwiched between supporting details.

- In a compilation of ideas from various sentences, each of which contains a critical element. It is up to the reader to piece these elements together to create the essence of meaning.

- Never explicitly stated, but implied by the information presented in the paragraph.

How, then, do you decide just what the main idea is? Ophelia H. Hancock, a specialist in improving reading skills for college students, suggests a three-step approach:[6]

1. *Search for the topic of the paragraph.* The topic of the paragraph is not the same thing as the main idea. Rather, it is the broad subject being discussed—for example, former President John F. Kennedy, hate crimes on campus, or the World Wide Web.

2. *Identify the aspect of the topic that is the paragraph's focus.* If the general topic is former President John F. Kennedy, the writer may choose to focus on any of literally thousands of aspects of that topic. Here are just a few: his health problems, his civil rights policies, his cabinet members, his effectiveness as a public speaker, his relationship with family.

3. *Find what the author wants you to know about the specific aspect being discussed, which is the main idea.* The main idea of a paragraph dealing with President Kennedy as a public speaker may be this:

> President Kennedy was a gifted, charismatic speaker who used his humor, charm, and intelligence to make the presidency accessible to all Americans during regularly televised presidential news conferences.

Recite

Once you finish reading a topic, stop and answer the questions you raised in the Q stage of SQ3R. You may decide to *recite* each answer aloud, silently speak the answers to yourself, tell or teach the answers to another person, or write your ideas and answers in brief notes. Writing is often the most effec-

TAKE ACTION

Find the Main Idea of a Paragraph

Use the three-step approach described on page 150 to find the main idea of the following paragraph:

Tone relates not so much to what you say as to how you say it. The tone of your writing has a major impact on what you are trying to communicate to your audience. Tone involves your choice of words interacting with your message. Have you ever reacted to someone's understanding of what you wrote with "That's not what I meant to say"? Your tone can be what has thrown your readers off track, although you can only be misunderstood if your writing is unclear or imprecise.[7]

- What is the topic of this paragraph?

  Markets

- What aspect of tone is being discussed?

  Organized.

- What main idea is being communicated?

  companie of business

- Now choose a meaty paragraph from one of the texts you are currently studying, and use the same questions to find the paragraph's main idea. How do these questions help you focus on the paragraph's most important points?

tive way to solidify what you have read because writing from memory checks your understanding.

"The best effect of any book is that it excites the reader to self-activity."

THOMAS CARLYLE

Keep your learning styles (Chapter 2) in mind when you explore different strategies. For example, an intrapersonal learner may prefer writing, while an interpersonal learner might want to recite answers aloud to a classmate. A logical–mathematical learner may benefit from organizing material into detailed outlines, while a musical learner might want to chant information aloud to a rhythm.

After you finish one section, read the next. Repeat the question–read–recite cycle until you complete the entire chapter. If you find yourself fumbling for thoughts, you may not yet "own" the ideas. Reread the section that's giving you trouble until you master its contents. Understanding each section as you go is crucial because the material in one section often forms a foundation for the next.

Review

Review soon after you finish a chapter. Reviewing, both immediately and periodically in the days and weeks after you read, is the step that solidifies your understanding. Chances are good that if you close the book after you read, you will forget much of what you learned. Here are some techniques for reviewing. Try many, and use what works best for you.

- Skim and reread your notes. Then, try summarizing them from memory.
- Answer the text's end-of-chapter review, discussion, and application questions.
- Quiz yourself, using the questions you raised in the Q stage. If you can't answer one of your own or one of the text's questions, go back and scan the material for answers.
- Create a chapter outline in standard outline form or think link form.
- Reread the preface, headings, tables, and summary.
- Recite important concepts to yourself, or record important information on a cassette tape and play it on your car's tape deck or your portable cassette player.
- Make flash cards that have an idea or word on one side and examples, a definition, or other related information on the other. Test yourself.
- Review and summarize in writing the material you have highlighted or bracketed. Your goal is to condense the material so that you can focus on the central ideas, setting the stage for critical thinking.
- Think critically: Break ideas down into examples, consider similar or different concepts, recall important terms, evaluate ideas, and explore causes and effects (see the next section for details).
- Discuss the concepts with a classmate or in a study group. Trying to teach study partners what you learned will pinpoint the material you know and what still needs work.
- Make think links that show how important concepts relate to one another.

If you need help clarifying your reading material, ask your instructor. Pinpoint the material you want to discuss, schedule a meeting during office hours, and bring a list of questions.

Refreshing your knowledge is easier and faster than learning it the first time. Set up regular review sessions; for example, once a week. Reviewing in as many different ways as possible increases the likelihood of retention. Critical reading may be the most important of these ways.

How can you *respond critically* to what you read?

Textbook features often highlight important ideas and help you determine study questions. As you advance in your education, however, many reading assignments—especially primary sources—will not be so clearly marked. You need critical-reading skills to select important ideas, identify examples that support them, and ask questions without the aid of any special features. The following suggestions will help you become a critical reader.

Ask Questions Based on the Mind Actions

The essence of critical reading, as with critical thinking, is asking questions. Instead of simply accepting what you read, seek a thorough understanding by questioning the material as you go along. Using the mind actions to formulate your questions is a key to success.

You can question any of the following components of reading material:

- the central idea of the entire piece
- a particular idea or statement.
- the examples that support an idea or a statement
- the proof of a fact
- the definition of a concept

Following are some ways to critically question reading material. Apply them to any component you want to question by substituting the component for the words *it* and *this*.

Similarity:	What does this remind me of or how is it similar to something else I know?
Difference:	What different conclusions are possible?
	How is this different from my experience?
Cause and effect:	Why did this happen or what caused this?
	What are the effects or consequences of this?
	What is the purpose of this material?
Example to idea:	How do I summarize this or what are the key ideas?
	What is the thesis or central idea?
Idea to example:	What evidence supports this or what examples fit this idea?
Evaluation:	How do I evaluate this? Is it useful or well constructed?
	Does this example support my thesis or central idea?
	Is this information or point of view important to my work? If so, why?

Engage Critical-Thinking Skills

Certain skills from Chapter 4—*distinguishing fact from opinion* and *examining new perspectives*—can help to deepen your understanding.

Use Knowledge of Fact and Opinion to Evaluate Arguments

You can evaluate any statement in your reading material, identifying it as fact or opinion and challenging how it is supported. You can also evaluate any argument you find in your reading material. In this case, *argument* refers to a persuasive case—a set of connected ideas supported by examples—that a writer makes to prove or disprove a point.

It's easy—and common—to accept or reject an argument outright, according to whether it fits with one's own opinions and views. If you ask questions about an argument, however, you can determine its validity and learn more from it.

Evaluating an argument involves two steps:

- evaluating the quality of the evidence
- evaluating whether the evidence adequately supports the point (whether the examples fit the idea)

Together, these evaluations help you see whether an argument works. If quality evidence (accurate input) combines with quality use of evidence (valid reasoning), you have a solid argument.

Evidence quality. Ask the following questions in order to see whether the evidence itself is accurate:

- What type of evidence is it—fact or opinion? Do the facts seem accurate?
- How is the evidence similar to or different from what I already believe to be true?
- Where is the evidence from? Are those sources reliable and free of bias?

Support quality. Ask these questions to determine whether you think the evidence successfully makes the argument:

- Do examples and ideas, and causes and effects, logically connect to one another?
- Do I believe this argument? How is the writer trying to persuade me?
- Are there enough pieces of evidence to support the central idea adequately?
- What different and perhaps opposing arguments seem just as valid?
- Has the argument evaluated all of the positive and negative effects involved?

Don't rule out the possibility that you may agree wholeheartedly with an argument. How-

RISING
TO THE CHALLENGE

Carly Eckart

Life can be extremely challenging. When Carly Eckart developed an eating disorder, partly in response to a family crisis, she had an experience that she now knows helped her to build strength that will serve her well in the years to come.

Sometimes it seems like life's struggles just keep piling up, testing your fortitude and helping you to build character. My father committed suicide in May of my seventh grade year, leaving me in a state of grief and confusion. I couldn't understand how he could take his own life, and I was ashamed that I hadn't paid attention to his drug problem and depression. I became unforgiving of myself and miserable; my depression and disgust at my imperfections consumed me.

I had always been an overachiever and put pressure on myself to perform, but soon I became obsessed with being the perfect student, athlete, and friend. By the end of the summer I developed an eating disorder. Subconsciously, I felt controlling my eating and weight would help me feel in control of my life again; instead, I felt hopeless and lost.

The deeper I fell into anorexia, the more out of control my life got. As an anorexic, I felt that eating something that was considered too fattening or high in calories would absolutely make me feel crazy. I wouldn't be able to go to sleep at night unless I ate under a certain amount of calories and exercised excessively. For me, living had become a chore, not a privilege. I had to stick to the rules I made for myself or else the monster inside would consume me.

By the end of my sophomore year of high school, after years of struggling with anorexia and bulimia, I had finally had enough. I had plans for my life, and I couldn't let my fears about myself and my life get in the way of doing great things. With the help of my friends and family, I overcame my eating disorders and moved on in my life. One thing I have learned is that you can't give up. You can't let your problems define your identity, and you also can't be too hard on yourself. A lot of times when I'd mess up during my recovery, I'd get really mad, and it made me take a step backward. I'd like myself less for messing up, so I'd have less motivation to do well in the future. What you have to do is set small, reasonable goals. You can't fix all of your problems all at once. Making slow progress is a lot better than cutting yourself off from your problem and then falling back on it before you're completely past it.

But, even more important than that, you have to love yourself. The food aspect of bulimia wasn't in any way the most important or serious aspect of the disease. It was all about my own self-image! If I had loved myself and been comfortable with the way I looked, then I wouldn't have started throwing up in the first place. Only once you accept the person that you are, with all of the good aspects and limitations, can you truly begin to overcome the problems that life throws your way.

If I could go back, I wouldn't change the way I've lived my life. All of the lessons I've learned and the strengths I've gained from my eating disorder are part of what makes me "me," and I love that. I've also learned how to work on things on my own, and to not need to always rely on other people for motivation or discipline. You know, no one made me recover—I had to make myself recover. That independence and assurance that I can do what I need to do to succeed makes me sure that I'll do great in college and in life.

Take a Moment to Consider . . .

- *What life challenge of yours has tested you and helped you become stronger.*
- *Something that inspires motivation in you in a healthy way—an idea, a goal, a person.*

ever, use critical thinking to make an informed decision.

For example, imagine that you are reading an article whose main argument is, "The dissolving of the family unit is the main cause of society's ills." You might examine the facts and examples the writer uses to support this statement, looking carefully at the cause-and-effect structure of the argument. You might question the writer's sources. You might think of examples that support the statement. You might find examples that disprove this argument, such as successful families that don't fit the traditional definition of family. Finally, you might think of opposing arguments, including the ideas and examples to support those arguments.

Examine New Perspectives

Many reading materials are written from a particular perspective. For example, if both a recording artist and a music censorship advocate were to write a piece about a controversial song created by that artist, their different perspectives would result in two very different pieces of writing.

To analyze perspective, ask questions like the following:

- What perspective is guiding this?
- Who wrote this and with what intent?
- How does the material's source affect its perspective?
- How is this perspective supported?
- What assumptions underlie this?
- What examples do not fit this assumption?

Think again about the example—the piece of writing claiming that "the dissolving of the family unit is the main cause of society's ills." Considering perspective, you might ask questions like these:

- What are the central opinions that influence this material?
- Who wrote this and why? Is it designed to communicate objective statistics or to promote a particular message?
- What is the source, and how does that affect the piece?

- What examples and evidence support the claim? Is the support valid? Do I feel comfortable with the perspective?
- What assumptions underlie this statement (e.g., assumptions about the definition of "family" or about what constitutes "society's ills")?
  - Can I think of examples (e.g., families or success stories) that do not fit these assumptions?

reflect

What is your most difficult college reading challenge? A challenge might be coping with a particular kind of material, thinking critically about what you read, handling a reading overload, or achieving a reading goal. Make a plan that addresses this challenge. Think about techniques from this chapter that might help, and discuss the steps you will take to incorporate them into your studying.

& respond

Seek Understanding

The fundamental purpose of all college reading is understanding. Think of your reading process as an archaeological dig. The first step is to excavate a site and uncover the artifacts, which corresponds to your initial survey and reading of the material. As important as the excavation is, the process is incomplete if you stop there. The second step is to investigate each item, evaluate what they all mean, and derive knowledge from what you discover. Critical reading allows you to complete that crucial second step.

Critical reading takes time and focus. Give yourself a chance at success by finding a time, place, and purpose for reading. Learn from others by working in pairs or groups whenever you can.

Why and how should you study with others?

Studying with a partner or in a group can enhance your learning in many ways. You benefit from shared knowledge, solidified knowledge, increased motivation, and increased teamwork ability.

"The wise person learns from everyone."

ETHICS OF THE FATHERS

do questions

Shared knowledge. To have individual students pass on their knowledge to each other in a study group requires less time and energy than for each of those students to learn all of the material alone.

Solidified knowledge. When you discuss concepts or teach them to others, you reinforce what you know and strengthen your critical thinking. Part of the benefit comes from simply repeating information aloud and rewriting it on paper, and part comes from how you think through information before you pass it on to someone else.

Increased motivation. When you study by yourself, you are accountable to yourself alone. In a study group, however, others see your level of work and preparation, which may increase your motivation.

Increased teamwork ability. The more you understand the dynamics of working with a group and the more experience you have at it, the more you build your ability to work well with others.

Students taking the same course, who decide to work together, may form a group that meets one or more times a week or right before exams. Instructors sometimes also initiate study groups for their students. Known as peer-assisted study sessions or supplemental instruction, these groups are especially common in math and science courses.

Leaders and Participants

Study groups and other teams rely on both leaders and participants to accomplish goals. Becoming aware of the roles each plays will increase your effectiveness.[8] Keep in mind that participants sometimes perform leadership tasks and vice versa. In addition, some teams shift leadership frequently during a project.

Being an Effective Participant

Some people are most comfortable when participating in a group that someone else leads. Participants, however, are "part owners" of the team process with a responsibility for, and a stake in, the outcome. The following strategies will help you become more effective in this role.

- *Get involved.* Let people know your views on decisions.
- *Be organized.* The more focused your ideas, the more other group members will take them seriously.
- *Be willing to discuss.* Be open to the opinions of others, even if they differ from your own. Always be respectful.
- *Keep your word.* Carry out whatever tasks you promise to do.

Being an Effective Leader

Some people prefer to initiate the action, make decisions, and control how things proceed. Leaders often have a "big-picture" perspective that allows them to envision how different aspects of a group project will come together. The following strategies help a leader succeed.

- *Define and limit projects.* The leader should define the group's purpose (e.g., brainstorming, decision making, or project collaboration) and limit tasks so that the effort remains focused.

TAKE ACTION

Form a Study Group

Take the lead in forming a study group for one of your courses:

- Course name: _____

- Study group members (names, phone numbers, e-mail addresses):

  Member #1 _____

  Member #2 _____

  Member #3 _____

  Member #4 _____

- Regular meeting time and place: _____

- Three strategies you plan to use to make the most of group time:

  Strategy #1: _____

  Strategy #2: _____

  Strategy #3: _____

- *Assign work and set a schedule.* A group functions best when everyone has an assigned task and when deadlines are clear.

- *Set meeting and project agendas.* The leader should, with advice from other group members, establish and communicate goals and define how the work will proceed.

- *Focus progress.* It is the leader's job to keep everyone on target and headed in the right direction.

  - *Set the tone.* If the leader is fair, respectful, encouraging, and hard working, group members are likely to follow the example.

  - *Evaluate results.* The leader should determine whether the team is accomplishing its goals on schedule. If the team is not moving ahead, the leader should make changes.

Group study can be effective if participants are disciplined and dedicated. Choosing a leader, meeting at regular times, and setting goals all help groups accomplish their work.

Strategies for Study Group Success

Every study group is unique. The way a group operates may depend on the members' personalities, the subject you study, the location of the group, and the size of the group. No matter what your particular group's situation, though, certain general strategies will help.

Choose a leader for each meeting. Rotating the leadership, among members willing to lead, helps all members take ownership of the group. If a leader has to miss class for any reason, choose another leader for that meeting.

Set long-term and short-term goals. At your first meeting, determine what the group wants to accomplish over the semester. At the start of each meeting, have one person compile a list of questions to address.

Adjust to different personalities. The art of getting along will serve you well no matter what you do.

Share the workload. The most important factor is a willingness to work, not a particular level of knowledge.

Set a regular meeting schedule. Try every week, every two weeks, or whatever the group can manage.

Create study materials for one another. Give each group member the task of finding a piece of information to compile, photocopy, and review for the other group members.

Help each other learn. Have group members teach pieces of information, make up quizzes for each other, or go through flash cards together.

Pool your note-taking resources. Compare notes with your group members and fill in any information you don't have. Try different note-taking styles (see Chapter 7 for more on note taking).

I apply past knowledge to new situations.

Your mind is not a blank slate. On the contrary, it is filled with information, ideas, and practical applications you have gained from a lifetime of experience and reading. Just as there is no need to relearn the alphabet every time you open a book, there is no need to start from ground zero—the absence of knowledge—when you encounter new ideas in your texts. Your challenge is to place these ideas in the context of what you already know.

The successful use of the SQ3R study method depends on this Habit of Mind. When you approach a new assignment, ask yourself, "Have I seen this material before? What do I already know about it?" Similarly, when you develop questions that expand your knowledge base, ask yourself, "How does this new material fit into what I already know?" Critical readers understand that knowledge is all interconnected—and that integrating the old with the new will bring understanding to the next level.

This Habit of Mind is essential as you move from lower-level to higher-level courses in your major—for example, from an Introduction to Business to a Marketing course. Embracing this habit will also enrich your learning in seemingly unrelated courses. By understanding 20th-century world history, for example, you will be better able to appreciate the paintings of Frida Kahlo, the novels of Richard Wright, and the music of Bob Dylan.

HABITS OF MIND
MIND
HABITS OF MIND

1. What will help you understand what you read?

Your life experiences, prior knowledge, family background, and other factors affect reading comprehension. You can boost your comprehension by making reading part of your daily routine, thinking positively about your ability to understand, thinking critically to capture meaning, and making extra efforts to build a better vocabulary.

2. How can you set the stage for reading?

You can help prepare yourself to read by taking an active, positive approach to every reading assignment and by choosing a setting that will minimize distractions. It is also important to define your purpose for reading. The four main purposes are comprehension (of both general ideas and specific examples), critical evaluation, practical application, and pleasure.

Expanding your vocabulary is also essential. Vocabulary-building techniques include analyzing word parts—prefixes, roots, and suffixes—and using a dictionary to learn the meanings of new words.

Finally, becoming a faster reader is an important goal because your reading requirements in college have increased so much. Common problems include word-by-word reading, lack of concentration, vocalization and subvocalization, limited vocabulary, unconscious regression, and slow recovery time.

3. How can SQ3R help you own what you read?

SQ3R, the process of surveying, questioning, reading, reciting, and reviewing, encourages active studying. Surveying refers to previewing a book before studying it. During the questioning phase, you write questions linked to chapter headings. During the reading stage, you read the material in order to answer these questions and take notes. During the reciting stage, you answer the questions you raised by reciting aloud or silently to yourself, telling another person, or writing the answers in a notebook. The review stage involves skimming and rereading your notes.

4. How can you respond critically to what you read?

Critical-reading skills help you select important ideas, identify supporting examples, and ask questions about any text, developing an understanding of the material through evaluation and analysis. Critical reading involves the use of SQ3R to "taste" the material, asking questions based on the mind actions, and engaging critical-thinking processes (establishing the truth of what you read, evaluating its arguments, and analyzing its perspective).

5. How and why should you study with others?

Studying with one or more people can enhance your learning and improve teamwork skills that will serve you well in the workplace. Benefits include shared and solidified knowledge, increased motivation, and an increased ability to work with others. Strategies for effective group study include setting goals, sharing the workload, setting a meeting schedule, and respecting one another.

Name   *Date*

CRITICAL THINKING
APPLYING LEARNING TO LIFE

Studying a Text Page

The following page is from the chapter "Groups and Organizations" in the sixth edition of John J. Macionis's *Sociology*.[9] Apply SQ3R as you read the excerpt. Using what you learned in this chapter about study techniques, complete the questions that follow (some questions ask you to mark the page itself).

1. Identify the headings on the page and the relationship between them. Mark primary-level headings with a #1, secondary headings with a #2, and tertiary (third-level) headings with a #3. Which heading serves as an umbrella for the rest?

   #2

2. What do the headings tell you about the content of the page?

   It means to be a tip of the chapter

3. After reading the chapter headings, write two study questions.
   A. _____

   _____
   B. _____

   _____

4. Using a marker pen, highlight key phrases and sentences. Write short marginal notes to help you review the material at a later point.

5. After reading this page, list three concepts that you need to study.
   A. _____
   B. _____
   C. _____

SOCIAL GROUPS

Virtually everyone moves through life with a sense of belonging; this is the experience of group life. A **social group** refers to *two or more people who identify and interact with one another.* Human beings continually come together to form couples, families, circles of friends, neighborhoods, churches, businesses, clubs, and numerous large organizations. Whatever the form, groups encompass people with shared experiences, loyalties, and interests. In short, while maintaining their individuality, the members of social groups also think of themselves as a special "we."

Groups, Categories, and Crowds

People often use the term "group" imprecisely. We now distinguish the group from the similar concepts of category and crowd.

Category. A *category* refers to people who have some status in common. Women, single fathers, military recruits, homeowners, and Roman Catholics are all examples of categories.

Why are categories not considered groups? Simply because, while the individuals involved are aware that they are not the only ones to hold that particular status, the vast majority are strangers to one another.

Crowd. A *crowd* refers to a temporary cluster of individuals who may or may not interact at all. Students sitting in a lecture hall do engage one another and share some common identity as college classmates; thus, such a crowd might be called a loosely formed group. By contrast, riders hurtling along on a subway train or bathers enjoying a summer day at the beach pay little attention to one another and amount to an anonymous aggregate of people. In general, then, crowds are too transitory and impersonal to qualify as social groups.

The right circumstances, however, could turn a crowd into a group. People riding in a subway train that crashes under the city streets generally become keenly aware of their common plight and begin to help one another. Sometimes such extraordinary experiences become the basis for lasting relationships.

Primary and Secondary Groups

Acquaintances commonly greet one another with a smile and the simple phrase, "Hi! How are you?" The response is usually a well scripted, "Just fine, thanks, how about you?" This answer, of course, is often more formal than truthful. In most cases, providing a detailed account of how you are *really* doing would prompt the other person to beat a hasty and awkward exit.

Sociologists classify social groups by measuring them against two ideal types based on members' genuine level of personal concern. This variation is the key to distinguishing *primary* from *secondary* groups.

According to Charles Horton Cooley (1864–1929), a **primary group** is a *small social group whose members share personal and enduring relationships.* Bound together by primary relationships, individuals in primary groups typically spend a great deal of time together, engage in a wide range of common activities, and feel that they know one another well. Although not without periodic conflict, members of primary groups display sincere concern for each other's welfare. The family is every society's most important primary group.

Cooley characterized these personal and tightly integrated groups as *primary* because they are among the first groups we experience in life. In addition, the family and early play groups also hold primary importance in the socialization process, shaping attitudes, behavior, and social identity.

Source: Sociology 6/E by Macionis, © 1997. Reprinted by permission of Pearson Education, Inc., Upper Saddle River, NJ.

TEAM BUILDING
COLLABORATIVE SOLUTIONS

Organizing a Study Group

Organize a study group with three or four members of your class. At the group's first meeting:

- Using the techniques you learned in Chapter 2, write a mission statement for the group and create a weekly schedule.

- Talk about the specific ways you will work together. Discuss which of the following methods you want to try in the group: pooling your notes, acting as tutors and students to teach each other difficult concepts; making up, administering, and grading quizzes for each other; creating study flash cards; using SQ3R to review required readings.

As an initial group exercise, try the following:

- Review the study questions that you wrote for the *Sociology* excerpt. Each person should select one question to focus on while reading (no two people should have the same question). Group members should then re-read the excerpt individually, thinking about their questions as they read and answering them in writing.

- When you have finished reading critically, gather as a group. Each person should take a turn presenting the question, the response or answer that was derived through critical reading, and any other ideas that came up while reading. The other members of the group may then present any other ideas to add to the discussion. Continue until all group members have had a chance to present what they worked on.

Over several weeks, try the group study methods you have chosen. Then, individually, evaluate the methods. Decide on those that worked best for you—that helped you master the course material—and those with little value. Come together as a group to share your evaluations, and revise the group's methods based on a consensus of what worked best.

personal IMPROVEMENT *plan*

I commit to three reading and studying strategies to improve my study skills.
From this chapter, I choose three strategies that I think will help me.

Strategy 1: _to search the chapter._

Strategy 2: _____

Strategy 3: _____

I choose one strategy to focus on (circle this strategy above) and I will:

■ describe my goal—what I want to gain from using this strategy.

_____

_____

_____

■ describe in detail how I plan to use the strategy.

_____

_____

_____

■ describe how I will measure my progress toward the goal this semester.

_____

_____

_____

Activate the Habit of Mind

HABITS OF MIND
MIND

Here's how I will *apply past knowledge to new situations* to achieve this goal:

_____

_____

_____

_____

SUGGESTED READINGS

Armstrong, William H. and M. Willard Lampe II. *Barron's Pocket Guide to Study Tips: How to Study Effectively and Get Better Grades.* New York: Barron's Educational Series, 1990.

Chesla, Elizabeth. *Reading Comprehension Success: In 20 Minutes a Day, Second edition,* Garden Grove, CA: Learning Express, 1998.

Frank, Steven. *The Everything Study Book.* Holbrook, MA: Adams Media, 1996.

Luckie, William R., Wood Smethurst, and Sarah Beth Huntley. *Study Power Workbook: Exercises in Study Skills to Improve Your Learning and Your Grades.* Cambridge, MA: Brookline Books, 1999.

Silver, Theodore. *The Princeton Review Study Smart: Hands-on, Nuts and Bolts Techniques for Earning Higher Grades.* New York: Villard Books, 1996.

INTERNET RESOURCES

Academictips.org (study tips and links) www.academictips.org/

How to Study (study advice with valuable links) www.howtostudy.com

Prentice Hall Student Success Supersite Study Skills: www.prenhall.com/success/

SQ3R Method (information on this important study method) www.u.arizona.edu/ic/wrightr/other/sq3r.html

ENDNOTES

1. Sherwood Harris, *The New York Public Library Book of How and Where to Look It Up.* Englewood Cliffs, NJ: Prentice Hall, 1991, p. 13.

2. Steve Moidel, *Speed Reading.* Hauppauge, NY: Barron's Educational Series, 1994, p. 18.

3. Ibid.

4. Francis P. Robinson, *Effective Behavior.* New York: Harper & Row, 1941.

5. John Mack Faragher, et al., *Out of Many,* 3rd ed. Upper Saddle River, NJ: Prentice Hall, p. xxxvii.

6. Ophelia H. Hancock, *Reading Skills for College Students,* 5th ed. Upper Saddle River, NJ: Prentice Hall, 2001, pp. 54–59.

7. Excerpted from Lynn Quitman Troyka, *Simon & Schuster Handbook for Writers,* 5th ed. Upper Saddle River, NJ: Prentice Hall, 1999, p. 12.

8. Louis E. Boone, David L. Kurtz, and Judy R. Block, *Contemporary Business Communication.* Englewood Cliffs, NJ: Prentice Hall, 1994, pp. 489–99.

9. John J. Macionis, *Sociology,* 6th ed. Upper Saddle River, NJ: Prentice Hall, 1997, p. 174.

Check those statements that apply to you right now:

- ◼ Although I listen to my instructors, I often do not remember what they say.

- ◼ Even when I study hard, I can do poorly on exams.

- ◼ When I hear something I don't agree with, I argue with the instructor in my head.

- ◼ I have a good memory, but I would like to make it even better.

- ◼ I use memory games to help me remember important information.

- ◼ I think that mnemonic devices will help me remember more of what I study.

Listening and Memory

CONCENTRATING TO MASTER KNOWLEDGE

Listening with understanding and empathy.

"People with this Habit of Mind are able **to take on the diverse perspectives of others**. They gently demonstrate their understanding and empathy by recapping, building on, clarifying, or giving examples."

—ART COSTA

*When you **appreciate the words of others through their perspective**, not your own, you are engaged in empathetic listening. As an empathetic listener, you will hear what others fail to hear—and the knowledge and insight you gain will add immeasurably to your education.*

In this chapter, you explore answers to the following questions:

■ How can you become a better listener?

■ How does memory work?

■ How does the learning process help you retain information?

■ What memory strategies can improve recall?

■ How can you use mnemonic devices to boost your memory power?

The learning process begins with receiving knowledge, often through listening, and ends with retaining knowledge, through memory. One way to learn actively is to be a skilled listener. You take in countless bits of information as you listen to instructors, fellow students, and others. Compare your listening ability to a camera. Even when you see an image through the viewfinder, you may not be able to tell what it is until you carefully focus the lens. Similarly, careful listening will allow you to clarify what you hear.

You'll need to remember much of what you hear during lectures, labs, and class discussions. Often, you will be tested on this information, because you need to retain it to continue to learn and function. Imagine that you're a nursing student: Your A on an anatomy exam is only useful if you can remember the location and functions of the kidneys when you meet a patient. This chapter will help you become actively involved in listening and remembering so that you can learn new material and hang on to it for the long term.

How can you become a better listener?

listening
A process that involves sensing, interpreting, evaluating, and reacting to spoken messages.

The act of hearing isn't quite the same as the act of **listening**. *Hearing* refers to sensing spoken messages from their source. *Listening* involves a complex process of communication. Successful listening occurs when the listener understands the speaker's intended message. In school and at home, poor listening may cause communication breakdowns and mistakes. Skilled listening, however, promotes progress and success. The good news is that listening is a teachable—and learnable—skill.

To see how complex listening can be, look at Figure 6.1. The left-hand column contains an excerpt from a typical classroom lecture on peer-group influence during adolescence, and the right-hand column records some examples of what an 18- or 19-year-old student might be thinking while the instructor is speaking. The column on the right reveals the complexity of listening, as well as some of the barriers that block communication.

As the figure shows, this student doesn't focus consistently on the information presented. Instead, she reacts to specific parts of the message and gets caught up in evaluating and judging what she hears. Understanding the listening process and why people may have trouble listening well can help you overcome these barriers.

Know the Stages of Listening

Listening is made up of four stages that build on one another: sensing, interpreting, evaluating, and reacting. These stages take the message from the speaker to the listener and back to the speaker (see Figure 6.2).

The complexity of listening.   FIGURE 6.1

A peer group is a social group made up of members with a lot in common. During adolescence, common interests often center on dating, popular music, clothing, and sports.

"Peer groups!" I've heard that term before. I'd better take notes; it'll probably be on the test.

The appeal of the group often comes from the fact that adults would not approve of what group members are doing. As a result, illicit activities—such as car racing, alcohol abuse, and drugs—are often the most popular.

What's this guy saying? That my friends and I do things just because our parents would object? Yeah, I guess I want to be different, but gimme a break! I don't drink and drive. I don't do drugs. I don't ignore my school work. Anyway, I'd better remember the connection between peer group popularity and adult disapproval. What were his exact words? I wish I remembered . . . on second thought maybe he has a point. I know kids who do things just to get a rise out of their parents.

Peer groups exert such a strong influence during adolescence because they give students the opportunity to form social relationships that are separate and apart from the one they have with their families. This is a time of rebellion and breaking away: a rough time for both adolescents and their parents.

Is it lunchtime yet? I'm really hungry! Stop thinking of food and start listening . . . back to work! Yeah, he's right, social relationships that have nothing to do with my family are important to me. I'd better write this down.

The good news for parents is that peer group pressure is generally strongest during adolescence. Teens achieve a greater balance between the influence of family and friends as the years pass. This doesn't make it any easier for parents trying to persuade their sons and daughters not to dye their hair green or pierce their eyebrows, but at least it tells them that the rebellion is temporary.

Why is he talking down to us? Why is he reassuring parents instead of focusing on how hard it is for teens to deal with life? He must be a parent himself . . . I wish those guys behind me would stop talking! I can't hear the lecture . . . there's a generation gap coming from the front of the room that's the size of the Grand Canyon! What's wrong with green hair and pierced eyebrows? He sounds like he knows all the answers and that we'll eventually see the light. I'm going to ask him how teens are supposed to act when they believe that their parents' values are wrong. Now, how should I word my question . . .

During the *sensation* stage (also known as hearing) your ears pick up sound waves and transmit them to the brain. For example, you are sitting in class and hear your instructor say, "The only opportunity to make up last week's test is Tuesday at 5:00 P.M."

In the *interpretation* stage, listeners attach meaning to a message. This involves understanding what is being said and relating it to what you already know. You relate this message to your knowledge of the test, whether you need to make it up, and what you are doing on Tuesday at 5:00 P.M.

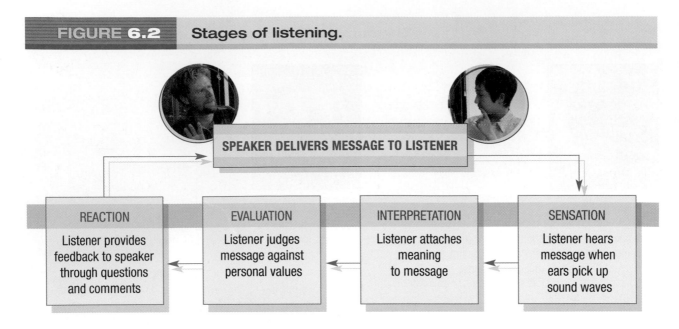

FIGURE 6.2   Stages of listening.

SPEAKER DELIVERS MESSAGE TO LISTENER

REACTION	EVALUATION	INTERPRETATION	SENSATION
Listener provides feedback to speaker through questions and comments	Listener judges message against personal values	Listener attaches meaning to message	Listener hears message when ears pick up sound waves

In the *evaluation* stage of listening, you decide how you feel about the message, whether, for example, you like it or agree with it. This involves evaluating the message as it relates to your needs and values. If the message goes against your values or does not fulfill your needs, you may reject it, stop listening, or argue in your mind with the speaker. In this example, if you do need to make up the test but have to work Tuesday at 5:00 P.M., you may evaluate the message as less than satisfactory. As you saw in Figure 6.1, what happens during the evaluation phase can interfere with listening.

The final stage of listening is a *reaction* to the message in the form of direct feedback. In a classroom, direct feedback often comes in the form of questions and comments. Your reaction, in this case, may be to ask the instructor if she can schedule another test time. If the student in Figure 6.1 actually asks a question, she will give the instructor the opportunity to clarify the lecture, or perhaps to add information.

Improving your listening skills involves two primary actions: managing listening challenges (maximizing the sensation stage) and becoming an active listener (maximizing the interpretation and evaluation stages).

For those who are deaf, effective listening involves a strong visual and physical component. Here, students at Gallaudet University use sign language as they communicate.

Manage Listening Challenges

Classic studies have shown that immediately after listening, students are likely to recall only half of what was said. This is partly due to such listening challenges as divided attention and distractions, the tendency to shut out the message, the inclination to rush to judgment, and partial hearing loss or learning disabilities.[1] As you will see next, there are ways to minimize these challenges.

Divided Attention and Distractions

Although you are capable of listening to more than one message at the same time, you may not completely hear or understand any of them. Learning to focus your attention—even as it is being pulled in different directions—is one of your most important listening challenges.

Internal and external distractions often divide your attention. *Internal distractions* include anything from hunger to headache to personal worries. Something the speaker says may also trigger a recollection that may cause your mind to drift. In contrast, *external distractions* include noises (whispering, police sirens) and excessive heat or cold. It can be hard to listen in an overheated room that is putting you to sleep.

Your goal is to reduce distractions so that you can concentrate on what you're hearing. Sitting near the front of the room where you can clearly see and hear will help, as will moving away from others who are chatting. You'll listen better if you are relaxed, comfortable, and alert. Work to concentrate on class when you're in class and save worrying about personal problems for later. Get enough sleep to stay alert, eat enough to avoid hunger pangs, and dress comfortably.

"No one cares to speak to an unwilling listener. An arrow never lodges in a stone: often it recoils upon the sender of it."

ST. JEROME

Shutting Out the Message

Although instructors are responsible for communicating information, they cannot force you to listen. The responsibility to listen consistently is in your hands. If students perceive that a subject is difficult or uninteresting, they may tune out and miss information that forms the foundation for what comes next. It's also tough to refocus after this kind of listening lapse.

One way to avoid this situation is to remind yourself that what your instructors say in class is valuable even if it is not obvious or not in the textbook. Instructors often present non-text material in class and include that material on tests. If you work to take in the whole message in class, you will be able to read over your notes later, compare your notes to what you learned in the text, and think critically about what is important. If you do experience a listening lapse, the best strategy is to refocus your concentration quickly on what is being said, instead of worrying about tuning out. Connect with a study buddy to clarify any material that you missed.

The Rush to Judgment

As Figure 6.1 illustrates, people may stop listening when they hear something they don't like. Their focus turns to their personal reactions and away from the content of the speaker's message. Students who disagree during a lecture often spend valuable class time figuring out how to word a question or comment in response.

reflect

Describe what goes through your head while you listen to an instructor with whom you disagree. Do you stop listening? Do you get caught up in an internal argument? Do you spend your time figuring out how to respond? Do your feelings hinder your ability to focus? Brainstorm ways of listening more effectively the next time this situation occurs.

& respond

Judgments also involve reactions to the speakers themselves. If you do not like your instructors or if you have preconceived notions about their ideas or cultural background, you may decide that their words have little value. Anyone whose words have ever been ignored because of race, ethnic background, gender, or disability understands how prejudice can interfere with listening.

Although it is human nature to stop listening, at times, in reaction to a speaker or message, this tendency can get in the way of your education. Before you give in to your inclination to tune out, think about this:

- An important part of your education involves using your critical-thinking skills to evaluate other points of view—even those radically different from your own. Stay open to the possibility that your instructor may say something to change your mind.

- No one is compelling you to like every instructor. But academic integrity requires that you listen respectfully. It is to your benefit to listen with an open mind.

Partial Hearing Loss and Learning Disabilities

If you have some level of hearing loss, seek out special services, including tutoring and equipment that can help you listen in class. For example, listening to a tape of a lecture at a higher-than-normal volume can help you hear things you missed in the classroom. Meeting with your instructor outside of class to clarify your notes may help. You may also wish to sit up close in class.

Other disabilities, such as attention deficit disorder (ADD) or a problem with processing spoken language, can add to listening difficulties. People with these problems may have trouble paying attention or understanding what they hear. While some find ways to compensate for their listening problems, others continue to struggle. If you have a disability that creates a listening challenge, seek help through your counseling or student health center, an advisor, or an instructor. An interview on page 46 with one of the authors deals directly with this problem.

Become an Active Listener

On the surface, listening seems like a passive activity: you sit back and listen as someone else speaks. Effective listening, however, is really an active process that involves setting a purpose for listening, asking questions, paying attention to **verbal signposts**, and knowing what helps and hinders listening.

Verbal signposts Spoken words or phrases that call your attention to the information that follows.

Set Purposes for Listening

In any situation, establish what you want to achieve through listening, such as understanding the material better or mastering a specific task. Many instructors state their purpose at the start of the class. A political science instructor might say, for example, "Today, we're going to talk about campaign financing." Listening carefully to the purpose and writing it down will help you focus on the message.

Ask Questions

A willingness to ask questions shows a desire to learn and is the mark of an active listener and critical thinker. *Clarifying* questions state your understanding of what you have just heard and ask if that understanding is correct. Whereas some clarifying questions focus on a key concept or theme ("So, some learning disorders can be improved with treatment?") others highlight specific facts ("Is it true that dyslexia can cause people to reverse letters and words?"). (For the role questions play in critical thinking, see Chapter 4.)

Although questions and comments turn you into an active participant, they may sometimes divert your attention from the speaker. One way to avoid this is to jot down your questions quickly and come back to them during a discussion period. When you know that your question is on paper, you can relax and listen to everything that is said.

Pay Attention to Verbal Signposts

Speakers' choice of words may tell you a lot about the information they consider important and help you predict test questions. For example, an idea described as "new and exciting" or "classic" is more likely to be on a test than one described as "interesting." Verbal signposts often involve transition words and phrases that help organize information, connect ideas, and indicate what is important and what is not. Let phrases like those in Table 6.1 direct your attention to the material that follows.

Know What Helps and Hinders Listening

Ralph G. Nichols, a pioneer in listening research, defined the characteristics of successful and unsuccessful listeners by studying 200 freshmen at the

Pay attention to verbal signposts.	TABLE 6.1

SIGNALS POINTING TO KEY CONCEPTS	SIGNALS OF SUPPORT
There are two reasons for this . . .	For example, . . .
A critical point in the process involves . . .	Specifically, . . .
Most important, . . .	For instance, . . .
The result is . . .	Similarly, . . .

SIGNALS POINTING TO DIFFERENCES	SIGNALS THAT SUMMARIZE
On the contrary, . . .	Finally, . . .
On the other hand, . . .	Recapping this idea, . . .
In contrast, . . .	In conclusion, . . .
However, . . .	As a result, . . .

TABLE 6.2   Factors that help and hinder listening.

LISTENING IS HELPED BY . . .	LISTENING IS HINDERED BY . . .
. . . making a conscious decision to work at listening; viewing difficult material as a listening challenge.	. . . caring little about the listening process; tuning out difficult material.
. . . fighting distractions through intense concentration.	. . . refusing to listen at the first distraction.
. . . continuing to listen when a subject is difficult or dry, in the hope that one might learn something interesting.	. . . giving up as soon as one loses interest.
. . . withholding judgment until hearing everything.	. . . becoming preoccupied with a response as soon as a speaker makes a controversial statement.
. . . focusing on the speaker's theme by recognizing organizational patterns, transitional language, and summary statements.	. . . getting sidetracked by unimportant details.
. . . adapting note-taking style to the unique style and organization of the speaker.	. . . always taking notes in outline form, even when a speaker is poorly organized, leading to frustration.
. . . pushing past negative emotional responses and forcing oneself to continue to listen.	. . . letting an initial emotional response disrupt listening.
. . . using excess thinking time to evaluate, summarize, and question what one just heard and anticipate what will come next.	. . . thinking about other things and, as a result, missing much of the message.

reflect

After reading Table 6.2, how would you describe your listening attitude? Be specific: note the factors that apply most often to you, and how these factors affect your ability to listen. Why do you think attitude is so important to listening success?

& respond

University of Minnesota over a nine-month period. His findings, summarized in Table 6.2, demonstrate that effective listening depends as much on a positive attitude as on specific skills.[2]

Although effective listening will enable you to acquire knowledge, retaining that knowledge demands that you remember what you hear, read, and study. A good memory is the result of skills that improve with practice.

How does memory work?

Your accounting instructor is giving a test tomorrow on key concepts involved in preparing income tax returns. You feel confident because you spent hours last week memorizing your notes from class lectures

TAKE ACTION

Change Your Listening Habits

Think about your personal listening habits in the classroom. Then complete the following:

- Look again at Table 6.2. Which habits, helpful or not so helpful, are part of your listening pattern?

  _____

  _____

- How do you react when you strongly disagree with something your instructor says—when you are convinced that you are "right" and your instructor is "wrong"?

  _____

  _____

- If one of the purposes of a college education is to open you to new ideas and opinions, how do feelings of being "right" affect your education?

  _____

  _____

- List two changes you could make in your listening habits that would improve your performance in college.

  1. _____

  2. _____

and from the text. Unfortunately, by the time you take the test, you may remember very little. This is not surprising, since most forgetting occurs within minutes after memorization.

In a classic study conducted in 1885, researcher Herman Ebbinghaus memorized a list of meaningless three-letter words such as CEF and LAZ. He then examined how quickly he forgot them. Within one hour he had forgotten more than 50 percent of what he had learned; after two days, he knew fewer than 30 percent of the memorized words. Although Ebbinghaus's recall of the nonsense syllables remained fairly stable after that, his experiment shows how fragile memory can be—even when you take the time and expend the energy to memorize information.[3]

If forgetting is so common, why do some people have better memories than others? Some may have an inborn talent for remembering. More often, though, they succeed because they have practiced and mastered techniques for improving recall.

How Your Brain Remembers: Short-Term and Long-Term Memory

Learning is a physical process—your brain undergoes physical changes when you hear, interpret, and work to remember a piece of information. Understanding how your brain commits information to memory will strengthen your ability to remember things.

Memories are stored in three different "storage banks" in your brain. The first, called *sensory memory*, is an exact copy of what you see and hear and lasts for a second or less. Certain information is then selected from sensory memory and moved into *short-term memory*, a temporary information storehouse that lasts no more than 10 to 20 seconds. You are consciously aware of material in your short-term memory. Unimportant information is quickly dumped. Important information is transferred to *long-term memory*—the mind's more permanent information storehouse.

Although all three stages of memory are important, targeting long-term memory will solidify learning the most. "Short-term—or working—memory is useful when we want to remember a phone number until we can dial or an e-mail address until we can type it in to the computer," says biologist James Zull. "We use short-term memory for these momentary challenges, all the time, every day, but it is limited in capacity, tenacity, and time."[4] Zull explains that short-term memory can only hold small amounts of information for brief periods of time. In addition, it is unstable—a distraction can easily bump information out of short-term memory.

How does the learning process help you retain information?

In order to retain information in long-term memory, your brain needs to move through the *learning process*. This process has four stages and relates directly to the stages of the listening process described on pages 169–170. Figure 6.3 illustrates the process.

1. *Experiencing* the material (*concrete experience*). Your brain takes in the information through one or more of your senses.
2. *Relating* the material to what you already know (*reflexive observation*). You reflect on the new information and connect it to previous knowledge.
3. *Forming* new ideas (*abstract hypothesis*). You come up with new insights from the combination of what you knew before and what you are learning now.
4. *Trying out and communicating* new ideas (*active testing*). You explore your ideas to see if they make sense and work.

Here's an example to illustrate the process.

1. In your Introduction to Business course, you hear the following information during the lecture: "During the economic bubble of the 1990s, ethical lapses were frequent at the highest levels of business. Among the major corporations involved in ethical abuses were Enron, Citibank, Merrill Lynch, and Tyco. Corporate executives at these companies bent the rules and ignored the law to maximize personal gain."

The stages of the learning process. **FIGURE 6.3**

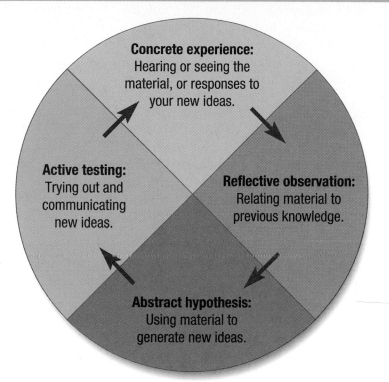

2. You think about the material in relation to what you know. First, you remember reading about the unethical practices of the billionaires of the 1930s, including J.P. Morgan and Andrew Carnegie, who built corporate empires and amassed personal fortunes—through unethical business practices. Second, you think about ethical and unethical behavior you have seen in people you know personally.

3. You form a new idea: Government regulations are necessary to curb the all-too-human tendency to bend rules for personal gain.

4. You try out your idea by talking to various students and thinking further about your own ideas.

   Result: Information about business ethics is solidly anchored in long-term memory.

Moving Knowledge into Long-Term Memory

Here are some pointers for how to use the learning process to anchor information in long-term memory:

Limit and organize the items you are processing. This involves two key activities that you perform during the observation stage of learning:

- *Separate main points from unimportant details.* Ask yourself: What is the most important information? Highlight only the key points in your texts, and write notes in the margins about central ideas. See the example in Figure 5.5 on page 149.

■ *Divide material into manageable sections.* Generally, when material is short and easy to understand, studying it from start to finish improves recall. With longer material, however, you may benefit from dividing it into logical sections, mastering each section, putting all the sections together, and then testing your memory of all the material. Actors take this approach when learning the lines of a play, and it can work just as well for students trying to learn new concepts.

Use critical thinking. Many of the critical-thinking mind actions encourage you to associate new information with your current knowledge. In this "abstract hypothesis" stage of the learning process, you reference and rearrange knowledge in your mind to form new relationships and ideas. Imagine that you have to remember information about a specific historical event—for example, the signing of the Treaty of Versailles, the agreement that ended World War II. You might put the mind actions to work in the following ways:

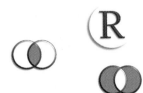

Recall everything that you know about the topic.

Think about how this event is *similar* to other events in history.

Consider what is *different* and unique about this treaty in comparison to other treaties.

Explore the *causes* that led up to this event, and look at the event's *effects*.

From the general *idea* of treaties that ended wars, explore other *examples* of such treaties.

Think about *examples* of what happened during the treaty signing, and from those examples come up with *ideas* about the tone of the event.

Looking at the facts of the event, *evaluate* how successful you think the treaty was.

Seek the big picture. When you look at the overall organization of a body of material, you will find a framework within which to remember the details. This corresponds to the active testing stage of the learning process—you try out your idea of the big picture, seeing if the details fit well into and support that idea. As you progress in your course work, fewer books will contain the structure your survey texts and classes have. When you cannot rely on the text or instructor for structure, looking for the big picture will help you shape your learning.

You are the creator of your own learning. Following are more suggestions to help you take responsibility for what you remember in the short and the long term.

What memory strategies can improve recall?

As a student, your job is to understand, learn, and remember information—everything from general concepts to specific details. The following strategies will help improve your recall.

Have Purpose and Intention

Why can you remember the lyrics to dozens of popular songs but not the functions of the pancreas? Perhaps this is because you *want* to remember the lyrics or you have an emotional tie to them. To achieve the same results at school, try to create in yourself the purpose and will to remember.

For example, as a student in a city-planning course, it may be easier for you to remember the complex rules surrounding federal, state, and local housing subsidies if you think about the families, including the children and the elderly, who benefit from these programs. If someone you know lives in a city housing project, the personal connection will probably make it easier to remember these rules.

Fear and boredom can stifle the will to remember. Deal directly with any fears. If you fear the material, for example, you might get to know the instructor during office hours, prepare more before class, or organize your notes better. To fight boredom, focus on how you need to know and use what you are learning. Boredom disappears when information becomes important to you.

Genuine interest and passion for a subject are invaluable memory tools. When you care about something, your brain responds differently, and learning is easier.

> *"The true art of memory is the art of attention."*

SAMUEL JOHNSON

Understand What You Memorize

Something that has meaning is easier to recall than something that makes little sense. This basic principle applies to everything you study—from biology and astronomy to history and English literature. Determine the logical connections in the information and use these connections to help you learn. For example, in a plant biology course, memorize plant families; in a history course, memorize events by linking them chronologically or in a cause-and-effect chain.

The best way to guarantee that concepts become part of your long-term memory is to understand them inside and out. With a depth of learning comes the framework on which to place related concepts. Thus, if you are having trouble remembering something new, think about how the new idea fits into what you already know. A simple example: If a new vocabulary word puzzles you try to identify the word's root, prefix, or suffix. Knowing that the root *bellum* means "war" and the prefix *ante* means "before" will help you recognize and remember that *antebellum* means "before the war."

Finally, use organizational tools, such as an outline or a think link (see Chapter 7 for more on these note-taking techniques), to record the material you want to recall and the logical connections among the elements. These tools will expose gaps in your understanding as they help you study and learn.

Recite, Rehearse, and Write

When you *recite* material, you repeat key concepts aloud, in your own words, to help you memorize them. *Rehearsing* is similar to reciting but is done

In lecture courses, listening carefully is an important aspect of improving your memory. Pay attention, focus on key points, and take effective notes.

silently. It is the process of mentally repeating, summarizing, and associating information with other information. *Writing* is reciting on paper. All three processes actively involve you in learning and memorizing material.

You will get the greatest benefit if you separate your learning into the following steps:

- Focus as you read on the key points you want to remember. These are usually found in the topic sentences of paragraphs. Then recite, rehearse, or write the ideas down.

- Convert each main idea into a key word or phrase—something that is easy to recall and that will set off a chain of memories that will bring you back to the original information. Write each key word or phrase on an index card.

- One by one, look at the key words on your cards and recite, rehearse, or write all the associated information you can recall. Check your recall against your original material.

Reciting, rehearsing, and writing involve much more than simply rereading material—that is, parroting words out loud, in your head, or on paper. Because rereading does not necessarily require any depth of involvement, you can reread without thinking or learning. However, you cannot help but think and learn as you convert text concepts into key points, rewrite key points as key words and phrases, and judge your learning by assessing what you know and what you still need to learn.

Study During Short, Frequent Sessions

Research has shown that you can improve your chances of remembering material if you learn it more than once. To get the most out of your study sessions, spread them over time. A pattern of short sessions followed by brief periods of rest is more effective than continual studying with little or no rest. Even though you may feel as though you accomplish a lot by studying for an hour without a break, you'll probably remember more from three 20-minute sessions. With this in mind, try studying during breaks in your schedule. Although studying between classes isn't for everyone, you may find that it can help you remember more information.

Sleep can actually aid memory because it reduces interference from new information. Since you can't always go to sleep immediately after studying for an exam, try postponing the study of other subjects until your exam is over. When studying for several tests at once, avoid studying two similar subjects back to back. Your memory is likely to be more accurate when you study history right after biology rather than, for example, chemistry after biology.

Practice the Middle

When you are trying to learn something, you usually study some material first, attack other material in the middle of the session, and approach still other topics at the end. The weak link in your recall is likely to be the material you study midway. It pays to give this material special attention in the form of extra practice.

Create Groupings

When items do not have to be remembered in any particular order, the act of **grouping** can help you recall them better. Say, for example, that you have to memorize these five 10-digit numbers:

9806875087   9876535703   7636983561   6724472879   3122895312

It may look impossible. If you group the numbers to look like telephone numbers, however, the job may become more manageable:

(980) 687–5087   (987) 653–5703   (763) 698–3561   (672) 447–2879
(312) 289–5312

In general, try to limit groups to around 10 items or fewer. It's hard to memorize more at one time.

> *Grouping*
> Forming digestible information segments that are easy to remember.

Use Flash Cards

Flash cards are a great visual memory tool. They give you short, repeated review sessions that provide immediate feedback, and they are portable, which gives you the flexibility to use them wherever you go. Use the front of a 3-by-5-inch index card to write a word, idea, or phrase you want to remember. Use the back for a definition, explanation, and other key facts. Figure 6.4 shows two flash cards used to study for a psychology exam.

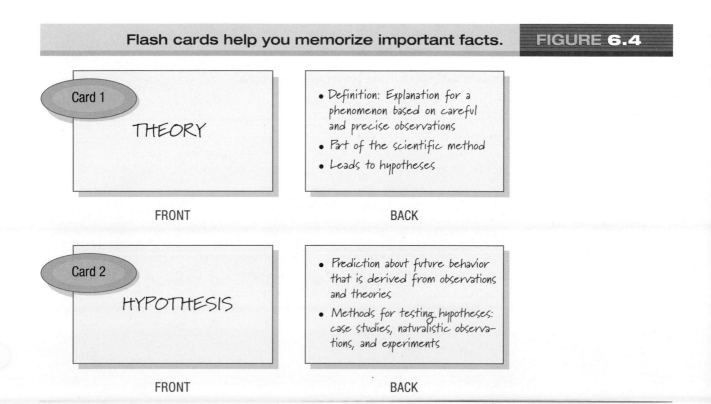

Flash cards help you memorize important facts.   **FIGURE 6.4**

Card 1

FRONT: THEORY

BACK:
- Definition: Explanation for a phenomenon based on careful and precise observations
- Part of the scientific method
- Leads to hypotheses

FRONT   BACK

Card 2

FRONT: HYPOTHESIS

BACK:
- Prediction about future behavior that is derived from observations and theories
- Methods for testing hypotheses: case studies, naturalistic observations, and experiments

FRONT   BACK

Here are some suggestions for making the most of your flash cards:

- *Use the cards as a self-test.* As you go through them, divide them into two piles—the material you know and the material you are learning.
- *Carry the cards with you and review them frequently.* You'll learn the most if you start using cards early in the course, well ahead of exam time.
- *Shuffle the cards and learn the information in various orders.* This will help you avoid putting too much focus on some information and not enough on other.
- *Test yourself in both directions.* First, look at the terms and provide the definitions or explanations. Then turn the cards over and reverse the process.
- *Reduce the stack as you learn.* You can eliminate cards as you are certain of your knowledge. Watching the pile get smaller is a reward that reinforces your motivation. As test time approaches, put all the cards together again for a final review.

Use Tape-Recorded Material

Questions on tape can work like audio flash cards. One method is to record short-answer study questions, leaving 10 to 15 seconds between questions for you to answer out loud. Recording the correct answer after the pause will give you immediate feedback. For example, part of a recording for a writing class might say, "The three elements of effective writing are . . . (10–15 seconds). . . topic, audience, and purpose."

TAKE ACTION
Analyze How Memorizing and Critical Thinking Help You Master Course Material

Identify the course you are most interested in this semester and the role memorization and critical thinking are likely to play in your success in the course. Then complete the following:

- Describe some material you will have to memorize.

  Learning to learn.

- Describe the specific ways in which you will use one or more of the critical-thinking mind actions to help you retain the material.

  Review the chapter

Working through every mind action might take time; you don't always have to use every one in every memory situation. Choose the ones that will help you most. The more information and ideas you can associate with the new item you're trying to remember, the more successful you will be.

How can you use mnemonic devices to boost memory power?

accronem

Certain performers entertain their audiences by remembering the names of 100 strangers or flawlessly repeating 30 ten-digit phone numbers. Although these performers probably have superior memories, they also rely on memory techniques, known as **mnemonic devices** (pronounced neh-MAHN-ick), for assistance.

Mnemonic devices depend on vivid associations (relating new information to other information). Instead of learning new facts by rote (repetitive practice), associations give you a "hook" on which to hang these facts and retrieve them later. Mnemonic devices make information familiar and meaningful through unusual, unforgettable mental associations and visual pictures.

There are different kinds of mnemonic devices, including visual images and associations and acronyms. Study how these devices work, then apply them to your own memory challenges. As you will see, these devices take time and effort to create, and you'll have to be motivated to remember the device itself. Because of this, it is smart to use mnemonic devices only when you really need them—for instance, to distinguish confusing concepts that consistently trip you up, to remember lists, or to recall items in order.

Mnemonic devices
Memory techniques that involve associating new information with information you already know.

Create Visual Images and Associations

When you link visual images to specific information, you strengthen the likelihood that you will remember the information. The best mental images often involve bright colors, three dimensions, action scenes, inanimate objects with human traits, ridiculousness, and humor.

> *"Memory is the stepping-stone to thinking, because without remembering facts, you cannot think, conceptualize, reason make decisions, create, or contribute."*
>
> **HARRY LORAYNE**

Turning information into mental pictures helps improve memory, especially for visual learners. To remember that the Spanish artist Picasso painted "The Three Women," you might imagine the women in a circle dancing to a Spanish song with a pig and a donkey (pig-asso). The more outlandish the image the better, since these images are the most memorable.

Here is another example: Say you are trying to learn some basic Spanish vocabulary, including the words *carta, rio,* and *dinero.* Instead of trying to learn these words by rote, you might come up with mental images such as those in Table 6.3 on page 186.

Use Visual Images to Remember Items in a List

Three mental imagery techniques will help you remember items in a list: taking a mental walk in a familiar place, forming an idea chain, and using the number/shape mnemonic.

Using the *mental walk* strategy, you imagine that you store new ideas in familiar locations. Say, for example, that for your biology course you have to remember the major endocrine glands, starting in the brain and working downward through the body. To do this, think of the route you take to the library. You pass the college theater, the science center, the bookstore, the cafeteria, the athletic center, and the social science building before reaching the library. At each spot along the route, you "place" the idea or concept you want to learn. You then link the concept with a similar-sounding word that brings to mind a vivid image (see Figure 6.5 on page 187):

- At the campus theater, you imagine bumping into the actor Brad **Pitt,** who is holding **two** cell phones and has a **terri**ble cold (pituitary gland).
- At the science center, you visualize Mr. Universe with bulging **thighs.** When you are introduced, you learn that his name is **Roy** (thyroid gland).
- At the campus bookstore, you envision a second Mr. Universe with his **thighs** covered in **mus**tard (thymus gland).
- In the cafeteria, you see an **ad** for **Dean Al** for president (adrenal gland).
- At the athletic center, you visualize a student throwing a ball into a **pan** and **cre**atures applauding from the bleachers (pancreas).
- At the social science building, you imagine receiving a standing **ovation** (ovaries).

RISING
TO THE CHALLENGE

Michael Sanders

After years of struggle with languages, peaking with a frustrated college teacher calling him "the only problem" in the class, Michael Sanders looked for a reason behind his trouble. A diagnosis provided fuel for improvement and inspiration for figuring out how to cope.

My experience with learning foreign languages at college has been disturbing and disheartening at best. During my sophomore and junior years, I was working to complete the college's foreign language requirement. When I was unable to complete several courses, I was evaluated . . . to determine whether I had certain processing weaknesses associated with language learning. [I] found that I have great difficulty processing novel language forms. I have very real problems in hearing individual syllables and the pronunciation of words in other languages, which makes it difficult for me to distinguish some words from others, and thus to participate actively in class.

Though I had these problems with languages in high school, I was unaware that they could be attributed to a learning disability. It was not until I went to college that my learning disability was identified. Because students at my university are required to complete the language requirement by the end of their sophomore year, I had been forced to take language courses term after term.

When I saw a pattern of problems developing over time in my language courses, I told my parents first. Their initial reaction was to tell me I should work harder. They instructed me to get a tutor, see my professor during his office hours, and check with the Academic Skills Center to see what I could do to improve my study habits. What they did not know was that I had long since done all of these things. Being unaware of what a language disability was and some of the problems associated with it, my parents . . . told me that I didn't do well because I didn't work hard enough. . . . I just think their lack of knowledge made them less likely to respond as I needed.

My girlfriend, who is bilingual, was . . . very supportive and tried to offer her assistance. Being of Spanish descent, Manuela speaks both English and Spanish fluently, and is also proficient in French. When I came to her with my problems, she offered all of the assistance that she could, including tutoring, special help with essays, and vocabulary exercises. But this didn't help much either—I continued to get low grades on my essays and fail my exams.

As I took more language courses and continued to have problems, I began to explain to my parents that I thought I had a learning disability. I told them what it was, describing my problems to them in terms of known problems associated with learning disabilities, and I asked for their advice. At this point, they began to respond in a different manner. When they learned that my lack of progress in languages was likely due to difficulties and weaknesses that to a certain extent I could not control, together we began to seek help in identifying and dealing with my problems.

I do not tell everyone that I have a learning disability explicitly, but many of them know at least that I have had problems with languages. The fact that my friendships rest on firm foundations reassures me emotionally and helps me deal with what is perceived as a disadvantage in a positive way. When I matriculated, I had no idea what lay in store for me. I was unaware of the difficulties I would encounter due to my learning disability. However, as I've progressed both academically and personally, I know I have experienced difficulties and problems that would have precluded my success if I had been of weaker character. These experiences have been critical factors in shaping who I am.

Take a Moment to Consider . . .

- *When someone's opinion of you has hurt or helped you, and how.*
- *What factors in your life have shaped who you are.*

- And at the library, you visualize sitting at a table taking a **test** that is **easy** (testes).

An *idea chain* is a memory strategy in which you form exaggerated mental images that are linked together to tell a story. The first image is connected to the second image, which is connected to the third image, and so on. Here, too, vivid, humorous images aid recall.

Imagine, for example, that you want to remember the seven mind actions that appear in the critical-thinking chapter: recall, similarity, difference, cause and effect, example to idea, idea to example, and evaluation. You can use the visual icons to form an idea chain that goes like this:

The letter R rolls down a hill (recall) and bumps into two similar intersecting circles (similarity) that start rolling and bump into two different intersecting circles (difference). Everything rolls past a sign with two circling arrows on it telling them to keep rolling (cause and effect), and then bumps into an "EX" at the bottom of the hill, which turns on a lightbulb (example to idea). That lightbulb shines on another "EX" (idea to example). The two "EX"s are sitting on either side of a set of scales (evaluation).

The *number/shape mnemonic* will help you remember items in a specific order by linking each to a vivid image that is associated with the number. Start by creating images in the forms of shapes for the numbers—in this case 1 through 10—like those in Table 6.4 on page 188. (These images can be used over and over again for different lists you need to remember.) Then link the shape you have associated with each number with the information you want to remember (see the right column in Table 6.4). In this case, the student is trying to remember the moons of the planet Uranus in order of their distance from the planet.

Create Acronyms

Another helpful association method involves the use of the **acronym.** In history class, you can remember the Allies during World War II—Britain, America, and Russia—with the acronym BAR. This is an example of a *word acronym,* because the first letters of the items you want to remember

TAKE ACTION

Create Your Own Mnemonic

Identify specific content you have to memorize for one of your courses. Then complete the following:

- Create a mnemonic device to help you memorize all the details. (If you need more space, use a separate sheet of paper.)

  _____

  _____

- Describe the types of visual images you used in the mnemonic. Were they humorous, ridiculous, or colorful?

  _____

  _____

- Why do you think these types of images help you?

  _____

  _____

TABLE 6.3   **Visual images aid recall.**

SPANISH WORD	DEFINITION	MENTAL IMAGE
carta	letter	A person pushing a shopping cart filled with letters into a post office.
rio	river	A school of sharks rioting in the river. One of the sharks is pulling a banner inscribed with the word *riot*. A killer shark bites off the *t* in riot as he takes charge of the group. "I'm the king of this river," he says.
dinero	money	A man is eating lasagna at a diner. The lasagna is made of layers of money.

Acronym
A word formed from the first letters of a series of words, created in order to help you remember the series.

spell a word. The word (or words) spelled don't necessarily have to be real words; see Figure 6.6 on page 188 for an acronym—the name Roy G. Biv—that will help you remember the colors of the spectrum.

Other acronyms take the form of an entire sentence in which the first letter of each word in each sentence stands for the first letter of the memorized term. This is called a *list order acronym*. For example, when science students want to remember the list of planets in order of their distance from the sun (Mercury, Venus, Earth, Mars, Jupiter, Saturn, Uranus, Neptune, and Pluto), they learn the sentence:

My **v**ery **e**legant **m**other **j**ust **s**erved **u**s **n**ine **p**ickles.

A mental walk. FIGURE **6.5**

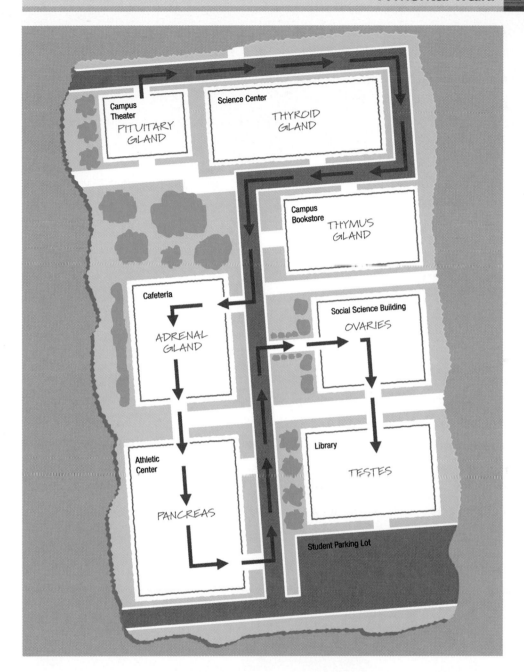

Here's another example, from music. Use this phrase to remember the notes that correspond to the lines on the treble clef (E, G, B, D, and F).

Every **G**ood **B**oy **D**oes **F**ine.

You can create your own acronyms. Suppose you want to remember the names of the first six presidents of the United States. You notice that the first letters of their last names—Washington, Adams, Jefferson, Madison, Monroe, and Adams—together read W A J M M A. To remember them, first you might add an e after the J and create a short nonsense word: *wajemma*. Then, to make sure you don't forget the nonsense word, you might picture the six presidents sitting in a row and wearing pajamas.

TABLE 6.4	Using the number/shape mnemonic to recall a sequenced list.	

NUMBER	YOUR IMAGE FOR THE NUMBER	ASSOCIATED IMAGES FOR THE MOONS OF URANUS IN THE ORDER OF THEIR DISTANCE FROM THE PLANET
1	A stick, pole, or arrow	A **cord** attached to a pole with a banner reading "I have a **deal** for **ya**" (closest moon is Cordelia)
2	A flexible goose-necked lamp twisted in the shape of a swan	An **oaf** sitting under a goose-necked lamp saying, "I **feel ya** pain." (second moon is Ophelia)
3	A pitcher's target with two spots—one for high pitches, the other for low pitches	A **bee** stings the pitcher's **ankle** (third moon is Bianca)
4	A sail on a sailboat	A water**cress** sandwich eaten by a sailor named **Ida** (fourth moon is Cressida)
5	Captain Hook's hook	Captain Hook chasing a man named **Desie** who **moans** after the hook claws his back (fifth moon is Desdemona)
6	A ball on the ground with a string loosely tied to it	A ball with a string covered with **jewel**s and a man nearby warning, "Don't touch **it yet.**" (sixth moon is Juliet)
7	A ski jump	A **Porsche** sports car racing over a ski jump (seventh moon is Portia)
8	An egg timer	A **rose** covered with **lint** against the backdrop of an egg timer (eighth moon is Rosalind)
9	The moon with a loose string attached to its side	The string attached to the moon is attached at the other end to a **bell** clanging in the **wind** (ninth moon is Belinda)
10	A shovel next to a hole	The shovel hitting a hockey **puck** into the hole (tenth moon is Puck)

FIGURE 6.6	Spectrum acronym.

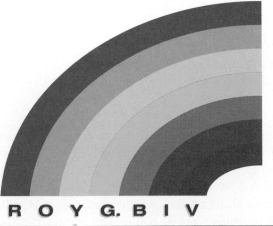

red
orange
yellow
green
blue
indigo
violet

R O Y G. B I V

Tap into these Multiple Intelligence strategies to develop more effective mnemonics.

INTELLIGENCE	SUGGESTED STRATEGIES	WHAT WORKS FOR YOU? WRITE NEW IDEAS HERE
Verbal–Linguistic	■ Develop a story line for the mnemonic first, then work on the visual images. ■ Choose language-based mnemonics such as word- or list-order acronyms.	
Logical–Mathematical	■ Think of a mnemonic device that flows logically from the material. ■ Develop three or four mnemonic device structures and use them repeatedly with different content.	
Bodily–Kinesthetic	■ Create a storyboard for your mnemonic on large pieces of paper. Tape them up on your walls as you memorize the material. ■ Record the mnemonic onto a tape and learn it as you walk between classes.	
Visual–Spatial	■ Focus on visual mnemonics such as mental walks and idea chains. ■ Use markers to add color to the images.	
Interpersonal	■ Work with a study partner to develop helpful mnemonics for the course. ■ Use the mnemonic to test each other on specific content.	
Intrapersonal	■ Take time alone to brainstorm ideas for the mnemonic. ■ After you develop the mnemonic, find a quiet spot to memorize the material.	
Musical	■ Play music while you are brainstorming ideas. ■ Create a mnemonic in the form of a musical rhyme.	
Naturalistic	■ Include images from nature in your mnemonic. ■ Learn the mnemonic while sitting outdoors.	

reflect

How do you react to the following statement: "We retain 10 percent of what we read, 20 percent of what we hear, 30 percent of what we see, 50 percent of what we hear and see, 70 percent of what we say, 90 percent of what we say and do." How can you use this insight to improve your ability to retain information?

& respond

Use Songs or Rhymes

Some of the classic mnemonic devices are rhyming poems that tend to stick in your mind effectively. One you may have heard is the rule about the order of "i" and "e" in spelling:

I before E, except after C, or when sounded like "A" as in "neighbor" and "weigh." Four exceptions if you please: either, neither, seizure, seize.

Make up your own poems or songs, linking tunes or rhymes that are familiar to you with information you want to remember. Thinking back to the "wajemma" example from the previous section, imagine that you want to remember the presidents' first names as well. You might set those first names—George, John, Thomas, James, James, and John—to the tune of "Happy Birthday." Or, to extend the history theme, you might use the first musical phrase of the National Anthem.

Improving your memory requires energy, time, and work. In school, it also helps to master SQ3R, the textbook study technique that was introduced in Chapter 5. By going through the steps in SQ3R and using the specific memory techniques described in this chapter, you will be able to learn more in less time—and remember what you learn long after exams are over.

I listen with understanding and empathy.

Think for a moment about what you hope to learn in school: Are you eager to gain new perspectives as you see things in new ways, or are you content to stay in your comfort zone, perhaps out of a reluctance to entertain ideas that challenge your values and beliefs? College is the place to stretch your mind—to go places intellectually that you never knew existed and to see things from the perspective of others, even those with whom you disagree.

The rewards of reining in your personal biases as you listen are immeasurable. Listening with understanding and empathy is a habit of mind that will help you become aware of other perspectives as you pursue your education. For example, although you will never be able to change your skin color, religious background, or country of origin, you can get a sense of what others experience—simply by paying close attention to what they say and to the emotional tone of their words.

It may take years to fine-tune your listening skills, even though, on the surface, listening comes naturally. Why? Because the best listeners focus on what is "said" beneath the words to uncover the essence of the person speaking. Start now, as you begin college, on this mind-expanding journey of uncovering deeper meaning as you interact with others.

HABITS OF MIND   MIND

REMEMBER!
the important points ∘∘∘

How can you become a better listener?

Listening involves managing listening challenges, including divided attention and distractions, the tendency to shut out all or part of the speaker's message, and the tendency to judge what you hear. Create a more positive listening environment by working to eliminate distractions, taking responsibility for listening, believing that what your instructors say is valuable, and making sure your emotions and opinions don't interfere with listening.

Effective listening is also active listening. You will become more involved with what you hear if you set a purpose for listening, ask questions, pay attention to verbal signposts, and know what helps and hinders listening.

How can you improve your memory?

Use specific memory strategies such as having purpose and intention; understanding what you memorize; reciting, rehearsing, and writing; focusing on important points while ignoring unimportant details; scheduling short, frequent study sessions; dividing material into manageable sections; practicing the material you learn in the middle of a study session; grouping material into easy-to-learn segments; using flash cards; and using tape-recorded material. Using critical thinking can also boost your memory power—mind actions like cause and effect and example to idea help you connect new information to what you already know.

How can you use mnemonic devices to boost memory power?

Mnemonic devices are memory techniques that associate new information with information you already know. The most effective mnemonics are linked to visual images. You can use visual images to remember items in a list by creating a memory walk or an idea chain. Acronyms, another type of mnemonic, are words formed from the first letters of words in a series. Songs or poems may help information stick in your mind through their use of music, rhythm, and rhyme.

Name   Date

CRITICAL THINKING
APPLYING LEARNING TO LIFE

Optimum Listening Conditions

Think of a recent situation (this semester or last semester) in which you were able to understand and retain most of what you heard in the classroom.

Describe the environment (course title, type of classroom setting, etc.).

_____

_____

Describe the instructor's style (lecture, group discussion, Q&A, etc.):

_____

_____

Describe your level of preparation for the class:

_____

_____

Describe your attitude toward the course:

_____

_____

Describe any barriers to listening that you had to overcome in this situation:

_____

_____

Now describe a classroom situation you recently experienced where you feel you did *not* retain information well.

_____

_____

Describe the environment (course title, type of classroom setting, etc.):

_____

_____

Describe the instructor's style (lecture, group discussion, Q&A, etc.)

_____

Describe your level of preparation for the class:

_____

Describe your attitude toward the course:

_____

Describe any barriers to listening that were present in this situation:

_____

Examine the two situations. Based on your descriptions, name two conditions that seem crucial for you to listen effectively and retain information.

_____

Describe one way in which you could have improved your listening and retention in the more difficult situation.

_____

Finally, using what you learned about mnemonic devices, create a mnemonic that allows you to remember what you consider the most important principles of listening. Write your mnemonic here.

_____

_____

TEAM BUILDING
COLLABORATIVE SOLUTIONS

Boost Your Memory

Gather as a class if your class is under 20 people, or divide into two groups if it is larger. Each person in your group should contribute at least one item to lay on a table, until there are a total of 20 items (try to avoid repeats). When all the items are laid out, allow one minute to look at them (use a watch or clock to time yourselves). Then cover the items, and, allowing five minutes, have each person list on paper as many as possible. Compare lists to the items to see how you did. Talk as a group about what you remembered and why, what you didn't remember and why, and what helped you remember.

You may also want to repeat the game using a mnemonic device "assignment." For example, create a new group of items; then allow five minutes to look at them and require everyone to develop an acronym or idea chain in that time. Then cover the items and make lists again. Finally, talk about whether this helped you remember more items.

personal IMPROVEMENT plan

I commit to three specific listening and memory strategies to improve my study skills.
From this chapter, I choose three strategies that I think will help me.

*Strategy 1:*_____

*Strategy 2:*_____

*Strategy 3:*_____

I choose one strategy to focus on (circle this strategy above) and I will:

■ describe my goal—what I want to gain by using this strategy.

_____
_____
_____
_____

■ describe in detail how I plan to use the strategy.

_____
_____
_____
_____

■ describe how I will measure my progress toward the goal this semester.

_____
_____
_____
_____

Activate the Habit of Mind

Here's how I will *listen with understanding and empathy* to achieve this goal:

_____
_____
_____

SUGGESTED READINGS

Higbee, Kenneth L. *Your Memory: How It Works and How to Improve It*. New York: Marlowe & Co., 2001.

Lorayne, Harry. *Super Memory—Super Student: How to Raise Your Grades in 30 Days*. Boston: Little, Brown & Company, 1990.

Lorayne, Harry. *The Memory Book: The Classic Guide to Improving Your Memory at Work, at School, and at play*. New York: Ballantine Books, 1996.

Robbins, Harvey A. *How to Speak and Listen Effectively*. New York: AMACOM, 1992.

Roberts, Billy. *Educate Your Memory: Improvement Techniques for Students of All Ages*. London: Allison &Busby, 2000.

Roberts, Billy. *Working Memory: Improving Your Memory for the Workplace*. London: London Bridge Trade, 1999.

Zull, James E. *The Art of Changing the Brain: Enriching Teaching by Exploring the Biology of Learning*. Sterling, VA: Stylus Publishing, 2002.

ENDNOTES

1. Ralph G. Nichols. "Do We Know How to Listen? Practical Helps in a Modern Age." *Speech Teacher* (March 1961), pp. 118–124.

2. Ibid.

3. Herman Ebbinghaus. *Memory: A Contribution to Experimental Psychology*, trans. H. A. Ruger and C. E. Bussenius. New York: Teachers College, Columbia University, 1885.

4. James Zull. *The Art of Changing the Brain: Enriching Teaching by Exploring the Biology of Learning*. Sterling, VA: Stylus Publishing, 2002.

INTERNET RESOURCES

About Memory: www.memory-key.com/

ForgetKnot: A Source for Mnemonic Devices: http://members.tripod.com/~ForgetKnot

THINKING IT THROUGH

Check those statements that apply to you right now:

- ☐ When I study my notes, I usually don't get much out of them.

- ☐ I use one note-taking system for every purpose.

- ☐ No matter how hard I try, I can never write down everything the instructor says.

- ☐ When I jot down notes on information I find in the library, they rarely help me when I look back at them later.

Taking Notes

RECORDING IMPORTANT IDEAS AND INFORMATION

Thinking flexibly.

"Flexible people draw upon a repertoire of problem-solving strategies and **tailor their style to the situation**, knowing when to be broad and global in their thinking and when to apply detailed precision."

—**ART COSTA**

*One of the hallmarks of a successful student is flexibility in the classroom. Your job is to learn from your instructors, no matter their teaching styles. To do this effectively, you'll learn to **tailor your notes to what is happening around you**—a challenge you can readily accomplish, but a challenge nonetheless.*

Every time you go to class, your ability to learn depends on your listening actively as you take in and absorb new information. Your success in retaining that information also depends on taking notes actively, recording information that you can study later. Similarly, when you conduct library or Internet research, note-taking skills will enable you to capture information from sources that will form the basis for papers and other assignments. With its focus on taking class and research notes, this chapter will help you master the note-taking skills you will need to succeed in college.

How does taking notes help you?

Note taking can be a challenge. You might feel that it prevents you from watching your instructor or that you can't write fast enough to get everything down. You may also be convinced that you can remember all that you need to know even when you don't take notes. The truth is that the act of note taking involves you in the learning process in many important ways. Taking clear notes that you can use to prepare for tests and as study tools can influence—and improve—your academic success (see Figure 7.1).

Because it is virtually impossible to take notes on everything you hear or read, the act of note taking encourages you to think critically and evaluate what is worth remembering. Asking yourself questions like the following will help you judge what is important enough to write down:

- Do I need this information?
- Is the information important to the lecture or reading, or is it just an interesting comment?
- Is the information fact or opinion? If it is opinion, is it worth remembering? (To explore this question, see Chapter 4.)

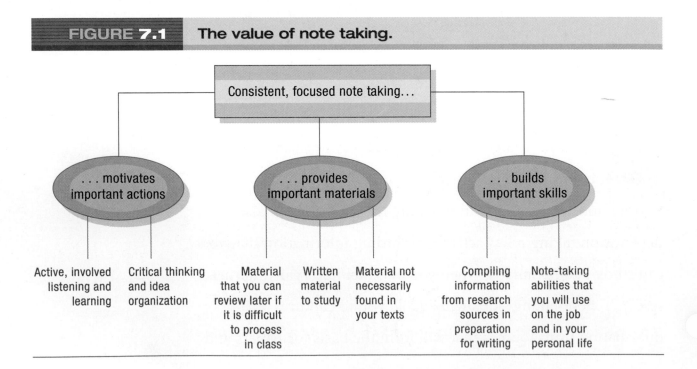

FIGURE 7.1 The value of note taking.

Consistent, focused note taking...

...motivates important actions | ...provides important materials | ...builds important skills

| Active, involved listening and learning | Critical thinking and idea organization | Material that you can review later if it is difficult to process in class | Written material to study | Material not necessarily found in your texts | Compiling information from research sources in preparation for writing | Note-taking abilities that you will use on the job and in your personal life |

Your responses will guide your note taking in class and help you decide what to study before an exam. Similarly, the notes you take while doing research will affect your research efforts. Learn what class notes and research notes are and how to use each to your advantage.

How can you make the most of class notes?

Class notes—the notes you take while listening to an instructor—may contain key terms and definitions, explanations of concepts and processes, or narratives of who did what to whom and when. If lectures include material that is not in your text, or if your instructor talks about specific test questions, your class notes become even more important as a study tool.

Prepare for Note Taking

Your class notes have two purposes: First, they should reflect what you heard in class, and second, they should be a resource for studying, writing, or comparing with your text material. Taking good class notes depends on good preparation.

Preview your reading material. More than anything else you can do, reading the text and other assigned materials *before* class will prepare you to understand your instructor's presentation and the class discussion. It will also give you the background to take effective notes. *For your own success, always complete your reading assignments before class.* The class syllabus should tell you when specific assignments are due. If you have any questions, ask your instructor.

Gather your supplies. Use separate pieces of 8½-by-11-inch paper for each class. If you use a three-ring binder, punch holes in handouts and insert them immediately following your notes for that day. If you take notes on a laptop, open the file containing your class notes right away.

Location, location, location. Find a comfortable seat where you can easily see and hear. Sitting near the front will minimize distractions. Be ready to write as soon as the instructor begins speaking.

Choose the best note-taking system. Select a system that is most appropriate for the situation. Later in the chapter, you will learn about different note-taking systems. Take the following factors into account when choosing one to use in any class:

reflect

Eighteenth-century German playwright Johann von Goethe said: "If you miss the first buttonhole, you will not succeed in buttoning up your coat." Describe how this quote applies to effective note taking and especially to the preparation you do before class. How will your first note-taking steps, including choosing the right note-taking style, affect your success?

& respond

> *"Education is learning what you didn't even know you didn't know."*

DANIEL BOORSTIN

- *The instructor's style.* (You'll be able to determine this style after a few classes.) Whereas one instructor may deliver organized lectures at a normal speaking rate, another may jump from topic to topic or talk very quickly.
- *The course material.* You may decide that an informal outline works best for a highly structured philosophy course, but that a think link is the right choice for a looser sociology course. Try a note-taking system for a few classes, then make adjustments.
- *Your learning style.* Choose strategies that make the most of your strong points and help boost weaker areas. A visual–spatial learner might prefer think links or the Cornell system; a thinker type might stick to outlines; an interpersonal learner might use the Cornell system and fill in the cue column in a study group setting (see Chapter 2 for a complete discussion of learning styles). You might even find that one system is best in class and another works best for review sessions.

Gather support. For each class, set up a support system with two students. That way, when you are absent, you can get the notes you missed from one or the other.

Record Information Effectively During Class

Because no one has time to write down everything, the following strategies will help you record what you feel is important in a format that you can review later. This is not a list of "musts." Rather, it is a source list of ideas to try as you work to find the note-taking system that works best for you.

Remember that the first step in note taking is to listen actively. Use the listening strategies described in Chapter 6 to make sure you are prepared to receive information.

- Date and identify each page. When you take several pages of notes, add an identifying letter or number to the date on each page: 11/27A, 11/27B, 11/27C, for example, or 11/27—1 of 3, 11/27—2 of 3, 11/27—3 of 3. This will help you keep track of page order.
- Add the specific topic of the lecture at the top of the page. For example:

  11/27A—U. S. Immigration Policy After World War II

  This suggestion will help you gather all your notes on the same topic when it is time to study.
- If your instructor jumps from topic to topic during a single class, it may help to start a new page for each new topic.

TAKE ACTION

Prepare to Take Notes in Your Most Challenging Class

In the spaces below, record the specific steps you will take to prepare to take notes in what you consider to be your most challenging course.

■ Course name and date of next class:

_____DL5001 · 10-18-07_____

■ List all the reading you must complete before class (Include pages from text and supplemental sources).

_____One Sentence_____

_____

■ Where do you intend to sit in class to focus your attention and minimize distractions?

_____

■ Which note-taking system is best suited for the class, and why?

_____

_____

■ Write the names and e-mail addresses of two classmates whose notes you can borrow if you miss a class:

_____

_____

■ Record whatever your instructor emphasizes. See Figure 7.2 for methods instructors use to call attention to information.

■ Write down all key terms and definitions. If, for example, your instructor is discussing the stages of mental development in children, as defined by psychologist Jean Piaget, your notes would define such terms as *sensorimotor* and *preoperational development*.

■ To save time, use short phrases instead of full sentences. For example, "Abraham Lincoln was elected president in the year 1860" becomes "Lincoln—elec. Pres. 1860."

■ Write down all questions raised by the instructor; these questions may appear on a test.

■ Leave one or more blank spaces between points. This "white space" will help you review your notes because information will be in

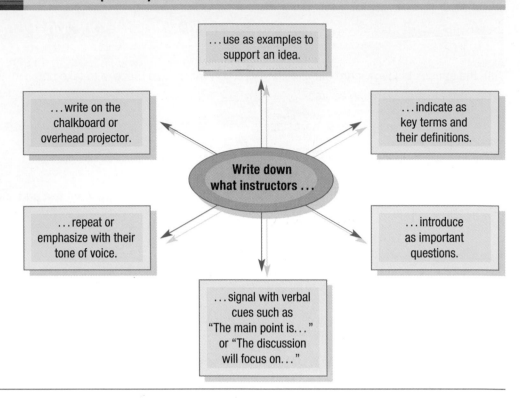

FIGURE 7.2   How to pick up on instructor cues.

...use as examples to support an idea.

...write on the chalkboard or overhead projector.

...indicate as key terms and their definitions.

Write down what instructors ...

...repeat or emphasize with their tone of voice.

...introduce as important questions.

...signal with verbal cues such as "The main point is..." or "The discussion will focus on..."

Sitting near students who are focused on their work will help you concentrate.

self-contained segments. (This suggestion does not apply if you are using a think link.)

- Draw pictures and diagrams that help illustrate ideas.

- Write quickly but legibly, perhaps using a form of personal shorthand. (See the section on shorthand in this chapter.)

- Indicate material that is especially important with a star, underlining, a highlighter pen, a different color pen, or capital letters.

- If you don't understand something, leave space and place a question mark in the margin. Then take advantage of your resources—ask the instructor to explain it after class, discuss it with a classmate, or consult your textbook—and fill in the blank when the idea is clear.

- Make your notes legible and organized—you can't learn from notes that you can't read or understand. Don't be fussy, however. Remember that you can always make improvements later.

- Consistency is important. Use the same system of indicating importance—such as indenting, spacing, or underlining—on each page of your notes. This will allow your mind to perceive key information with a minimum of effort.[1]

- Consider that your notes are part, but not all, of what you need to learn. Using your text to add to your notes after class makes a superior, "deeper and wider" set of information to study.

Taking Notes During Extended Class Discussion

In many classrooms, instructors interact with students during extended discussion periods. One student may say something, then another, and finally the instructor may summarize the comments or link them together to make a point. Frequently, class discussion periods have tremendous value, but just as frequently information is presented in a disorganized, sometimes chaotic way. Here are some suggestions for recording what you need to know during these discussions:

- Listen carefully to everyone who speaks. Jot down important or interesting points and ignore points that seem unrelated to the lesson.
- Listen for idea threads that weave through the comments students make. These threads may signal an important point.
- Listen for ideas the instructor picks up on and emphasizes. Listen for encouraging comments to students, such as "You make a great point," "I like your idea," and so on.
- Take notes when the instructor rephrases and clarifies a student's point.
- Try using a think link as your note-taking system, since discussions often take the form of brainstorming sessions. A think link will help you connect ideas that come at you from different perspectives and in different voices.
- Finally, if you are unsure, ask the instructor (during the discussion or in office hours) whether a student's statement is important.

Review and Revise Your Notes

Even the most comprehensive notes in the world won't do you any good unless you review them. The crucial act of reviewing helps you solidify the information in your memory so that you can recall it and use it. It also helps you link new information to information you already know, which is a key step in building new ideas. The review-and-revision stage of note taking should include time for planning, critical thinking, adding information from other sources, summarizing, and working with a study group.

Plan a Review Schedule

Use what you learned in Chapter 6 about memory strategies to plan your review time as strategically as possible.

Review within a day of the lecture. Plan your first review for the day following the lecture. Reviewing while the material is still fresh in your mind will help your recall. You don't have to spend hours focusing on every word. Just set some time aside to reread your notes and perhaps write questions and comments on them. If you know you have an hour between classes, for example, that would be an ideal time to work in a quick review.

reflect

What methods do you use to review your notes? How do you review your notes for a test that will happen soon? How do you prepare for a comprehensive exam that will require you to review material you studied several months ago? Are the same review methods effective for both situations?

& respond

Review regularly. Try to schedule times during the week for reviewing notes from that week's class meetings. For example, if you know you are free from 2 P.M. to 5 P.M. every Tuesday and Thursday, plan to review notes from two courses on Tuesday and from two others on Thursday. Having a routine helps assure that you will look at material regularly.

Review with an eye toward tests. Step up your efforts before a test. Schedule longer review sessions, call a study group meeting, and review more frequently. Shorter sessions of intense review work interspersed with breaks may be more effective than long hours of continuous studying. Some students find that recopying their notes before an exam or at an earlier stage helps cement key concepts in memory.

Read and Rework Using Critical Thinking

The critical-thinking mind actions will help you make the most of your notes.

 Recall. Read your notes to learn the information, clarify points, write out abbreviations, and fill in missing information.

 Similarity. Consider what similar facts or ideas the information brings to mind. Write them in the page margins or white space.

 Difference. Consider how the information differs from what you already know. Is there a discrepancy you should examine? If something seems off base, could you have written it down inaccurately?

 Cause and effect. Look for cause-and-effect connections. You might even want to use another color pen to draw a line linking related ideas or facts on the page.

 Example to idea. Think about what new ideas you can form from the information in your notes. If any come to mind, write them in your notes or on a separate page.

 Idea to example. Think carefully about what the ideas in your notes mean. Do the examples in your notes support or negate them? Add new examples as you review.

 Evaluation. Use your evaluation skills to select and underline or highlight important ideas and information. Think about why they are important and make sure you understand them completely.

Revise Using Other Sources

Revising and adding to your notes using material from your texts, other required course readings, and the Internet is one of the best ways to build your understanding and link new information to information you already know. Try using the following critical-thinking actions when you add to your notes:

- Brainstorm and write down examples from other sources that illustrate central ideas in your notes.

- Pay attention to similarities between your text materials and class notes (ideas that appear in both are probably important to remember).
- Think of facts or ideas from the reading that can support and clarify ideas from your notes.
- Consider what in your class notes differs from your reading, and why.
- Write down any new ideas that come up when you are reviewing your notes.
- Look at cause-and-effect connections between material from your notes and the reading material. Note how ideas, facts, and examples relate to one another.

Summarize

Writing a summary of your notes is another important review technique. Summarizing involves critically evaluating which ideas and examples are most important and then rewriting the material in a shortened form, focusing on those important ideas and examples.

You may prefer to summarize as you review, with the notes in front of you. If you are using the Cornell system (see page 208), you would summarize in space at the bottom of the page. Other ideas include summarizing on a separate page that you insert in your binder, or summarizing on the back of the previous page.

Another helpful review technique is to summarize your notes from memory after you review them. This will give you an idea of how well you have retained the information. You may even want to summarize as you read, then summarize from memory, and compare the two summaries.

Work with Study Groups

When you work with a study group, you have the opportunity to review both your personal notes and those of other members of the class. This can be an enormous help if, for example, you lost concentration during part of a lecture and your notes don't make sense. You and another student may even have notes that contradict each other or have radically different information. When this happens, try to reconstruct what the instructor said and, if necessary, bring in a third group member to clear up the confusion. See Chapter 5 for more on effective studying in groups.

"When love and skill work together, expect a masterpiece."

JOHN RUSKIN

What note-taking system should you use?

You will benefit most from the system that feels most comfortable to you and makes the most sense for the course content. For example, you might take notes in a different style for a history class than for a

reflect

Consider trying a note-taking strategy you have never used before. For example, how willing are you to try the Cornell system or a think link if you have always used an outline? How willing are you to give a new system a fair test over a period of weeks or months? Brainstorm ways of opening yourself to new strategies that may improve your note-taking and other study skills.

& respond

foreign language class. The most common note-taking systems include outlines, the Cornell system, and think links.

Taking Notes in Outline Form

When a reading assignment or lecture seems well organized, you may choose to take notes in outline form. Outlining means constructing a line-by-line representation, with certain phrases set off by varying indentations, showing how concepts, facts, and examples are related.

Formal Versus Informal Outlines

Formal outlines indicate ideas and examples with Roman numerals, uppercase and lowercase letters, and numbers. The rules of formal outlines require at least two headings on the same level. That is, if you have a IIA, you must also have a IIB. Similarly, if you have a IIIA1, you must also have a IIIA2. In contrast, informal outlines show the same associations but replace the formality with a system of consistent indenting and dashes. Figure 7.3 shows the

FIGURE 7.3   The structure of an outline.

FORMAL OUTLINE	INFORMAL OUTLINE
TOPIC	TOPIC
I. First Main Idea	First Main Idea
A. Major supporting fact	—Major supporting fact
B. Major supporting fact	—Major supporting fact
1. First reason or example	—First reason or example
2. Second reason or example	—Second reason or example
a. First supporting fact	—First supporting fact
b. Second supporting fact	—Second supporting fact
II. Second Main Idea	Second Main Idea
A. Major supporting fact	—Major supporting fact
1. First reason or example	—First reason or example
2. Second reason or example	—Second reason or example
B. Major supporting fact	—Major supporting fact

difference between the two outline forms. Many students find that using informal outlines is better for in-class note taking. Figure 7.4 shows how a student has used the structure of a formal outline to write notes on the topic of civil rights legislation.

When you use an outline to write class notes, you may have trouble when an instructor rambles or jumps from point to point. The best advice in this case is to abandon the outline structure for the time being. Focus instead on taking down whatever information you can and on drawing connections between key topics. After class, try to restructure your notes and, if possible, rewrite them in outline form.

Guided Notes

From time to time, an instructor may give you a guide, usually in the form of an outline, to help you take notes in class. This outline may be on the board, on an overhead projector, or on a handout that you receive at the beginning of class.

Rewriting notes after class will help you remember and understand the material.

Sample formal outline.　　**FIGURE 7.4**

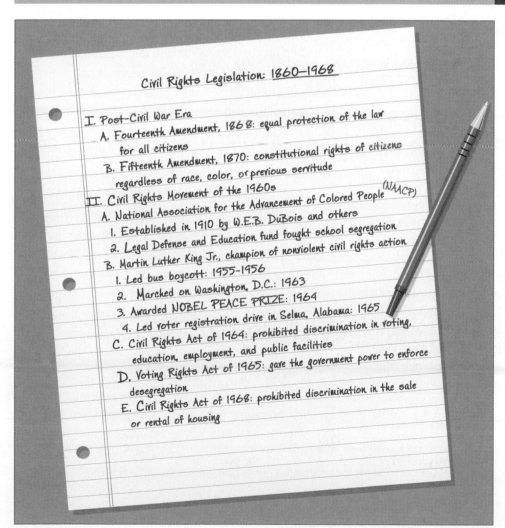

Civil Rights Legislation: 1860–1968

I. Post-Civil War Era
  A. Fourteenth Amendment, 1868: equal protection of the law for all citizens
  B. Fifteenth Amendment, 1870: constitutional rights of citizens regardless of race, color, or previous servitude

II. Civil Rights Movement of the 1960s
  A. National Association for the Advancement of Colored People (NAACP)
    1. Established in 1910 by W.E.B. DuBois and others
    2. Legal Defense and Education fund fought school segregation
  B. Martin Luther King Jr., champion of nonviolent civil rights action
    1. Led bus boycott: 1955-1956
    2. Marched on Washington, D.C.: 1963
    3. Awarded NOBEL PEACE PRIZE: 1964
    4. Led voter registration drive in Selma, Alabama: 1965
  C. Civil Rights Act of 1964: prohibited discrimination in voting, education, employment, and public facilities
  D. Voting Rights Act of 1965: gave the government power to enforce desegregation
  E. Civil Rights Act of 1968: prohibited discrimination in the sale or rental of housing

Although guided notes help you follow the lecture and organize your thoughts during class, they do not replace your own notes. Because they are usually no more than a basic outline of topics, they require that you fill in the details. If your mind wanders because you think that the guided notes are all you need, you may miss important information.

When you receive guided notes on paper, write directly on the paper if there is room. If not, use a separate sheet and write on it the outline categories that the guided notes suggest. If the guided notes are on the board or overhead, copy them, leaving plenty of space in between for your own notes.

Using the Cornell Note-Taking System

The Cornell note-taking system, also known as the T-note system, was developed by Walter Pauk at Cornell University and is now used throughout the world.[2] The system consists of three sections on ordinary notepaper.

- *Section 1,* the largest section, is on the right. Record your notes here in whatever form is most comfortable for you.
- *Section 2,* to the left of your notes, is the *cue column.* Leave it blank while you read or listen, then fill it in later as you review. You might fill it with comments that highlight main ideas, clarify meaning, suggest examples, or link ideas and examples. You can even draw diagrams. Many students use this column to raise questions that they will ask themselves when they study. By placing specific questions in the cue column, you can help yourself focus on critical details.
- *Section 3,* at the bottom of the page, is known as the *summary area.* Here you briefly summarize the notes on the page. Use this section during the review process to reinforce concepts and provide an overview of what the notes say.

Create this note-taking structure before class begins. Picture an upside-down letter *T* as you follow these directions:

- Start with a sheet of standard loose-leaf paper. Label it with the date and title of the lecture.

RISING
TO THE CHALLENGE

Uriel Portillo

Junior, Music Education, Trinity International University

Having a talent for something doesn't necessarily mean that you will succeed in that subject. When he entered college, Uriel Portillo found out that his way of learning music didn't earn him easy A's. Fortunately, with help and determination, he has found his own path to success.

Music is in my blood. My family always played music, so I was exposed to it and played many instruments without much formal training. My involvement in music continued in high school. I spent a lot of time playing for the school worship team where I played the timbales (a Latin percussion instrument) and picked up the drums and then the bass. Between playing music and basketball (my other passion), I just did what I needed to do to get by in school.

Fortunately I had a mentor during this time. My friend's father, the school principal and a good musician, became my friend. He knew that I wasn't excited to be in school, but he convinced me that taking education seriously would help me with my future. I knew that I wanted to go into music education since I got a lot of satisfaction from showing my friends how to play instruments. I saw that music was a great way to help people feel good about themselves. After graduating from high school, I enrolled at Trinity, which has a strong music program.

College was very different from high school. My first class, Music History, took me by surprise. The instructor gave lectures that were packed with information, and expected that students should already be somewhat familiar with it. However, I didn't recognize any of those 16th-century musicians. I had trouble taking notes and would always miss important things.

My trouble understanding the material showed on the tests. Around this time, I had decided on my primary instrument, the saxophone, but was having trouble learning it in such a formal setting. I wasn't good at reading music, and I was used to learning instruments by just playing. After the first semester, I wasn't doing so well in the music program and my advisor urged me to cut out the music part of my major and just concentrate on education. I knew that he thought that I couldn't cut it in the music department, but I was determined to prove him wrong. To do this, I had to change my attitude and make learning a priority.

The first thing I did was ask for help. Even though my music history teacher had high expectations, she was very willing to help me understand the material. She would ask me questions to find out what my understanding was, and then correct me if I was wrong or missing something. I also tried to find out what my learning style was and adjust my study habits. Since I did best in hands-on classes, I realized that I was a kinesthetic learner. So when I was trying to understand something in my music theory class, I would get out an instrument and figure it out that way. I also learned some new study tricks, like mnemonic devices. I can remember dates better if I associate them with basketball players' numbers.

Even with these tricks, pursuing my passion still involved plain old hard work. In order to prove that I could learn the saxophone, I spent up to 20 hours a week practicing. I had to give up some of my free time during the school year, including playing basketball, which could give me injuries that might keep me from playing music. It also took patience since it didn't feel like I was getting better right away.

Since I'm normally pretty laid back, all this studying didn't come naturally to me, but it has really paid off so far. I managed to raise my grade point average one whole point in the last two years. Also, I did my first recital this year, and really impressed my music history teacher with my improvement. One of the best sax players in the school was so impressed by how fast I'd learned to play that he told me he'd have to start asking me for pointers soon!

Take a Moment to Consider . . .

- *A mentor who has made a difference in your life, and in what way.*
- *How you may have been inspired to achieve in order to "prove someone wrong," and how that felt.*

- To create the *cue column*, draw a vertical line about 2½ inches from the left side of the paper. End the line about 2 inches from the bottom of the sheet.
- To create the *summary area*, start at the point where the vertical line ends (about 2 inches from the bottom of the page) and draw a horizontal line that spans the entire paper.

Figure 7.5 shows how a student used the Cornell system to take notes in a business course.

Creating a Think Link

A *think link,* also known as a mind map, is a visual form of note taking. When you draw a think link, you diagram ideas by using shapes and lines that link ideas and supporting details and examples. The visual design makes the connections easy to see, and the use of shapes and pictures extends the material beyond just words. Many learners respond well to the power of **visualization**. You can use think links to brainstorm ideas for paper topics as well.

To create a think link, start by circling or boxing your topic in the middle of a sheet of paper. Next, draw a line from the topic and write the name of one major idea at the end of the line. Circle that idea also. Then, jot down specific facts related to the idea, linking them to the idea with lines. Continue the process, connecting thoughts to one another by using circles, lines, and words. Figure 7.6 shows a think link on social stratification (a sociology concept) that follows this particular structure.

You can design any kind of think link that feels comfortable to you. Examples include stair steps showing connected ideas that build toward a conclusion, or a tree shape with roots as causes and branches as effects. Look back to Figure 7.1 for a type of think link sometimes referred to as a "jellyfish."

A think link may be difficult to construct in class, especially if your instructor talks quickly. In this case, use another note-taking system during class. Then, make a think link as part of the review process.

FIGURE 7.5   Notes taken with the Cornell system.

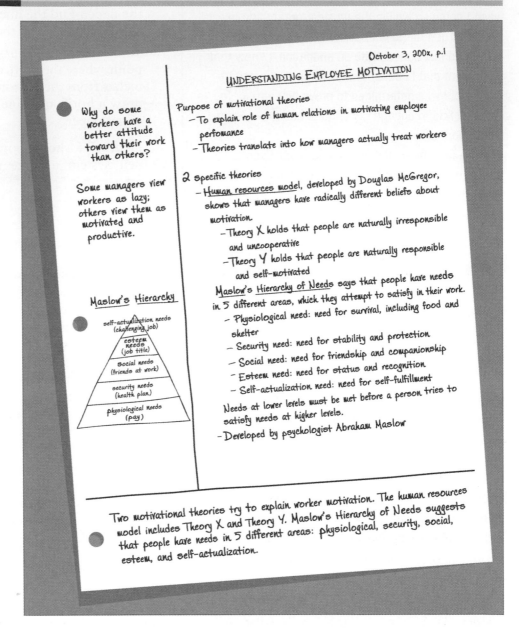

October 3, 200x, p.1

UNDERSTANDING EMPLOYEE MOTIVATION

Why do some workers have a better attitude toward their work than others?

Some managers view workers as lazy; others view them as motivated and productive.

Maslow's Hierarchy

- self-actualization needs (challenging job)
- esteem needs (job title)
- social needs (friends at work)
- security needs (health plan)
- physiological needs (pay)

Purpose of motivational theories
—To explain role of human relations in motivating employee performance
—Theories translate into how managers actually treat workers

2 specific theories
—Human resources model, developed by Douglas McGregor, shows that managers have radically different beliefs about motivation.
   —Theory X holds that people are naturally irresponsible and uncooperative
   —Theory Y holds that people are naturally responsible and self-motivated

Maslow's Hierarchy of Needs says that people have needs in 5 different areas, which they attempt to satisfy in their work.
   — Physiological need: need for survival, including food and shelter
   — Security need: need for stability and protection
   — Social need: need for friendship and companionship
   — Esteem need: need for status and recognition
   — Self-actualization need: need for self-fulfillment
Needs at lower levels must be met before a person tries to satisfy needs at higher levels.
—Developed by psychologist Abraham Maslow

Two motivational theories try to explain worker motivation. The human resources model includes Theory X and Theory Y. Maslow's Hierarchy of Needs suggests that people have needs in 5 different areas: physiological, security, social, esteem, and self-actualization.

Other Visual Note-Taking Strategies

Several other note-taking strategies will help you organize your information and are especially useful to visual learners. These strategies may be too in-volved to complete quickly during class, so you may want to use them when taking notes on a text chapter or when rewriting your notes for review.

Time lines. A time line can help you organize information—such as dates of French Revolution events or eras of different psychology practices—into chronological order. Draw a vertical or horizontal line on the page and con-nect each item to the line, in order, noting the dates.

Tables. Tables throughout this text show information through vertical or horizontal columns. Use tables to arrange information according to categories.

Visualization
The interpretation of verbal ideas through the use of mental visual images.

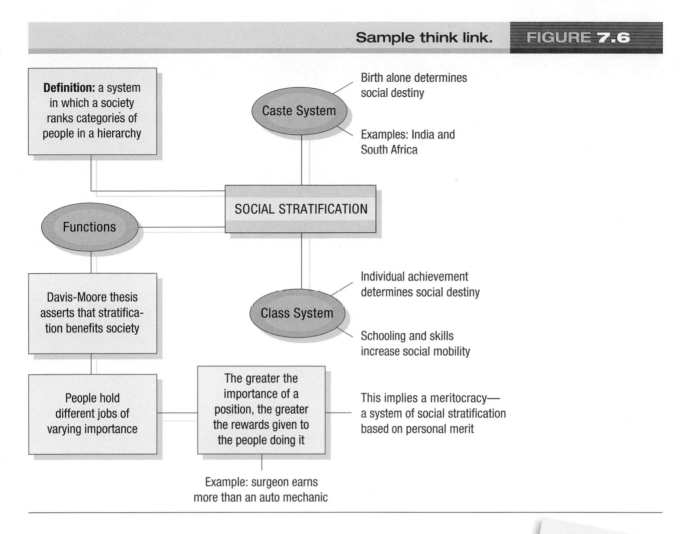

Sample think link.   FIGURE 7.6

Definition: a system in which a society ranks categories of people in a hierarchy

SOCIAL STRATIFICATION

Caste System
- Birth alone determines social destiny
- Examples: India and South Africa

Functions

Davis-Moore thesis asserts that stratification benefits society

Class System
- Individual achievement determines social destiny
- Schooling and skills increase social mobility

People hold different jobs of varying importance

The greater the importance of a position, the greater the rewards given to the people doing it

This implies a meritocracy— a system of social stratification based on personal merit

Example: surgeon earns more than an auto mechanic

Hierarchy charts. Charts showing the **hierarchy** of information can help you visualize how each piece fits into the hierarchy. A hierarchy chart could show levels of government, for example, or levels of scientific classification of animals and plants.

Once you choose a note-taking system, your success will depend on how well you use it. Personal shorthand will help you make the most of whatever system you choose.

What can you do to take notes faster?

Using some personal **shorthand** (not standard secretarial shorthand) can help you push your pen faster. Because you are the only intended reader, you can misspell and abbreviate words in ways that only you understand.

The only danger with shorthand is that you might forget what your writing means. To avoid this problem, review your shorthand notes while your abbreviations and symbols are fresh in your mind. If there is any confusion, spell out words as you review.

Hierarchy
A graded or ranked series.

Shorthand
A system of rapid handwriting that employs symbols, abbreviations, and shortened words to represent words, phrases, and letters.

TAKE ACTION

Course by Course Note-Taking Strategies

The following questions will encourage you to think about the note-taking strategies that are best for you and most effective in each of your classes.

- What note-taking strategies fit most comfortably with your learning style?
  (Consult the Multiple Intelligence Strategies for Note-Taking on page 215.)

  _____

  _____

- List each of your courses below and briefly describe its content:

  Course 1: _____

  _____

  Course 2: _____

  _____

  Course 3: _____

  _____

  Course 4: _____

  _____

- Briefly explain the instructor's teaching style for each course:

  Course 1: _____

  _____

  Course 2: _____

  _____

  Course 3: _____

  _____

  Course 4: _____

  _____

- Taking these factors into consideration, name the note-taking system best suited to each course:

  Course 1: _____

  _____

  Course 2: _____

  _____

  Course 3: _____

  _____

  Course 4: _____

  _____

Here are some suggestions that will help you master this important skill:

1. Use standard abbreviations in place of complete words.

w/	with	cf	compare, in comparison to
w/o	without	ff	following
→	means; resulting in	Q	question
←	as a result of	p.	page
↑	increasing	*	most important
↓	decreasing	<	less than
∴	therefore	>	more than
∵	because	=	equals
≈	approximately	%	percent
+ or &	and	△	change
—	minus; negative	2	to; two; too
NO. or #	number	vs	versus; against
i.e.	that is	e.g.	for example
etc.	and so forth	c/o	care of
ng	no good	lb	pound

2. Shorten words by removing vowels from the middle of words.

prps   =   purpose
lwyr   =   lawyer
cmptr   =   computer

3. Substitute word beginnings for entire words.

assoc   =   associate; association
info   =   information
subj   =   subject

4. Form plurals by adding *s* to shortened words.

prblms   =   problems
drctrys   =   directories
prntrs   =   printers

5. Make up your own symbols and use them consistently.

b/4   =   before
4tn   =   fortune
2thake   =   toothache

6. Use standard or informal abbreviations for proper nouns such as places, people, companies, scientific substances, events, and so on.

DC   =   Washington, D.C.
H_2O =   water
Moz.   =   Wolfgang Amadeus Mozart

7. If you know you are going to repeat a particular word or phrase often throughout a class, write it out once at the beginning of the class and then establish an abbreviation for the rest of your notes. For example, if you are taking notes on the rise and fall of Argentina's former first lady Eva Peron, you might start out by writing "Eva Peron (EP)" and then use "EP" as you continue.

TAKE ACTION

Evaluate and Improve Your Notes

At your college or community library, you'll find books and lectures on tape. Choose a tape with an academic or study-skills topic that interests you—for example, a book that examines memory-improvement techniques. Then listen to 15 minutes of the tape, taking notes in your personal shorthand as you listen. Reread your notes to determine if you effectively recorded the content. Then answer these questions:

■ What note-taking system did you use? Was it the right choice for the speaker and the content? Why or why not?

_____

_____

_____

■ Evaluate the effectiveness of your shorthand:

Did your shorthand enable you to record the material? _____

Can you make sense of your notes? _____

What changes can you make to improve speed and legibility?

_____

_____

■ Now listen to the next 15 minutes of the tape. This time, change your note-taking style to reflect what you learned in the first 15-minute session. How do these notes compare to the first set of notes?

_____

_____

Finally, throughout your note taking, remember that the primary goal is for you to generate materials that help you learn and remember information. No matter how sensible any note-taking strategy, abbreviation, or system might be, it won't do you any good if it doesn't help you reach that goal. Keep a close eye on what works for you and stick to it.

If you find that your notes aren't comprehensible, legible, or focused, think critically about how you might improve them. Can't read your notes? You might just have been too sleepy, or you might have a handwriting issue. Lots of confusing gaps in the information? You might be distracted in class, have an instructor who jumps around in the lecture, or have a deeper lack of understanding of the course material. Put your problem-solving skills to work and address your note-taking issues, brainstorming solutions from the variety of strategies in this chapter. With a little time and effort, your notes will truly become a helpful learning tool in school and beyond.

As you will see next, doing research in college—at the library and on the Internet—will require that you learn how to take effective research notes. (Chapter 10 examines library and Internet research in depth.)

MULTIPLE PATHWAYS TO LEARNING

MULTIPLE INTELLIGENCE STRATEGIES *for* Note Taking

Note taking is a critical learning tool. The tips below will help you retain information for both the short and long term.

INTELLIGENCE	SUGGESTED STRATEGIES	WHAT WORKS FOR YOU? WRITE NEW IDEAS HERE
Verbal–Linguistic	■ Rewrite important ideas and concepts in class notes from memory. ■ Write summaries of your notes in your own words.	
Logical–Mathematical	■ Organize the main points of a lecture or reading using outline form. ■ Make charts and diagrams to clarify ideas and examples.	
Bodily–Kinesthetic	■ Make note taking as physical as possible—use large pieces of paper and different colored pens. ■ When in class, choose a comfortable spot where you have room to spread out your materials and shift body position when you need to.	
Visual–Spatial	■ Take notes using colored markers. ■ Rewrite lecture notes in think link format, focusing on the most important and difficult points from the lecture.	
Interpersonal	■ Whenever possible, schedule a study group right after a lecture to discuss class notes. ■ Review class notes with a study buddy. See what you wrote that he or she missed and vice versa.	
Intrapersonal	■ Schedule some quiet time as soon as possible after a lecture to reread and think about your notes. If no class is meeting in the same room after yours and you have free time, stay in the room and review there.	
Musical	■ Play music while you read your notes. ■ Write a song that incorporates material from one class period's notes or one particular topic. Use the refrain to emphasize the most important concepts.	
Naturalistic	■ Read or rewrite your notes outside. ■ Review notes while listening to a nature CD—running water, rain, forest sounds.	

What are research notes and how can you use them?

Research notes are the notes you take while gathering information to answer a research question. Research notes take two forms: source notes and content notes.

Source notes are the preliminary notes you take as you review available research. They include vital bibliographic information, as well as a short summary and critical evaluation of the work. Write these notes when you consider a book or article interesting enough to look at again. They do not signal that you have actually read something all the way through, only that you plan to review it later.

Each source note should include the author's full name; the title of the work; the edition (if any); the publisher, year, and city of publication; issue and/or volume number when applicable (such as for a magazine); and the page numbers you consulted. Many students find that index cards work best for source notes. See Figure 7.7 for an example of how you can write source notes on index cards.

The second type of research notes is *content notes*. Unlike source notes, content notes provide an in-depth look at the source, taken during a thorough reading. Use them to record the information you need to write your draft. Here are some suggestions for taking effective content notes:

- When a source looks promising, begin reading it and summarizing what you read. Use standard notebook paper that fits into a three-ring binder. This gives you space to write, as well as the flexibility to

FIGURE 7.7   Sample source note.

LORENZ, KONRAD. *King Solomon's Ring.* New York: Crowell, 1952, pp. 102–122.

Summary: Descriptions of the fascinating habits of various animals and birds.

Evaluation: Although this book is old, it's a classic! Added pluses: the author can be funny and provocative.

rearrange the pages into any order that makes sense. (If you prefer using large index cards for content notes, choose 5-by-6-inch or 5-by-8-inch sizes.)

- Include bibliographic information and page numbers for every source.
- Limit each page to a single source.
- If you take notes on more than one subject from a single source, create a separate page for each subject.
- If the notes on a source require more than one page, label the pages and number them sequentially. For example, if the source is *Business Week* magazine, your pages might be labeled BW1, BW2, and so on.
- Identify the type of note that appears on each page. State whether it is a summary in your own words, a quotation, or a **paraphrase**.
- Write your summary notes in any of the note-taking systems described earlier in the chapter.

Notations that you make directly on photocopies of sources—marginal notes, highlighting, and underlining—can supplement your content notes. Say, for example, that you are writing a paper on the psychological development of adolescent girls. During your research, you photocopy an article by Dr. Carol Gilligan, an expert in the field. On the photocopy, you highlight important information and make marginal notes that detail your immediate reactions to some key points. Then, you take content notes on the article. When it is time to write your paper, you have two different and helpful resources to consult.

If you use photocopies as your primary reference without making any of your own content notes, you may have more work to do when you begin writing because you will need to spend time putting the source material in your own words. Writing paraphrases and summaries in content notes ahead of time will save you some work later in the process.

Whether you are taking notes in class or while doing research, there are different note-taking systems from which you can choose. Select the ones that work best for you, depending on the material and the instructor's or writer's style. Doing this will not only provide you with material to study from but also actually help you understand, absorb, and retain the information.

Paraphrase
A restatement of a written text or passage in another form or other words; often used to clarify meaning.

I will think flexibly.

In the best of all possible worlds, every instructor would come to class ready to deliver a well-organized presentation and have a dynamic speaking style that captures your interest. In this same idyllic world, every instructor's style would mesh perfectly with your note-taking style so that you can comfortably record everything of value.

The reality of the classroom is often very different. Throughout college, you will meet a range of instructors who have good days and bad days—just like anyone else. Moreover, even gifted instructors may sometimes use a stream-of-consciousness style that leaves you scribbling ferociously as you try to take notes that make sense.

Your success in the classroom depends, in part, on recording key concepts, on taking down examples and supporting data, and on writing down problems and solutions. Taking effective notes during a freewheeling presentation is possible only with flexibility. Open yourself up to different note-taking techniques, even if you've used one technique for as far back as you can remember. Having the flexibility to adjust your note-taking style to the situation will help ensure that your notes will help you learn.

REMEMBER!
the important points ○○○

How does note taking help you?

Notes help you learn when you are in class, doing research, or studying. The positive effects of taking notes include having written study material and becoming an active and involved listener. Note taking encourages you to think critically and to evaluate what is worth remembering. The notes you take during library research record what you learn from the sources you consult.

How can you make the most of class notes?

Class notes may contain critical definitions, explanations of difficult concepts, and narratives of events. Taking comprehensive class notes requires pre-class preparation, the skill to report accurately what you hear during class, and a commitment to review the notes after class, using critical thinking.

Which note-taking system should you use?

You can choose among several note-taking systems for class and research. These include formal or informal outlining, the Cornell system, and think links. Your goal is to use a system that feels comfortable and that fits the special needs of the situation. For example, the Cornell system or informal outlining may work best during class, whereas think links and formal outlining may be most useful for rewriting your notes during review sessions.

What can you do to take notes faster?

Note taking often requires rapid writing, especially in class. Using a version of personal shorthand, which replaces words with shorter words or symbols, will help you accurately record what the instructor says. To avoid the problem of forgetting what your shorthand means, review your notes while the abbreviations and symbols are fresh in your mind, and spell out words as you review.

What are research notes and how can you use them?

Research notes, the notes you take while gathering information to answer a research question, consist of source notes and content notes. Source notes are preliminary notes that you take as you briefly review available research. Content notes provide an in-depth, critical look at each source. Index cards work well for both source notes and content notes. Marginal notes and highlighting on photocopied research materials are also helpful.

Name   Date

CRITICAL THINKING
APPLYING LEARNING TO LIFE

Using Your Class Notes and Text to Study for an Exam

To evaluate the role your class notes play when you are learning information for an exam, take the following steps in one or more of your courses:

- Well in advance, make sure you understand what will be covered on the exam. Ask your instructor for clarification if you are confused.

- Start your studying by reviewing and learning the material in your class notes.

- Proceed to review the assigned text pages as well as material from other sources. Use SQ3R as a study tool (see Chapter 5). (This should not be the first time you read the assigned pages. As you learned in this chapter, reading the text *before* class is essential for getting the most out of the lecture and learning the material.)

- After you learn the material—but before your exam—evaluate the role your class notes played in your studying and their helpfulness to you by answering the following questions.

1. How important were your notes in learning the material?

   _____

   _____

2. Did your notes clarify important text concepts, did they cover material not found in the text, or both?

   _____

   _____

3. What does your answer to the previous question tell you about your instructor's teaching style and what he or she expects you to do independently to learn the material?

   _____

   _____

Your next step is to take the exam and evaluate the role your class notes played in your performance. The following will guide your analysis:

1. Evaluate how much of the material on the test was based on class lectures and discussions rather than just on the text. Then analyze how you did on these class-based questions. What does this analysis tell you about the effectiveness of your notes?

_____

_____

2. Evaluate how much of the test was based on your text rather than on ideas introduced in class. Then analyze how you did on these questions. What does this analysis tell you about the effectiveness of your method for studying your text?

_____

_____

3. Based on your analysis, describe three ways to improve your class notes before the next exam.

_____

_____

4. Finally, describe three ways to improve your method of studying your text and notes.

_____

_____

TEAM BUILDING
COLLABORATIVE SOLUTIONS

Create a Note-Taking Team

In your most demanding course, choose two people you can turn to for the class notes you may miss due to absence and to clarify notes that you took but that are confusing. Before a class, the three of you should agree to take a full set of notes and to schedule time after class to compare the results. It may help to photocopy all the notes to make comparisons easier.

As you compare, focus on the following characteristics of the notes:

- Legibility to the note taker and to other team members
- Completeness (Did you all record the same information? If not, why not?)
- Organizational effectiveness to the note taker and to other team members
- Value of the notes as a study aid to the note taker and to other team members

Now among the three of you, discuss specific ways to improve your personal note-taking skills so that you can rely on each other's notes in a crunch. Your goal is not to use your classmates' notes as a crutch, but to develop a support network to help you do the best you can in class.

Now put your agreement to the test. Follow the same procedure for another session of the same course and judge everyone's improvement as well as areas that need work.

personal
IMPROVEMENT
plan

I commit to three note-taking strategies to improve my study skills.
From this chapter, I choose three strategies that I think will help me.

Strategy 1: _____

Strategy 2: _____

Strategy 3: _____

I choose one strategy to focus on (circle this strategy above) and I will:

■ describe my goal—what I want to gain from using this strategy.

_____

_____

_____

■ describe in detail how I plan to use the strategy.

_____

_____

_____

_____

■ describe how I will measure my progress toward the goal this semester.

_____

_____

_____

_____

Activate the Habit of Mind

Here's how I will *think flexibly* to achieve this goal:

_____

_____

_____

_____

SUGGESTED READINGS

DePorter, Bobbi and Mike Hernacki. *Quantum Notes: Whole-Brain Approaches to Note-Taking*. Chicago: Learning Forum, 2000.

Dunkel, Patricia A., Frank Pialorsi, and Joane Kozyrez. *Advanced Listening Comprehension: Developing Aural & Note-Taking Skills*. Boston: Heinle & Heinle, 1996.

Klein, Brock and Matthew Hunt. *The Essential Workbook for Library and Internet Research Skills*. New York: McGraw-Hill, 1999.

Lebauer, R. Susan. *Learn to Listen, Listen to Learn: Academic Listening and Note-Taking*. Upper Saddle River, NJ: Prentice Hall, 2000.

Levin, Leonard. *Easy Script Express: Unique Speed Writing Methods to Take Fast Notes and Dictation*. Chicago: Legend Publishing, 2000.

INTERNET RESOURCES

Study Skills Guide: College of Saint Benedict/Saint John's University (important note-taking tips): **www.csbsju.edu/academicadvising/helplist.html**

Academic Skills Center—Notetaking Systems from California Polytechnic State University, San Luis Obispo (solid note-taking advice): **www.sas.calpoly.edu/asc/ssl/notetaking.systems.html**

ENDNOTES

1. William H. Armstrong and M. Willard Lampe II. *Pocket Guide to Study Tips,* 3rd ed. Hauppage, NY: Barron's Educational Series, Inc., 1990, p. 56.

2. Walter Pauk. *How to Study in College*, 7th ed. Boston: Houghton Mifflin, 2001, pp. 236–41.

THINKING IT THROUGH

Check those statements that apply to you right now:

■ Before an exam, I try to find out as much as I can about what will be covered and tailor my studying accordingly.

■ I get tense before and during exams, and I think the tension hurts my grades.

■ As soon as the instructor hands out the exam, I begin answering the questions.

■ I look for qualifying words—*always*, *never*, *sometimes*, and so forth—in short-answer questions since these words can change a question's meaning.

■ When I answer an essay question, I try to plan my response before I begin writing.

■ I don't really look at my answers after I get tests back, no matter the grades.

t Test Taking

DEVELOPING A WINNING STRATEGY FOR TEST SUCCESS

IN THIS CHAPTER

In this chapter, you explore answers to the following questions:

- How can preparation improve test performance?

- How can you work through test anxiety?

- What general strategies can help you succeed on tests?

- How can you master different types of test questions?

- How can you learn from test mistakes?

Taking responsible risks.

"Flexible people tend to go beyond established limits; they 'live on the edge' of their competence. . . . However, they do not behave impulsively. Their **risks are calculated.** They draw on past knowledge, are thoughtful about consequences, and have a well-trained sense of which risks are worthwhile."

—ART COSTA

*Every time you register for a new course, you are taking a responsible risk that may result in success or disappointment on class tests. Despite the risk, it is worth it to **put yourself out there.** If you are committed to learning, you will succeed by studying hard and mastering helpful test-taking techniques.*

For a runner, a race is equivalent to a test because it measures ability at a given moment. Doing well in a race requires training similar to the studying you do for exams. The best runners—and test takers—understand that they train not just for the race or test, but to achieve a level of competence that they will use in other settings.

While very few students look forward to exams—most students take them only because they have to—exams are actually an important part of the learning process. Why? Because they force you to focus on a body of material and learn it well enough to demonstrate mastery—to your instructor and yourself. Smart test preparation results in real learning that you take with you from course to course and into your career and life. When you show what you know on tests, you achieve concrete educational goals and develop confidence that you can perform well again and again. Exams also help you gauge your progress in a course and, if necessary, improve your efforts.

As you will see in this chapter, test taking is about preparation, persistence, and strategy. It's also about conquering fears, paying attention to details, and learning from mistakes.

How can preparation improve test performance?

Without even realizing it, you prepare for exams every day of the semester. By staying on top of class assignments, completing readings and projects, and participating in class discussions, you are actively learning what you need to know. Early and continual preparation—doing what you have to do for every class—is also the best way to retain what you learn and do well on exams.

When an exam is announced, the following strategies will help you prepare for exam day:

Identify Test Type and Material Covered

Before you begin studying, find out as much as you can about the test, including:

- *The topics the test will cover:* Will it cover everything since the semester began or will it be limited to a narrow topic?
- *The types of questions on the test:* Objective (multiple choice, true–false, sentence completion), subjective (essay), or a combination?
- *The material you will be tested on:* Will the test cover only what you learned in class and in the text, or will it also cover outside readings?

Your instructors may answer many of these questions. They may tell you the question format and the topics that will be on the test. Some instructors may even drop hints about possible test questions, either directly ("I might ask a question on this subject on your next exam") or more subtly ("One of my favorite theories is . . . ").

Here are a few other strategies for predicting what may be on a test.

Use SQ3R to identify what's important. Often, the questions you write and ask yourself when you read assigned materials may be part of the test. Textbook study questions are also good candidates.

Talk to people who already took the course. Try to assess test difficulty, whether tests focus primarily on assigned readings or class notes, what materials are usually covered, and what types of questions are asked. Also ask about instructors' preferences. If you learn that the instructor pays close attention to specific facts, for example, use flash cards to drill yourself on details. If he or she emphasizes a global overview, focus on conceptualization and example-to-idea thinking (see Chapter 4).

Examine old tests, if the instructor makes them available. You may find them in class, on-line, or on reserve in the library. If you are unsure of whether your instructor or the student grapevine is the source of these exams, ask your instructor directly. Using old exams without the instructor's permission is a form of cheating.

Old tests will help you answer the following questions:

- Does the instructor focus on examples and details, general ideas and themes, or a combination?
- Can you do well through straight memorization or should you take a critical-thinking approach?
- Are the questions straightforward or confusing and sometimes tricky?
- Do the tests require that you integrate facts from different areas in order to draw conclusions?

After taking the first exam in the course, you will have a better idea of what to expect.

Create a Study Plan and Schedule

Now choose what you will study. Go through your notes, texts, related primary sources, and handouts, and set aside materials you don't need. Then prioritize the remaining materials. Your goal is to focus on information that is most likely to be on the exam.

Next, use your time-management skills to prepare a schedule. Consider all of the relevant factors—your study materials, the number of days

reflect

Think about the relationship between testing and mastering something new. Do you think you would learn as much if you didn't have to take tests? Why or why not? If you "need" tests as a motivator, do you consider that a strength or weakness? Why or why not? As you reflect, think about something you recently mastered—like cooking a great omelet or playing a new song on your guitar—and how "getting it right" made you feel. Consider whether you think mastering course material will give you similar feelings of satisfaction.

& respond

until the test, and the time you can study each day. If you establish your schedule ahead of time and write it in a date book, you are more likely to follow it.

Schedules may vary widely according to the situation. For example, if you have three days before the test and no other obligations during that time, you might set two 2-hour study sessions during each day. On the other hand, if you have two weeks before a test, classes during the day, and work three nights a week, you might spread out your study sessions over the nights you have off during those two weeks.

Prepare Through Careful Review

A thorough review will give you the best shot at remembering the material you are studying. Use the following strategies when you study:

Use SQ3R. The reading method you studied in Chapter 5 provides an excellent structure for reviewing your reading materials.

- *Surveying* gives you an overview of topics.
- *Questioning* helps you focus on important ideas and determine what the material is trying to communicate.
- *Reading* (or, in this case, rereading) reminds you of the ideas and supporting information.
- *Reciting* helps to anchor the concepts in your head.
- *Reviewing*, such as quizzing yourself on the Q-stage questions, summarizing sections you highlight, making flash cards for important concepts, and outlining text chapters, helps solidify learning.

Review your notes. The following techniques will help you review your notes before an exam:

Taking a pretest in a test-like setting can be an effective review technique.

- *Time your reviews carefully.* Review notes for the first time within a day of the lecture, if you can, and then review again closer to the test day.
- *Mark up your notes.* Reread them, filling in missing information, clarifying points, writing out abbreviations, and highlighting key ideas.
- *Organize your notes.* Consider adding headings and subheadings to your notes to clarify the structure of the information. Rewrite them using a different organizing structure—for example, an outline if you originally used a think link.
- *Summarize your notes.* Evaluate which ideas and examples are most important, then rewrite your notes in shortened form, focusing on those ideas and examples. Summarize your notes in writing or with a summary think link. Try summarizing from memory as a self-test.

Complete the following checklist for each exam to define your study goals, get organized, and stay on track:

Course: _____ Instructor: _____

Date, time, and place of test: _____

Type of test (e.g., is it a midterm or a minor quiz?) _____

What instructor said about the test, including types of test questions, test length, and how much the test counts toward your final grade:

_____

_____

Topics to be covered on the test, in order of importance:

1. _____
2. _____
3. _____
4. _____
5. _____

Study schedule, including materials you plan to study (texts, class notes, homework problems, and so forth) and dates you plan to complete each:

Material   **Completion Date**

1. _____   _____
2. _____   _____
3. _____   _____
4. _____   _____
5. _____   _____

Materials you are expected to bring to the test (e.g., textbook, sourcebook, calculator).

_____

_____

Special study arrangements (such as plan study group meetings, ask the instructor for special help, get outside tutoring).

_____

_____

Life-management issues (e.g., rearrange work hours):

_____

_____

Source: Adapted from Ron Fry, *"Ace" Any Test*, 3rd ed. Franklin Lakes, NJ: Career Press, 1996, pp. 123–24.

Think critically. Using the techniques discussed in Chapter 4, approach test preparation as a critical thinker, working to understand material rather than just to repeat facts. As you study, try to analyze causes and effects, look at issues from different perspectives, and connect concepts that, on the surface, appear unrelated. This work will increase your understanding and probably result in higher test grades. Critical thinking is especially important for essay tests that require you to develop and support a thesis.

"The secret of a leader lies in the tests he has faced over the whole course of his life and the habit of action he develops in meeting those tests."

GAIL SHEEHY

Take a Pretest

Use questions from your textbook to create your own pretest. Most textbooks include end-of-chapter questions. If your course doesn't have an assigned text, develop questions from your notes and assigned outside readings. Old homework problems will also help you target your areas of weakness. Choose questions that are likely to be covered on the test, then answer them under test-like conditions—in a quiet place, with no books or notes to help you (unless your exam is open book), and with a clock to tell you when to quit.

Prepare Physically

Most tests ask you to work efficiently under time pressure, so try to be at your best. A good night's sleep will leave you rested and alert and improve your ability to remember the material you studied the night before.

Eating right is also important. Sugar-laden snacks bring up your energy, only to send you crashing down much too soon. Also, too much caffeine can add to your tension and make it difficult to focus. Eating nothing leaves you drained, but too much food can make you sleepy. The best advice is to eat a light, well-balanced meal before a test. When time is short, grab a quick-energy snack such as a banana, orange juice, or a granola bar.

Make the Most of Last-Minute Studying

Cramming—studying intensively and around the clock right before an exam—often results in information going into your head and popping right back out shortly after the exam is over. *If learning is your goal, cramming is not a good idea.* The reality, however, is that nearly every student crams during college, especially during midterms and finals when time is short. Use these hints to make the most of this intensive study time:

- *Review your flash cards.* If you use flash cards, review them one last time.
- *Focus on crucial concepts.* Don't worry about the rest. Resist reviewing notes or texts page by page.

Cramming
Hasty, last-minute preparation for an examination.

MULTIPLE PATHWAYS TO LEARNING

MULTIPLE INTELLIGENCE STRATEGIES *for* Test Preparation

If the topic or format of a test challenges your stronger or weaker intelligences, these tips will help you make the most of your time and abilities.

INTELLIGENCE	SUGGESTED STRATEGIES	WHAT WORKS FOR YOU? WRITE NEW IDEAS HERE
Verbal–Linguistic	■ Think of and write out questions your instructor may ask on a test. Answer the questions and then try rewriting them in a different format (essay, true–false, and so on). ■ Underline important words in review questions or practice questions.	
Logical–Mathematical	■ Make diagrams of review or practice questions. ■ Outline the key steps involved in topics on which you may be tested.	
Bodily–Kinesthetic	■ Review out loud. Recite concepts, terms and definitions, important lists, dates, and so on. ■ Create a sculpture, model, or skit to depict a tough concept that will be on your test.	
Visual–Spatial	■ Create a think link to map out an important topic and its connections to other topics in the material. Study it and redraw it from memory a day before the test. ■ Make drawings related to possible test topics.	
Interpersonal	■ Form a study group and encourage each other. ■ In your group, come up with as many possible test questions as you can. Ask each other these questions in an oral exam format.	
Intrapersonal	■ Brainstorm test questions. Then, come back to them after a break or even a day's time. On your own, take the sample "test" you developed. ■ Make time to review in a solitary setting.	
Musical	■ Play music while you read if it does not distract you. ■ Study concepts by reciting them to rhythms you create or to music.	
Naturalistic	■ Bring your text, lecture notes, and other pertinent information to an outdoor spot that inspires you and helps you to feel confident, and review your material there.	

- *Create a last-minute study sheet.* On a single sheet of paper, write down key facts, definitions, formulas, and so on. If you prefer visual notes, use think links to map out ideas and supporting examples.
- *Arrive early.* Study the sheet or your flash cards until you are asked to clear your desk.

After your exam, evaluate how cramming affected how much you remember. Within a few days, you will probably recall very little—a reality that will work against you in advanced courses that build on this knowledge and in careers that require it. Since cramming is not in your long-term best interest, think about starting to study earlier before your next exam.

Whether you cram or not, you may experience anxiety on test day. Following are some ideas for how to handle test anxiety when it strikes.

How can you work through test anxiety?

A certain amount of stress can be a good thing. Your body is alert, and your energy motivates you to do your best. Some students, however, experience incapacitating stress before and during exams, especially midterms and finals, that results in lower grades.

Test anxiety can cause sweating, nausea, dizziness, headaches, and fatigue. It can reduce your ability to concentrate and make you feel overwhelmed and depressed. You can minimize your anxiety by preparing thoroughly and building a positive attitude. (Chapter 9 includes additional techniques for dealing with anxiety before math tests.)

Test anxiety
A bad case of nerves that makes it hard to think or remember during an exam.

Preparation

The more confident you feel about the material, the better you will perform on test day. In this sense, consider all the preparation and study information in *Keys to Effective Learning* as test-anxiety assistance. Also, finding out what to expect on the exam will help you feel more in control. Seek out information about the material that will be covered, the question format, the length of the exam, and the points assigned to each question.

Creating a detailed study plan builds your knowledge as it combats anxiety. Divide the plan into small tasks. As you finish each, you gain a sense of accomplishment, confidence, and control. Instead of worrying about the test, take active steps that will help you succeed.

Attitude

Maintaining a positive attitude is also important. Here are ways to maintain an attitude that will help you succeed.

- *See the test as an opportunity to learn.* All too often, students view tests as contests that they either "win" or "lose." However, if you see a test as a signpost along the way to a greater goal, mastering the material will be more important than "winning."

- *Understand that tests measure performance, not personal value.* Your grade does not reflect your ability to succeed. Whether you get an A or an F, you are still the same person.

- *Appreciate your instructor's purpose.* To instructors, exams are opportunities for students to show what they know, not chances for the instructor to make students' life difficult. They want to help you succeed, so don't hesitate to visit them during office hours and send e-mail questions to clarify material before tests.

- *Seek study partners who challenge you.* Find study partners who can inspire you to do your best. Try to avoid people who are also anxious, because you may pick up their negative feelings. (For more on study groups, see Chapter 5.)

- *Set yourself up for success.* Expect progress and success—not failure. Take responsibility for creating success through your work and attitude. Know that, ultimately, you are responsible for the outcome.

- *Practice relaxation.* When you feel test anxiety mounting, breathe deeply, close your eyes, and visualize positive mental images such as getting a good grade and finishing with time to spare. Try to ease muscle tension— stretch your neck, tighten and then release your muscles.

- *Practice positive self-talk.* Tell yourself that you can do well, that studying will pay off in the form of a good grade, and that it is normal to feel anxious, particularly before an important exam. As you walk into the testing room, give yourself a pep talk that builds confidence—something like, *"I know this stuff, and I'm going to show everyone what I know."* Also, slay the perfection monster inside of you by telling yourself, *"I don't have to get a perfect score."*

reflect

Do you experience test anxiety? Describe how tests generally make you feel (you might in-clude an example of a specific test situation and what happened). Identify your specific test-taking fears, and write out your plan to overcome fears and self-defeating behaviors. If test anxiety isn't a problem, what do you think contributes to your pre-test calm?

& respond

Test Anxiety and the Returning Student

If you're returning to school after years away, you may question your ability to learn. To deal with these feelings, focus on what you have learned through life experience. For example, managing work and a family requires strong time-management, planning, and communication skills that can help you plan study time, juggle school responsibilities, and interact with students and instructors.

"Fear is nature's warning sign to get busy."

HENRY C. LINK

In addition, your life experiences will give abstract classroom concepts real meaning. For example, workplace relationships may help you understand social psychology concepts, and refinancing your home mortgage may help you grasp the importance of interest-rate swings—a key concept in economics. Feeling good about the knowledge and skills you have acquired over the years will improve your ability to achieve your goals.

Parents who have to juggle child care with study time can find the challenge especially difficult before a test. Here are some suggestions that might help:

- *Find help.* This is especially important with younger children. Ask a relative or friend to watch the children during study time, or arrange for your child to visit a friend. Consider trading baby-sitting hours with another parent, hiring a baby-sitter who will come to your home, or enrolling your child in day care.

    - *Plan activities.* Also important if you have younger children is a supply of games, books, and videos they can use to play quietly while you study.

    - *Tell your children why the test is important.* When your children are school-aged, they will understand concrete reasons why study time is important. For example, doing well in school might mean a high-paying job after graduation, which, in turn, can mean more money for family vacations.

    - *Explain the time frame.* Tell school-aged children your study schedule and when the test will occur. Plan a reward after your test—going for ice cream, seeing a movie, or having a picnic.

Preparing for an exam sets the stage for taking the exam. You are ready to focus on methods to help you succeed when the test begins.

What general strategies can help you succeed on tests?

Even though every test is different, there are general strategies that will help you handle almost all tests, including short-answer and essay exams. Chapter 9 includes additional techniques to strengthen your performance on math and science tests.

Write Down Key Facts

Before you even look at the test, write down key information—including formulas, rules, and definitions—that you studied recently. Use the back of the question sheet or some scrap paper for your notes. (Be sure your instructor knows that you made these notes after the test began.) Recording this information at the start prevents your forgetting it.

Begin with an Overview of the Exam

Although exam time is precious, spend a few minutes at the start of the test getting a sense of the questions—how many there are in each section, what types, and their point values. Use this information to schedule your time. For example, if a two-hour test is divided into two sections of equal point value—an essay section with four questions and a short-answer section with 60 questions—you can spend an hour on the essays (15 minutes per question) and an hour on the short-answer section (one minute per question). As you calculate, think about the level of difficulty of each section. If you think you can handle the short-answer questions in less than an hour, budget more time for the essays.

Read Test Directions

Reading test directions carefully can save you trouble. For example, although a history test of 100 true-or-false questions and one essay may look straightforward, the directions may tell you to answer 80 of the 100 questions or that the essay is optional. If the directions indicate that you are penalized for incorrect answers—meaning that you lose points instead of simply not gaining points—avoid guessing unless you're fairly certain.

When you read directions, you may learn that some questions or sections are **weighted** more heavily than others. For example, the short-answer questions may be worth 30 points, whereas the essays are worth 70. In this case, it's smart to spend more time on the essays than the short answers. To stay aware of the specifics of the directions, circle or underline key words and numbers.

Weighted
Given a higher or lower point value.

Mark Up the Test Questions

Marking up the test in order to highlight key words and instructions will help you avoid careless errors. As you read each question, circle qualifiers, such as *always, never, all, none,* and *every;* verbs that communicate specific test instructions; and concepts that are tricky or need special attention. If you are prohibited from writing on the test, mark these words lightly with a pencil, and erase the marks at the end of the exam.

Take Special Care on Machine-Scored Tests

Use the right pencil (usually a number 2) on machine-scored tests, and mark your answer in the correct space, filling the space completely. Periodically, check the answer number against the question number to make sure they match. If you mark the answer to question 4 in the space for question 5, not only will your response to question 4 be wrong, but also your responses to all subsequent questions will be off by a line. To avoid this problem, put a small dot next to any number you skip and plan to return to later.

Neatness counts on these tests because the computer can misread stray pencil marks or partially erased answers. If you mark two answers to a question and only partially erase one, the computer will read both responses and charge you with a wrong answer.

Because you have access to the text material, an open-book exam tests your ability to connect and analyze ideas and examples.

Work from Easy to Hard

Begin with the easiest questions, and try to answer them quickly. This will boost your confidence and leave more time for questions that require greater effort. Mark difficult questions as you reach them, and return to them after you answer the questions you know.

Watch the Clock

Keep track of how much time is left and how you are progressing. Some students are so concerned about time that they rush through the test and have time left over. Instead of leaving early, spend the remaining time refining and checking your work. You may correct inadvertent errors, change answers, or add more information to an essay.

Master the Art of Intelligent Guessing

When you are unsure of an answer on a short-answer test, you can leave it blank or guess. As long as you are not penalized for incorrect answers, guessing helps you. "Intelligent guessing," writes Steven Frank, an authority on student studying and test taking, "means taking advantage of what you do know in order to try to figure out what you don't. If you guess intelligently, you have a decent shot at getting the answer right."[1]

First, eliminate all the answers you know—or believe—are wrong. Try to narrow your choices to two possible answers; then choose the one you think is more likely to be correct. Strategies for guessing the correct answer on a multiple-choice test are discussed later in this chapter.

When you check your work at the end of the test, ask yourself whether you would make the same guesses again. Chances are that you will leave your answers alone, but you may notice something that changes your mind—a qualifier that affects meaning, a recalled fact that enables you to answer the question without guessing, or a miscalculation in a math problem.

Use Critical Thinking to Avoid Errors

Critical thinking can help you work through questions and avoid errors. Following are some critical-thinking strategies to use during a test:

- 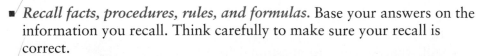*Recall facts, procedures, rules, and formulas.* Base your answers on the information you recall. Think carefully to make sure your recall is correct.
- 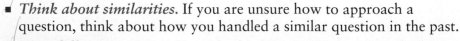*Think about similarities.* If you are unsure how to approach a question, think about how you handled a similar question in the past.
- *Note differences.* Especially with objective questions, items that seem different from the material you studied may clue you in to answers you can eliminate.
- *Think through causes and effects.* For a numerical problem, think about how you plan to solve it and see if the answer—the effect of your plan—makes sense. For an essay question that asks you to analyze a condition or situation, consider both what caused it and what effects it has.

- *Find the best idea to match the example(s) given.* For a numerical problem, decide what formula (idea) best applies to the example or examples (the data of the problem). For an essay question, decide what idea applies to, or links, the examples given.

- *Support ideas with examples.* When answering an essay question, be sure to back up your ideas with supporting examples.

- *Evaluate each test question.* In your initial approach to a question, decide what kinds of thinking will best help you solve it. For example, essay questions often require cause-and-effect and idea-to-example thinking, whereas objective questions often benefit from thinking about similarities and differences.

Maintain Academic Integrity

When you take a test honestly, following all the rules of the test, you strengthen the principle of trust between students and instructors, which is at the heart of academic integrity (see Chapter 1). You also receive an accurate reading of how much you know and how much you still need to learn. Finally, you reinforce the habit of honesty.

Cheating as a strategy to pass a test or get a better grade robs you of the opportunity to learn the material on which you are being tested, which, ultimately, is your loss. It also makes fair play between students impossible. When one student studies hard for an exam and another cheats and both get the same high grade, the efforts of the hard-working student are diminished. It is important to realize that cheating jeopardizes your future at college if you are caught. You may be seriously reprimanded—or even expelled—if you violate your school's code of academic integrity.

Now that you have explored these general strategies, you can use what you've learned to address specific types of test questions.

How can you master different types of test questions?

Every type of test question has a different way of finding out how much you know about a subject. For **objective questions**, you choose or write a short answer, often making a selection from a limited number of choices. Multiple-choice, fill-in-the-blank, matching, and true-or-false questions fall into this category. **Subjective questions** demand the same information recall as objective questions, but they also require you to plan, organize, draft, and refine a response. All essay questions are subjective.

Figure 8.1 shows samples of real test questions from western civilization, macroeconomics, Spanish, and biology college texts published by Pearson Education. Included are multiple-choice, true–false, fill-in-the-blank, matching, and essay questions, including a short-answer essay. Seeing these questions firsthand will help you feel more comfortable with testing formats and question types when you take your first exams.

objective questions
Short-answer questions that test your ability to recall, compare, and contrast information and link ideas to examples.

Subjective questions
Essay questions that require you to express your answer in terms of your personal knowledge and perspectives and to formulate responses.

FIGURE 8.1   Real test questions from real college texts.

From Chapter 29, "The End of Imperialism," in *Western Civilization: A Social and Cultural History*, 2nd edition.[2]

■ **MULTIPLE-CHOICE QUESTION**

India's first leader after independence was:

A. Gandhi   B. Bose   C. Nehru   D. Sukharno   *(answer: C)*

■ **FILL-IN-THE-BLANK QUESTION**

East Pakistan became the country of _____ in 1971.

A. Burma   B. East India   C. Sukharno   D. Bangladesh   *(answer: D)*

■ **TRUE–FALSE QUESTION**

The United States initially supported Vietnamese independence.   T   F   *(answer: false)*

■ **ESSAY QUESTION**

Answer one of the following:

1. What led to Irish independence? What conflicts continued to exist after independence?
2. How did Gandhi work to rid India of British control? What methods did he use?

From Chapter 6, "Unemployment and Inflation," in *Macroeconomics: Principles and Tools*, 3rd edition.[3]

■ **MULTIPLE-CHOICE QUESTION**

If the labor force is 250,000 and the total population 16 years of age or older is 300,000, the labor-force participation rate is

A. 79.5%   B. 83.3%   C. 75.6%   D. 80.9%   *(answer: B)*

■ **FILL-IN-THE-BLANK QUESTION**

Mike has just graduated from college and is now looking for a job, but has not yet found one. This causes the employment rate to _____ and the labor-force participation rate to _____.

A. increase; decrease   C. stay the same; stay the same

B. increase; increase   D. increase; stay the same   *(answer: C)*

■ **TRUE/FALSE QUESTION**

The Consumer Price Index somewhat overstates changes in the cost of living because it does not allow for substitutions that consumers might make in response to price changes.   T   F   *(answer: true)*

■ **SHORT-ANSWER ESSAY QUESTION**

During a press conference, the Secretary of Employment notes that the unemployment rate is 7.0%. As a political opponent, how might you criticize this figure as an underestimate? In rebuttal, how might the Secretary argue that the reported rate is an overestimate of unemployment?

(Possible answer: The unemployment rate given by the secretary might be considered an underestimate because discouraged workers, who have given up the job search in frustration, are not counted as unemployed. In addition, full-time workers may have been forced to work part-time. In rebuttal, the secretary might note that a portion of the unemployed have voluntarily left their jobs. Most workers are unemployed only briefly and leave the ranks of the unemployed by gaining better jobs than they had previously held.)

From: Mosaicos: Spanish as a World Language, 3rd edition.[4]

■ **MATCHING QUESTION**

You are learning new words and your teacher asks you to think of an object similar to or related to the words he says. His words are listed below. Next to each word, write a related word from the box below.

el reloj	el cuaderno	el pupitre	una computadora
el televisor	la tiza	el lápis	la mochila

1. el escritorio _____

2. el bolígrafo _____

3. la videocasetera _____

4. la pizarra _____

5. el libro _____

(answers: 1. el pupitre; 2. el lápis; 3. el televisor; 4. la tiza; 5. el cuaderno)

■ **ESSAY QUESTION**

Your mother always worries about you and wants to know what you are doing with your time in Granada. Write a short letter to her describing your experience in Spain. In your letter, you should address the following points:

1. What classes you take

2. When and where you study

3. How long you study every day

4. What you do with your time (mention three activities)

5. Where you go during your free time (mention two places)

From Chapter 13, "DNA Structure and Replication," in *Biology: A Guide to the Natural World*, 2nd edition. [5]

■ **MULTIPLE-CHOICE QUESTION**

What units are bonded together to make a strand of DNA?

A. chromatids   B. cells   C. enzymes   D. nucleotides   E. proteins   *(answer: D)*

■ **TRUE–FALSE QUESTION**

Errors never occur in DNA replication, because the DNA polymerases edit out mistakes.   T   F

(answer: false)

■ **FILL-IN-THE-BLANK QUESTION**

In a normal DNA molecule, adenine always pairs with _____ and cytosine always pairs with_____.   *(answers: thymine; guanine)*

■ **MATCHING QUESTION**

Match the scientist and the approximate time frames (decades of their work) with their achievements.

Column 1	Column 2
____ 1. Modeled the molecular structure of DNA	A. George Beadle and Edward Tatum, 1930s and 1940s
____ 2. Generated X-ray crystallography images of DNA	B. James Watson and Francis Crick, 1950s
____ 3. Correlated the production of one enzyme with one gene	C. Rosalind Franklin and Maurice Wilkins, 1950s

(answers: 1–B; 2–C; 3–A)

Multiple-Choice Questions

Multiple-choice questions are the most popular type of question on standardized tests. The following strategies can help you answer them:

- *Carefully read the directions.* Directions can be tricky. For example, whereas most test items ask for a single correct answer, some give you the option of marking several choices that are correct. For some tests, you might be required to answer only a certain number of questions.

- *Read each question thoroughly.* Then look at the choices, and try to answer the question. This strategy reduces the possibility that the choices will confuse you.

- *Underline key words and phrases.* If the question is complicated, try to break it down into small sections that are easy to understand.

Examples of the kinds of questions you might encounter in a Psychology course[6] (the correct answer follows each question).

1. Arnold is at the company party and has had too much to drink. He releases all of his pent-up aggression by yelling at his boss, who promptly fires him. Arnold normally would not have yelled at his boss, but after drinking heavily he yelled because

    A. parties are places where employees are supposed to be able to "loosen up"

    B. alcohol is a stimulant

    C. alcohol makes people less concerned with the negative consequences of their behavior

    D. alcohol inhibits brain centers that control the perception of loudness   *(answer: C)*

2. Which of the following has not been shown to be a probable cause of or influence on the development of alcoholism in our society?

    A. intelligence   C. personality

    B. culture   D. genetic vulnerability   *(answer: A)*

3. Geraldine is a heavy coffee drinker who has become addicted to caffeine. If she completely ceases her intake of caffeine over the next few days, she is likely to experience each of the following EXCEPT

    A. depression   C. insomnia

    B. lethargy   D. headaches   *(answer: C)*

Are the following questions true or false?

1. Alcohol use is clearly related to increases in hostility, aggression, violence, and abusive behavior.   *(true)*

2. Marijuana is harmless.   *(false)*

3. Simply expecting a drug to produce an effect is often enough to produce the effect.   *(true)*

4. Alcohol is a stimulant.   *(false)*

- *Pay attention to words that could throw you off.* For example, it is easy to overlook negatives in a question ("Which of the following is *not* . . . ").

- *If you don't know the answer, eliminate answers that you know or suspect are wrong.* Your goal is to leave yourself with two possible answers, which would give you a 50–50 chance of making the right choice. To eliminate choices, ask yourself:
  - *Is the choice accurate on its own terms?* If there's an error in the choice—for example, a term that is incorrectly defined—the answer is wrong.
  - *Is the choice relevant?* An answer may be accurate, but it may not relate to the essence of the question.
  - *Are there any qualifiers?* Absolute qualifiers, like *always, never, all, none,* or *every,* often signal an exception that makes a choice incorrect. For example, the statement "Normal children always begin talking before the age of two" is untrue (most normal children begin talking before age two, but some start later). Analysis has shown that choices containing conservative qualifiers (e.g., *often, most, rarely,* or *may sometimes be*) are often correct.
  - *Do the choices give clues?* Does a puzzling word remind you of a word you know? If you don't know a word, does any part of the word—its prefix, suffix, or root—seem familiar?

- *Make an educated guess by looking for patterns.* The ideal is to know the material so well that you don't have to guess, but that isn't always possible. Test-taking experts point to patterns in multiple-choice questions that may help you. Here is their advice:
  - Consider the possibility that a choice that is *more general* than the others is the right answer.
  - Consider the possibility that a choice that is *longer* than the others is the right answer.
  - Look for a choice that has a *middle value in a range* (the range can be from small to large or from old to recent). It is likely to be the right answer.
  - Look for two choices that have *similar meanings.* One of these answers is probably correct.
  - Look for answers that *agree grammatically with the question.* For example, a fill-in-the-blank question that has an *a* or *an* before the blank gives you a clue to the correct answer.

  Keep in mind that these and other patterns may not apply to the specific questions you encounter on tests.

- *Make sure you read every word of every answer.* Instructors have been known to include answers that are almost right, except for a single word. Focus especially on qualifying words such as *always, never, tend to, most, often,* and *frequently.*

- *When questions are keyed to a reading passage, read the questions first.* This will help you focus on the information you need to answer the questions.

True-or-False Questions

True-or-false questions test your knowledge of facts and concepts. Read them carefully to evaluate what they are asking. If you're stumped, guess (unless you're penalized for wrong answers).

Look for qualifiers in true-or-false questions—such as *all, only,* and *always* (the absolutes that often make a statement false) and *generally, often, usually,* and *sometimes* (the conservatives that often make a statement true)—that can turn a statement that would otherwise be true into one that is false or vice versa. For example, "The grammar rule 'I before E except after C' is *always* true" is false, whereas "The grammar rule 'I before E except after C' is *usually* true" is true. The qualifier makes the difference.

Matching Questions

Matching questions ask you to match the terms in one list with the terms in another list, according to the directions. For example, the directions may tell you to match a communicable disease with the pathogen that usually causes it. The following strategies will help you handle these questions.

- *Make sure you understand the directions.* The directions tell you whether each answer can be used only once or more than once.

- *Work from the column with the longest entries.* The left-hand column usually contains terms to be defined or questions to be answered, while the right-hand column contains definitions or answers. As a result, entries in the right-hand column are usually longer than those on the left. Reading the items on the right only once each will save time as you attempt to match them with the shorter phrases on the left.

- *Start with the matches you know.* On your first run-through, mark these matches immediately with a penciled line, waiting to finalize your choices after you've completed all the items. Keep in mind that if you can use an answer only once, you may have to change answers if you reconsider any of your original choices.

- *Finally, tackle the matches you're not sure of.* On your next run-through, focus on the more difficult matches. Look for clues and relationships you might not have thought of at first. Think back to class lectures, notes, and study sessions and try to visualize the correct response.

  Consider the possibility that one of your sure-thing answers is wrong. If one or more phrases seem to have no correct answer, look back at your easy matches to be sure that you did not jump too quickly. See if another phrase can be used instead, thus freeing up an answer for use in another match.

- *A final suggestion:* If you are left with two matches—two on the left and two on the right—and you really don't know the correct matches, you could pair them randomly, giving yourself an even chance of getting both right—or both wrong. Alternatively, you could give the same answer to both matches. That way, at least one of the matches will be correct.

> *"A little knowledge that acts is worth infinitely more than much knowledge that is idle."*
>
> **KAHLIL GIBRAN**

Fill-in-the-Blank Questions

Fill-in-the-blank questions, also known as sentence completion questions, ask you to supply one or more words or phrases with missing information that completes the sentence. These strategies will help you make the right choices.

- *Be logical.* Insert your answer; then reread the sentence from beginning to end to be sure it is factually and grammatically correct and makes sense.

- *Note the length and number of the blanks.* These are important clues but not absolute guideposts. If two blanks appear right after one another, the instructor is probably looking for a two-word answer. If a blank is longer than usual, the correct response may require additional space. However, if you are certain of an answer that doesn't seem to fit the blanks, trust your knowledge and instincts.

- *Pay attention to how blanks are separated.* If there is more than one blank in a sentence and the blanks are widely separated, treat eachone separately. Answering each as if it were a separate sentence-completion question increases the likelihood that you will get at least one answer correct. Here is an example:

When Toni Morrison was awarded the _____ Prize for Literature, she was a professor at _____ University.
(Answer: Morrison received the Nobel Prize and is a professor at Princeton University.)

In this case, and in many other cases, your knowledge of one answer has little impact on your knowledge of the other answer.

- *Think out of the box.* If you can think of more than one correct answer, put them both down. Your instructor may be impressed by your assertiveness and creativity.

- *Make a guess.* If you are uncertain of an answer, make an educated guess. Use qualifiers like *may, sometimes,* and *often* to increase the chance that your answer is at least partially correct. Have faith that after hours of studying, the correct answer is somewhere in your subconscious mind and that your guess is not completely random.

Examples of questions you might encounter in an Astronomy course[7] (correct answers follow questions).

1. A _____ is a collection of hundreds of billions of stars.   *(galaxy)*

2. Rotation is the term used to describe the motion of a body around some _____.   *(axis)*

3. The solar day is measured relative to the sun; the sidereal day is measured relative to the _____.

   (stars)

4. On December 21, known as the_____, the sun is at its_____.

   (winter solstice; southernmost point)

Essay Questions

An essay question allows you to express your knowledge and views more extensively than a short-answer question. With the freedom to express your views, though, comes the challenge to demonstrate your ability to organize and express that knowledge clearly. Questions that require short, subjective explanations—no longer than a paragraph or two—also require clear thinking and clear writing.

The following steps will help improve your responses to essay questions. Many of these guidelines reflect methods for approaching any writing assignment. That is, you undertake an abbreviated version of the writing process as you plan, draft, revise, and edit your response (see Chapter 10). The primary differences here are that you are writing under time pressure and that you are working from memory.

1. Start by reading the questions. Decide which to tackle (if there's a choice). Then focus on what each question is asking and the mind actions you need to use. Read the directions carefully and do everything asked. Some essay questions may contain more than one part, so it is important to budget your time. For example, if you have one hour to answer three question sections, you might budget 20 minutes for each section, and break that down into writing stages, three minutes for planning, 15 minutes for drafting, two minutes for revising and editing).

2. Watch for action verbs. Certain verbs can help you figure out how to think. Figure 8.2 explains some words commonly used in essay questions. Underline these words as you read, clarify what they mean, and use them to guide your writing.

3. Plan. Brainstorm ideas and examples. Create an informal outline, as shown in Figure 8.3, or a think link to map your ideas and list your supporting examples. (See Chapter 10 for a discussion of these organizational devices.)

4. Draft. Start with a thesis statement that states clearly what your essay will say. Then, devote one or more paragraphs to the main points in your outline. Back up the general statement that starts each paragraph with evidence in the form of examples, statistics, and so on. Use simple, clear language, and look back at your outline to make sure you cover everything. Wrap it up with a short, pointed conclusion. Since you probably won't have time for redrafting, try to be as complete and organized as possible as you write.

TAKE ACTION

Write to the Verb

On essay tests, focusing on the action verbs in test instructions can mean the difference between giving instructors what they want and answering questions that were never asked. This exercise will help you read essay instructions accurately.

■ Start by choosing a topic you learned about in this text—for example, the Habit of Mind presented in each chapter or the critical-thinking mind actions. Write your topic here:

_____

_____

■ Then put yourself in the role of your instructor, and write instructions for an essay question in the course. Use one of the action verbs in Figure 8.2 to frame the question. For example, "List the Habits of Mind presented in *Keys to Effective Learning*," or "Analyze the importance of understanding how your mind works."

_____

_____

■ Now choose three other action verbs from Figure 8.2, and use each to rewrite the instructions.

1. _____

2. _____

3. _____

■ Finally, analyze how each new verb changes the focus of the essay.

1. _____

_____

2. _____

_____

3. _____

FIGURE 8.2   Common action verbs on essay tests.

Analyze—Break into parts and discuss each part separately.	**Explain**— Make the meaning of something clear, often by making analogies or giving examples.
Compare—Explain similarities and differences.	**Illustrate**—Supply examples.
Contrast—Distinguish between items being compared by focusing on differences.	**Interpret**—Explain your personal view of facts and ideas and how they relate to one another.
Criticize—Evaluate the positive and negative effects of what is being discussed.	**Outline**—Organize and present the main examples of an idea or sub-ideas.
Define—State the essential quality or meaning. Give the common idea.	**Prove**—Use evidence and argument to show that something is true, usually by showing cause and effect or giving examples that fit the idea to be proven.
Describe—Visualize and give information that paints a complete picture.	**Review**—Provide an overview of ideas and establish their merits and features.
Discuss—Examine in a complete and detailed way, usually by connecting ideas to examples.	**State**—Explain clearly, simply, and concisely, being sure that each word gives the image you want.
Enumerate/List/Identify—Recall and specify items in the form of a list.	**Summarize**—Give the important ideas in brief.
Evaluate—Give your opinion about the value or worth of something, usually by weighing positive and negative effects, and justify your conclusion.	**Trace**—Present a history of the way something developed, often by showing cause and effect.

FIGURE 8.3   Informal outline made during essay test.

Roles of BL in IC
1. To contradict or reinforce words
   —e.g., friend says "I'm fine"
2. To add shades of meaning
   —saying the same sentence in 3 diff. ways
3. To make lasting 1st impression
   —impact of nv cues and voice tone greater than words
   —we assume things abt person based on posture, eye contact, etc.

5. Revise. Make sure you answer the question completely and include all of your points. Look for ideas you left out, general statements that are poorly supported, paragraphs with faulty structure, extraneous material, and confusing sentences. You can add new material in the margins, indicating with an arrow where it fits, or you can indicate that inserts can be found on separate pages. If you have more than one insert, label each to avoid confusion (e.g., Insert #1, Insert #2, etc.).

As you check over your essay, ask yourself these questions:

- Does your essay begin with a clear thesis statement, and does each paragraph start with a strong topic sentence that supports the thesis?
- Have you provided the support necessary in the form of examples, statistics, and relevant facts to prove your argument?
- Are your logical connections sound and convincing?
- Have you covered all the points in your outline?
- Is your conclusion an effective wrap-up?
- Does every sentence effectively communicate your point?

6. Edit. Check for mistakes in grammar, spelling, punctuation, and usage. No matter your topic, being technically correct in your writing makes your work more impressive.

Neatness is a crucial factor in essay writing. No matter how good your ideas are, if your instructor can't read them, they won't help you get a good grade. You might consider printing and skipping every other line if you know your handwriting is a problem. Avoid writing on both sides of the paper, since it is harder to read. If your handwriting is dismal, ask if it is possible to take the test on a laptop computer.

To answer the third essay question, one student created the planning outline shown in Figure 8.3. Notice that abbreviations and shorthand help the student write quickly. It is much faster to write *"Roles of BL in IC"* than *"Roles of Body Language in Interpersonal Communication"* (see Chapter 7 for strategies for taking shorthand notes). Figure 8.4 on page 250 shows the student's essay, including the word changes and inserts she made while revising the draft.

Here are some examples of essay questions you might encounter in an Interpersonal Communication course. In each case, notice the action verbs from Figure 8.2.

1. Summarize the role of the self-concept as a key to interpersonal relationships and communication.

2. Explain how internal and external noise affects the ability to listen effectively.

3. Describe three ways that body language affects interpersonal communication.

Oral Exams

In an oral exam, your instructor asks you to present verbal responses to exam questions or to discuss a pre-assigned topic. Exam questions may be similar to essay questions on written exams. They may be broad and general or focused on a narrow topic, which you are expected to explore in depth.

You may never have had an oral exam in college—and you may never have one. Nevertheless, mastering oral-exam skills will help you feel more comfortable answering questions in class and taking part in class discussions. Some instructors consider your class participation when determining your course grade.

Students with learning disabilities that affect their writing may need to take all their exams orally. If you have a disability that fits into this category, speak with your advisor and instructors to set up an examination system that works for you.

Here are a few strategies to remember when taking oral exams. Refer also to the section in Chapter 10 on oral presentations for other ideas.

- *Plan your presentation.* Brainstorm your topic if it is pre-assigned, narrow it with the prewriting strategies you will learn in Chapter 10, determine your central idea or argument, and write an outline that will be the basis of your talk. Draft an outline of your thoughts using "trigger" words or phrases that will remind you of what you want to say.

- *Practice your presentation.* Use notes on index cards to keep on target. Do a test run with friends or alone—consider audiotaping or videotaping yourself to find out how you look and sound—and pay attention to the clock if you have a time limit. Try to practice in the place where you will be speaking, and ask about where your instructor will sit and what will be around you, such as a podium, table, chair, or white board.

- *Be prepared for questions.* Anticipate questions that may come up, and plan your responses.

RISING
TO THE CHALLENGE

Anonymous
Student in Denver, Colorado

In people's lives, events and situations occur that change the way they think about how they live. This student was fortunate to learn a huge lesson about life and herself when, as a high school student, she was diagnosed with bipolar disorder.

I come from a Hispanic family. My parents wanted to give me and my sisters what they never had. From an early age, I recognized their sacrifices and hard work and figured I owed it to them to work just as hard. I had it in my mind early on that I had to be the best.

When I was accepted to a private high school in Denver and awarded a scholarship, I felt like high school would be nothing but smooth sailing. However, I was dead wrong. High school turned out to be one of the biggest shocks of my life. I was no longer the kid who had the best GPA, as I had always been before. I was struggling to pass my classes for the first time in my life. To make matters worse, I hadn't made any friends.

The most devastating part of my high school career came at the end of my first semester. On my first report card, I had made a C in my math class. It may as well have been an F. From that moment on, I committed myself to working on nothing but schoolwork. I worked nonstop, getting up early to study, staying after school for help, and studying from the time I got home until I went to bed.

Pretty soon I stopped sleeping. I worked through the night to get ahead in the lesson plans. During school, I started leaving class because I felt it was pointless to listen to a lecture on a lesson I had already learned. I had been sent to detention several times and was on the verge of being suspended. When I walked out of history class one day, my history teacher sent me to the school psychologist that day instead of to detention.

The psychologist asked me first of all why I was leaving class. I told him that school was pointless because I was teaching myself. He asked why I argued with my teachers. I told him that I was smarter than they are. He asked me last what I did for fun, who my friends were, and how I was sleeping. I snapped at him saying that I didn't have any friends, I thought doing anything for fun was pointless because it takes me away from working, and that I didn't sleep.

That night the psychologist told my parents that I needed to be tested for mental disorders. He said that it was possible that I was in a state of mania, and could be either hypomanic or bipolar. A few days later, I finally went to sleep. I didn't wake up the next day to go to school, and didn't return to school for three days. I had completely lost my motivation to work. A few days later, my mother literally dragged me into the doctor's office. From talking to me about what I felt like a few weeks earlier and how I was feeling then, he was able to diagnose me with bipolar disorder. I had been in a manic phase for about two months. Now I was in a depressive stage.

After weeks of blood tests, I was finally given lithium to balance the chemicals in my brain and to level out the manic peaks and depressive valleys that come with being bipolar. Then, during therapy, I was able to learn to recognize and accept my weaknesses. I saw tutors to help me organize my life, and saw counselors to help me relearn how to be social and how to ask others for help. With therapy and regular medication, my life became more balanced. I still managed to graduate high school with honors. I've learned that my best is good enough for me and for everyone else. Perhaps what makes people unique and beautiful is not being the best of everything, but doing your best at everything.

Take a Moment to Consider . . .

- *When you have, and have not, done your best in school and what resulted in each case.*

- *A situation or problem you have now that could improve with help from a human resource—counselor, tutor, health professional, or advisor.*

- *Be physically and mentally ready.* Get a good night's sleep before the exam so you'll speak with energy. Avoid drinking too much coffee or any alcohol. Take deep breaths, and have some water handy. Visualize your own success—see yourself speaking with knowledge, confidence, and poise.

No matter what kind of test you take, you may be tempted never to think about it again after you leave the testing room. If you take the time to examine your results, however, you can learn a great deal from your mistakes.

How can you learn from test mistakes?

The purpose of a test is to see how much you know, not merely to assign a grade. Rather than ignoring mistakes, examine them and learn from them as you learn from mistakes on the job and in relationships. Working through your mistakes helps you avoid repeating them on another test. The following strategies will help.

Try to identify patterns in your mistakes. Look for the following:

- *Careless errors.* In your rush to complete the exam, did you misread the question or directions, blacken the wrong box on the answer sheet, skip a question, write illegibly?

- *Conceptual or factual errors.* Did you misunderstand a concept or never learn it? Did you fail to master certain facts? Did you skip part of the text or miss classes in which ideas were covered?

Find the time to rework the questions you got wrong. Based on instructor feedback, try to rewrite an essay, recalculate a math problem from the original question, or redo questions following a reading selection. If you discover a pattern of careless errors, promise yourself that you'll be more careful and that you'll save time to double-check your work.

FIGURE 8.4   Response to an essay question.

QUESTION: Describe three ways that body language affects interpersonal communication.

Body language plays an important role in interpersonal communication and helps shape

the impression you make. Two of the most important functions of body language are to

, especially when you meet ^ someone for the first time

contradict and reinforce verbal statements. When body language contradicts verbal

language, the message ~~conveyed~~ *delivered* by the body is dominant. For example, if a friend tells

you that she is "fine," but her posture is slumped, *her eye contact minimal,* and her facial expression troubled, you

have every reason to wonder whether she is telling the truth. If the same friend tells

you that she is feeling fine and is smiling, walking with a bounce in her step, and has

direct eye contact, her body language is ~~telling the truth.~~ *accurately reflecting and reinforcing her words.*

The nonverbal cues that make up body language also have the power to add shades

of meaning. Consider this statement: "This is the best idea I've heard all day." If you

were to say this three different ways—in a loud voice while standing up; quietly while

sitting with arms and legs crossed and looking away; and while ~~maintening~~ *maintaining* eye contact

and taking the receiver's hand—you might send three different messages.

Finally, the impact of nonverbal cues can be greatest when you meet someone for

the first time. When you meet someone, you tend to make assumptions based on nonverbal

Although first impressions emerge from a combination of nonverbal cues, tone of voice, and choice of words, nonverbal elements (cues and tone) usually come across first and strongest.

behavior such as posture, eye contact, gestures, and speed and style of movement.

In summary, nonverbal communication plays a ~~crusial~~ *crucial* role in interpersonal relationships.

It has the power to send an accurate message that may ~~destroy~~ *belie* the speaker's words,

offer shades of meaning, and set the tone of a first meeting.

After reviewing your mistakes, fill in your knowledge gaps. If you made mistakes on questions because you didn't know or understand them, develop a plan to learn the material. Solidifying your knowledge can help you on future exams and in life situations that involve the subject you're studying. You might even consider asking to retake the exam. The score might not count, but you may find that focusing on learning, rather than on grades, can improve your knowledge.

Talk to your instructors. You can learn a lot by talking with your instructor about specific mistakes on short-answer questions or about a weak essay. Respectfully ask the instructor to explain comments he or she made on your paper. If you are not sure why you were marked down on an essay, ask what you could have done to improve your grade. Take advantage of this opportunity to determine how to do better on the next exam.

If you fail a test, don't throw it away. Keep it as a reminder that many students have been in your shoes and that you have room to improve if you supply the will to succeed.

reflect

Lao-tzu, the Chinese Taoist philosopher who lived around 600 B.C.E., said the following:

"Failure is the foundation of success, and the means by which it is achieved." What do you think Lao-tzu meant? How do you think the statement will help you the next time you do poorly on a test? As you write, think about the importance of a positive attitude and perseverance in overcoming your obstacles.

& respond

TAKE ACTION

Learn from Your Mistakes on a Recent Exam

Analyze an exam on which your performance fell short of your expectations. If possible, choose an exam that contains different types of objective and subjective questions. With the test and answer sheet in hand, answer the following questions:

- Identify the types of questions on which you got the most correct answers (e.g., matching, essay, multiple choice).

  _____ matching _____

- Identify the types of questions on which you made the greatest number of errors.

  _____ Fill in a blank _____

- Look closely at your errors to try to identify patterns—for example, did you misread test instructions, or did you ignore qualifiers that changed the questions' meaning? What did you find?

  _____ misread directions. _____

  _____

- Finally, what are two actions you pledge to take during your next exam to avoid the same problems?

  Action 1: _____

  Action 2: _____

I take responsible risks.

There is a voice inside nearly every student's head that expresses reluctance to take on new academic challenges because of the fear of failing tests: "If you don't try it, you won't be wrong," the voice says, "but if you try it and you are wrong, you will look stupid." If this voice sounds familiar, think for a moment about why you are in school. Are you there to get an A on every test, or are you there to master new concepts, gain competence in new areas, and enrich your mind and your potential? Your answer should reflect what is in your long-term best interest.

Because testing is an inherent part of your education, responsible risk-taking is too. That is, on every test, you put your knowledge—and a bit of yourself—on the line. Ironically, taking tests moves you forward even as it causes you to feel unbalanced.

Take comfort in knowing that test anxiety is understandable as you are asked to show mastery of new and often difficult material. Work to overcome this anxiety by learning the concrete test-taking skills presented in this chapter. These skills will help you gain the significant rewards that can come from the risks you have taken.

REMEMBER!
the important points ○○○

How can preparation improve test performance?

Preparation strategies that can help improve test performance include identifying test type and coverage, choosing appropriate study materials, setting a study plan and schedule, reviewing (using SQ3R, notes, and critical thinking), taking a pretest, getting enough sleep and eating well, and making the most of last-minute studying.

How can you work through test anxiety?

Good preparation helps minimize test anxiety. Before each test, find out what material will be covered, the types of questions, and the length of the test. Your next step is to create a detailed study plan that will enable you to master all the material before the test. A positive attitude will also help alleviate anxiety.

What general strategies can help you succeed on tests?

Methods that will help improve your performance on almost every test include writing down key information as soon as the test begins, taking time to skim the exam and get an overview, reading the directions, working from the easiest questions to the hardest, keeping track of time as you work, learning to guess intelligently, knowing how to fill out machine-scored tests, and using critical thinking to avoid errors.

How can you master different types of test questions?

Objective questions (multiple choice, true-or-false, matching, and fill-in-the-blank) use a short-answer format to test your ability to recall, compare, and contrast information. Subjective questions—essay questions—require you to express your knowledge and perspective, usually in written form, using an abbreviated version of the writing process. Oral exams require both skill in answering subjective questions and skill in public speaking.

How can you learn from test mistakes?

Test mistakes can show you where you may need to strengthen your knowledge. When you get your test back, look for careless errors, as well as those that involve concepts and facts. Instead of taking your mistakes as a defeat, treat them as an opportunity to understand what happened and to avoid repeating the same errors.

BUILDING SKILLS
FOR SUCCESSFUL LEARNING

Name   Date

CRITICAL THINKING
APPLYING LEARNING TO LIFE

Analysis of How You Perform on Tests

First, look at the potential problems listed here. Circle the ones that you feel are factors that hurt your performance on exams. Fill in the blanks with any key problems not listed.

Incomplete preparation	Confusion about directions
Fatigue	Test anxiety
Feeling rushed during the test	_____
Weak understanding of concepts	_____
Poor guessing techniques	

Pick your two most significant problems. For each, brainstorm ways to minimize the problem as you move forward. Include specific strategies you learned in this chapter.

Problem 1: _____

_____

Solutions: _____

_____

_____

_____

Problem 2: _____

_____

Solutions: _____

_____

_____

_____

TEAM BUILDING
COLLABORATIVE SOLUTIONS

Test-Preparation Study Group

Form a study group with two or three other students in one of your academic courses. (You may have to meet immediately before or after the class to avoid scheduling problems.) Ask each group member to record everything he or she does to prepare for the next exam, including:

- learning what to expect on the test (topics and material that will be covered, types of questions that will be asked)
- examining old tests
- creating and following a study schedule and checklist
- using SQ3R to review material
- taking a pretest
- getting a good night's sleep before the exam
- doing last-minute cramming
- mastering general test-taking strategies
- mastering test-taking strategies for specific types of test questions (multiple choice, true-or-false, matching, fill-in-the-blank, essay)

After the exam, meet together to compare preparation regimens. What important differences can you identify in the group members' routines? How might different routines have affected test performance and outcome? On a separate piece of paper, for your own reference, write down what you learned from the habits of your study mates that may help you as you prepare for up-coming exams.

personal
IMPROVEMENT
plan

I commit to three test-taking strategies to improve my study skills.
From this chapter, I choose three strategies that I think will help me.

Strategy 1: _____

Strategy 2: _____

Strategy 3: _____

I choose one strategy to focus on (circle this strategy above) and I will:

- describe my goal—what I want to gain from using this strategy.

  _____

  _____

  _____

- describe in detail how I plan to use the strategy.

  _____

  _____

  _____

  _____

- describe how I will measure my progress toward the goal this semester.

  _____

  _____

  _____

  _____

Activate the Habit of Mind

Here's how I will *take responsible risks* to achieve this goal:

_____

_____

_____

_____

SUGGESTED READINGS

Browning, William G., Ph.D. *Cliffs Memory Power for Exams*. Lincoln, NE: Cliffs Notes Inc., 1990.

Frank, Steven. *Test Taking Secrets: Study Better, Test Smarter, and Get Great Grades*. Holbrook, MA: Adams Media Corporation, 1998.

Fry, Ron. *"Ace" Any Test*, 3rd ed. Franklin Lakes, NJ: Career Press, 1996.

Hamilton, Dawn. *Passing Exams: A Guide for Maximum Success and Minimum Stress*. Herndon, VA: Cassell Academic, 1999.

Kesselman, Judy and Franklynn Peterson. *Test Taking Strategies*. New York: NTC/Contemporary Publishing, 1981.

Luckie, William R. and Wood Smethurst. *Study Power: Study Skills to Improve Your Learning and Your Grades*. Cambridge, MA: Brookline Books, 1997.

INTERNET RESOURCES

Prentice Hall Student Success Supersite (testing tips in study skills section): www.prenhall.com/success

Florida State University (list of sites offering information on test-taking skills): http://osi.fsu.edu/hot/testtaking/skills.htm

NetStudy Aids.com (study aids, skills, guides, and techniques): www.netstudyaids.com

Test-Taking Tips—Help for Studying: www.testtakingtips.com

University of Minnesota Duluth (study strategies home page): www.d.umn.edu/student/loon/acad/strat/

ENDNOTES

1. Steven Frank. *The Everything Study Book*. Holbrook, MA: Adams Media Corporation, 1996, p. 208.

2. Margaret L. King. *Western Civilization: A Social and Cultural History*, 2nd ed. Upper Saddle River, NJ: Pearson Education, 2003. Questions from *Instructor's Manual and Test Item File* by Dolores Davison Peterson. Used with permission.

3. Arthur O'Sullivan and Steven M. Sheffrin. *Macroeconomics: Principles and Tools*, 3rd ed. Upper Saddle River, NJ: Pearson Education, 2003. Questions from *Test Item File 2* developed by Linda Ghent. Used with permission.

4. Matilde Olivella de Castells, Elizabeth Guzmán, Paloma Lupuerta, and Carmen García. *Mosaicos: Spanish as a World Language*, 3rd ed. Upper Saddle River, NJ: Prentice Hall, 2002. Questions from *Testing Program* by Mark Harpring. Used with permission.

5. David Krogh. *Biology: A Guide to the Natural World*, 2nd ed. Upper Saddle River, NJ: Prentice Hall, 2002. Questions from *Test Item File* edited by Dan Wivagg. Used with permission.

6. Charles G. Morris, *Understanding Psychology*, 3rd ed. Upper Saddle River, NJ: Prentice Hall, 1996. Questions are from *Test Item File* by Gary W. Piggrem. Used with permission.

7. Questions from Eric Chaisson and Steve McMillan, *Astronomy Today*, 2nd ed. Upper Saddle River, NJ: Prentice Hall, 1996, p. 27. Used with permission.

Quantitative Learning

BECOMING COMFORTABLE WITH MATH AND SCIENCE

IN THIS CHAPTER

In this chapter, you explore answers to the following questions:

■ Why do you need to be able to think quantitatively?

■ How can you master math and science basics?

■ How can you overcome math anxiety?

■ What techniques will improve your performance on math and science tests?

■ How can you "read" visual aids?

Striving for accuracy and precision.

"People who value accuracy, precision, and craftsmanship **take time to check over their products**. They review the rules by which they are to abide and the models and visions they are to follow . . . and confirm that their finished product conforms exactly." —**ART COSTA**

*Approaching math and science with **precision and a focus on accuracy** will get you far. You will have the best chance at solving a numerical problem if you approach it with care and deliberateness—focus on the rules, work to be accurate, and carefully check your work.*

A solid grasp of *quantitative thinking*—thinking in terms of measurable quantities—is a must for success in math and science. However, biology, math, and computer science majors aren't the only people who need quantitative skills. Because working with numbers means solving problems, it builds logic and follow-through—two skills that will help you solve problems in *all* academic areas. This chapter will give you

an overview of quantitative thinking and offer basic problem-solving strategies.

You will also learn how to approach math and science in a positive way. When asked about working with numbers, many students report that they "hate math" or were "never any good at science." Developing a positive attitude is a key step toward a successful relationship with numbers. The chapter will help you examine and address math anxiety and show you how you can gain an understanding of visual aids to enhance your math and science learning.

Why do you need to be able to think quantitatively?

Math moves you from questions to solutions as it reinforces critical thinking. Consider the following practical examples of problems requiring quantitative thinking:

- You make $2,000 per month in your job. How do you determine how you allocate your money to pay your bills?
- You want to carpet your house. However, many of the rooms and hallways are not regularly shaped. How do you determine how much carpet you need to buy?
- You are trying to schedule your classes for next semester. Each of your classes is only offered at certain times. How do you go about making the best possible schedule?

As these examples demonstrate, everyone needs a certain comfort and competence in math. These skills can be broken down into the following broad areas.

- *Arithmetic.* Many everyday tasks require arithmetic (numerical computations such as addition, subtraction, multiplication, and division, plus the use of fractions and other ratios). You are using arithmetic when you calculate how much tuition you can cover in a semester or figure out what to tip in a restaurant.
- *Algebra.* A knowledge of **algebra** is needed almost as frequently as arithmetic. You use algebra when you figure out the interest on a loan or compute your GPA. Algebra involves determining an unknown value using known values.

Algebra
A generalization of arithmetic in which letters representing unknown quantities are combined, often with other numbers, into equations according to the rules of arithmetic.

- *Geometry.* The most important uses of geometry occur in determining areas and volumes. However, geometric ideas occur in many other forms. Examples of geometry in everyday life include determining how closely you can pass a car and packing a suitcase so that it can close.

- *Probability and statistics.* A knowledge of basic **probability** and **statistics** is needed for understanding the relevance and importance of the overwhelming amount of statistical information you encounter. For example, if a woman reads breast cancer statistics, her knowledge of statistics and probability can help her determine her risk of getting the disease. Careers such as actuarial or genetic science demand a strong background in these subjects, and some areas of business, economics, and engineering require strong skills as well.

- *Calculus and differential equations.* Calculus and differential equations are needed for most engineering fields, business and economics, physics, and astronomy. Many problems in which a rate of change is involved require calculus and differential equations. Problems that involve work, water pressure, areas, and volumes also use calculus.

- *Sciences.* Biology, anatomy, and other sciences directly related to the human body can help you to better manage your health through a greater understanding of how your body works. Chemistry can help you figure out how to substitute ingredients in a recipe and understand the chemical makeup of any medications you are taking and the interactions that are possible. A knowledge of physics can help you appreciate how airplanes fly and automobiles stop.

Ultimately, both math and science are relevant to your other subjects because they aid problem solving and critical thinking. When you put your brain through the paces of mathematical and scientific problem solving, you are building the kind of critical-thinking ability that you can apply to problem solving in any subject. You'll be using the same analytical process when you write an essay on the causes of an historical event or reconcile different perspectives in a philosophy course.

Probability
The study of the chance that a given event will occur.

Statistics
Collection, analysis, and interpretation of numerical data.

How can you master math and science basics?

reflect

Think about and describe when in the past week you have used any aspect of quantitative thinking—basic calculations in your checkbook, geometrical thinking for how to rearrange a room, adding up a tip, and so forth. Be comprehensive. Then write down what thoughts come to mind when you look at your list of "numbers encounters."

Companion Website

& respond

Certain thinking strategies will help improve your ability to think quantitatively. Mastering math and science basics is easier when you take a critical approach to the classroom, the textbook, studying and homework, and word problems.

Many different college courses will require you to think quantitatively.

Classroom Strategies

When you are taking a math or science class, there are two primary ingredients for success:

- *Be prepared.* Before class, read the material that will be covered that day. This allows you to build a base of knowledge, providing a context in which to ask questions about the material.

- *Be in class.* Take notes, focusing on the central ideas and connecting supporting examples (especially sample problems) to those ideas. Highlight items or examples that confuse you so that you can go back and focus on them later. Also, ask questions—participating in this way will help you retain and apply what you are learning.

College math and science are quite different from high school courses—and the differences require you to be more focused and diligent about attending class and keeping up with homework. Among the differences you may notice are the following:

- Courses are faster-paced.
- Assignments are crucial (although they may not always be collected).
- Class time may be more focused on theories and ideas than on problem solving.
- Class size might be considerably larger, with smaller lab sections.
- Technological proficiency may be important (allowing you to use graphing calculators or software specific to the course).

How to Approach Your Textbook

Math and science textbooks move sequentially (later chapters build on concepts and information introduced in previous chapters). Your command of later material depends on how well you learned material in earlier chapters. Use these strategies to get the most from your textbooks:

- *Interact with math material critically through writing.* Math textbooks are problem-and-solution based. As you read, take notes of examples on a pad of paper. If problem steps are left out, as they often are, work them out on your pad. Draw sketches as you read to help visualize the material. Try not to move on until you understand the example and how it relates to the central ideas. Write down questions you want to ask your instructor or fellow students.

- *Pay attention to formulas.* In any math or science textbook, note the formulas that are given. Evaluate whether these formulas are important and recall whether the instructor emphasized them. In some classes you are responsible for gathering all formulas through your reading; in others, the instructors will provide them. Read the assigned material to prepare for homework.

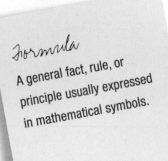

formula
A general fact, rule, or principle usually expressed in mathematical symbols.

■ *Use memory skills with science material.* Science textbooks are often packed with vocabulary specific to that particular science (for example, a chapter in a psychobiology course may give medical names for the parts of the brain). To remember what you read, use mnemonic devices, test yourself with flash cards, and rehearse aloud or silently (see Chapter 6). Selective highlighting and writing summaries of your readings, perhaps in table format, will also help.

"The proper and immediate object of science is the acquirement, or communication, of truth."

SAMUEL TAYLOR COLERIDGE

Because many sciences rely on a base of mathematical knowledge, your math reading strategies will help you understand and remember the formulas that may appear in your science reading. As with math, make sure you understand the principles behind each formula, and do as many problems as you can to solidify your knowledge.

Studying and Homework

When it comes to studying and doing homework in math and science courses, more is better.

■ *Review materials.* Review your class notes as soon as possible after each class. Have the textbook alongside and compare the lecture information to the book. Fill in missing steps in the instructor's examples before you forget them.

■ *Do problems, problems, and more problems.* Working through problems is critical for math courses, as well as math-based science courses such as chemistry and astronomy, because it provides examples that will help you understand concepts and formulas. Plus, becoming familiar with a group of problems will help you apply what you know to similar problems on other assignments and tests.

■ *Fight frustration strategically.* Do not expect to complete every problem without effort. If you are stuck on a problem, go on to another one. If you hit a wall, take a break to clear your head. If you have done the assigned homework but still don't feel secure, do additional problems.

■ *Work with others.* Other people's perspectives can often help you break through a mental block. Even if your math and science classes have lab sessions, try to set up study groups outside of class. Do as much of your homework as you can and then meet to discuss the homework and work through additional problems. Be open to other perspectives, and don't hesitate to ask other students to explain their thought processes in detail.

■ *Focus on learning styles.* Use strategies that activate your strengths. For example, a visual learner might draw pictures to illustrate problems, and an interpersonal learner might organize a study group. Musical learners might even make up songs describing math concepts—Barbara Aaker wrote 40 of them for her students at the Community College of Denver, and they have helped musical learners retain difficult concepts. Figure 9.1 gives one of her algebra songs. The Multiple Intelligence grid on page 272 offers more ideas.

Word Problems

Because word problems are the most common way you will encounter quantitative thinking throughout your life, being able to solve them is crucial. Word problems can be tough, however, because they force you to translate between two languages—English and mathematics. Although math is a precise language, English and other living languages are not so precise. This difference in precision makes the process of translating difficult.

Steps to Solving Word Problems

Translating English or any other language into math takes a lot of practice. George Polya, in his 1945 classic *How to Solve It*, devised a four-step method for attacking word problems.[1] The basic steps reflect the general problem-solving process you explored in Chapter 4, and they will work for any word problem, whether in a math or science course.

1. *Understand the individual elements of the problem.* Read the problem carefully. Understand what it is asking. Know what information you have. Know what information is missing. Draw a picture, if possible. Translate the given information from words into mathematical language (e.g., numbers, symbols, formulas).

FIGURE 9.1	A musical approach to math.

"How Much Is That X in the Equation?"

(to the tune of "How Much Is That Doggie in the Window?")

How much is that *x* in the equation?
What value will make it be true?
To find the *x* and get the solution
The numbers attached we **undo**.

The **connector** is plus or minus seven,
To find *x* we have to **undo**.
Just write below both sides—make it even.
We **undo** to find the *x* value.

If multiply or divide is showing,
The **connector** tells what has been done.
To **undo** is where we still are going—
We're trying to get *x* alone.

Source: Reprinted with permission. Barbara Aaker, *Mathematics: The Musical.* Denver: Crazy Broad Publishing, 1999.

2. *Name and explore potential solution paths.* Think about similar problems that you understand and how those were solved. Consider whether this problem is an example of a mathematical idea that you know. In your head, try out different ways to solve the problem to see which may work best.

3. *Carry out your plan.* Choose a solution path and solve the problem. Check each of your steps.

4. *Review your result.* Check your answer, if possible. Make sure you've answered the question the problem is asking. Does your result seem logical in the context of the problem? Are there other ways to do the problem?

TAKE ACTION

Get the Most from Your Textbook

From a textbook in a math or science course you are now taking, choose a chapter that you are about to cover in class. Do the following to maximize your understanding of the material:

1. Read the chapter now, before its material is covered in class. Take notes. Check this box when you have read it through. ☒

2. Identify and work through two of the most difficult concepts or formulas to understand. Develop a game plan to gain a greater understanding, basing your plan on what will help most—memory techniques, study groups, problems, a chat with an instructor, and so forth.

   A. Note the concept or formula.

   to think quantitatively...

   Briefly describe your game plan here.

   to think before taking action.

   Check the box when you have put your plans into action, and indicate whether they helped.

   Work done? ☒   How did it help?   _Pattern_

   B. Note the concept or formula:

   Pattern

   Briefly describe your game plan here.

   first look specifically in pattern and then prosedode.

   Check the box when you have put your plans into action, and indicate whether they helped.

   Work done? ☐   How did it help? _____

Different problem-solving strategies will be useful to you when solving word problems. Evaluate which strategy will work best on a given problem and then apply the strategy. The following section outlines several problem-solving strategies by working through word problem examples.[2]

Problem-Solving Strategies

Strategy 1. Look for a pattern. G. H. Hardy (1877–1947), an eminent British mathematician, described mathematicians as makers of patterns and ideas. The search for patterns is one of the best strategies in problem solving. When you look for a pattern, you think inductively, observing a series of examples and determining the general idea that links the examples together.

Example: Find the next three entries in the following:

a. 1, 2, 4, ____, ____, ____

b. O, T, T, F, F, S, S, ____, ____, ____

Solutions to Example:

a. When trying to identify patterns, you may find a different pattern than someone else. This doesn't mean yours is wrong. Example *a* actually has several possible answers. Here are two:

1. Each succeeding term of the sequence is twice the previous term. In that case, the next three values would be 8, 16, 32.

2. The second term is 1 more than the first term and the third term is 2 more than the second. This might lead you to guess the fourth term is 3 more than the third term, the fifth term is 4 more than the fourth term, and so on. In that case, the next three terms are 7, 11, 16.

b. Example *b* is a famous pattern that often appears in puzzle magazines. The key to it is that "O" is the first letter of *one*, "T" is the first letter of *two*, and so on. Therefore, the next three terms would be E, N, and T for *eight*, *nine*, and *ten*.

Strategy 2. Make a table. A table can help you organize and summarize information. This may enable you to see how examples form a pattern that leads you to an idea and a solution.

Example: How many ways can you make change for a half dollar using only quarters, dimes, nickels, and pennies?

Solutions to Example: You might construct several tables and go through every possible case. You could start by seeing how many ways you can make change for a half dollar without using a quarter, which would produce the following tables:

Quarters	0	0	0	0	0	0	0	0	0	0	0	0	0	0	0	0	0	0
Dimes	0	0	0	0	0	0	0	0	0	0	0	1	1	1	1	1	1	1
Nickels	0	1	2	3	4	5	6	7	8	9	10	0	1	2	3	4	5	6
Pennies	50	45	40	35	30	25	20	15	10	5	0	40	35	30	25	20	15	10

Quarters	0	0	0	0	0	0	0	0	0	0	0	0	0	0	0	0	0	0
Dimes	1	1	2	2	2	2	2	2	2	3	3	3	3	3	4	4	4	5
Nickels	7	8	0	1	2	3	4	5	6	0	1	2	3	4	0	1	2	0
Pennies	5	0	30	25	20	15	10	5	0	20	15	10	5	0	10	5	0	0

There are 36 ways to make change for a half dollar without using a quarter. Using one quarter results in this table:

Quarters	1	1	1	1	1	1	1	1	1	1	1	1
Dimes	0	0	0	0	0	0	1	1	1	1	2	2
Nickels	0	1	2	3	4	5	0	1	2	3	0	1
Pennies	25	20	15	10	5	0	15	10	5	0	5	0

Using one quarter, you get 12 different ways to make change for a half dollar. Lastly, using two quarters, there's only one way to make change for a half dollar. Therefore, the solution to the problem is that there are 36 + 12 + 1 = 49 ways to make change for a half dollar using only quarters, dimes, nickels, and pennies.

Strategy 3. Identify a subgoal. Breaking the original problem into smaller and possibly easier problems may lead to a solution to the original problem. This is often the case in writing a computer program.

Example: Arrange the nine numbers 1, 2, 3, . . . , 9 into a square subdivided into nine sections in such a way that the sum of every row, column, and main diagonal is the same. This is called a *magic square*.

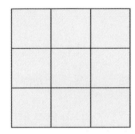

Solution to Example: The sum of any individual row, column, or main diagonal has to be one-third the sum of all nine numbers (or else they wouldn't be the same). The sum of 1 + 2 + 3 + 4 + 5 + 6 + 7 + 8 + 9 = 45. Therefore, each row, column, and main diagonal needs to sum to 45/3 = 15. Now, you need to see how many ways you can add three of the numbers from 1 to 9 and get 15. When you do this, you should get:

9 + 1 + 5 = 15	8 + 3 + 4 = 15
9 + 2 + 4 = 15	7 + 2 + 6 = 15
8 + 1 + 6 = 15	7 + 3 + 5 = 15
8 + 2 + 5 = 15	6 + 4 + 5 = 15

Now, looking at your magic square, notice that the center position will be part of four sums (a row, a column, and the two main diagonals). Looking back at your sums, you see that 5 appears in four different sums, therefore 5 is in the center square.

Now, in each corner, the number there appears in three sums (row, column, and a diagonal). Looking through your sums, you find that 2, 4, 6, and 8 each appear in three sums. Now, you need to place them in the corners in such a way that your diagonals add up to 15.

2		6
	5	
4		8

Then, to finish, all you need to do is fill in the remaining squares so that 15 is the sum of each row, column, and main diagonal. The completed square is as follows:

2	7	6
9	5	1
4	3	8

Strategy 4. Examine a similar problem. Sometimes a problem you are working on has similarities to a problem you've already read about or solved. In that case, it is often possible to use a similar approach to solve the new problem.

Example: Find a magic square using the numbers 3, 5, 7, 9, 11, 13, 15, 17, and 19.

Solution to Example: This problem is very similar to the example for Strategy 3. Approaching it in the same fashion, you find that the row, column, and main diagonal sum is 33. Writing down all the possible sums of three numbers to get 33, you find that 11 is the number that appears four times, so it is in the center.

	11	

The numbers that appear three times in the sums and will go in the corners are 5, 9, 13, and 17. This now gives you:

13		17
	11	
5		9

Finally, completing the magic square gives you:

13	3	17
15	11	7
5	19	9

"The word impossible is not in my dictionary."

NAPOLEON

Strategy 5. Work backward. With some problems, you may find it easier to start with the perceived final result and work backward.

Example: In the game of "Life," Carol had to pay $1,500 when she was married. Then, she lost half the money she had left. Next, she paid half the money she had for a house. Then, the game was stopped, and she had $3,000 left. With how much money did she start?

Solution to Example: Carol ended up with $3,000. Right before that she paid half her money to buy a house. Because her $3,000 was half of what she had before her purchase, she had 2 × $3,000 = $6,000 before buying the house. Prior to buying the house, Carol lost half her money. This means that the $6,000 is the half she didn't lose. So, before losing half her money, Carol had 2 × $6,000 = $12,000. Prior to losing half her money, Carol had to pay $1,500 to get married. This means she had $12,000 + $1,500 = $13,500 before getting married. Because this was the start of the game, Carol began with $13,500.

Strategy 6. Draw a diagram. Drawing a picture is often an aid to solving problems, especially for visual learners. Although pictures are especially useful for geometrical problems, they can be helpful for other types of problems as well.

Example: There were 20 women at a round table for dinner. Each woman shook hands with the woman to her immediate right and left. At the end of the dinner, each woman got up and shook hands with everybody except those who sat on her immediate right and left. How many handshakes took place after dinner?

Solution to Example: To solve this with a diagram, it might be a good idea to examine several simpler cases to see if you can determine a pattern of any kind that might help. Starting with two or three people, you can see there are no handshakes after dinner because everyone is adjacent to everyone else.

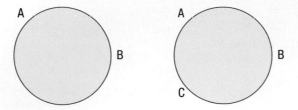

Now, in the case of four people, we get the following diagram, connecting those people who shake hands after dinner:

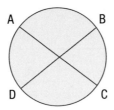

In this situation, you see there are two handshakes after dinner, AC and BD. In the case of five people, you get this picture:

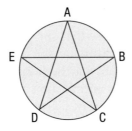

In this case, you have five after-dinner handshakes: AC, AD, BD, BE, and CE. Six people seated around a circle gives the following diagram:

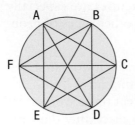

In this diagram, there are now a total of nine after-dinner handshakes: AC, AD, AE, BD, BE, BF, CE, CF, and DF. By studying the diagrams, you realize that if there are N people, each person would shake N–3 people's hands after dinner. (They don't shake their own hands or the hands of the two people adjacent to them.) Because there are N people that would lead to N(N–3) after-dinner handshakes. However, this would double-count every handshake, because AD would also be counted as DA. Therefore, there are only half as many actual handshakes. So, the correct number of handshakes is [N(N–3)]/2. So finally, if there are 20 women, there would be 20(17)/2 = 170 after-dinner handshakes.

Strategy 7. Translate words into an equation.   This strategy is often used in algebra.

Example: A farmer needs to fence a rectangular piece of land. He wants the length of the field to be 80 feet longer than the width. If he has 1,080 feet of fencing available, what should the length and width of the field be?

Solution to Example: The best way to start this problem is to draw a picture of the situation and label the sides.

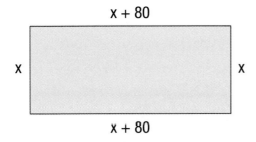

Let x represent the width of the field and $x + 80$ represent the length of the field. The farmer has 1,080 feet of fencing and he will need $2x + 2(x + 80)$ feet of fencing to fence his field. This gives you the equation:

$$2x + 2(x + 80) = 1080$$

Multiplying out:	$2x + 2x + 160 = 1080$
Simplifying and subtracting 160:	$4x = 920$
Dividing by 4:	$x = 230$
Therefore,	$x + 80 = 310$
As a check, you find that	$2(230) + 2(310) = 1080$

These sample problems are designed to boost your ability to think critically through some basic math strategies. If they have made you feel anxious, however, you will benefit from some information about math anxiety.

MULTIPLE PATHWAYS TO LEARNING

MULTIPLE INTELLIGENCE STRATEGIES *for* Working with Numbers

When math and science get tough, look to your strongest intelligences to figure out ways to cope.

INTELLIGENCE	SUGGESTED STRATEGIES	WHAT WORKS FOR YOU? WRITE NEW IDEAS HERE
Verbal–Linguistic	■ Convert numerical problems and formulas into word problems whenever possible. When you have word problems, convert them into numbers to help solidify the relationship between words and the numbers they signify.	
Logical–Mathematical	■ Practice. Do both assigned and extra problems. ■ Focus on process. Make sure you understand any formula you use; then, carefully work through each step of the process used to solve the problem.	
Bodily–Kinesthetic	■ Find physical representations of problems. Use pennies; cut up an apple; measure lengths; drive distances. ■ For hands-on experience, look for science classes with a strong laboratory component. ■ When several instructors teach sections of the course, find out who is best at giving concrete examples.	
Visual–Spatial	■ Draw visual aspects of problems—geometrical shapes, grids, matrices—and use plenty of space. ■ Circle important items in the descriptions of problems. ■ Draw out word problems, including writing out the formulas.	
Interpersonal	■ Go over homework problems with a study group each week. Pass around your solutions and discuss them. ■ Take advantage of your instructor's office hours. Schedule a time to talk about concepts that are giving you trouble.	
Intrapersonal	■ Find a solitary spot to do your reading or homework. ■ Take quiet breaks when you hit a roadblock. Take a walk or a nap; see if this helps you think of a new approach.	
Musical	■ Listen to and study music whenever possible. The rhythms and notes of music are based in mathematics; musical experience can enhance quantitative abilities.	
Naturalistic	■ When you need science credits, look for courses in biological sciences or botany. ■ Find patterns and categorize information whenever possible.	

TAKE ACTION

Tackle a Word Problem

Read this word problem:

When using a stair climber, Eric burns 9.6 calories per minute. When he walks on the treadmill, he burns 5.3 calories per minute. If Eric has 50 minutes to exercise and wants to burn 350 calories, how many minutes should he spend on each machine?

Work through the problem here, and use additional pages if you need to. Indicate the equation you came up with. Finally, name the strategy or strategies that you used.

To Study and Homework because it will keep me to successs in class.

[The answer can be found on the last page of this chapter.]

Adapted from The Math Forum @ Drexel, an online community for mathematics education (http://mathforum.org/).

How can you overcome math anxiety?

Math anxiety is often a result of common misconceptions about math, such as the notion that people are born with or without an ability to think quantitatively, or the idea that "real" quantitative thinkers solve problems quickly in their heads. Some students feel that they can't do any math at all and, as a result, may give up without asking for help.

Math anxiety most commonly occurs right before or during an exam. A student getting ready to take a test or reading a particular problem on a test experiences rising anxiety or even what can be described as "blanking out." This can happen on exams for other subjects, but it seems to occur especially

Math anxiety
Any of several uncomfortable, high-stress feelings that appear in relation to quantitative thinking.

TAKE ACTION

Explore Your Math Anxiety

Answer the following statements by marking a number from 1 (Disagree) to 5 (Agree).

1. ___3___ I don't like math classes, and haven't since high school.

2. ___5___ I do okay at the beginning of a math class, but I always feel it will get to the point where it is impossible to understand.

3. ___2___ I can't seem to concentrate in math classes. I try, but I get nervous and distracted and think about other things.

4. ___4___ I don't like asking questions in math class. I'm afraid that the teachers or the other students will think I'm stupid.

5. ___2___ I stress out when I'm called on in math class. I seem to forget even the easiest answers.

6. ___5___ Math exams scare me far more than any of my other exams.

7. ___2___ I can't wait to finish my math requirement so that I'll never have to do any math again.

Scoring Key: 28–35: You suffer from full-blown math anxiety.

   21–27: You are coping, but you're not happy about mathematics.

   14–20: You're doing okay.

   7–13: So what's the big deal about math? You have very little problem with anxiety.

Source: Freedman, Ellen (March 1997). *Test Your Math Anxiety* (on-line). Available: http://fc.whyy.org/CCC/alg1anxtest.htm (March 1998).

often in tests involving quantitative thinking. The best strategies include practice, using your resources, taking responsibility for your quantitative learning, and knowing your rights as a quantitative learner.

- *Practice.* The best way to overcome test-time anxiety is to practice quantitative thinking to increase your confidence. Keeping up with your homework, attending class, preparing well for tests, and doing extra problems will help you feel confident because they increase your familiarity with the material. Figure 9.2 shows additional ways to reduce math anxiety.

- *Use resources.* Your school can provide help with math and science courses. Most schools have math or science learning labs, tutors, or computer programs that can help you practice difficult quantitative processes. You can visit your instructor during office hours or present a lab assistant or TA with your questions. Sometimes you will even have an extra review session set up by an instructor or TA so that students can ask questions before a major test. Don't hesitate to make the most of these helpful resources.

Ten ways to reduce math anxiety.   FIGURE 9.2

1. Overcome your negative self-image about math.
2. Ask questions of your teachers and your friends, and seek outside assistance.
3. Math is a foreign language—practice it often.
4. Don't study mathematics by trying to memorize information and formulas.
5. READ your math textbook.
6. Study math according to your personal learning style.
7. Get help the same day you don't understand something.
8. Be relaxed and comfortable while studying math.
9. "TALK" mathematics. Discuss it with people in your class. Form a study group.
10. Develop a sense of responsibility for your own successes and failures

Source: Freedman, Ellen (March 1997). *Ten Ways to Reduce Math Anxiety* [on-line]. Available: http://fc.whyy.org/CCC/algl/reduce.htm (March 1998).

■ *Take responsibility.* Even though math anxiety is a real problem, students must take some responsibility for their responses to quantitative thinking. You can't change the math experiences you have had in the past, but you can make choices about how to respond to quantitative material from here on out. The following responsibilities are worded as intention statements; use them for focus and motivation.[3]

- I will attend all classes and do my homework.
- I will seek extra help when necessary, from an instructor, a tutor, or a fellow student.
- I will speak up in class when I have questions.
- I will be realistic about my abilities and will work to improve them.
- I will approach quantitative thinking with an open mind, not assuming the worst.

■ *Know your rights.* Finally, along with being a responsible student, you also have rights regarding your mathematical learning. These include:[4]

- the right to learn at your own pace
- the right to ask questions
- the right not to understand
- the right to be treated as a competent person
- the right to believe you are capable of thinking quantitatively

reflect

Reflect on your high school experiences in math and science. What is your perception of your level of achievement in math and science classes? What attitudes toward quantitative learning did you form at that time, and why? Have these attitudes helped or hurt you?

& respond

Beyond working to control your math anxiety, several other techniques will help you do your very best when you are tested on your math skills.

What techniques will improve your performance on math and science tests?

In addition to the general strategies for test taking that you have explored, here are several additional techniques that can help you achieve better results on math and science exams.

Theorem
A formula or statement, often mathematical, proposed or accepted as a demonstrable truth.

- *Read through the exam first.* When you first get an exam, read through every problem quickly. Make notes on how you might attempt to solve the problem, if something occurs to you immediately.

- *Analyze problems carefully.* Categorize problems according to type. Take all the "givens" into account, and write down any formulas, **theorems,** or definitions that apply before you begin your calculations. Focus on what you want to find or prove, and take your time—precision demands concentration. If some problems seem easier than others, do them first in order to boost your confidence.

Estimate
To calculate the approximate amount of; to make a rough or preliminary calculation.

- Estimate *before you begin to come up with an approximate solution.* Then, work the problem and check the solution against your guess. The two answers should be close. If they're not, recheck your calculations. You may have made a simple calculation error.

- *Break the calculation into the smallest possible pieces.* Go step by step and don't move on to the next step until you are clear about what you've done so far.

- *Recall how you solved similar problems.* Past experience can give you valuable clues to how a particular problem should be handled.

- *Draw a picture to help you see the problem.* This can be a diagram, a chart, a probability tree, a geometric figure, or any other visual image that relates to the problem at hand.

"People seldom see the halting and painful steps by which the most insignificant success is achieved."

ANNIE SULLIVAN

- *Be neat.* When it comes to numbers, mistaken identity can mean the difference between a right and a wrong answer. A 4 that looks like a 9, for example, can mean trouble.

- *Use the opposite operation to check your work.* When you come up with an answer, work backward to see if you are right. Use subtraction to check your addition; use division to check multiplication; and so on.

- *Look back at the questions to be sure you did everything that was asked.* Did you answer every part of the question? Did you show all the required work? Be as complete as you possibly can.

Group work in a lab setting gives students a chance to learn from one another.

Quantitative information often appears in visual form, in any of a number of visual aid formats. Whether visual aids appear on a website, in a magazine article that your instructor photocopied for use in a course, or in a textbook, they help to clarify quantitative concepts.

How can you "read" visual aids?

Visual aids such as tables and charts clarify numeric information through a visual format, often summarizing concepts found in the text. Especially for visual-dominant learners, what doesn't "click" when read in a text form often makes sense as part of a table or chart. Because tables and charts usually involve quantitative information, they are commonly used to present mathematical and scientific concepts.

Visual aids highlight statistical comparisons that show:

- *Trends over time* (e.g., the number of televisions per household in 1997 as compared to the number in 1957)

- *Relative rankings* (e.g., the size of the advertising budgets of four consumer products companies)

- *Distributions* (e.g., students' performance on standardized tests by geographic area)

- *Cycles* (e.g., the regular upward and downward movement of the nation's economy)

Knowing what to look for in visual aids will help you learn to "read" the information they present. The major types of visual aids are tables and charts.

reflect

Noted scientist Louis Pasteur said that "Chance favors only the prepared mind." What does this

mean to you? How does it relate to your approach to math and science classes? If you agree with Pasteur what can you do to make sure that you have a "prepared mind"?

& respond

Tables. The two basic types of tables are data tables and word tables. Data tables present numerical information—for example, the number of students taking a standardized test in 50 states. Word tables summarize and consolidate complex information, making it easier to study and evaluate. Look at Table 10.2 on page 293 for an example of a word table.

Charts. Also known as graphs, charts present numerical data in visual form to show associations among the data. Types of charts include pie charts, bar charts, and line charts. The *pie chart* presents data as wedge-shaped sections of a circle to show the relative size of each item as a percentage of the whole. *Bar charts* consist of horizontal bars of varying lengths to show the relative as well as absolute quantities. Whereas pie charts compare individual parts to the whole, bar charts compare items to one another. Finally, *line charts* show trends. The horizontal axis often shows a span of time, and the vertical axis frequently represents a specific measurement such as dollars.

Figure 9.3 gives an example of each type of chart, showing data from the U. S. Digest of Education Statistics. The pie chart shows where schools got their operating funds during a particular academic year. The bar chart shows how many students got degrees in certain fields of study during three academic years. Finally, the line chart shows enrollment in public and private colleges from 1960 through 2000.

Tables and charts help you to understand quantitative information. They are valuable study aids that can enhance your comprehension of what you read.

RISING
TO THE CHALLENGE

Dr. Baruj Benacerraf

Immunologist and Professor at Harvard University, Winner of the 1980 Nobel Prize in Physiology and Medicine

When you face difficulty, looking to your family and yourself for support can get you through it. Through his family's encouragement and his own perseverance, the dyslexic Dr. Benacerraf became an internationally known immunologist and winner of the Nobel Prize.

I was born in Caracas, Venezuela, of Spanish–Jewish ancestry. My primary and secondary education was in French, but I pursued my later education in the United States. I have dyslexia, which took me a long time to realize, because when I was young, it was a disorder that was not easily identified.

When I lived in Paris as a child, I had to repeat a year of school. I couldn't spell very well and I wrote slowly. I was constantly getting the lowest grades in writing and literature. The first few years of school were difficult because they depended so heavily on these skills. My family put a high value on achievement and encouraged me to do better.

Because I was perceived to be lazy and incompetent, not many teachers were willing to help me. I had to make progress by myself. To work through the slowness with reading, I would wake up at four in the morning and read in bed. That was how I became acquainted with the world. I also learned to have a good memory because with my slow reading I only had time to read things once. Although I could never learn how to spell, I have been saved by the computer because of the spell check. Now I have written 600 papers.

I became very successful at school because I made up for my shortcomings by being successful at other things, like mathematics and science. When I passed the French baccalaureate (high school) exam, I got the lowest grade in French and the highest in mathematics. In college and medical school I received high grades. When you have a problem, it's important that you realize you're not stupid, you simply have been given other advantages. For instance, I can see space in three dimensions, better than anyone else I know. It comes with being dyslexic.

I was not diagnosed with dyslexia until I was an adult, when it started appearing in my daughter. My daughter inherited the disorder and has been very successful as a urologist. My grandson also has the same problem with reading, but they learned earlier that he had it and therefore could react better to it. By then I knew how to help him not to struggle. I taught him how to read by syllables and advised him to read a lot. My daughter complained that I was too tough on her—when she got a 95, I said, "Why not 100?" But eventually she realized what I was trying to do. This was the recipe that I followed: always aim for the highest. My grandson will soon graduate from Harvard, summa cum laude.

I spent most of my life in science, and I had the luck of being awarded the Nobel Prize for Medicine, of which I am very proud. There are two things I have been most satisfied with. First, if there is a problem, I can find insight into how to solve it when everyone else gives up. Second, I have trained a large number of scientists, now very successful, who have become a family of mine. So now I have two families, genetic and intellectual. It is a fulfilling and wonderful legacy.

To others who have a learning disability, I would tell them the same thing I told my daughter and grandson: to work really hard. The world is full of challenges, and it is up to you to meet them. I say, always be your own best critic—you don't have to listen to other people to gain a sense of how you're doing. You must look at yourself with a very, very critical eye to be sure you can improve. The only person you can depend on to improve you is yourself.

Take a Moment to Consider . . .

- *What you have been most satisfied with in your life thus far.*

- *How you would like to improve yourself, and what you think you need to do to make this improvement.*

FIGURE 9.3 — Charts make information visual.[5]

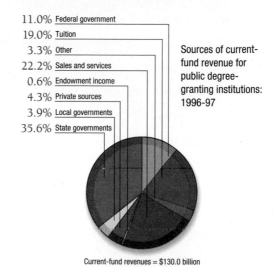

Pie Chart

11.0% Federal government
19.0% Tuition
3.3% Other
22.2% Sales and services
0.6% Endowment income
4.3% Private sources
3.9% Local governments
35.6% State governments

Sources of current-fund revenue for public degree-granting institutions: 1996-97

Current-fund revenues = $130.0 billion

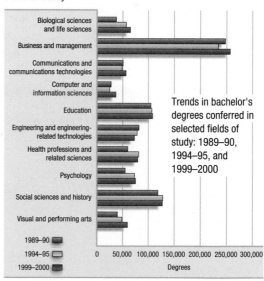

Bar Chart

Fields of study

Biological sciences and life sciences
Business and management
Communications and communications technologies
Computer and information sciences
Education
Engineering and engineering-related technologies
Health professions and related sciences
Psychology
Social sciences and history
Visual and performing arts

1989–90
1994–95
1999–2000

0   50,000 100,000 150,000 200,000 250,000 300,000
Degrees

Trends in bachelor's degrees conferred in selected fields of study: 1989–90, 1994–95, and 1999–2000

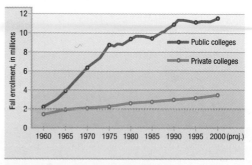

Line Chart

Fall enrollment, in millions

Public colleges
Private colleges

1960 1965 1970 1975 1980 1985 1990 1995 2000 (proj.)

Enrollment in degree-granting institutions: 1960–61 to 2000–01

I strive for accuracy and precision.

Although accuracy and precision are important in many different subjects, they have particular value in math and science. Complete a step of an algebra problem inaccurately, and your answer will be incorrect. Complete a step of a biology lab project imprecisely, and your results will be off. In class, of course, the consequences of inaccuracy are reflected in low grades; in life, the consequences could show in a patient's health or in the calculation of widely used data such as jobless rates.

Working accurately and precisely with numbers requires time, focus, attention to detail, and striving for high quality. Lots of practice with problems—essential for developing precision—requires that you take your time. Checking over the details of your work—key for assuring accuracy—demands focus. Furthermore, consistently striving for high quality will help you to be consistent and to base your work on solid understanding of concepts rather than counting on guesses and luck. The quality you are capable of will shine through if you focus on precision and accuracy in your work.

REMEMBER!
the important points ...

Why do you need to be able to think quantitatively?

Practical problems that come up from time to time, such as in personal finances or scheduling, require quantitative thinking. Many everyday tasks require skills such as arithmetic, algebra, geometry, and statistics. Most important, math is a problem-solving discipline; when you perform mathematical and scientific problem solving, you build critical-thinking skills that you can apply to any problem in school, work, or life.

How can you master math and science basics?

Mastering the basics involves classroom focus (being prepared and asking questions), textbook focus (taking careful notes, noting formulas, working problems), and studying and homework focus (doing as many problems as you can, even outside of assigned homework). Solve word problems (the most common problems) by following the four-step method: Understand the problem, name and explore potential solution paths, carry out your solution plan, and review your result. Other helpful word-problem strategies include looking for a pattern, making a table, drawing a diagram, working backward, and examining a similar problem.

How can you overcome math anxiety?

Math anxiety is a high-stress feeling appearing in relation to quantitative thinking. It is often a result of common misconceptions such as the notion that people are born with or without an ability to do math. Strategies to overcome math anxiety include extensive practice, using human and text resources, taking responsibility for your quantitative learning, and knowing your rights as a quantitative learner.

What techniques will improve your performance on math and science tests?

General test-taking strategies certainly apply. In addition, consider analyzing problems carefully, estimating before beginning a problem, breaking a calculation into the smallest possible pieces, recalling how you solved similar problems, drawing a picture to help you see a problem, using an opposite operation to check your work, writing neatly, and making sure you did everything a question asks.

How can you "read" visual aids?

Visual aids, including tables and charts, highlight statistical comparisons (including trends over time, relative rankings, distributions, and cycles) and summarize information. Reading visual aids depends on understanding their value as learning tools and on learning how tables and charts are constructed and the messages they convey.

BUILDING SKILLS
FOR SUCCESSFUL LEARNING

Name _____   Date _____

CRITICAL THINKING
APPLYING LEARNING TO LIFE

Problem Strategies and Reactions

Using a math or science book, copy down two questions from the text. For each question, name a problem-solving strategy or strategies from this chapter that will help you solve the problem. Solve the problem on a separate piece of paper. Afterward, state here why you chose the strategies you did. Are there other ways to solve the same problem?

Problem 1: _____

_____

_____

Strategies: _____

_____

_____

_____

Problem 2: _____

_____

_____

Strategies: _____

_____

_____

_____

   Think about how doing these problems, and working on other math and science problems, makes you feel. Evaluate your level of math anxiety by responding to the following statements as accurately as possible.

1. When I make an error on a math problem, I

_____

_____

2. When I'm unable to solve a particular problem, I

ask to a instructor or go over my notes.

3. When I'm able to solve a difficult problem, I feel

unable to keep going to solve other Problem

4. One thing I enjoy about doing math is

doing each step of a problem.

5. Working on mathematics makes me feel

bad, because numbers are not my thing.

TEAM BUILDING
COLLABORATIVE SOLUTIONS

The Study Group Approach to Quantitative Learning

Choose one or two people from one of your math or science classes—fellow students with whom you feel comfortable working. Use problems from your assigned text.

1. *Choose one problem.* Each of you work on the same problem separately. After finishing the problem, come together to share your methods. Discuss how each of you approached the problem. What steps did you each take in solving the problem? What strategies did you use? How did you check to see if your procedures were correct?

2. *Now pick a different problem on which to work together.* After solving this problem, discuss your problem-solving process. Did you learn more or less by working together as compared to working separately? Were you able to solve the problem faster by working together than you did when you worked alone? Did you gain a better understanding of the problem by working together?

3. *Generalize your experiences to discuss attitudes about math and science.* What do each of you do to overcome challenges? What positive steps do you each take in problem solving?

personal IMPROVEMENT plan

I commit to three specific quantitative learning strategies to improve my math and science skills. From this chapter, I choose three strategies that I think will help me.

Strategy 1: _____

Strategy 2: _____

Strategy 3: _____

I choose one strategy to focus on (circle this strategy above) and I will:

- describe my goal—what I want to gain by using this strategy.

  _____
  _____
  _____

- describe in detail how I plan to use the strategy.

  _____
  _____
  _____
  _____

- describe how I will measure my progress toward the goal this semester.

  _____
  _____
  _____
  _____

Activate the Habit of Mind

Here's how I will *strive for precision and accuracy* to achieve this goal:

_____
_____
_____
_____
_____

SUGGESTED READINGS

Gralla, Preston, Sarah Ishida (Illustrator), Mina Reimer (Illustrator), and Steph Adams. *How the Internet Works: Millennium Edition.* Indianapolis, IN: Que, 1999.

Hart, Lynn and Deborah Najee-Ullich. *Studying for Mathematics.* New York: HarperCollins College Publishers, 1997.

Lerner, Marcia. *Math Smart: Essential Math for These Numeric Times.* New York: Villard Books, 1995.

Polya, George. *How to Solve It.* London: Penguin, 1990.

INTERNET RESOURCES

Algebra Online: www.algebra-online.com

Professor Freedman's Math Help: www.mathpower.com

Math.com—The World of Math Online: www.math.com

Math Forum @ Drexel: http://mathforum.org

Math Homework Help:
    http://erols.com/bram/column2.html

Answer to Take Action

Here is the solution to the word problem on page 273:

20 minutes on the stair climber and

30 minutes on the treadmill.

ENDNOTES

1. George Polya. *How to Solve It.* London: Penguin, 1990.

2. Rick Billstein, Shlomo Libeskind, and Johnny W. Lott. *A Problem Solving Approach to Mathematics for Elementary School Teachers.* Example 1-1 (p. 5); problem 2 (pp. 21–22); problem 3 (pp. 22–24); problem 4 (pp. 26–27); and problem set 1-2, #21 (p. 35). Copyright © 1993 by Addison-Wesley Publishing Company, Inc. Reprinted by permission of Pearson Education, Inc.

3. Adapted from Acker, Kathy (March 1997). *Math Anxiety Code of Responsibilities* [on-line]. Available: http://fc.whyy.org/CCC/alg1/code.htm (March 1998).

4. Sheila Tobias. *Overcoming Math Anxiety.* New York: W. W. Norton & Company, 1993, pp. 226–27.

5. Pie chart source: U. S. Department of Education, National Center for Education Statistics, Integrated Postsecondary Education Data System, "Finance FY97" survey. Bar chart source: U. S. Department of Education, National Center for Education Statistics, Higher Education General Information Survey, "Degrees and Other Formal Awards Conferred" survey, and Integrated Postsecondary Education Data System, "Completions" surveys. Line chart source: U. S. Department of Education, National Center for Education Statistics, Higher Education General Information Survey, "Fall Enrollment in Institutions of Higher Education," "Degrees and Other Formal Awards Conferred," and "Financial Statistics of Institutions of Higher Education" surveys; and Integrated Postsecondary Education Data System, "Fall Enrollment," "Completions," and "Finance" surveys.

THINKING IT THROUGH

Check those statements that apply to you right now:

- ■ When I do library research, I hunt around until I find information; I don't use a research plan.

- ■ I use the Internet all the time and am comfortable finding information on it.

- ■ When I write, I try to think about who will read my work and what they need to know.

- ■ My goal is to be able to write a perfect paper the first time around.

- ■ I am very careful to avoid plagiarizing the works of other writers.

- ■ When I revise and edit a paper, I consider many different things including tone, organization, language, sentence and paragraph structure, spelling, and grammar.

- ■ I rarely or never proofread what I write.

Researching and Writing

10

GATHERING AND COMMUNICATING IDEAS

IN THIS CHAPTER

In this chapter you explore answers to the following questions:

- How can you make the most of your library?

- How can you do research on the Internet?

- What are the elements of effective writing?

- What is the writing process?

- How can you deliver an effective oral presentation?

Thinking and communicating with clarity and precision.

HABITS OF MIND
MIND

"Language and thinking are closely entwined. . . . Intelligent people **strive to communicate accurately** in both written and oral form, taking care to define terms and to use precise language, correct names, universal labels, and apt analogies." —ART COSTA

*The benefits of clear, precise writing are immeasurable—not only in school, but in everything you do. When you write clearly, you show others that you care enough **to use language properly and to organize your thoughts**. You leave a lasting impression of intelligence.*

Research and writing are powerful learning and communication tools that are at the heart of your education. Through library and Internet research, you gather information from sources all over the world. Through writing, you communicate information and perspective to others. Whether you write an essay in English class or a chemistry lab report, the writing process will help you clarify and sharpen your thinking.

287

This chapter has two goals: to help you improve your skill in finding information at your college library and on the Internet, and to reinforce some of the writing basics that most students also study in English composition courses. In school and in your career, researching and writing are essential to success.

How can you make the most of your library?

Alibrary is a home for information; consider it the "brain" of your college. Your challenge is to find what you need quickly and efficiently.

Start with a Road Map

Most college libraries are bigger than high school and community libraries, so you may feel lost on your first few visits. Make your life easier by learning how your library is organized.

- *Circulation desk.* All publications are checked out at the circulation desk, which is usually near the library entrance.

- *Reference area.* Here you'll find reference books, including encyclopedias, directories, dictionaries, almanacs, and atlases. You'll also find librarians and other library employees who can direct you to information. Computer terminals, containing the library's catalog of holdings, as well as on-line bibliographic and full-text databases, are usually part of the reference area.

- *Book area.* Books—and, in many libraries, magazines and journals in bound or boxed volumes—are stored in the *stacks*. A library with "open stacks" allows you to search for materials on your own. In a "closed-stack" system, a staff member retrieves materials for you.

- *Periodicals area.* Here you'll find recent issues of popular and scholarly magazines, journals, and newspapers. Most college libraries collect **periodicals** ranging from *Time* to the *New England Journal of Medicine*. Because unbound periodicals are generally not circulated, you may find photocopy machines nearby where you can copy pages.

- *Audiovisual materials areas.* Many libraries have special areas for video, art and photography, and recorded music collections.

- *Computer areas.* Computer terminals, linked to databases and the Internet, may be scattered throughout the building or set off in particular areas. You may be able to access these databases and the Internet from computer labs and writing centers. Many college dorm rooms are also

Periodicals
Magazines, journals, and newspapers that are published on a regular basis throughout the year.

wired for computer access, enabling students to connect via their personal computers.

■ *Microform areas.* Most libraries have microform reading areas. Microforms are materials printed in reduced size on film, either *microfilm* (a reel of film) or *microfiche* (a sheet or card of film), that is viewed through special machines. Many microform reading machines can print hard copies of images.

To learn about your college library, take a tour or training session. Almost all college libraries offer orientation sessions on how to locate books, periodicals, and databases and use the Internet. If your school has more than one library, explore each one you intend to use.

A road map of library resources may also be available on your library's web page, which usually can be accessed from any terminal on campus, including those in student dormitories. Library web pages usually contain online catalogs from your college and other associated colleges, on-line databases, and phone numbers and e-mail addresses for reference librarians.

Getting to know your library will help you spend less time locating materials and more time on your research.

Learn How to Conduct an Information Search

The most successful and timesaving library research involves following a specific *search strategy*—a step-by-step method for finding information that takes you from general to specific sources. Starting with general sources usually works best because they provide an overview of your research topic and can lead you to more specific information and sources. For example, an encyclopedia article on the archaeological discovery of the Dead Sea Scrolls—manuscripts written between 250 B.C.E. and 68 C.E. that trace the roots of Judaism and Christianity—may mention that one of the most important books on the subject is *Understanding the Dead Sea Scrolls,* edited by Hershel Shanks (New York: Random House, 1992). This book, in turn, leads you to 13 experts who wrote specialized text chapters.

Narrowing your topic is critical to research success because broad topics yield too much data. Here, instead of using the topic "Dead Sea Scrolls" in your search, consider narrowing it. For example:

■ How the Dead Sea Scrolls were discovered by Bedouin shepherds in 1947
■ The historical origins of the scrolls
■ The process archaeologists used to reconstruct scroll fragments

Conducting a Keyword Search

To find materials related to your topic, conduct a *keyword search* of the library database—a method for locating sources through the use of topic-related words and phrases. To narrow your topic and reduce the number of

TABLE 10.1   How to perform an effective keyword search.

IF YOU ARE SEARCHING FOR . . .	DO THIS	EXAMPLE
A word	Type the word normally.	Aid
A phrase	Type the phrase in its normal word order (use regular word spacing) or surround the phrase with double quotation marks.	financial aid or "financial aid"
Two or more keywords without regard to word order	Type the words in any order, surrounding the words with quotation marks. Use *and* to separate the words.	"financial aid" and "scholarships"
Topic A or topic B	Type the words in any order, surrounding the words with quotation marks. Use *or* to separate the words.	"financial aid" or "scholarships"
Topic A but not topic B	Type topic A first within quotation marks, and then topic B within quotation marks. Use *not* to separate the words.	"financial aid" not "scholarships"

"hits," add more keywords. For example, instead of searching through the broad category *art*, focus on *French art* or, more specifically, *nineteenth-century French art*.

Keyword searches use natural language, rather than specialized classification vocabulary. Table 10.1 provides tips to help you use the keyword system. The last three entries describe how to use "or," "and," and "not" to narrow searches with what is called Boolean logic.

As you search, keep in mind that:

- double quotes around a word or phrase will locate the exact term you entered ("financial aid").

- using uppercase or lowercase does not affect the search (*Scholarships* will find *scholarships*).

- singular terms will find the plural (*scholarship* will find *scholarships*).

"Seeing research as a quest for an answer makes clear that you cannot know whether you have found something unless you know what it is you are looking for."

LYNN QUITMAN TROYKA

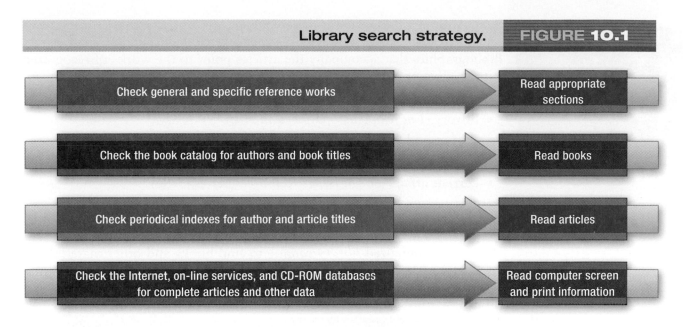

Library search strategy.   FIGURE 10.1

Check general and specific reference works	→	Read appropriate sections
Check the book catalog for authors and book titles	→	Read books
Check periodical indexes for author and article titles	→	Read articles
Check the Internet, on-line services, and CD-ROM databases for complete articles and other data	→	Read computer screen and print information

Conducting Research Using a Search Strategy

Knowing where to look during each phase of your search helps you find information quickly and efficiently. A successful search strategy often starts with general references and moves to more specific references (see Figure 10.1).

Use General Reference Works

Begin your research with *general reference works*. These works cover many different topics in a broad, nondetailed way. General reference guides are often available on-line or on **CD ROM**.

Among the works that fall into the general reference category are these:

- Encyclopedias such as the multivolume *Encyclopedia Americana* and the single-volume *New Columbia Encyclopedia*
- Almanacs such as the *World Almanac and Book of Facts*
- Yearbooks such as the *McGraw-Hill Yearbook of Science and Technology* and the *Statistical Abstract of the United States*
- Dictionaries such as *Webster's New World College Dictionary*
- Biographical reference works such as the *New York Times Biographical Service*, *Webster's Biographical Dictionary*, and various editions of *Who's Who*
- Bibliographies such as *Books in Print* (especially the *Subject Guide to Books in Print*)

Scan these sources for an overview of your topic. Bibliographies at the end of encyclopedia articles may also lead to important sources.

CD-ROM

A compact disk, containing words and images in electronic form, that can be read by a computer (CD-ROM stands for "compact disk read-only memory").

Search Specialized Reference Works

Turn next to *specialized reference works* for more specific facts. Specialized reference works include encyclopedias and dictionaries that focus on a narrow

field. Although the entries in these volumes are short summaries, they focus on critical ideas and on the keywords you need to conduct additional research. Bibliographies that accompany the articles point to the works of recognized experts. Examples of specialized reference works, organized by subject, include the following:

- history (*Encyclopedia of American History*)
- science and technology (*Encyclopedia of Biological Sciences*)
- social sciences (*Dictionary of Education*)
- current affairs (*Social Issues Resources Series [SIRS]*)

Browse Through Books on Your Subject

Use the computerized *library catalog* to find books and other materials on your topic. The catalog tells you which publications the library owns and where they can be found and is searchable in multiple ways, including by author, title, and subject. For example, to find *The Artist's Way: A Spiritual Path to Higher Creativity* by Julia Cameron in your library you could search by author: *Cameron, Julia* (last name first); by title: *The Artist's Way* (or just *Artist's Way*); or by subject: *creative ability, self-actualization,* or *creation.*

Each catalog listing refers to the library's classification system, which in turn tells you exactly where the publication can be found. The Dewey Decimal and Library of Congress systems are among the most common classification systems. Getting to know your library's system will help save time and trouble.

Use Periodical Indexes to Search for Periodicals

Periodicals, a valuable source of current information, include journals, magazines, and newspapers. *Journals* are written for readers with specialized knowledge. Whereas *Newsweek* magazine may run a general-interest article on AIDS research, the *Journal of the American Medical Association* may print the original scientific study for an audience of doctors and scientists. Many libraries display periodicals that are up to a year or two old, and they usually convert older copies to microfilm or microfiche. Many full-text articles are also available on computer databases.

Periodical indexes lead you to specific articles. The *Reader's Guide to Periodical Literature*, available in print and on CD-ROM, indexes general information sources including articles in hundreds of general-interest publications. Look in the *Infotrac* family of databases (available on-line or on CD-ROM) for other periodical indexes such as *Health Reference Center* and *General Business File*. Another periodical database family—*Ebsco Host*—catalogs general and health-related periodicals.

Indexing information is listed in the *Standard Periodical Directory, Ulrich's International Periodicals Directory,* and *Magazines for Libraries*. Each database also lists the magazines and periodicals it indexes. Because there is no all-inclusive index for technical, medical, and scholarly journal articles, you'll have to search indexes that specialize in narrow subject areas. Such indexes also include *abstracts* (article summaries). Among the available indexes are *ERIC* (*Educational Resources Information Center*), the *Humanities Index, Index Medicus,* and *Psychological Abstracts*. You'll also find separate newspaper indexes in print, in microform, on CD-ROM, or on-line.

Almost no library owns all of the publications listed in these and other specialized indexes. However, journals that are not part of your library's collection or that are not available in full-text form on-line may be available through an interlibrary loan, which allows patrons to request materials from other libraries. The librarian will help you arrange the loan.

Ask the Librarian

Librarians can assist you in solving research problems. They can help you locate unfamiliar or hard-to-find sources, navigate catalogs and databases, and uncover research shortcuts. Say, for example, you are researching a gun-control bill that is currently before Congress, and you want to contact groups on both sides of the issue. The librarian may lead you to the *Encyclopedia of Associations*, which lists the National Rifle Association, a pro-gun organization, and Handgun Control Inc., a gun-control group. By contacting these groups or visiting their websites, you can find information on current legislation. Table 10.2 lists additional reference sources that are available on-line.

TABLE 10.2	Valuable on-line reference sources.

IF YOU WANT TO SEARCH . . .	VISIT THIS INTERNET ADDRESS
Copyrighted books in print	Amazon.com: www.amazon.com
	Barnes and Noble: www.barnesandnoble.com
Encyclopedia entries	Encarta: http://encarta.msn.com
Magazine and newspaper articles	AJR Newslink: http://newslink.org
Primary source documents	Library of Congress American Memory: http://lcweb2.loc.gov/ammem/mdbquery.html
Federal legislation	Thomas: Legislative Information on the Internet: http://thomas.loc.gov
Biographies	Biographical Dictionary: www.s9.com/biography
	Biography.com: www.biography.com/search
	Biography-Center: www.biography-center.com
	Lives: www.amillionlives.com
Maps	Perry-Castañeda Library Map Collection: www.lib.utexas.edu/maps/index.html
	Maptech MapServer (topo): http://mapserver.maptech.com
Country profiles	Atlapedia Online: www.atlapedia.com/online/country_index.htm
	Kiosk: Journal of Geopolitics: http://FowlerLibrary.com/Kiosk
U.S. population and economic data	U. S. Census Bureau: U. S. Department of Commerce: www.census.gov/index.html
Company information	Thomas Register: www.thomasregister.com

Librarians are not the only helpful people in the library. For simplicity's sake, this book uses the term *librarian* to refer to both librarians and other staff members who are trained to help. Here are some tips that will help you get the advice you are seeking from the librarian.

■ *Be prepared and be specific.* Instead of asking for information on the American presidency, focus on the topic you expect to write about in your American history paper—for example, how President Franklin D. Roosevelt's physical disability may have affected his leadership during World War II.

■ *Ask for help when you can't find a specific source.* For example, when a specific book is not on the shelf, the librarian may direct you to another source that works as well.

■ *Ask for help with computer and other equipment.* Librarians are experts in using the library's computers and other equipment, so turn to them if you encounter a technical problem you can't solve.

TAKE ACTION

Discover Your College Library

Take an actual or a virtual tour of your college's library system. Then complete the following:

■ Look for the areas mentioned under the heading "Start with a Road Map." How does your library compare to what is described here?

_____

_____

_____

■ Now find a list of Internet resources. What search engines, directories, and databases are emphasized at your library?

_____

_____

_____

■ In which of the courses you are taking this semester are you likely to conduct a search strategy at the library to complete an assignment? In which are you likely to conduct an Internet search? Describe why your research decisions would differ.

_____

_____

_____

_____

The library is one of your college's most valuable resources, so take advantage of it. Your library research and critical-thinking skills give you the ability to collect information, weigh alternatives, and make decisions. These skills last a lifetime and may serve you well if you choose one of the many careers that require research ability. The library is not your only research resource, however. The Internet is becoming a primary research tool for both school and work.

How can you do research on the Internet?

The *Internet* is a computer network that links organizations and people around the world. A miracle of technology, it can connect you to billions of information sources almost instantaneously.

Because of its widespread reach, the Internet is an essential research tool—if used wisely. This section will help you make the most of the time you spend on-line now and in the future. As the Internet becomes more important, it opens up a world of opportunities—for example, it may be the medium through which you continue your studies via on-line courses, do your work in a home-based office, purchase products and services, find medical information, book airline and hotel reservations, investigate potential employers, file your taxes, make investments, and more.

Internet research depends on your critical judgment. Bob Kieft, library director at Haverford College in Pennsylvania, says that students must "think critically and independently about the sources they use, be curious and imaginative about the projects they are working on, be open to the topic in ways that lead them to ask good questions, and bring their analytical powers to bear. . . . What students know about technology is less important than how they think about their work."[1]

The Basics

With a basic knowledge of the Internet, you can access facts and figures, read articles and reports, purchase products, download files, send messages electronically via e-mail, and even "talk" to people in real time. Following is some information that you should know.

■ *Access.* Users access the Internet through Internet Service Providers (ISPs). Some ISPs are commercial, such as America Online or Earthlink. Others are linked to companies, colleges, and other organizations. When you sign up with an ISP, you choose a *screen name,* which is part of your online address.

■ *Information locations.* Most information is displayed on *websites,* cyberspace locations developed by companies, government agencies, organizations, and individuals. Together, these sites make up the *World Wide Web.* By visiting particular websites, you can research topics as well as buy and sell products. Other locations where information resides include *newsgroups* (collections of messages from people interested in a particular topic), *FTP sites* (File Transfer Protocol sites that allow users to download files), and other non-web sites (Gopher sites) that provide access to databases or electronic library holdings.

■ *Finding locations.* The string of text and numbers that identifies an Internet site is called a *URL* (Universal Resource Locator). Look at the Internet Resources list at the end of this chapter, or any other, for some examples of URLs. You can type in a URL to access a specific site. Many websites include *hyperlinks*—URLs, usually underlined and highlighted in color, that when clicked on will take you directly to another web location.

Using Search Directories and Search Engines

Search directories are large lists of websites sorted by category, much as Yellow Pages directories organize business telephone numbers. Information is accessible through keyword searches. When searching, try a search directory first, since the results may be more manageable than those provided by a search engine. Some of the most popular and effective search directories include Google (www.google.com), Yahoo! (www.yahoo.com), MSN Search (www.msnsearch.com), Overture (www.overture.com), and Excite (www.excite.com).

Among the search directories aimed at academic audiences are the Librarian's Index to the Internet (www.lii.org), Infomine (www.infomine.com), and Academic Info (www.academicinfo.com).

Each search directory has particular features. Some have different search options (simple search, advanced search); some are known for having strong lists of sites for particular topics; some have links that connect you to lists of sites that fall under particular categories. The search directory's website will help you learn how best to use the directory.

Slightly different from search directories, *search engines* search for keywords through the entire Internet—newsgroups, websites, and other resources—instead of just websites. This gives you wider access but may yield an enormous list of "hits" unless you know how to limit your search effectively. Some useful search engines include: Alta Vista (http://altavista.com), HotBot (www.hotbot.com), Ask (www.ask.com), and Lycos (www.lycos.com). As with search directories, each search engine includes helpful search tools and guides.

Search Strategy

The World Wide Web has been called "the world's greatest library, with all its books on the floor." With no librarian in sight, you need to master a basic search strategy that will help you avoid becoming overwhelmed while researching on-line.

1. *Think carefully about what you want to locate.* University of Michigan professor Eliot Soloway recommends phrasing your search in the form of a question—for example, *What vaccines are given to children before age 5?* Then he advises identifying the important words in the question (*vaccines, children, before age 5*) as well as other related words (*chicken pox, tetanus, polio, shot, pediatrics,* and so on). This will give you a collection of terms to use in different combinations as you search.[2]

2. *Use a search directory to isolate sites under your desired topic or category.* Save the sites that look useful. Most Internet software has a "bookmark" or "favorites" feature for recording sites you want to find again.

3. *Explore these sites to get a general idea of what's out there.* If the directory takes you where you need to go, you're in luck. More often in academic research, you will need to dig deeper. Use what you find in the search directory to notice useful keywords and information locations.

4. *Move on to a search engine to narrow your search.* Use your keywords in a variety of ways to uncover as many possibilities as you can. Make sure your keywords are spelled correctly.

   ■ Vary word order if you are using more than one keyword (for example, search under *education, college, statistics* and *statistics, education, college*).

   ■ Use *Boolean operators*—the words "and," "not," and "or"—in ways that limit your search (see Table 10.1 for tips for using keywords in library searches).

5. *Evaluate the list of links that appears.* If there are too many, narrow your search by using more keywords or more specific keywords (*Broadway* could become *Broadway* AND "*fall season*" AND *2004*). If there are too few, broaden your search by using fewer or different keywords.

6. *When you think you are done, start over.* Choose another search directory or search engine and perform your search again. Why? Because different systems access different sites.

Use Critical Thinking to Evaluate Every Source

It is up to you to evaluate the truth and usefulness of the information you find on the Internet. Since the Internet is largely an uncensored platform for free-flowing information, you must decide which sources have value and which should be ignored. It takes time and experience to develop the instincts you need to make these evaluations, so talk to your instructor if you have questions about specific sources.

If you are informed about the potential pitfalls of Internet research and use critical thinking to avoid them, you will get the most from your time and effort. Use the following strategies to analyze the value of each source.[3]

■ *Ask questions about the source.* Is the author a recognized expert? Does he or she write from a particular perspective that may bias the presentation? Is the source recent enough for your purposes? Where did the author get the information? Are the sources reliable?

■ *Broaden your questioning.* Note the website's name and the organization that creates and maintains the site. Is the organization reputable? Is it known as an authority on the topic you are researching? If you are not sure of the source, the URL will usually give you a clue. For example, URLs ending in .edu originate at an educational institution, and .gov sites originate at government agencies.

Take time to critically evaluate what you read on the Internet.

■ *Evaluate the material.* Evaluate the content of an Internet source the way you would any other material you read. See if sources are noted and if they are sources you trust. Is the source a published document (newspaper article, professional journal article, etc.), or is it simply one person's views? Can you verify the data by comparing it to other material? Pay attention, also, to writing quality. Texts with grammatical and spelling errors, poor organization, or factual mistakes are likely to be unreliable.

■ *Be prepared for Internet-specific problems.* The nature of the Internet causes particular problems for researchers, including constantly changing information (new information arrives daily; old information may not be removed or updated) and technology problems (websites may move, be deleted, or have technical problems that deny access). Try to budget extra time to handle problems and to investigate whether information is current.

Take advantage of the wealth of material the Internet offers—but be picky. Always remember that your research will only be as strong as your critical thinking. If you work hard to ensure that your research is solid and comprehensive, the product of your efforts will speak for itself.

Combining Library and Internet Searches

For many research projects, it makes good sense to combine library and Internet resources. Head to the library when:

■ You are conducting in-depth research, requiring an historical perspective. Older information is more likely to be at the library than on the web.

■ You want to verify the authenticity of what you discover on the Internet.

■ You need personal, face-to-face help from a librarian.

■ You feel more comfortable navigating the established library system than the tangle of Internet sites.

Whatever source you use—and wherever you find that source—it is wrong to claim that work written by others is your own. As you will see later in this chapter, plagiarism devalues your work and may result in repercussions that jeopardize your education.

Whether you are zapping electronic mail across the globe or using a pencil and pad to write a research paper, the success of your communication depends on your ability to write. In the next section, you will explore ways to improve your writing.

reflect

Describe your research style at the library: Is it quick and dirty, thorough and scholarly, detective-like and cunning? Now describe your style when you conduct Internet research. If your style differs in these settings, why do you think this is the case? What can you do to improve your research skills in both settings?

& respond

What are the elements of effective writing?

Becoming an effective writer is so crucial to your education that most schools require students to pass a semester- or year-long writing course in the English department. Many schools also make available self-directed writing labs in which students can practice and hone specific skills. The overview presented here is intended to reinforce some of the basics you will learn in these settings. The focus of this material is on writing a research paper, but you can apply much of what you learn to other writing assignments. These skills will also help you when you take essay exams and prepare for oral exams (see Chapter 8).

Good writing depends on and reflects clear thinking and is influenced greatly by reading. Exposing yourself to the works of other writers introduces you to new concepts and perspectives as it helps you discover different ways to express ideas.

Every writing situation is unique, depending on your purpose, topic, and **audience**. Your goal is to understand each element before you begin.

reflect

Identify a piece of writing that you recently read that captured your attention. (It could be a

 work of literature, a biography, a magazine or newspaper article, or even a section from one of your college texts.) Describe, in detail, why it was effective. Did it communicate ideas you never thought of before? Did it arouse buried or unfamiliar feelings? Did it inspire you to action? Why? What can you learn from this piece that you can apply to your own writing?

& *respond*

Writing Purpose

Writing without a clear purpose is like driving without a destination. You'll get somewhere, but chances are it won't be the right place. Therefore, when you write, always decide what you want to accomplish before you start. The two most common writing purposes are to inform and to persuade.

Informative writing presents and explains ideas in an unbiased way. A research paper on how hospitals process blood donations informs readers without trying to mold opinions. Most newspaper articles, except on the opinion and editorial pages, are examples of informative writing.

Persuasive writing attempts to convince readers to adopt a point of view. For example, as the health editor of a magazine, you might write a column to persuade readers to give blood. Examples of persuasive writing include newspaper editorials, business proposals, and books with a point of view.

Audience
The reader or readers of any piece of written material.

Knowing Your Audience

In almost every case, a writer creates written material so that others can read it. The writer and audience are partners in this process. Knowing who your audience is helps you communicate successfully.

Key Questions About Your Audience

In school, your primary audience is your instructors. For many assignments, instructors want you to assume that they are *typical readers* who know little about your topic and need full explanations. In contrast, *informed readers* know your subject and require less information. Ask yourself some or all of the following questions to help you determine how much information your readers need:

- Who are my readers? Are they instructors or fellow students?
- How much do they know about my topic? Are they experts or beginners?
- Are they interested, or do I have to convince them to read my material?
- Can I expect readers to have open or closed minds about my topic?

Your answers will help you shape what you write. Remember, communication is successful only when readers understand the message you intend. Effective and successful writing involves following specific steps in the writing process.

What is the writing process?

The writing process for research papers and essays gives you the opportunity to state and rework your thoughts until you express yourself clearly. The four main parts of the process are planning, drafting, revising, and editing. Critical thinking plays an important role throughout.

Planning

Prewriting strategies
Techniques for generating ideas about a topic and finding out how much you already know before you start your research and writing.

Planning gives you a chance to think about what to write and how to write it. Planning involves brainstorming for topic ideas, using **prewriting strategies** to define and narrow your topic, conducting research, writing a thesis statement, and writing a working outline. Although these steps are listed in sequence, in real life they overlap one another as you plan your document.

Open Your Mind Through Brainstorming

Whether your instructor assigns a specific topic (the unfolding relationships between mothers and daughters in Amy Tan's novel *The Joy Luck Club*), a partially defined topic (novelist Amy Tan), or a general category within which you make your own choice (Asian-American authors), you should brainstorm to develop topic ideas. Brainstorming is a creative technique that involves generating ideas about a subject without making judgments (see Chapter 4).

First, let your mind wander. Write down anything on the assigned subject that comes to mind, in no particular order. Then, organize that list into an outline or think link that helps you see the possibilities more clearly. To make the outline or think link, separate the items you've listed into general ideas or categories and sub-ideas or examples. Then, associate the sub-ideas or examples with the ideas they support or fit.

Figure 10.2 shows a portion of an outline that student Michael B. Jackson constructed from a brainstorming list. The assignment is a five-paragraph essay on a life-changing event. Here Michael chose to brainstorm the topic of "boot camp"; then he organized his ideas into categories.

Part of a brainstorming outline.   FIGURE 10.2

> <u>A LIFE-CHANGING EVENT</u>
> — family
> — childhood
> → military
>   — travel
>   → boot camp
>   — physical conditioning
>   • swim tests
>   • intensive training
>   • ENDLESS push-ups!
>   — Chief who was our commander
>   — mental discipline
>   • military lifestyle
>   • perfecting our appearance
>   — self-confidence
>   • walk like you're in control
>   • don't blindly accept anything

Narrow Your Topic Through Prewriting Strategies

Next, narrow your topic, focusing on the specific sub-ideas and examples from your brainstorming session. Explore one or more of these with prewriting strategies such as brainstorming, freewriting, and asking journalists' questions.[4] Prewriting strategies help you decide which of your possible topics you would most like to pursue.

Brainstorming. The same process you used to generate ideas also helps you narrow your topic. Write down your thoughts about the possibility you have chosen, and then organize them into categories, noticing any patterns that appear. See if any of the sub-ideas or examples might make good topics.

Freewriting. When you freewrite, you write whatever comes to mind without censoring ideas or worrying about grammar, spelling, punctuation, or organization. Freewriting helps you think creatively and gives you an opportunity to begin integrating the information you know. Freewrite on the sub-ideas or examples you created to see if you want to pursue them. Here is a sample of freewriting:

Boot camp for the Coast Guard really changed my life. First of all, I really got in shape. We had to get up every morning at 5 A.M., eat breakfast, and go right into training. We had to do endless military-style push-ups, but we later found out that these have a purpose, to prepare us to hit the deck in the event of enemy fire. We had a lot of aquatic tests, once we were awakened at 3 A.M. to do one in full uniform! Boot camp also helped me to feel confident about myself and be disciplined. Chief Marzloff was the main person who made that happen. He was tough but there was always a reason. He got angry when I used to nod my head whenever he would speak to me, he said that made it seem like I was blindly accepting whatever he said, which was a weakness. From him I have learned to keep an eye on my body's movements when I communicate. I learned a lot more from him too.

Asking journalists' questions. When journalists start working on a story, they ask themselves: Who? What? Where? When? Why? and How? You can use these *journalists' questions* to focus your thinking. Ask these questions about any sub-idea or example to discover what you may want to discuss.

Who?   Who was at boot camp? Who influenced me the most?

What?   What about boot camp changed my life? What did we do?

When?   When in my life did I go to boot camp and for how long?

Where?   Where was camp located? Where did we spend our day-to-day time?

Why?   Why did I decide to go there? Why was it such an important experience?

How?   How did we train in the camp? How were we treated? How did we achieve success?

As you prewrite, keep paper length, due date, and other requirements (such as topic area or purpose) in mind. These requirements influence your choice of a final topic. For example, if you have a month to write an informative 20-page paper on a learning disability, you might discuss the symptoms, effects, and treatment of attention deficit disorder. If you have a week to write a five-page persuasive essay, you might write about how elementary school students with ADD need special training.

Prewriting helps you develop a topic broad enough to give you something with which to work but narrow enough to be manageable. Prewriting also helps you see what you know and what you don't know. If your assignment requires more than you already know, you may need to do research.

Conduct Research

In some cases, prewriting strategies may generate all the ideas and information you need. In other writing situations, you will have to do research. Try doing your research in stages. In the first stage, look for a basic overview that can lead to a thesis statement. In the second stage, go into more depth, tracking down information that helps you fill in gaps and complete your thoughts.

As you research, create source notes and content notes on index cards. These help you organize your work, keep track of your sources, and avoid **plagiarism**, which is discussed in detail later in this chapter. (Source notes and content notes are examined in Chapter 7.)

Write a Thesis Statement

Your work has prepared you to write a thesis statement, the central message you want to communicate to readers. The thesis statement states your subject and point of view, reflects your writing purpose and audience, and acts as the organizing principle of your paper. Here is an example from Michael's paper:

Plagiarism
The act of using someone else's exact words, figures, unique approach, or specific reasoning without giving appropriate credit.

Topic:	Coast Guard boot camp
Purpose:	To inform
Audience:	Instructor who probably knows little about the topic
Thesis statement:	Chief Marzloff, our Basic Training Company Commander at the U.S. Coast Guard Basic Training Facility, shaped my life through physical conditioning, developing self-confidence, and instilling strong mental discipline.

TABLE 10.3	Preparation checklist.	

DATE DUE	TASK	IS IT COMPLETE?
	Brainstorm	
	Define and narrow	
	Use prewriting strategies	
	Conduct research if necessary	
	Write thesis statement	
	Write working outline	
	Complete research	

A thesis statement is just as important in a short document, such as a letter, as it is in a long paper. For example, when you write a job application letter, a clear thesis statement helps you tell the recruiter why you should be hired.

Write a Working Outline

The final step in the preparation process is writing a working outline. Use this outline as a loose guide instead of a final structure. As you draft your paper, your ideas and structure may change. Only by allowing changes to occur do you get closer to what you really want to say. Some students prefer a formal outline structure, while others like to use a think link.

Create a Checklist

Use the checklist in Table 10.3 to make sure your preparation is complete. Under Date Due, create your own writing schedule, giving each task an intended completion date. Work backward from the date the assignment is due and estimate how long it will take to complete each step. Refer to Chapter 3 for time-management skills that will help you schedule your writing process.

You'll probably move back and forth among the tasks on the schedule. You might find yourself doing two and even three things on the same day. Stick to the schedule as best you can, while balancing the other demands of your life, and check off your accomplishments as you complete them.

Drafting

A *first draft* involves putting ideas down on paper for the first time—but not the last. You may write many versions of the assignment until you are satisfied. Each version moves you closer to saying exactly what you want in the way you want to say it.

FIGURE **10.3**	The "writing sandwich."

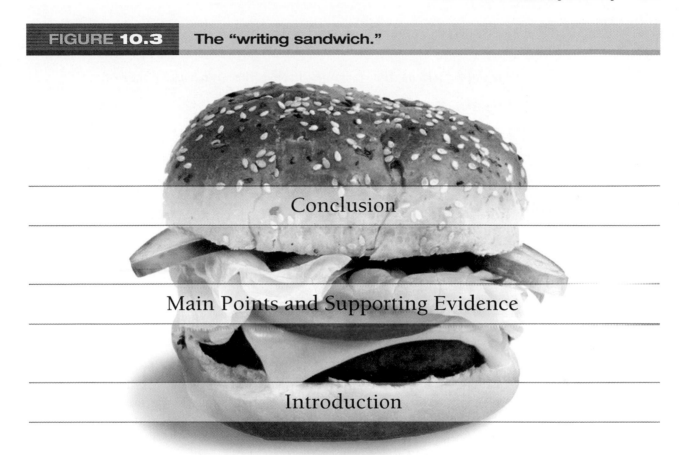

Conclusion

Main Points and Supporting Evidence

Introduction

The process of writing a first draft includes freewriting, crafting an introduction, organizing the ideas in the body of the paper, formulating a conclusion, citing sources, and soliciting feedback. When you think of drafting, it might help to imagine that you are creating a kind of "writing sandwich." The bottom slice of bread is the introduction, the top slice is the conclusion, and the sandwich stuffing is made of central ideas and supporting evidence (see Figure 10.3).

Freewriting Your Draft

Take everything that you have developed in the planning stages and freewrite a rough draft. For now, don't consciously think about your introduction, conclusion, or the structure within the paper's body. Simply focus on getting your ideas out onto paper. When you have the beginnings of a paper, you can start to shape it into something with a more definite form. First, work on how you want to begin.

Writing an Introduction

The introduction tells readers what the rest of the paper contains, and includes a thesis statement. On the next page, for example, is a draft of an introduction for Michael's paper about the Coast Guard. The thesis statement is underlined at the end of the paragraph.

> Chief Marzloff took on the task of shaping the lives and careers of the youngest, newest members of the U.S. Coast Guard. During my eight weeks in training, he was my father, my instructor, my leader, and my worst enemy. He took his job very seriously and demanded that we do the same. <u>The Chief was instrumental in conditioning our bodies, developing our self-confidence, and instilling mental discipline within us.</u>

When you write an introduction, use one or more *hooks* to catch your readers' attention and encourage them to read further. Useful hooks include relevant anecdotes, quotations, dramatic statistics, or questions that encourage thinking. Always link your strategy to your thesis statement. After you craft an introduction that establishes the purpose of your paper, make sure the body fulfills that purpose.

Creating the Body of a Paper

The body of the paper contains your central ideas and supporting evidence. *Evidence*—proof that informs or persuades—consists of facts, statistics, examples, and expert opinions.

Look at the array of ideas and evidence in your draft in its current state. Think about how you might group evidence with the particular ideas it supports. Then, try to find a structure that helps you organize your ideas and evidence into a clear pattern. Here are some strategies to consider:

- *Arrange ideas by time.* Describe events in order or in reverse order.
- *Arrange ideas according to importance.* Start with the idea that carries the most weight and move to less important ideas. Or move from the least important to the most important idea.
- *Arrange ideas by problem and solution.* Start with a specific problem and then discuss solutions.

You might want to use "chain-link support"—a set of reasons that build on one another. Be sure to consider arguments that oppose yours, and consider presenting evidence that answers such arguments.

Writing the Conclusion

Your conclusion is a statement or paragraph that summarizes the information that is in the body of your paper and critically evaluates what is important about it. Try one of the following strategies:

- Summarize main points (if material is longer than three pages)
- Relate a story, statistic, quotation, or question that makes the reader think
- Call the reader to action
- Look to the future

Try not to introduce new facts or restate what has already been proven ("I have shown that violent cartoons are linked to violence in children"). Let your ideas in the body of the paper speak for themselves. Readers should feel that they have reached a natural point of completion.

"Omit needless words. . . . This requires not that the writer make all his sentences short, or that he avoid all detail and treat his subjects only in outline, but that every word tell."

WILLIAM STRUNK, JR.[5]

Avoiding Plagiarism: Crediting Authors and Sources

When you write a research paper, you often incorporate ideas from other sources into your work. These ideas are the writer's *intellectual property*. Using another writer's words, content, unique approach, or illustrations without crediting the author is called *plagiarism* and is illegal and unethical. It is just as serious as any other theft and may have unpleasant consequences. Most colleges have stiff penalties for plagiarism, as well as for any other cheating offense.

The following techniques will help you properly credit sources and avoid plagiarism:

- *Make source notes as you go.* Plagiarism often begins accidentally during research. You may forget to include quotation marks around a quotation, or you may intend to cite or paraphrase a source but never do. To avoid forgetting, write detailed source and content notes as you research. Try writing something like "*Quotation from original; rewrite later*" next to quoted material you copy into notes, and add bibliographic information (title, author, source, page number, etc.) so you don't spend hours trying to locate it later.

- *Learn the difference between a quotation and a paraphrase.* A quotation repeats a source's exact words, which are set off from the rest of the text by quotation marks. A paraphrase is a restatement of the quotation in your own words. A restatement requires that you completely rewrite the idea, not just remove or replace a few words. A paraphrase may not be acceptable if it is too close to the original. Figure 10.4 illustrates the difference.

- *Use a citation even for an acceptable paraphrase.* Take care to credit any source that you quote, paraphrase, or use as evidence. To credit a source, write a footnote or endnote that describes it, using the format preferred by your instructor. Writing handbooks, such as the *Simon &*

FIGURE 10.4   Avoid plagiarism by learning how to paraphrase.

QUOTATION

"The most common assumption that is made by persons who are communicating with one another is... that the other perceives, judges, thinks, and reasons the way he does. Identical twins communicate with ease. Persons from the same culture but with a different education, age, background, and experience often find communication difficult. American managers communicating with managers from other cultures experience greater difficulties in communication than with managers from their own culture."*

UNACCEPTABLE PARAPHRASE (The underlined words are taken directly from the quoted source.)

When we communicate, we assume that the person to whom we are speaking <u>perceives, judges, thinks, and reasons the way</u> we do. This is not always the case. Although <u>identical twins communicate with ease, persons from the same culture but with a different education, age, background, and experience often</u> encounter communication problems. Communication problems are common among American managers as they attempt to <u>communicate with managers from other cultures.</u> They experience greater communication problems than when they communicate <u>with managers from their own culture.</u>

ACCEPTABLE PARAPHRASE

Many people fall into the trap of believing that everyone sees the world exactly as they do and that all people communicate according to the same assumptions. This belief is difficult to support even within our own culture as African-Americans, Hispanic-Americans, Asian-Americans, and others often attempt unsuccessfully to find common ground. When intercultural differences are thrown into the mix, such as when American managers working abroad attempt to communicate with managers from other cultures, clear communication becomes even harder.

*Source of quotation: Lynn Quitman Troyka, *Simon & Schuster Handbook for Writers* (Upper Saddle River, NJ: Prentice Hall, 1996).

Schuster Handbook for Writers by Lynn Quitman Troyka, explain the two standard documentation styles from the American Psychological Association (APA) and the Modern Language Association (MLA).

■ *Understand that lifting material off the Internet is plagiarism.* Words in electronic form belong to the writer just as words in print form do. Even though it is easy to cut and paste sections from a source document onto a paper you are writing, you are committing plagiarism through this act.

Instructors who have received plagiarized papers have identified the following types of plagiarism. They consider a paper to be plagiarized when a student

■ submits a paper from a website that sells or gives away research papers.

■ buys a paper from a non-Internet service.

■ hands in a paper written by a fellow student at the college or a family member.

- copies material in a paper directly from a source without proper quotation marks or source citation.
- paraphrases material in a paper from a source without proper source citation.

Students who choose to plagiarize place their academic careers at risk, in part because the cheating is easy to discover. Increasingly, instructors are using anti-plagiarism software programs to find strings of words that are identical to those in a database. Many instructors put all student papers through the program, whereas others look for clues of plagiarism, such as unusual formatting, specialized jargon, advanced vocabulary and sentence structure, inconsistencies in bibliographic citations, and missing assignment parts.

TAKE ACTION

Avoid Plagiarism

Plagiarism is a growing problem on campuses. Take some time to think about this act, and then complete the following:

- Consider the ethics of plagiarism. Why is plagiarism considered an offense that involves both stealing and lying? Describe how you look at it.

- Citing sources indicates that you respect the ideas of others. List two additional ways that accurate source citation strengthens your writing and makes you a better student.

1.
2.

- What specific penalties for plagiarism are described in your college handbook? How do you feel about risking these penalties?

- Many experts believe that researching on the Internet is behind many acts of plagiarism. How do you respond to this view?

TABLE 10.4	First draft checklist.	
DATE DUE	TASK	IS IT COMPLETE?
	Freewrite a draft	
	Plan and write the introduction	
	Organize the body of the paper	
	Include research evidence in the body	
	Plan and write the conclusion	
	Check for plagiarism and rewrite passages to avoid it	
	Credit sources	
	Solicit feedback	

Make a commitment to hand in your own work and to uphold the highest standards of academic integrity. Never put off your assignment until the last possible moment so that you feel crushed by the pressure and willing to compromise your ethics in order to meet your deadline. The compromise is never worth making, and you risk being caught.

Continue Your Checklist

Create a checklist for your first draft (see Table 10.4). The elements of a first draft do not have to be written in order. In fact, many writers prefer to write the introduction after the body of the paper, so the introduction reflects the paper's content and tone. Whatever order you choose, make sure your schedule allows you to get everything done—with enough time left over for revisions.

Revising

When you revise, you critically evaluate the word choice, paragraph structure, and style of your first draft. Be thorough as you add, delete, replace, and reorganize words, sentences, and paragraphs. You may want to print your draft and correct the hard copy before you make changes on the computer. If your instructor evaluates an early draft of your paper, incorporate his or her revision suggestions into the final product. If you disagree with an important point, schedule a conference to talk it over.

Some classes include a peer review process in which students read one another's work and offer suggestions. Many schools also have tutors in writing or learning centers who can act as peer readers

reflect

The great boxing champion Muhammad Ali once said, "Inside of a ring or out, ain't nothing wrong with going down. It's staying down that's wrong." Apply Ali's sentiments to the process of improving your writing. When you work hard on a draft and an instructor tells you that your paper requires major revisions, how do you feel? Do you give up or try even harder to succeed?

Companion Website

& respond

The techniques below allow you to access your power as a writer by uncovering valuable research sources and clearly communicating what you really want to say.

INTELLIGENCE	SUGGESTED STRATEGIES	WHAT WORKS FOR YOU? WRITE NEW IDEAS HERE
Verbal–Linguistic	■ Read many resources and take comprehensive notes on them. Summarize the main points from your resources. ■ Interview someone about the topic and take notes.	
Logical–Mathematical	■ Take notes on 3×5 cards and organize them according to topics and subtopics. ■ Create a detailed, sequential outline of your writing project, making sure that your argument is logical if your assignment requires persuasive writing.	
Bodily–Kinesthetic	■ Pay a visit to numerous sites that hold resources you need or that are related to your topic—businesses, libraries, etc. ■ After brainstorming ideas for an assignment, take a break involving physical activity. During the break, think about your top three ideas and see what insight occurs to you.	
Visual–Spatial	■ Create full-color charts as you read each resource or interview someone. ■ Use think link format or another visual organizer to map out your main topic, subtopics, and related ideas and examples. Use different colors for different subtopics.	
Interpersonal	■ Discuss material with a fellow student as you gather it. ■ Pair up with a classmate and become each other's peer editors. Read each other's first drafts and next-to-final drafts, offering constructive feedback.	
Intrapersonal	■ Take time to mull over any assigned paper topic. Think about what emotions it raises in you, and why. Let your inner instincts guide you as you begin to write. ■ Schedule as much research time as possible.	
Musical	■ Play your favorite relaxing music while you brainstorm topics for a writing assignment.	
Naturalistic	■ Pick a research topic that relates to nature. ■ Build confidence by envisioning your writing process as a successful climb to the top of a mountain.	

FIGURE 10.5   Sample first draft with revision comments.

Of the changes that ~~happened to us,~~ the physical transformation is the ~~biggest.~~ *most evident* ~~When~~

military recruits undergo

~~*Too much*~~   *Maybe—* upon my January arrival at the training facility,

~~we arrived at the training facility, it was January, cold and cloudy. At the time,~~ I was a

little thin, but I had been working out and thought that I could physically do anything.

Oh boy, was I wrong! The Chief said to us right away: "Get down, maggots!" Upon this   *← his trademark phrase*

command, we all to drop to the ground and do military-style push-ups. Water survival tac-

were   *endless*

tics were also part of the training ~~that we had to complete.~~ Occasionally, my dreams of

← unnecessary

home were interrupted at 3 a.m. when we had a surprise aquatic test. Although we ~~didn't~~

resented

~~feel too happy about~~ this sub-human treatment at the time, we learned to appreciate how

mention how chief was involved

the conditioning was turning our bodies into fine-tuned machines.   *say more about this*
(swimming in uniform incident?)

---

of a draft before it is finalized. Figure 10.5 shows a paragraph from Michael's first draft, with revision comments added.

The elements of revision include being a critical writer, evaluating paragraph structure, and checking for clarity and conciseness.

Being a Critical Writer

Critical thinking helps you move beyond restating what you learned from other sources to creating your own perspective.

Use the mind actions to guide your revision. Ask yourself questions that can help you evaluate ideas, develop original insights, and be complete and clear. Here are some examples of questions you may ask:

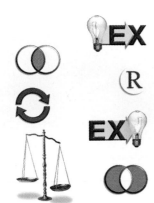

- Are these examples clearly connected to the idea?

- Am I aware of similar concepts or facts that can act as support?

- What else can I recall that can help to support this idea?

- In evaluating a situation, have I clearly indicated causes and effects?

- What new idea comes to mind when I think about these facts?

- How do I evaluate any effect, fact, or situation?

- Are there different arguments that I should address here?

Critical thinking can also help you evaluate the content and form of your paper. As you start your revision, ask yourself these questions:

- Will my audience understand my thesis and how I've supported it?

- Does the introduction prepare the reader and capture attention?
- Is the body of the paper organized effectively?
- Is each idea fully developed, explained, and supported by examples?
- Are my ideas connected to one another through logical transitions?
- Do I have a clear, concise, simple writing style?
- Does the paper fulfill the requirements of the assignment?
- Does the conclusion provide a natural ending to the paper?

If your paper contains arguments, use critical thinking to make sure they are well constructed and convincing. Using what you know from the discussion in Chapter 4, think through your arguments and provide solid support with facts and examples.

Evaluating Paragraph Structure

Make sure that each paragraph has a *topic sentence* that states the paragraph's main idea (a topic sentence does for a paragraph what a thesis statement does for an entire paper). The rest of the paragraph should support the idea with evidence. Most topic sentences are at the start of the paragraph, although sometimes topic sentences appear elsewhere. The topic sentence in the following paragraph is underlined:

Chief Marzloff played an integral role in the development of our self-confidence. He taught us that anything less than direct eye contact was disrespectful to both him and ourselves. He encouraged us to be confident about our own beliefs and to think about what was said to us before we decided whether to accept it. Furthermore, the Chief reinforced self-confidence through his own example. He walked with his chin up and chest out, like the proud parent of a newborn baby. He always gave the appearance that he had something to do and that he was in complete control.

Examine how paragraphs flow into one another by evaluating your transitions—the words, phrases or sentences that connect ideas. Among the words and phrases that are helpful are *also, in addition*, and *next*. Similarly, *finally, as a result*, and *in conclusion* tell readers that a summary is on its way.

Checking for Clarity and Conciseness

Aim to say what you want to say clearly and concisely. Try to eliminate extra words and phrases. Rewrite wordy phrases in a more straightforward, conversational way. For example, write "if" instead of "in the event that," and "now" instead of "at this point in time."

> *"See revision as 'envisioning again.' If there are areas in your work where there is a blur or vagueness, you can simply see the picture again and add the details that will bring your work closer to your mind's picture."*
>
> **NATALIE GOLDBERG**

Editing

Editing involves correcting technical mistakes in spelling, grammar, and punctuation, as well as checking for consistency in such elements as abbreviations and capitalizations. Editing comes last, after you are satisfied with your ideas, organization, and writing style. If you use a computer, start with the grammar check and spell check to find mistakes, realizing that you still need to check your work. Although a spell checker won't pick up the mistake in the sentence, "They are not hear on Tuesdays," someone who is reading for sense will.

Look also for *sexist language*, which characterizes people according to gender. Sexist language often involves the male pronouns *he*, *him*, or *his*. For example, "An executive often spends hours a day going through his e-mail" implies that executives are always men. A simple change to a plural subject eliminates the problem: "Executives often spend hours each day going through their e-mail." Try to be sensitive to words that slight women. *Mail carrier* is preferable to *mailman, student* to *coed*.

Proofreading is the last editing stage and happens after your paper is in its final form. Proofreading means reading every word and sentence for accuracy. Look for technical mistakes, run-on sentences, and sentence fragments. Look for incorrect word usage and unclear references.

Work hard to make your paper look good. If possible, type every paper before submitting it to your instructor. If you don't have a computer or printer of your own, complete the assignment at your school's computer lab. If your typing skills are weak, self-directed typing programs may also be available at the lab.

A Final Checklist

You are now ready to complete your revising and editing checklist. All the tasks listed in Table 10.5 should be complete before you submit your paper. Figure 10.6 shows the final version of Michael's paper.

TAKE ACTION

Revise and Edit

Revising and editing are necessary before submitting a paper. Think about these processes, and then complete the following:

■ Based on instructor feedback, what are your writing strengths? Be specific.

_____

_____

■ Based on instructor feedback, what kinds of errors do you consistently make when you draft a paper? What part of your paper generally requires the most revision work?

_____

_____

Identify three steps you can take to minimize these errors.

1. _____

2. _____

3. _____

■ Do you think it is necessary to incorporate all your instructor's recommendations into your final draft? Why or why not?

_____

_____

_____

■ Since "neatness counts" when you submit a paper, identify two ways you plan to improve the appearance of your next paper.

1. _____

2. _____

Your final paper reflects your efforts. Ideally, you have a piece of work that shows your writing ability and that communicates interesting and important ideas.

You can use your improved writing and research skills to craft effective speeches and oral presentations. Being an effective speaker will work to your advantage in school, your community, and your career.

FIGURE 10.6   **Sample final version of paper.**

Michael B. Jackson   March 19, 2004
BOYS TO MEN

His stature was one of confidence, often misinterpreted by others as cockiness. His small frame was lean and agile, yet stiff and upright, as though every move were a calculated formula. For the longest eight weeks of my life, he was my father, my instructor, my leader, and my worst enemy. His name is Chief Marzloff, and he had the task of shaping the lives and careers of the youngest, newest members of the U.S. Coast Guard. As our Basic Training Company Commander, he took his job very seriously and demanded that we do the same. Within a limited time span, he conditioned our bodies, developed our self-confidence, and instilled within us a strong mental discipline.

Of the changes that recruits in military basic training undergo, the physical transformation is the most immediately evident. On my January arrival at the training facility, I was a little thin, but I had been working out and thought that I could physically do anything. Oh boy, was I wrong! The Chief wasted no time in introducing me to one of his trademark phrases: "Get down, maggots!" Upon this command, we were all to drop to the ground and produce endless counts of military-style push-ups. Later, we found out that exercise prepared us for hitting the deck in the event of enemy fire. Water survival tactics were also part of the training. Occasionally, my dreams of home were interrupted at about 3 A.M. when our company was selected for a surprise aquatic test. I recall one such test that required us to swim laps around the perimeter of a pool while in full uniform. I felt like a salmon swimming upstream, fueled only by natural instinct. Although we resented this subhuman treatment at the time, we learned to appreciate how the strict guidance of the Chief was turning our bodies into fine-tuned machines.

Beyond physical ability, Chief Marzloff also played an integral role in the development of our self-confidence. He would often declare in his raspy voice, "Look me in the eyes when you speak to me! Show me that you believe what you're saying!" He taught us that anything less was an expression of disrespect. Furthermore, he appeared to attack a personal habit of my own. It seemed that whenever he would speak to me individually, I would nervously nod my head in response. I was trying to demonstrate that I understood, but to him, I was blindly accepting anything that he said. He would roar, "That is a sign of weakness!" Needless to say, I am now conscious of all bodily motions when communicating with others. The Chief also reinforced self-confidence through his own example. He walked with his square chin up and chest out, like the proud parent of a newborn baby. He always gave the appearance that he had something to do, and that he was in complete control. Collectively, the methods that the Chief used were all successful in developing our self-confidence.

Perhaps the Chief's greatest contribution was the mental discipline that he instilled in his recruits. He taught us that physical ability and self-confidence were nothing without the mental discipline required to obtain any worthwhile goal. For us, this discipline began with adapting to the military lifestyle. Our day began promptly at 0500 hours, early enough to awaken the oversleeping roosters. By 0515 hours, we had to have showered, shaved, and perfectly donned our uniforms. At that point, we were marched to the galley for chow, where we learned to take only what is necessary, rather than indulging. Before each meal, the Chief would warn, "Get what you want, but you will eat all that you get!" After he made good on his threat a few times, we all got the point. Throughout our stay, the Chief repeatedly stressed the significance of self-discipline. He would calmly utter, "Give a little now, get a lot later." I guess that meant different things to all of us. For me, it was a simple phrase that would later become my personal philosophy on life. The Chief went to great lengths to ensure that everyone under his direction possessed the mental discipline required to be successful in boot camp or in any of life's challenges.

Chief Marzloff was a remarkable role model and a positive influence on many lives. I never saw him smile, but it was evident that he genuinely cared a great deal about his job and all the lives that he touched. This man single-handedly conditioned our bodies, developed our self-confidence, and instilled a strong mental discipline that remains in me to this day. I have not seen the Chief since March 28, 1992, graduation day. Over the years, however, I have incorporated many of his ideals into my life. Above all, he taught us the true meaning of the U.S. Coast Guard slogan, "Semper Peratus" (Always Ready).

TABLE 10.5	Revising and editing checklist.	
DATE DUE	**TASK**	**IS IT COMPLETE?**
	Check the body of the paper for clear thinking and adequate support of ideas	
	Finalize introduction and conclusion	
	Check spelling, usage, and grammar	
	Check paragraph structure	
	Make sure language is clear and concise	
	Check punctuation and capitalization	
	Check transitions	
	Eliminate sexist language	
	Get feedback from peers and/or instructor	

How can you deliver an effective oral presentation?

In school, you may be asked to deliver a speech, take an oral exam, or present a team project. Even when you ask a question or make a comment in class, you are using public-speaking skills.

The public-speaking skills that you learn for *formal* presentations help you make a favorable impression in *informal* settings, such as when you meet with an instructor, summarize a reading for your study group, or participate in a planning session at work. When you are articulate, others take notice.

Prepare as for a Writing Assignment

Speaking in front of others involves preparation, strategy, and confidence. Planning a speech is similar to planning a piece of writing: you must know your topic and audience and think about presentation strategy, organization, and word choice. Specifically, you should:

- *Think through what you want to say and why.* What is your purpose—to make or refute an argument, present information, entertain? Have a goal for your speech.
- *Plan.* Take time to think about who your listeners are and how they are likely to respond. Then, get organized. Brainstorm your topic—narrow it with prewriting strategies, determine your thesis, write an outline, and do research.
- *Draft your thoughts.* Draft your speech. Illustrate ideas with examples, and show how examples lead to ideas. As in writing, have a clear

beginning and end. Start with an attention-getter and conclude with a wrap-up that summarizes your thoughts and leaves your audience with something to remember.

- *Integrate visual aids.* Think about building your speech around visual aids including charts, maps, slides and photographs, and props. Learn software programs such as PowerPoint to create presentation graphics.

With computer-generated presentations, your motto should be "Less is more." Although it's tempting to use all the options available for adding sound, animation, and fancy backgrounds, too many effects can distract your audience from the message you want to convey.

Finally, keep in mind that the rules governing plagiarism of written information also apply to graphic images. If you import graphics from websites into your own presentation, you must cite your source, either directly on the slide or on a reference sheet accompanying the presentation.

Practice Your Performance

The element of performance distinguishes speaking from writing. Here are some tips to keep in mind:

- *Know the parameters.* How long do you have? Where will you be speaking? Be aware of the setting—where your audience will be and available props (e.g., a podium, table, a blackboard). If you plan to use electronic equipment such as a microphone or an overhead projector, run a test before the presentation to make sure these tools are in working order.

- *Use index cards or notes.* Reduce your final draft to "trigger" words or phrases that remind you of what you want to say. Refer to the cards and to your visual aids during your speech.

RISING
TO THE CHALLENGE

Kevin Leman
Counselor and Public Speaker,
Tucson, Arizona

You can't always judge a person by past performance. Kevin Leman was near the bottom of his high school class and dropped out of college twice. Later, with the help of inspiring people in his life, he graduated and became a nationally known writer and psychologist.

Kevin Leman was the most un-interested screwball of a student you ever met. "My high school guidance counselor told me he couldn't get me admitted to reform school, much less college," Leman admits. Growing up in western New York, he was the youngest of three siblings. His sister was the captain of the cheerleading squad; his brother was the high school football hero. And young Kevin was, as he describes himself, "the best at being the worst." "My mother was in high school more than I was," he recalls. "I was never there. I'd cut school. She always went to those meetings they had, you know, and she'd come home with the standard story—'If only Kevin would apply himself . . . '"

Herein lay the problem: Leman really didn't know how to apply himself. He graduated near the bottom of his class, with SAT scores to match. "They were in the zero percentile—which is pretty hard to do, just by the mathematics alone," he said. And he still remembers one of his college rejection letters, which read, "Most regrettably, Kevin's record does not support admission, which our studies show could lead to his failure. We must decline his application." Although he made it into another school, he was thrown out a year later. Leman seemed destined for academic failure and found a job as a janitor at the local hospital.

It was here that destiny took an unexpected turn. At the hospital he met Sande Buchheit, a nurse's assistant, who would later become his wife. Sande believed in Leman and introduced him to other people who had vision for their lives. He began to believe that there was some purpose to life and his motivation blossomed. Next, he decided to enroll at the University of Arizona.

"I was walking on campus," he recalls, "not really knowing where I was, and I found this guy named Robert Leonard, a professor. He sat down with me and went way beyond what you'd expect. He got the catalog out and spent two hours with me, showing me exactly what I needed to do."

To his astonishment, Leman made the dean's list the first semester. In that moment, Leman discovered one of the beauties of life: Every day offers a chance to make a new start. He decided he wanted to be a psychologist based, in part, on his earlier run-in with his high school guidance counselor who told him reform school was too high to shoot for. "I remember thinking, 'He's a counselor?'" Ironically, Leman dedicated his first book to this man.

Leman credits much of his success to the power of mentoring. When speaking about one of his professors from the U of A, Leman says, "He was a guy who changed my life. He taught me how to work with people, and he taught me that I could turn kids' behavior around, in some cases in a matter of days. I'm very grateful to him."

Kevin Leman is living proof that anyone can be a success. Today he has a private practice as a psychologist and counselor and is a nationally known authority on family issues. He has written 21 popular psychology books that have sold in the millions. He has also been a featured guest on shows like *The Today Show* and *Oprah*. "Looking back on my UA experience," he says, "I felt like I belonged. I had people there who cared about me, and that made all the difference."

Take a Moment to Consider . . .

- *When you've experienced a "turning point" in your life.*

- *What you might write about if you were to write books that helped and informed others.*

This story has been rewritten with permission from Dan Huff, whose original article, "The Living Proof," first appeared in *Arizona Alumnus*, Spring 2001.

- *Pay attention to the physical.* Your body position, voice, and clothing contribute to the impression you make. Your goal is to look and sound good and to appear relaxed. Try to make eye contact with your audience, and walk around if you are comfortable presenting in that way.

- *Practice ahead of time.* Do a test run with friends or alone. If possible, practice in the room where you will speak. Audiotape or videotape your practice sessions and evaluate your performance.

- *Be yourself.* When you speak, you express your personality through your words and presence. Don't be afraid to add your own style to the presentation. Take deep breaths. Smile. Know that you can speak well and that your audience wants to see you succeed. Finally, envision your own success.

In preparing to speak, envision your own success.

I think and communicate with clarity and precision.

Not only will clear writing make a strong impression on your instructors—and increase the likelihood of a good grade—it will also change the way you think. Clear writing forces you to test the connections among your ideas as you ask, "Does this make sense?" "Am I proving my case?" "Have I given evidence to support my conclusions?" "Have I backed up my opinion with a solid argument?" "Is there more to add?"

Writing also forces you to pay attention to the needs of your readers, since the purpose of writing is to communicate with others. By its very nature, communication involves a sender and a receiver, and successful communication occurs only when the reader understands exactly what the writer is trying to say.

The writing process you learned in this chapter requires a disciplined approach—the discipline to plan, to draft, and to revise and edit your words. The result you can expect is a clearer, more precise paper that shows the time and care you took to get it right. The result you might not expect is a sharper mind that has been enriched by clear logic and by your striving for words that say exactly what you mean.

REMEMBER!
the important points ○○○

How can you make the most of your library?

Start by taking a real or virtual orientation or tour of your college library system. Most libraries contain one or more areas dedicated to reference materials, books, periodicals, audiovisual materials, and microfilm. To find the information you need, use a library search strategy—a step-by-step method that moves from general to specific sources. Becoming familiar with library classification systems, consulting librarians, and using critical thinking to evaluate sources will help you conduct a successful search.

How can you conduct research on the Internet?

To use the Internet as a research tool, you will need to learn how to access the World Wide Web through such search directories as Google and Yahoo! and search engines as AltaVista and HotBot. A step-by-step search strategy will help you locate information and gather reliable sources. Because the Internet lacks safeguards to keep out false or misleading information, it is especially important to be a critical, skeptical researcher.

What are the elements of effective writing?

The three primary elements are purpose, topic, and audience. Start by defining your writing purpose: to inform or persuade. Then, decide who your readers are and what they know about the topic, so that you can tailor your message to their needs. Your goal is to write in a complete and organized manner so that your audience can follow your ideas easily.

What is the writing process?

The writing process includes planning, drafting, revising, and editing. During the planning stage, you brainstorm, define and narrow your topic, begin research, write a thesis statement, create a working outline, and complete your research. Drafting involves freewriting, writing an introduction, organizing the ideas in the body of the paper, formulating a conclusion, and citing sources. During the revision stage, you evaluate and improve your first draft by asking critical-thinking questions, evaluating paragraph structure, and aiming for clear and concise language. Finally, during the editing stage you correct spelling, grammar, punctuation, and usage.

How can you deliver an effective oral presentation?

Public speaking requires careful preparation. You must know your audience, draft your remarks, and prepare props or visual aids. Public speaking also requires that you practice, just as you would any performance.

Name   Date

CRITICAL THINKING
APPLYING LEARNING TO LIFE

Audience Analysis

As a reporter for your college newspaper, you have been assigned the job of writing a story about some part of campus life. You submit the following suggestions to your editor-in-chief:

- The campus parking lot squeeze: too many cars and too few spaces.
- Drinking on campus: Is the problem getting better or worse?
- Diversity: how students accept differences and live and work together.

Your editor-in-chief asks you the following questions about reader response (consider that your different "audiences" include students, faculty and administrators, and community members):

1. Which subject would likely appeal to all audiences at your school and why?

   _____

   _____

   _____

2. How would you adjust your writing according to how much readers know about the subject?

   _____

   _____

   _____

3. For each topic, name the audience (or audiences) that you think would be most interested. If you think one audience would be equally interested in more than one topic, you can name an audience more than once.

   Campus parking lot _____

   Drinking on campus _____

   Student diversity _____

4. How can you make a specific article interesting to a general audience?

   _____

   _____

   _____

Prewriting

Choose a topic you are interested in and know something about—for example, college sports or handling stress. Narrow your topic; then, use the following prewriting strategies to discover what you already know about the topic and what you would need to learn if you had to write an essay about the subject for one of your classes (if necessary, continue this prewriting exercise on a separate sheet of paper):

Brainstorm your ideas.

_____

_____

_____

_____

_____

_____

Freewrite.

_____

_____

_____

_____

_____

_____

_____

Ask journalists' questions.

_____

_____

_____

_____

_____

_____

Writing a Thesis Statement

Write two thesis statements for each of the following topics. The first statement should inform the reader, and the second should persuade. In each case, use the thesis statement to narrow the topic.

1. The rising cost of a college education
   A. Thesis with an informative purpose:

   _____

   _____

   B. Thesis with a persuasive purpose:

   _____

   _____

2. Handling test anxiety

   A. Thesis with an informative purpose:

   _____

   _____

   B. Thesis with a persuasive purpose:

   _____

   _____

TEAM BUILDING
COLLABORATIVE SOLUTIONS

Team Research

Join with three other classmates and decide on two relatively narrow research topics that interest all of you and that you can investigate by spending no more than an hour in the library. The first topic should be current and in the news—for example, safety problems in sport utility vehicles (SUVs), body piercing, or the changing U.S. family. The second topic should be more academic and historical—for example, the polio epidemic in the 1950s, the Irish potato famine, or South African apartheid.

Working alone, team members should use the college library and the Internet to research both topics. Set a research time limit of no more than one hour per topic. The goal should be to collect a list of sources for later investigation. When everyone is through, the group should come together to discuss the research process. Among the questions group members should ask each other are:

- How did you "attack" and organize your research for each topic?
- What research tools did you use to investigate each topic?
- How did the nature of your research differ from topic to topic? Why do you think this was the case?
- How did your use of library and Internet resources differ from topic to topic?

- Which research techniques yielded the best results? Which techniques led to dead ends?

Next, compare the specific results of everyone's research. Analyze each source for what it is likely to yield in the form of useful information. Finally, come together as a group and discuss what you learned that might improve your approach to library and Internet research.

personal
IMPROVEMENT
plan

I commit to three research or writing strategies to improve my study skills.
From this chapter, I choose three strategies that I think will help me.

<u>Strategy 1:</u> _____

<u>Strategy 2:</u> _____

<u>Strategy 3:</u> _____

I choose one strategy to focus on (circle this strategy above) and I will:

■ describe my goal—what I want to gain from using this strategy.

_____

_____

_____

■ describe in detail how I plan to use the strategy.

_____

_____

_____

_____

■ describe how I will measure my progress toward the goal this semester.

_____

_____

_____

_____

Activate the Habit of Mind

HABITS OF MIND
MIND

Here's how I will *think and communicate with clarity and precision* to achieve this goal:

_____

_____

_____

_____

SUGGESTED READINGS

Becker, Howard S. *Tricks of the Trade: How to Think About Your Research While You're Doing It*. Chicago: University of Chicago Press, 1998.

Booth, Wayne C., Gregory G. Columb, and Joseph M. Williams. *The Craft of Research*. Chicago: University of Chicago Press, 1995.

Cameron, Julia. *The Right to Write: An Invitation into the Writing Life*. New York: Putnam, 1999.

Gibaldi, Joseph and Phyllis Franklin. *MLA Handbook for Writers of Research Papers*, 5th ed. New York: Modern Language Association of America, 1999.

LaRocque, Paula. *Championship Writing: 50 Ways to Improve Your Writing*. Oak Park, IL: Marion Street Press, 2000.

Markman, Peter T. and Roberta H. Markman. *10 Steps in Writing the Research Paper*, 5th ed. New York: Barron's Educational Series, 1994.

Strunk, William, Jr. and E. B. White. *The Elements of Style*, 4th ed. New York: Allyn and Bacon, 2000.

Troyka, Lynn Quitman. *Simon & Schuster Handbook for Writers*, 5th ed. Upper Saddle River, NJ: Prentice Hall, 1999.

Walsch, Bill. *Lapsing into a Comma: A Curmudgeon's Guide to the Many Things That Can Go Wrong in Print—and How to Avoid Them*. New York: Contemporary Books, 2000.

Williams, Joseph M. *Style: Ten Lessons in Clarity and Grace*. Chicago: University of Chicago Press, 2003.

INTERNET RESOURCES

Prentice Hall Student Success SuperSite—study skills section (valuable information on writing and research): www.prenhall.com/success

National Writing Centers Association (a collection of writing labs and writing centers on the web): http://iwca.syr.edu

Online Writing Lab—Purdue University: http://owl.english.purdue.edu

How to Organize a Research Paper and Document It with MLA Citations (specific citation rules from the Modern Language Association): www.geocities.com/Athens/Oracle/4184

Online Resources for Writers (a comprehensive website for writers that includes multiple links) http://webster.commnet.edu/writing/writing. htm

Plagiarism Q&A (information students need to know to avoid plagiarism): www.ehhs.cmich.edu/~mspears/plagiarism.html

A Student's Guide to WWW Research: Web Searching, Web Page Evaluation, and Research Strategies (a comprehensive site developed at St. Louis University) www.slu.edu/departments/english/research

ENDNOTES

1. Joyce Kasman Valenza, "Skills That College Freshmen Need," *The Philadelphia Inquirer*, April 26, 2001, p. NA.

2. Lori Leibovich, "Choosing Quick Hits Over the Card Catalog," *The New York Times*, August 10, 2000, p. 1.

3. Floyd H. Johnson (May 1996), "The Internet and Research: Proceed with Caution" (on-line). Available at www.lanl.gov/SFC/96/posters.html#johnson (August 2000).

4. Analysis based on Lynn Quitman Troyka, *Simon & Schuster Handbook for Writers*. Upper Saddle River, NJ: Prentice Hall, 1996, pp. 22–23.

5. *The Elements of Style*, Strunk and White, © 2000. Reprinted by permission of Pearson Education, Inc.

Multiple Choice. Circle or highlight the answer that seems to fit best.

1. When in class, you should choose a note-taking system that
   A. suits the instructor's style, the course material, and your learning style.
   B. you've used in other classes successfully.
   C. matches what you use when you study outside of class.
   D. is recommended by your instructor.

2. A library search strategy takes you from
   A. specific reference works to general reference works.
   B. general reference works to specific reference works.
   C. encyclopedias to almanacs.
   D. encyclopedias to the Internet.

3. When answering an essay question on a test, you should
   A. spend most of your time on the introduction because the grader sees it first.
   B. skip the planning steps if your time runs short.
   C. use the four steps of the writing process but take less time for each step.
   D. write your essay and then rewrite it on another sheet or booklet.

4. Strategies to overcome math anxiety include all of the following **except**
   A. avoiding courses with any mathematical content.
   B. seeking help from your instructor or working with a tutor or classmate.
   C. asking questions in class.
   D. being conscientious about your responsibilities to do your homework and attend class.

5. Being able to recognize the meaning of prefixes, roots, and suffixes will help you
   A. do well when you study a foreign language.
   B. understand the meaning of words and remember information.
   C. create visual aids.
   D. identify your purpose for reading.

6. Strategies for using flash cards to help memory do **not** include
   A. testing yourself on one side of the cards only.
   B. using the cards as a self-test.
   C. shuffling the cards and learning the information in various orders.
   D. carrying cards with you and reviewing them frequently.

Fill-in-the-Blank. Complete the following sentences with the appropriate word(s) or phrase(s) that best reflect what you learned in the chapter. Choose from the items that follow each sentence.

1. In the Cornell note-taking system, the section on the left, called the _____, is used for filling in comments and diagrams as you review. (cue column, summary area, main body)

2. A _____ is a memory technique that works by connecting information you are trying to learn with simpler or familiar information. (mnemonic device, acronym, idea chain)

3. _____ encourages you to put your _____ ideas on paper and is an important part of the _____ process. (Freewriting/uncensored/planning, Editing/polished/planning, Researching/censored/editing)

4. SQ3R stands for Survey, Question, Read, _____, and Review. (Reread, Retell, Recite)

5. It is important to be sensitive to _____ verbs on essay tests. (action, passive, static)

6. One of the best math problem-solving strategies is to look for a _____. (solution, clue, pattern)

Essay Questions. The following essay questions will help you learn to organize and communicate your ideas in writing, just as you must do on an essay test. Before you begin answering a question, spend a few minutes planning (brainstorm possible approaches, write a thesis statement, jot down main thoughts in outline or think link form). To prepare yourself for actual test conditions, limit your writing time to no more than 20 minutes per question.

1. Describe the steps of the reading strategy SQ3R. What is involved in each step? How does each step contribute to your understanding of reading material?

2. Write an essay that supports or rejects all or part of the following statement: "*The tests you take in college not only help ensure that you acquire important skills and knowledge, but also help prepare you for the day-to-day learning demands that are associated with twenty-first century careers.*" If possible, support your position with references to career areas that interest you.

SUCCESS
BREAKTHROUGH

Oprah Winfrey
Talk Show Host and Media Superstar

Although media superstar Oprah Winfrey is one of the richest and most famous women in the world, she started life in poverty. She might have achieved little had it not been for the support of her grandmother and father and her determination to make something more of her life. Humble beginnings, a broken family, and personal tragedies did not stop Winfrey from realizing her dreams.

Born to poor, young, unwed parents, Oprah Winfrey began life on a Mississippi pig farm. She was cared for by her paternal grandmother, who recognized her remarkable intelligence and taught her to read, and love reading, at a very young age. By the age of three, Winfrey had already taken her first steps toward becoming a public personality, performing readings and recitations for her church congregation.

Winfrey's life changed dramatically—and for the worse—when her mother returned and decided to rear her six-year-old daughter. During the time with her mother, Winfrey was sexually abused, sometimes by trusted family members. Winfrey told no one about the abuse; instead, she internalized her pain and shame with wild, self-destructive behaviors that included running away from home. Too wild for her mother to handle, Winfrey was sent to live with her father.

Her father instituted a regimen of strict discipline right away. He gave her a curfew and made sure she wore respectable clothes and spoke properly. Because he saw education as the key to success, he required her to read five books every two weeks and write weekly book reports, memorize lists of vocabulary words, and learn about successful African Americans. When Winfrey brought home a report card full of C's, her father told her that the grades were unaccept-

able because she was capable of much more. Proud of her own intelligence, and getting the positive attention that she needed, Winfrey took her father's message to heart. She began believing in herself and learned that excellence was the best defense against racism and sexism.

Soon Winfrey got her first job as a reporter for a Nashville radio station and then a scholarship to Tennessee State University, where she earned a degree in broadcasting. At the age of 19, she became the youngest person and the first African-American woman to anchor the news at Nashville's WTVF-TV. She then moved to Baltimore to be a news anchor and to host a talk show. The talk show was a hit and lasted for eight years before Winfrey left it to take over a failing Chicago talk show. Audiences were captivated by her warm, conversational style, and within a year, the show skyrocketed to number one in the ratings. *The Oprah Winfrey Show,* as the program was now called, entered syndication and became the highest-rated talk show in television history and winner of multiple Emmy Awards.

The talk show success was only a starting point for Winfrey's later work as an actress, creator, producer, and chairperson of her media production company, Harpo, Inc. Her vision and drive also brought her success in publishing and the health and fitness industry. Through her support of educational, social, and philanthropic organizations, she has tried to help others achieve better lives.

Winfrey's influence is far more than she could have ever dreamed possible during her troubled youth in Mississippi. Refusing to define herself as a victim or to dwell on her limitations and mistakes, she took charge of her life and made history as a woman, as an African American, and as an extraordinary individual.

Take a Moment to Consider . . .

- *Why "victimhood" is incompatible with personal achievement and life success.*
- *How friends and loved ones have the ability to nurture talent that would otherwise go to waste.*

Information about Oprah Winfrey's life from *Everybody Loves Oprah! Her Remarkable Life Story,* by Norman King. New York: William Morrow & Co., 1987.

SUCCESS
Breakthrough

Stephen Hawking
Physicist and Author

Stephen Hawking found his calling as a physicist and channeled his genius only after he was crippled by a devastating neurological illness. His success is the achievement of his extraordinary will and a tribute to the power of love.

Stephen Hawking never cut a promising figure as a young student in England. Awarded a scholarship to Oxford University, where he specialized in physics for his bachelor's degree, Hawking was not a diligent student. Bored with the curriculum, he worked very little and experimented with drinking and rowdy pranks. Only his enormous intelligence and intuition for the subject got him through, and he was awarded the University Physics Prize in his second year.

He had barely begun his doctoral work in general relativity and cosmology at Cambridge University when serious health problems appeared. First he noticed that he frequently bumped into things, fell for no reason, and slurred his speech. Over Christmas break his parents convinced him to see a doctor. After two weeks of testing, it was clear that Hawking was in the early stages of amyotrophic lateral sclerosis (ALS), more commonly known as Lou Gehrig's disease. The incurable disease affects motor neurons, killing people by slowly wasting the body. The process causes no pain, and leaves the brain untouched—except for the torture of experiencing a total loss of physical control and the anticipation of a slow and certain death.

Hawking's health deteriorated quickly and physicians advised him that he would not live long enough to finish his doctoral work. With little hope to sustain him, he lapsed into depression until, during a routine hospital stay, he met a desperately ill young boy with leukemia who made a strong impression on him. Realizing that there were people more seriously ill than he, Hawking regained enough hope to return to his work.

However, it was his relationship with Jane Wilde that helped him break out of his depression and believe that there was something important to live for. With Jane's love and support, Hawking became determined to get his doctorate so they could marry. He achieved both goals and stayed on at Cambridge as a professor.

Hawking's health steadily deteriorated to near total paralysis and confinement to a wheelchair, but with his newfound positive attitude, his career rocketed to success. Indeed, he once remarked that his disease actually contributed to his career by giving him the ability to think about physics and the universe. Hawking's primary research has been on the subject of black holes, although some of his work focused on unifying Einstein's theory of general relativity with quantum theory. In addition, he has made contributions to understanding the basic laws governing the universe.

A sudden case of pneumonia necessitated a tracheotomy operation that, in Hawking's own words, "saved my life but took away my voice." Fellow Cambridge professor David Mason fitted a voice synthesizer and computer to his wheelchair, allowing him to speak again. Overcoming this just as he had the ALS, Hawking has continued to pursue research, writing, and teaching.

Hawking is the author of seven books written with other physicists and eight independent works. He achieved worldwide fame after the publication of *A Brief History of Time*, which dominated the bestseller list for 236 weeks. People worldwide became used to seeing Hawking in his wheelchair, speaking through his synthesizer about his work. His personal achievements in the face of daunting obstacles demonstrate his belief that every day is worth living for the promise it brings.

Take a Moment to Consider . . .

- *When a friend or family member helped support you through rough times and what that meant to you.*
- *The challenges people with disabilities face and what you can do, on a personal level, to offer hope and help to a disabled person.*

Information about Stephen Hawking's life from Stephen Hawking; A Life in Science, by Michael White and John Gribbin. Washington, D.C.: Joseph Henry Press, 2002; www.top-biography.com/9132-Stephen%20Hawking/life.htm; www-gap.dcs.st-and.ac.uk/~history/ Mathematicians/Hawking.html.

PART III
CREATING LIFE SUCCESS

11 *Relating to Others*
COMMUNICATING IN A DIVERSE WORLD

12 *Wellness, Career, and Money*
BUILDING SKILLS FOR LIFE SUCCESS

THINKING IT THROUGH

Check those statements that apply to you right now:

■ When I think of diversity, I think of different races and ethnic groups.

■ I'm not quite sure why diversity should be important to me.

■ I'm entitled to my opinions about different groups of people.

■ I try not to judge people based on generalizations about their group identity.

■ I am aware of my personal communication style and try to change it in different situations.

■ I avoid conflict because it makes me uncomfortable.

■ I don't think about the different roles I play in groups. I just take things as they come.

334

Relating to Others

COMMUNICATING IN A DIVERSE WORLD

Questioning and posing problems.

"One of the characteristics that distinguishes humans from other forms of life is our **inclination and ability to find problems to solve**. Effective problem solvers know how to ask questions to fill in the gaps between what they know and what they don't know." **—ART COSTA**

Asking questions—and avoiding making assumptions before you hear the answers—is an essential way to learn about people and to generate successful communication. Through asking questions you can define communication issues and work toward solving them.

As society continually grows more diverse, colleges enroll students of all sorts of backgrounds, religions, races, ethnicities, ages, and lifestyles. Students often try activities and groups until they find the right fit. As you explore and look for a place that feels like home, being an effective communicator will help you maintain productive relationships with those around you. Positive interactions with all kinds of people leads to respect for others and strong teamwork skills, both key ingredients for success in school and beyond.

In this chapter, you investigate how your ability to maintain an open mind can positively affect the way in which you perceive and relate to others. You examine how having a strong network of relationships can help you grow and progress toward your goals. Special attention is paid to the choices minority students face. You explore how to communicate effectively, investigating different styles, ways to address communication problems, and methods for handling conflict. Finally, you look at how to enhance your personal relationships.

How do you experience diversity?

Whether you grew up in a small town, a suburb, or a large city, inevitably you will encounter people who are nothing like anyone you've ever met. With society becoming more diverse, the likelihood of these encounters is increasing. As Figure 11.1 shows, the population of the United States not only grew by nearly 27.5 million between 1990 and 2000, it also became more of a "gorgeous mosaic"—a metaphor first coined by David Dinkins, New York City's first African-American mayor, to describe the city's diversity.

According to the 2000 census, one in four Americans is a minority group member, compared with one in five in 1980. And, for the first time, with the census allowing people to choose categories from an array of racial identities—white, black, Asian, American Indian, Alaska native, Pacific Islander and Hawaiian native, or "some other race"—Americans now describe themselves in terms of 63 different racial categories, compared with only five in 1990.[1]

Diversity on Campus

College campuses reflect society, so diversity on campus is on the upswing. Most students will notice different races and ethnicities around them at school, and projections are for greater population shifts to come. As Figure 11.2 shows, whereas white students made up 71 percent of the student population in 1995, their percentage is expected to drop to 63 percent in 2015. During the same 20-year period, Hispanic-American and Asian-American students will grow more numerous, while African-American enrollment will hold steady at

FIGURE **11.1**

Minorities are changing the face of the United States.

FIGURE **11.2**

How the student body is expected to change by 2015.

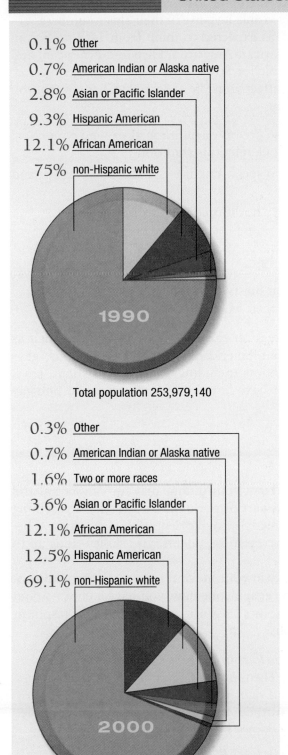

0.1% Other

0.7% American Indian or Alaska native

2.8% Asian or Pacific Islander

9.3% Hispanic American

12.1% African American

75% non-Hispanic white

1990

Total population 253,979,140

0.3% Other

0.7% American Indian or Alaska native

1.6% Two or more races

3.6% Asian or Pacific Islander

12.1% African American

12.5% Hispanic American

69.1% non-Hispanic white

2000

Total population 281,421,906

Source: U.S. Census Bureau. Data from 2000 Census of the Population.

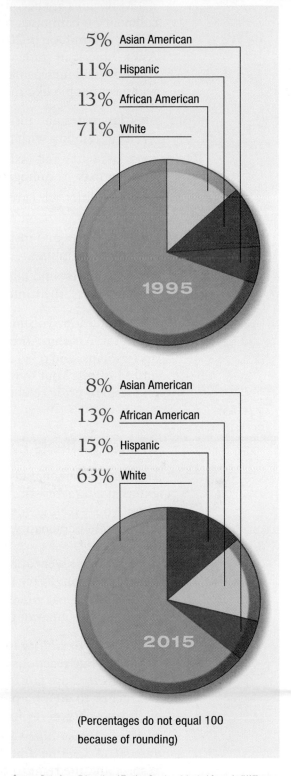

5% Asian American

11% Hispanic

13% African American

71% White

1995

8% Asian American

13% African American

15% Hispanic

63% White

2015

(Percentages do not equal 100 because of rounding)

Source: Data from Educational Testing Service. Adapted from Jodi Wilgoren, "Swell of Minority Students Is Predicted at Colleges," *The New York Times* May 24, 2000, A16.

about 13 percent. Some areas show even more dramatic trends. By 2015, whites will be a *minority* on campuses in California, the District of Columbia, Hawaii, and New Mexico.[2]

Minorities are becoming more visible because of their sheer numbers. Enrollment on campuses nationwide is expected to jump from 14.3 million in 1997 to 19 million in 2015, with African-American, Hispanic-American, and Asian-American students responsible for 80 percent of the growth.

How will increasing diversity affect your life at school? Chances are, you will meet people like the following:

- Classmates and instructors who are bi- or multiracial or who come from families with more than one religious tradition.
- Classmates and instructors who speak English as a second language and who may be immigrants.
- Classmates who are older than "traditional" 18- to 22-year-old students.
- Classmates and instructors who are in wheelchairs, and those with other disabilities.
- Classmates who adopt different lifestyles—often expressed in the way they dress, their interests, and their leisure activities.

In addition, you may see posters on campus for diverse clubs, such as those for African Americans, Asian Americans, Hispanic Americans, gays and lesbians, and religious organizations including those for Christians, Jews, and Muslims. Your school may also have campus-wide ethnic, racial, and gay and lesbian pride celebrations.

Diversity Affects Everyone

Diversity is personal in two ways. First, your unique makeup of internal and external characteristics makes you part of the quilt of diversity. Everything about you—your gender, race, ethnicity, sexual orientation, age, physical being, unique personality, religious orientation, talents, and skills—adds up to who you are.

Second, you encounter diversity in your inevitable interactions with people around you. Every time you meet someone new, you have a choice about how to relate—or whether to relate at all. Consider two important responsibilities as you analyze your options:

- *Your responsibility to yourself is to consider your feelings carefully.* Observe your reactions to others. Then, use critical thinking to make decisions that are fair to others and right for you. No one can force you to interact or to adopt a particular attitude. It's important to feel comfortable with your choices, as long as they do not hurt anyone.

- *Your responsibility to others is to treat people with tolerance and respect.* Accepting others comes down to being able to grant them your respect and the right to their own opinions. In addition to having basic tolerance, being open-minded rather than closed-minded about others will help your relationships thrive (Table 11.1 compares some open-minded and

TABLE 11.1	The value of an open-minded approach to diversity.		
YOUR ROLE	**SITUATION**	**CLOSED-MINDED APPROACH**	**OPEN-MINDED APPROACH**
Fellow student	For an assignment, you are paired with a student old enough to be your mother.	You assume the student will be closed off to the modern world. You think she might preach to you about how to do the assignment.	You get to know the student as an individual. You stay open to what you can learn from her experiences and knowledge.
Friend	You are invited to dinner at a friend's house. When he introduces you to his partner, you realize that he is gay.	You are turned off by the idea of two men in a relationship. You make an excuse to leave early. You avoid your friend after that evening.	You have dinner with the two men and make an effort to get to know more about what their lives are like and who they are individually and as a couple.
Employee	Your new boss is of a different racial and cultural background from yours.	You assume that you and your now boss don't have much in common and you think he will be distant and uninterested in you.	You rein in your assumptions, knowing they are based on stereotypes, and approach your new boss with an open mind.

closed-minded responses). Although you won't like every person you meet, take the time to make a fair decision based on what you learn about the inner person rather than the exterior characteristics.

"Minds are like parachutes. They only function when they are open."

SIR JAMES DEWAR

Prejudice, stereotyping, and discrimination often get in the way of fairness to others. As you read more about these topics, think about how your problem-solving skills can help you overcome these barriers to honest communication.

How can critical thinking help you explore diversity?

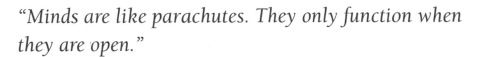

Negative responses to diversity are based on prejudice and stereotypic thinking. These responses, in turn, can lead to discrimination and hate. As you read, think about what you can do to prevent some of the worst parts of human nature from taking hold within yourself and others.

TAKE ACTION

Diversity Awareness

Being able to respond to the people you meet as individuals rather than group members requires that you become more aware of personal characteristics, starting with your own. Brainstorm six words or phrases that describe you (e.g. Cuban American, blonde, laid-back, only child, 24 years old, musician, fraternity member, basketball player, and so on).

1. _Latin American_
2. _college students_
3. _Full employee_
4. _white skin_
5. _skinny_
6. _social with family._

Now describe a person you've met recently who is a member of a group with which you have little experience. In order to help you react to this person more as an individual than as a member of a group, try to focus on personal as well as group characteristics, just as you did when you described yourself.

she is intelligence, friendly, hard work, and keep following her goal.

Understand Prejudice, Discrimination, and Hate

Prejudice
A preconceived judgment or opinion, formed without just grounds or sufficient knowledge.

Prejudice occurs when people *prejudge* others, usually on the basis of characteristics such as gender, race, sexual orientation, and religion. Particular prejudices are so pervasive that they have their own names: *racism* (prejudice based on race), *sexism* (prejudice based on sex), and *ageism* (prejudice based on age) are just a few. Here are some reasons why people judge others before they know anything about them:

- *Family and culture.* Children learn attitudes, including intolerance, superiority, and hate, from their parents, peers, and community.

- *Fear of differences.* When people who grew up in the midst of prejudice encounter others from different backgrounds, those differences can be unsettling.

- *Insecurity and jealousy.* When things go wrong, it is easier to blame others than to take responsibility. Similarly, in the face of insecurity, it can be easier to devalue others than to examine personal flaws.

- *Experience.* One bad experience with a person of a particular race or religion may lead someone to condemn all people with the same background, even though the condemnation is illogical. Prejudice may also stem from having no experience with members of a minority group. Some people find it easy to think the worst in the absence of information.

Prejudice Is Based on Stereotypes

A **stereotype** is an assumption made, without proof or critical thinking about the characteristics of a person or group of people. Although stereotypes can be "positive" or "negative," as the examples in Table 11.2 show, even "positive" stereotypes aren't always harmless or true. Stereotypes are the foundation for prejudiced thinking.

What are some reasons for stereotypes?

- *A desire for patterns and logic.* People often try to make sense of the world by using the labels, categories, and generalizations that stereotypes provide.

- *The media.* The more people see stereotypical images—the airhead beautiful blonde, the jolly fat man—the easier it is to believe that stereotypes are universal.

- *Laziness.* Labeling a group according to a characteristic they seem to have in common takes less energy than exploring unique qualities within individual group members.

Stereotypes communicate a message of disrespect and prevent relationships from growing. It is hard to experience the personality, character, talents, sense of humor, or intelligence of others if you paste stereotypical labels on them.

Prejudice Causes Discrimination

Prejudice—and the stereotypes it is based on—can lead to discrimination. *Discrimination* is made up of concrete actions that deny people equal employment, educational, and housing opportunities, and treat people as second-class citizens. As Sheryl McCarthy, an African-American columnist for *New York Newsday*, a daily newspaper, explains, "Nothing is quite so basic and clear as having a cab go right past your furiously waving body and pick up the white person next to you."[3]

Federal law forbids discrimination: You cannot be denied basic opportunities and rights because of your race, creed, color, age, gender, national or ethnic origin, religion, marital status, potential or actual pregnancy, or potential or actual illness or disability (unless the illness or disability prevents you from performing required tasks and unless accommodations are not possible).

Unfortunately, the law is often broken, and many people suffer the impact of discrimination. Some people don't report violations, fearing reprisals. Others aren't aware that discrimination has occurred or that there are laws to protect them from its consequences.

The many faces of prejudice and discrimination appear on college campuses. Students may not want to work with students of other races. Members of campus clubs may reject prospective members because of their religion. Outsiders may harass students attending gay and lesbian alliance meetings. Students may find that instructors judge

With an effort to keep open minds, people from different cultures can find common ground.

> ### Stereotype
> A standardized mental picture that represents an oversimplified opinion or uncritical judgment.

TABLE 11.2	Positive and negative stereotypes involve generalizations that may not be true.

POSITIVE STEREOTYPE	NEGATIVE STEREOTYPE
All women are nurturing.	Women are too emotional for business.
African Americans are the best athletes.	African Americans do poorly in school.
Hispanic Americans are very family oriented.	Hispanic Americans have too many kids.
White people are successful in business.	White people are cold and power hungry.
Gay people are artistic.	Gay people sleep around.
Because people with disabilities have been through so much, they are sensitive to the suffering of others.	People with disabilities can't hold jobs.
Older people have wisdom.	Older people can't learn new skills.
Asian Americans are good in math and science.	Asian Americans are poor leaders.

their abilities and attitudes according to their gender, weight, or body piercings. Actions like these block mutual understanding and respect and can derail students' focus on their education.

Hate crime

A crime motivated by a hatred of a specific characteristic thought to be possessed by the victim.

Hate Crimes: The Awful Consequences of Prejudice

When prejudice turns violent and ugly, it often manifests itself in **hate crimes** directed at racial, ethnic, and religious minorities and homosexuals:

- In Wyoming in 1998, Matthew Shepard, a gay college student, was kidnapped and tied to a fence where his captors beat and abandoned him. He died of his injuries.

- In 1999, Eric Harris and Dylan Klebold opened fire in Columbine High School in Littleton, Colorado, killing 12 students and one teacher and wounding others. Their writings revealed their desire to harm minorities, athletes, and others different from them.

- In 1999, Buford O. Furrow entered the North Valley Jewish Community Center near Los Angeles, California, and shot three preschool children and two adults because they were Jewish. He then shot and killed a Filipino-American letter carrier.

The increase in hate crimes in recent years—particularly the substantial rise of these crimes on college campuses—is alarming. According to the latest statistics compiled by the U.S. Department of Education, campus hate crimes increased from 1,312 in 1997 to 2,067 in 1999, with more than 90 percent of the offenses involving assaults.[4] The

reflect

Write about a time or period in your life when you felt stereotyped—in regard to gender, age, race ethnicity, appearance, weight, financial status, disability, or some other factor. Describe the situation or event, how it made you feel, and any actions you or anyone else took as a result. How did this event change you?

& respond

increase is linked, in part, to the Internet, which has given a "safe haven" to groups that espouse hate.

Be Part of the Solution

As you know from Chapter 4, the best and most lasting solutions come when you address the causes rather than the effects of behavior. Therefore, the best way to fight discrimination and hate crimes is to work to eliminate prejudice.

Start With Yourself

If one person can think more expansively, both that person and the world will benefit. *Think critically about any prejudices you have.* Ask yourself: Am I prejudiced against any group or groups? How did I develop this prejudice? How does it affect me and others? How can I change the way I think?

Dr. Martin Luther King, Jr. believed in the power of critical thinking to change ingrained attitudes. He said:

> The tough-minded person always examines the facts before he reaches conclusions: in short, he postjudges. The tender-minded person reaches conclusions before he has examined the first fact; in short, he prejudges and is prejudiced. . . . There is little hope for us until we become tough minded enough to break loose from the shackles of prejudice, half-truths, and downright ignorance.[5]

As you think critically, realize that the opinions of family, friends, and the media may sometimes lead you to adopt attitudes that you haven't thought through. Think about the attitudes you *want* to hold and make choices that are right for you and fair to others.

Try to avoid judgments based on external characteristics. If you meet a woman in a wheelchair, make the effort to learn who she really is. She may be an accounting major, a daughter, and a mother. She may love baseball, politics, and science fiction novels. These characteristics—not just her wheelchair—describe who she is.

Cultivate relationships with people different from yourself. Through personal experience and reading, find out how other people live and think, and see what you can learn from them. Then, if you are inclined take concrete actions: Choose a study partner from a different ethnic or racial background. Go to synagogue with a Jewish friend; go to a mosque with a Muslim friend.

Explore who you are. Learn about your personal ethnic and cultural heritage by talking with family and reading. Then, share your knowledge with others.

Learn from history. Read about the atrocities of slavery, the Holocaust, and the "ethnic cleansing" in Kosovo. Cherish your freedom and seek continual improvement at home and in the world.

Be sensitive to the needs of others. Ask yourself what you would feel and do if you were in another person's shoes.

Help others in need. Newspaper columnist Sheryl McCarthy wrote about an African American who, in the midst of the 1992 Los Angeles riots, saw an Asian-American man being beaten and helped him to safety: "When asked why he risked grievous harm to save an Asian man he didn't even know, the African-American man said, 'Because if I'm not there to help someone else, when the mob comes for me, will there be someone there to save me?'"[6]Continue the cycle of kindness.

Take personal responsibility. Avoid blaming problems on people who are different from you.

Recognize that people everywhere have the same basic needs. Everyone loves, thinks, hurts, hopes, fears, and plans. Strive to find out what is special about others instead of how they fit your preconceived idea of who they are. People are united through their essential humanity.

Encountering Others Who Are Prejudiced

What should you do when someone you know makes prejudiced remarks or discriminates against you or others? It can be hard to stand up to someone, even though right—and the law—are on your side. You may choose to say nothing, make a small comment, or get help. If you approach an authority, start with the person who can most directly affect the situation—an instructor or supervisor. At each decision stage, weigh all of the possible positive and negative effects and evaluate whether the action is wise for you and others.

It is everyone's responsibility to sound the alarm on hate crimes. Let the authorities know if you suspect that a crime is about to occur. Join campus protests. Express your opinion by writing letters to the editor of your school newspaper and attend lectures sponsored by the Anti-Defamation League and other organizations that encourage acceptance and tolerance.

How can minority students make the most of college?

Who fits into the category of "minority student" at your school? The term *minority* includes students of color; students who are not part of the majority Christian sects; and gay, lesbian, and bisexual students. However, even for members of these groups, there is no universal "minority" experience. Each person's experiences are unique.

Most colleges have special organizations and support services for minority groups. Among these are specialized student associations, cultural centers, arts groups with a minority focus, residence halls for minority students, minority fraternities and sororities, and political-action groups. Your involve-

TAKE ACTION

Building peace and acceptance is a step-by-step, person-by-person process. Look at the "Be Part of the So-lution" section and make it personal. Choose three of the strategies and rewrite them, making them specific to your situation and intention. For example, "Help others in need" might become "Sign up to tutor in the Writing Center." Check the box for each when you have completed the task or, if it is ongoing, when you have begun the change.

1. ☐ _____

_____

_____

2. ☐ _____

_____

3. ☐ _____

_____

_____

ment with these groups depends on how comfortable you are within a com-munity of students who share your background and how much you want to extend your social connections.

Define Your Experience

When you start school, it's natural to gravitate to people with whom you share common ground. You may choose to live with a roommate from the same background, sit next to other minority students in class, or attend minority-related social events and parties. However, if you define your *entire* college experience by these ties, you may limit your understanding of others and thereby your opportunities for growth.

Many minority students adopt a fairly balanced approach, involving themselves in activities with members of their group as well as with the col-lege mainstream. For example, a student may be a member of the African-American Students Association and also join clubs for all students such as the campus newspaper or an athletic team. Both worlds have much to offer.

To make choices as a minority student on campus, ask yourself these questions:

■ Do I want to focus my social interactions on people who share my background? How much time do I want to spend pursuing minority-

reflect

Imagine that you must change either your gender or your racial ethnic group. Which would you change and why? What do you anticipate would be the positive and negative effects of the change—in your social life, in your family life, on the job, and at school?[7]

& respond

related activities? Do I want to focus my studies on a minority-related field, such as African-American studies?

- Do I want to minimize my ties with my minority group and be "just another student"? Will I care if other minority students criticize my choices?
- Do I want to spend part of my time among people who share my background and part with students from other groups?

You may feel pressured to make certain choices based on what your peers do—but if these decisions go against your gut feelings, they are almost always a mistake. Your choice should be right for you, especially because it will determine many of your college experiences. Plus, the attitudes and habits you develop now may have implications for the rest of your life—in your choice of friends, where you decide to live, your work, and even your family. Think long and hard about the path you take, and always follow your head and heart.

Understand Stereotype Vulnerability

Stereotype vulnerability happens when minority students avoid facing a problem because they think that admitting it perpetuates a group stereotype.[8] For example, an immigrant to the United States may resist going to tutoring in English for fear of seeming like an ignorant foreigner. In another aspect of stereotype vulnerability, people refuse help because they believe that these offerings are motivated by pity. "He feels sorry for me because of my disability." Defensive responses like these are based on assumptions about what the other person is thinking.

If you see stereotype vulnerability in yourself, you may be cutting yourself off from helpful assistance and communication. If you need help, try to approach someone who can give it—and try to avoid making assumptions about why that person is helping you. You may discover that the helper will see you not as a representative of a group but as an individual.

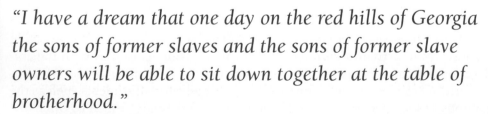

"I have a dream that one day on the red hills of Georgia the sons of former slaves and the sons of former slave owners will be able to sit down together at the table of brotherhood."

MARTIN LUTHER KING, JR.

The concept of diversity examined so far in this chapter has focused on the need to accept and embrace the multiculturalism that defines the

United States and students' experiences in college. However, some forms of diversity are more subtle, including differences in the way people communicate. While one person may be direct and disorganized, another may be analytic and organized, and a third may hardly say a word. Just as there is diversity in skin color and ethnicity, there is also diversity in the way people communicate.

Accepting diversity includes accepting differences in communication style and working to understand them. This is especially important because successful relationships depend on effective communication. If you strive to express yourself clearly and to interpret what others say in the way they intend, you can connect with people in all aspects of your life.

How can you communicate effectively?

Clear spoken communication promotes success at school, at work, and in your personal relationships. Clarity comes from understanding communication styles, learning to give and receive criticism, becoming knowledgeable about body language, working through communication problems, and using specific techniques for effective oral presentations.

Adjusting to Communication Styles

When you speak, your goal is for listeners to receive the message as you intended. Problems arise when one person has trouble "translating" a message coming from someone with a different style of communication.

Your knowledge of the Personality Spectrum (see Chapter 2) will help you understand different styles of communication. Particular communication styles tend to accompany dominance in particular dimensions. Recognizing specific styles in yourself and others will help you communicate more effectively.

Identifying Your Styles

Following are some communication styles that tend to be associated with the four dimensions in the Personality Spectrum. No one style is better than another. Successful communication depends on understanding your personal style and becoming attuned to the styles of others.

Thinker-dominant communicators focus on facts and logic. As speakers, they tend to rely on logic to communicate ideas and prefer quantitative concepts to those that are conceptual or emotional. As listeners, they often do best with logical messages. They may also need time to process what they have heard before responding. Written messages—on paper or via e-mail—are often useful because writing can allow for time to put ideas together logically.

Organizer-dominant communicators focus on structure and completeness. As speakers, they tend to deliver well-thought-out, structured messages that fit into an organized plan. As listeners, they often appreciate a well-organized message that has tasks defined in clear, concrete terms. As with Thinkers, a written format is often an effective form of communication to or from an Organizer.

Giver-dominant communicators focus on concern for others. As speakers, they tend to cultivate harmony and work toward closeness in their relationships. As listeners, they often appreciate messages that emphasize personal connection and address the emotional side of the issue. Whether speaking or listening, they often favor direct, in-person interaction over written messages.

Adventurer-dominant communicators focus on the present. As speakers, they tend to convey a message as soon as the idea arises and then move on to the next activity. As listeners, they appreciate up-front, short, direct messages that don't get sidetracked. Like Givers, they tend to communicate and listen more effectively in person.

Use this information not as a label but as a jumping-off point for your self-exploration. Just as people tend to demonstrate characteristics from more than one Personality Spectrum dimension, communicators may demonstrate different styles. Think about the communication styles associated with your dominant Personality Spectrum dimensions. Consider, too, how you tend to communicate and how others generally respond to you. Are you convinced only in the face of logical arguments? Are you attuned most to feelings? Use what you discover to get a better idea of what works best for you.

Speakers Adjust to Listeners

Listeners may interpret messages in ways you never intended. Think about how you can address this problem as you read the following example involving a Giver-dominant instructor and a Thinker-dominant student (the listener):

> Instructor: "Your essay didn't communicate any sense of your personal voice."
>
> Student: "What do you mean? I spent hours writing it. I thought it was on the mark."

- *Without adjustment:* The instructor ignores the student's need for detail and continues to generalize. Comments like, "You need to elaborate. Try writing from the heart. You're not considering your audience," might confuse or discourage the student.
- *With adjustment:* Greater logic and detail will help. For example, the instructor might say: "You've supported your central idea clearly, but you didn't move beyond the facts into your interpretation of what they mean. Your essay reads like a research paper. The language doesn't sound like it is coming directly from you."

MULTIPLE PATHWAYS TO LEARNING

MULTIPLE INTELLIGENCE STRATEGIES *for* Communication

Using techniques corresponding to your stronger intelligences boosts your communication skills both as a speaker and as a listener.

INTELLIGENCE	SUGGESTED STRATEGIES	WHAT WORKS FOR YOU? WRITE NEW IDEAS HERE
Verbal–Linguistic	■ Find opportunities to express your thoughts and feelings to others—either in writing or in person. ■ Remind yourself that you have two ears and only one mouth. Listening is more important than talking.	
Logical–Mathematical	■ Allow yourself time to think through solutions before discussing them—try writing out a logical argument on paper and then rehearsing it orally. ■ Accept the fact that others may have communication styles that vary from yours and that may not seem logical.	
Bodily–Kinesthetic	■ Have an important talk while walking or performing a task that does not involve concentration. ■ Work out physically to burn off excess energy before having an important discussion.	
Visual–Spatial	■ Make a drawing or diagram of points you want to communicate during an important discussion. ■ If your communication is in a formal classroom or work setting, use visual aids to explain your main points.	
Interpersonal	■ Observe how you communicate with friends. If you tend to dominate the conversation, brainstorm ideas about how to communicate more effectively. ■ Remember to balance speaking with listening.	
Intrapersonal	■ When you have a difficult encounter, take time alone to evaluate what happened and to decide how you can communicate more effectively next time. ■ Remember that, in order for others to understand clearly, you may need to communicate more than you expect to.	
Musical	■ Play soft music during an important discussion if it helps you, making sure it isn't distracting to the others involved.	
Naturalistic	■ Communicate outdoors if that is agreeable to all parties. ■ If you have a difficult exchange, imagine how you might have responded differently had it taken place outdoors.	

Listeners Adjust to Speakers

As a listener, you can improve understanding by being aware of stylistic differences and translating the message into one that makes sense to you. The following example of an Adventurer-dominant employee speaking to an Organizer-dominant supervisor shows how adjusting can pay off.

> Employee: "I'm upset about the e-mail you sent me. You never talked to me directly and you let the problem build into a crisis. I haven't had a chance to defend myself."

- *Without adjustment:* If the supervisor is annoyed by the employee's insistence on direct personal contact, he or she may become defensive: "I told you clearly what needs to be done, and my language wasn't a problem. I don't know what else there is to discuss."
- *With adjustment:* In an effort to improve communication, the supervisor responds by encouraging the in-person, real-time exchange that is best for the employee. "Let's meet after lunch so you can explain to me how you believe we can improve the situation."

Although adjusting to communication styles helps you speak and listen more effectively, you also need to understand the nature of criticism and learn to handle criticism as a speaker and listener.

Constructive
Promoting improvement or development.

Constructive and Nonconstructive Criticism

Criticism can be either **constructive** or nonconstructive. *Constructive criticism* involves goodwill suggestions for improvement, promoting the hope that things will be better. In contrast, *nonconstructive criticism* focuses on what went wrong, doesn't offer alternatives or help, and is often delivered negatively, creating bad feelings and defensiveness.

Consider a case in which someone has continually been late to study group sessions. The group leader can comment in either of these ways:

- *Constructive.* The group leader talks privately with the student: "I've noticed that you've been late a lot. We count on you, because our success depends on what each of us contributes. Is there a problem that is keeping you from being on time? Can we help?"
- *Nonconstructive.* The leader watches the student arrive late and says, in front of everyone, "Nice to see you could make it. If you can't start getting here on time, there's really no point in your coming."

Which comment would encourage you to change your behavior? When offered constructively and carefully, criticism can help bring about important changes.

While at school, your instructors will criticize your class work, papers, and exams. On the job, criticism comes primarily from supervisors and coworkers. No matter the source, positive comments can help you grow as a person. Be open to what you hear, and always remember that most people want to help you succeed.

Offering Constructive Criticism

When offering constructive criticism, use the following strategies to be effective:

- *Criticize the behavior rather than the person.* Avoid personal attacks—they inevitably result in defensive behavior. In addition, make sure that a behavior is within a person's power to change. Chronic lateness can be changed if the person has poor time-management skills; it can't be changed if a physical disability slows the person down.

- *Define the problematic behavior specifically.* Try to focus on the facts, substantiating with specific examples, minimizing emotions, and avoiding additional complaints. People can hear criticisms better if they are discussed one at a time.

- *Suggest new approaches.* Talk about different ways of handling the situation. Help the person see options he or she may have never considered.

- *Use a positive approach and hopeful language.* Express the conviction that changes will occur and that the person can turn the situation around.

- *Stay calm and be brief.* Avoid threats, ultimatums, and accusations. Use "I" messages that help the person see how his or her actions are affecting you.

- *Offer help in changing the behavior.* Do what you can to make the person feel supported.

Receiving Criticism

When you find yourself on criticism's receiving end, use the following techniques:

- *Use critical thinking to analyze the comments.* Listen carefully, and then carefully evaluate what you heard. Does it come from a desire to help or from jealousy or frustration? Try to let nonconstructive comments go without responding.

- *If the feedback is constructive, ask for suggestions on how to change your behavior.* Ask, "How would you like me to handle this in the future?"

- *Summarize the criticism and your response to it.* Make sure everyone understands the situation in the same way.

- *Plan a specific strategy.* Decide how to change and take concrete steps to make it happen.

Criticism, as well as other thoughts and feelings, may be communicated through nonverbal communication. You will become a more effective communicator if you understand what body language may be saying.

The Role of Body Language

Considered by many to be the most "honest" form of communication because of its capacity to express people's real feelings, body language often reveals a

TAKE ACTION

Giving Criticism Positively

Think for a moment: What situation in your life could be improved if you were able to offer constructive criticism to a friend or family member? Briefly describe the situation here, noting the improvement you are seeking:

relationship with my

Imagine that you have a chance to speak to this person. First describe the setting—time, place, atmosphere—where you think you would be most successful:

Now develop your "script." Keeping in mind what you know about constructive criticism, freewrite what you would say. If you get stuck, think about how you would want someone to talk to you if you were the one receiving the criticism.

Finally, if you can, make your plan a reality. Will you do it? ☒ Yes ☐ No
If you do have the conversation, note here: Was it worth it? ☐ Yes ☒ No

great deal though gestures, eye movements, facial expressions, body positioning and posture, touching behaviors, vocal tone, and use of personal space. Although reading body language is far from an exact science, understanding its basics will help you use it to your advantage as you speak and listen.

Figure 11.3 shows examples of body language that are associated with specific meanings in our culture. Keep in mind that culture influences how body language is interpreted. For example, in the United States, looking away from someone may be a sign of anger or distress; in Japan, the same behavior is usually a sign of respect.

How Body Language Works

Here are some important principles of body language.

Nonverbal communication strongly influences first impressions.
First impressions emerge from a combination of verbal and nonverbal cues. Nonverbal elements, including tone of voice, posture, eye contact, and speed and style of movement, usually come across first and strongest.

Body language provides possible communication clues.   FIGURE 11.3

Firm handshake:
capability, friendliness

Body turned away:
lack of interest

Hands on hips:
readiness, toughness

Open sitting posture:
interest or agreement

Body language can reinforce or contradict verbal statements.
When you greet a friend with a smile and a strong handshake, your body language reinforces your words of welcome. When, on the other hand, your body language contradicts your words, your body generally tells the real story.

Nonverbal cues shade meaning. The statement, *"This is the best idea I've heard all day,"* can mean different things depending on vocal tone. Said sarcastically, the words may mean that the speaker considers the idea a joke. In contrast, the same words said while sitting with your arms and legs crossed and looking away may communicate that you dislike the idea, but are unwilling to say so.

Using Body Language to Your Advantage

The following strategies will help you maximize your awareness of body language so that you can use it—as a speaker and a listener—to your advantage.

- *Become aware.* Pay attention to what other people are really saying through their nonverbal cues and to what you communicate through your own cues.
- *Match your words with your body language.* Try to monitor your personal body language when you deliver important messages. For example, if you really want to communicate satisfaction to an instructor, look the instructor in the eye and speak enthusiastically.
- *Note cultural differences.* Cultural factors influence how nonverbal cues are interpreted. For example, in Arab cultures, casual acquaintances

Awareness of body language contributes to successful cross-cultural communication.

Assertive
Able to declare and affirm one's own opinions while respecting the rights of others to do the same.

stand close together when speaking, while in the United States, the same distance is reserved for intimate conversation. With any cross-cultural conversation, you can discover what seems appropriate by paying attention to what the other person does on a consistent basis.

No matter how much you know about verbal and nonverbal communication, you will still encounter communication problems. Here are strategies for solving some common ones.

Solving Communication Problems

Although every communication situation is different, many communication problems have common threads that are easy to identify. If you experience any of the problems described, try applying these strategic fixes.

Problem: Being too passive or aggressive in the way you communicate.

Solution: Take the middle ground. Be assertive.

No matter what your dominant learning styles, you tend to express yourself in one of three ways—through *aggressive, passive,* and *assertive* communication. The **assertive** style will help you communicate in the clearest, most productive way. Assertive communicators are likely both to get their message across and to give listeners the opportunity to speak, without attacking others or sacrificing their own needs.

By contrast, aggressive communicators focus primarily on their own needs. They can become angry and impatient when those needs are not immediately satisfied. Passive communicators deny themselves power by focusing almost exclusively on the needs of others, often experiencing unexpressed frustration and tension in the process.

Table 11.3 compares the characteristics of these communicators. Assertive behavior strikes a balance between aggression and passivity.

To become more assertive, aggressive communicators should take time before speaking, use "I" statements that accept personal responsibility, listen to others, and avoid giving orders. Similarly, passive communicators who want to become more assertive might try to acknowledge anger or hurt, express opinions, exercise their right to make requests, and know that their ideas and feelings are important.

Problem: Attacking the receiver.

Solution: Send "I" messages.

When a conflict arises, often the first instinct is to pinpoint what someone else did wrong. Unfortunately, accusations put others on the defensive as they shut down communication.

"I" messages help you communicate your needs rather than attacking someone else. Creating these messages involves nothing more than some sim-

TABLE 11.3	Assertiveness fosters clear communication.	
AGGRESSIVE	**PASSIVE**	**ASSERTIVE**
Loud, heated arguing	Concealing one's own feelings	Expressing feelings without being nasty or overbearing
Physically violent encounters	Denying one's own anger	Acknowledging emotions but staying open to discussion
Blaming, name-calling, and verbal insults	Feeling that one has no right to express anger	Expressing oneself and giving others the chance to express themselves equally
Walking out of arguments before they are resolved	Avoiding arguments	Using "I" statements to defuse arguments
Being demanding: "Do this"	Being noncommittal: "You don't have to do this unless you really want to . . ."	Asking and giving reasons: "I would appreciate it if you would do this, and here's why . . ."

ple rephrasing: "You didn't lock the door!" becomes "I felt uneasy when I came to work and the door was unlocked." Similarly, "You never called last night" becomes "I was worried about you when I didn't hear from you last night."

"Do not use a hatchet to remove a fly from your friend's forehead."

CHINESE PROVERB

"I" statements soften the conflict by highlighting the effects that the other person's actions have on you, rather than focusing on the person or the actions themselves. When you focus on your own responses and needs, the receiver may feel freer to respond, perhaps offering help and even acknowledging mistakes.

Problem: Choosing bad times to communicate.

Solution: Be sensitive to the cues in your environment.

When you have something to say, choose a time when you can express yourself clearly. Spoken too soon, ideas can come out sounding nothing like you intended. Left simmering too long, your feelings can spill over into other issues. Rehearsing mentally or talking your thoughts through with a friend can help you choose the most effective strategy, words, and tone.

Good timing also requires sensitivity to your listener. Even a perfectly worded message won't get through to someone who isn't ready to receive it. If you try to talk to your instructor when she is rushing out the door, she won't pay attention to what you are saying. If a classmate calls to discuss a project while you are cramming for an exam, his point will be lost. Pay attention to mood as well. If a friend had an exhausting week, it's smart to wait before asking a favor.

One of the biggest barriers to successful communication is conflict, which can result in anger and even violence. With effort, you can manage conflict successfully and stay away from those who cannot.

Handling Conflict

Conflicts, both large and small, arise when there is a clash of ideas or interests. You may have small conflicts with a housemate over a door left unlocked. You may have major conflicts with your partner about finances or with an instructor about a failing grade. Conflict, as unpleasant as it can be, is a natural element in the dynamic of getting along with others.

Conflict Resolution Strategies

When handled poorly, conflicts create anger and frustration. All too often, people deal with these negative feelings through avoidance (a passive tactic that shuts down communication) or escalation (an aggressive tactic that often leads to fighting). Conflict resolution strategies use calm communication and critical thinking to avoid extreme reactions. Think through conflicts using what you know about problem solving (see Chapter 4):

1. *Identify and analyze the problem.* Determine the severity of the problem by looking at its effects on everyone involved. Then, find and analyze its causes.

2. *Brainstorm possible solutions.* Consider as many angles as you can, without judgment. Try to apply what you did in similar situations.

3. *Explore each solution.* Evaluate each solution, including its possible benefits and risks. Look at options from the perspective of others as you try to determine which would cause the least stress. Make sure everyone has a chance to express an opinion.

4. *Choose, carry out, and evaluate the solution you decide is best.* Translate the solution into actions, and then evaluate what happens. Decide whether you made the best choice, and make mid-course corrections, if necessary.

Goodwill and motivation will aid your efforts to resolve conflict. Also helpful is a determination to focus on the problem rather than on placing blame and an effort to calm anger. All people get angry at times—at people, events, and themselves. However, excessive anger—out-of-control, loud, irrational, and sometimes physical—has the power to contaminate relationships, stifle communication, and turn friends and family away.

Managing Anger

People who continually respond to disappointments and frustrations by shouting, cursing, or even physically lashing out find that emotions get in the way of personal happiness and school success. It is hard to concentrate on

American history when you are raging over being cut off in traffic. It is hard to focus during a study group if you can't let go of your anger with a group member. Psychologists report that angry outbursts do nothing to resolve problems and may actually make things worse. What can you do when you feel yourself losing control or when anger turns into rage that you just can't drop? First, remember that it doesn't help to explode. Then, try some of these anger-management techniques.

Relax. Calm down by breathing deeply while slowly repeating a calming word or phrase, such as "Take it easy" or "It's just not worth it" or "Relax."

Try to change the way you process what is happening. Instead of reacting in anger to the frustration of being closed out of a course, say to yourself, "I'm frustrated and upset, but it's not the end of the world. I'll talk to my advisor about taking the course next semester. Getting angry is not going to get me a seat in the class."

Change your environment. Take a walk, go to the gym, see a movie. Take a break from what's upsetting you. If you can build break time into your daily schedule, you'll be better able to handle problems without blowing up.

Change your language. Language can inflame anger, so turn your language down a notch. Instead of barking orders to your lab partner, such as "Give me the flask! I need it now!" say, "Zack, I need the flask in about ten seconds—could you pass it to me please?" The person to whom you are talking is more likely to do what you ask if you stay in control.

Think before you speak. When angry, most people tend to say the first thing that comes to mind, even if it's mean. Inevitably, this escalates the hard feelings and the intensity of the argument. Instead, count to 10—slowly, if necessary—until you are in control.

Try not to be defensive. No one likes to be criticized. While it's natural to respond by fighting back, it's also self-defeating. Instead, try to hear the message that's behind the criticism. Ask questions to make sure you understand the other person's point. If you focus on the problem—and if the other person works with you—anger is more likely to take a back seat.

Do your best to solve a problem, but remember that not all problems can be solved. Analyze a challenging situation, make a plan, resolve to do your best, and begin. If you fall short, you will know you did all you could and be less likely to turn your frustration into anger.

reflect

In 1934, due to her opposition to the Nazi regime, international journalist Dorothy Thompson was the first American correspondent expelled from Nazi Germany. She once stated: "Peace is not the absence of conflict but the presence of creative alternatives for responding to conflict." Do you agree or disagree? How do you come to peace in your own situations of conflict?

Companion Website

& respond

Get help if you can't keep your anger in check. If you try these techniques and still find yourself lashing out, you may need the help of a counselor. Many schools have licensed mental health professionals available to students who take the initiative to set up an appointment.

Anger directed primarily at women sometimes takes the form of sexual harassment. When this anger turns violent, it involves partners in destructive relationships. Anger also fuels rape, including date rape.

Sexual Harassment

The facts. Both men and women can be victims of sexual harassment, although the most common targets are women. Sexual harassment covers a wide range of behavior, divided into the following types:

- *Quid pro quo harassment* refers to a request for some kind of sexual favor or activity in exchange for something else. It is a kind of bribe or threat. ("If you don't do X for me, I will fail you/fire you/make your life miserable.")
- *Hostile environment harassment* indicates any situation where sexually charged remarks, behavior, or items cause discomfort. Harassment of this type ranges from lewd jokes to the display of pornography.

How to cope. If you feel degraded by anything that goes on at school or work, address the person who you believe is harassing you, or speak to an authority. Try to avoid assumptions—perhaps the person is unaware that the behavior is offensive. On the other hand, the person may know exactly what is going on. Either way, you are entitled to ask the person to stop.

Violence in Relationships

The facts. Violent relationships among students are increasing. Here are some statistics from the Corporate Alliance to End Partner Violence.[9]

RISING
TO THE CHALLENGE

Gustavo Minaya
Student at Essex Community College, Baltimore, Maryland

Making a connection with others can be difficult, especially if you start out feeling exceptionally different. Gustavo Minaya spoke no English when he came to the completely unfamiliar United States as a child. Through learning and getting involved in activities, he has found his niche.

I am native of Peru. When I was six years old, my mother told me that we were going to America for a better life. My father was already living in the U. S. so my mother went to the embassy to apply for a visa, but our visa was denied. In desperation, she decided to hire "coyotes." These are people who know secret routes to the United States. Their job was to help us cross the border.

Our journey began at night with cold train rides. At different points, we stopped to eat or to get on a different train. Along the way other families joined us. At the Mexico—Texas border, the "coyotes" instructed us to walk under a highway. Once we were out again in the open, everyone began running for the U. S. border. Helicopters were circling overhead with their search lights on, and people were shouting. It was pandemonium.

Exhausted, we made it across the border and onto a van, where people were stacked on top of each other. At another border check, my mother and I were arrested and taken into custody by immigration officers who took our fingerprints. They arranged to have us transported to an emergency shelter run by the American Red Cross. Meanwhile, my dad completed the paperwork for legal immigration, and we joined him a few months later.

Of course, I didn't know English. When I started school in the second grade I looked different from the other kids, and I sounded different because of my accent. Some of the kids picked on me. I cried a lot back then. The next year I took English as a Second Language (ESL) classes. Gradually, I learned English and began to feel like I fit in.

When I look back over my experiences, I believe the one thing that has helped me adjust to the changes is friendliness. I like to make people laugh, and I go into things with a positive attitude. Being friendly with other students, and people in general, has helped me gain a sense of belonging.

My main advice to international students who want to make the most of their education is to participate in campus activities. You can join a club or work on campus, maybe at the school store or library. This way you meet new people, and you'll learn English faster. You can't fit in if you isolate yourself.

Participation is also important for developing leadership skills. I look at clubs and other campus activities as opportunities to enhance my education. For example, I joined the International Student Association (ISA) and am now the president. During the meetings, I give my ideas and show my support by volunteering for projects. I've discovered that one of my strengths is bringing people together for a good cause.

I'm very proud of my parents for how hard they worked to make a better life for me and my brothers and sisters. In my native country of Peru, you can work as hard as you want, but it gets you nowhere. Some of the smartest people there are taxicab drivers because they can't find jobs doing anything else. Here, if you are willing to work, you can have a profession and achieve what you want. I plan to achieve as much as I can.

Take a Moment to Consider . . .

- *What important opportunity you feel that living in this country offers you, whether you are an immigrant or native-born.*

- *How you plan to gain a sense of belonging at your school.*

- One in five college students has experienced and reported at least one violent incident while dating, from being slapped to more serious violence.

- In three out of four violent relationships, problems surface after the couple has dated for a while.

- In six out of ten cases, drinking and drugs are associated with the violence.

Women in their teens and twenties, who make up the majority of women in college, are more likely to be victims of domestic violence than older women, for a number of reasons. First, when trouble occurs, students are likely to turn to friends, rather than professional counselors or the law. Second, peer pressure makes them uneasy about leaving the relationship; they would rather be abused than alone. And finally, because of their inexperience in dating, they may believe that violent relationships are "normal."[10]

How to cope. Start by recognizing the warning signs of impending violence, including controlling behavior, unpredictable mood swings, personality changes associated with alcohol and drugs, and outbursts of anger. If you see a sign, think about ending the relationship.

If you are being abused, your safety and sanity depend on seeking help. Call a shelter or abuse hotline. Seek counseling at your school or at a community center. If you need medical attention, go to a clinic or hospital emergency room. If you believe that your life is in danger, get out and get a restraining order that requires your abuser to stay away from you.

Rape and Date Rape

The facts. Any intercourse or anal or oral penetration by a person against another person's will is defined as rape. Rape is primarily a controlling, violent act of rage, not a sexual act.

Rape, especially acquaintance rape or **date rape**, is a problem on many campuses. Any sexual activity during a date that is against one partner's will constitutes date rape, including situations where one partner is too drunk or drugged to give consent. Currently appearing on campuses is a drug called Rohypnol, known as Roofies, that is sometimes used by date rapists to sedate their victims and is difficult to detect in a drink.

Campus Advocates for Rape Education (C.A.R.E.), an organization at Wheaton College, describes the collateral damage caused by date rape. "One's trust in a friend, date, or acquaintance is violated. As a result, a victim's fear, self-blame, guilt, and shame are magnified because the assailant is known."[11]

How to cope. Beware of questionable situations or drinks when on a date with someone you don't know well or who seems unstable or angry. Clearly communicate what you want and don't want to do. If you are raped, get medical attention immediately. Next, talk to a close friend or counselor. Consider reporting the incident to the police or to campus officials. Whether or not you take legal action, continue to get help through counseling, a rape survivor group, or a hotline.

Your ability to communicate and manage conflict has a major impact on your relationships with friends and family. Successful relationships are built on self-knowledge, good communication, and hard work.

How do you make the most of personal relationships?

Personal relationships with friends, classmates, spouses and partners, and parents can be sources of great satisfaction and inner peace. Relationships have the power to motivate you to do your best in school, on the job, and in life.

When things go wrong with relationships, however, nothing in your world may seem right. You may be unable to eat, sleep, or concentrate. Because of this, relationship strategies are all-around survival strategies.

Use Positive Relationship Strategies

Here are some strategies for improving your personal relationships.

Make personal relationships a high priority. Life is meant to be shared. In some marriage ceremonies, the bride and groom share a cup of wine, symbolizing that the sweetness of life is doubled by tasting it together and the bitterness is cut in half when shared by two.

Invest time. You devote time to education, work, and sports. Relationships benefit from the same investment. In addition, spending time with people you like can relieve stress.

Spend time with people you respect and admire. Life is too short to hang out with people who bring you down or encourage you to do things that go against your values. Develop relationships with people whose choices you admire and who inspire you to fulfill your potential.

Date rape
Sexual assault perpetrated by the victim's escort during an arranged social encounter.

If you want a friend, be a friend. If you treat others with the kind of loyalty and support that you appreciate yourself, you are likely to receive the same in return.

Work through tensions. Negative feelings can fester when left unspoken. Get to the root of a problem by discussing it, compromising, forgiving, and moving on.

Take risks. It can be frightening to reveal your deepest dreams and frustrations, to devote yourself to a friend, or to fall in love. However, if you open yourself up, you stand to gain the incredible benefits of companionship, which for most people outweigh the risks.

Find a pattern that suits you. Some students date exclusively and commit early. Some students prefer to socialize in groups. Some students date casually. Be honest with yourself—and others—about what you want in a relationship.

Keep personal problems in their place. Try to separate your problems from your schoolwork. Mixing the two may hurt your performance, while doing nothing to solve your problem.

If a relationship fails, find ways to cope. When an important relationship becomes strained or breaks up, use coping strategies to help you move on. Some people need time alone; others need to be with friends and family. Some seek counseling. Some throw their energy into school or exercise. Some cry. Whatever you do, believe that in time you will emerge from the experience stronger.

Choose Communities That Enhance Your Life

Personal relationships often take place in the context of communities, or groups, that include people who share your interests—for example, martial arts groups, bridge clubs, sororities, fraternities, athletic teams, and political groups. So much of what you accomplish in life is linked to your network of personal contacts.

If you affiliate with communities that are involved in positive activities, you are more likely to surround yourself with responsible and character-rich people who may become your friends and professional colleagues. You may find among them your future spouse or partner, your best friend, a person who helps you land a job, your doctor, accountant, real estate agent, and so on.

If you find yourself drawn toward communities that encourage negative and even harmful behavior, such as gangs or groups that haze pledges, stop and think before you commit. Be aware of cliques that bring out negative qualities including aggression, hate, and superiority. Use critical thinking to analyze why you are drawn to these groups and, if necessary, to resist the temptation to join. If you are already involved and want out, stand up for yourself and be determined.

I question and pose problems.

Though it's human to make assumptions about people based on their characteristics or background, such assumptions can cause problems as minimal as a casual misunderstanding or as damaging as a war. Asking questions is the essential "anti-assumption" strategy. If you ask someone a question, and really listen to the answer, you will find out how the person truly thinks or feels about an issue—and how what they say may differ from what you might have assumed. Asking questions also opens the lines of communication and fosters an honest exchange of ideas.

When encountering confusion in any relationship, intelligent questioners will ask the kinds of questions that will uncover a problem, should one exist: "Why did I receive that grade?" "Why did he treat me that way?" "Why didn't she understand my response?" When answering these questions reveals a problem, you then have the opportunity to solve it and thereby to improve the communication and the relationship in a way that you could not have seen before your investigation. Questioning and posing problems has the potential to take your communication to a new level of success.

How can critical thinking help you explore diversity?

Your analytical and problem-solving skills will help you understand prejudice and avoid its effects—stereotyping and discrimination. Prejudice occurs when people prejudge others, usually on the basis of external characteristics. It is based on stereotypes—assumptions about the characteristics of a group. Prejudice causes discrimination—concrete actions that deny people equal treatment in situations involving housing, employment, and so on. Hate crimes show the most violent side of prejudice. Thinking critically about diversity will help you break down the barriers that prevent successful communication. Be part of the solution by doing what you can to address and eliminate prejudice.

How can minority students make the most of college?

There is no universal "minority" experience—students who fit into the category of "minority" have many choices on campus in terms of activities, organizations, and courses of study. It's helpful for minority students to define how much they want to focus on people and issues that reflect their background, and how much they want to seek out experiences that are not necessarily minority-focused. It's also helpful to understand and work against stereotype vulnerability—the tendency to avoid facing a problem because it may reinforce a group stereotype.

How can you communicate effectively?

Clear spoken communication promotes success in all areas of your life. Considering communication styles that reflect the Thinker, Giver, Organizer, and Adventurer types will help you understand how you and others communicate. Trying to criticize constructively and receive criticism thoughtfully will help you find good solutions. Other important communication strategies include understanding body language, being an assertive communicator, using "I" messages, and communicating at ideal times. When communication problems lead to conflict, use a conflict resolution strategy based on the problem-solving plan. Managing anger is also essential to conflict resolution. When anger has a sexual aspect, such as with sexual harassment or date rape, specific strategies will help you avoid—or if necessary cope with—such situations.

How do you make the most of personal relationships?

Personal relationships are a significant part of your life—when they go well, they enhance your energy, and when they go wrong, they can derail your focus and concentration. To make the most of them, use positive relationship strategies such as investing time, working through tensions, taking risks, and finding patterns that suit you. It's also important to choose communities—groups, clubs, teams, and so forth—that enhance your life and promote positive activities.

BUILDING SKILLS
FOR SUCCESSFUL LEARNING

Name _____ Date _____

CRITICAL THINKING
APPLYING LEARNING TO LIFE

Diversity Discovery

Express your own personal diversity. Describe yourself in response to the following questions:

How would you identify yourself? Write words or short phrases that describe you.

_____
_____
_____
_____

Name one or more facts about yourself that would not be obvious to someone who just met you.

_____
_____
_____

Name two values or beliefs that govern how you live, what you pursue, or with whom you associate.

_____
_____
_____

Describe a particular choice you have made that tells something about who you are.

_____
_____
_____

Now, join with a partner in your class. Choose someone you don't know well. Your goal is to communicate what you have written to your partner and for your partner to communicate to you in the same way. Talk to each other for 10 minutes, and take notes on what the other person says. At the end of that period, join together as a class. Each person will describe his or her partner to the class.

Name something you learned about your partner that intrigued or even surprised you.

_____

_____

_____

What did you learn that went against any assumptions you may have made about that person?

_____

_____

_____

On your own time, reflect on how this exercise may have altered your perspective on yourself and others.

TEAM BUILDING
COLLABORATIVE SOLUTIONS

Problem Solving Close to Home

Divide into groups of two to five students. Assign one group member to take notes. Discuss the following questions, one at a time:

1. What are the three largest problems my school faces with regard to how people get along with and accept others?

2. What could my school do to deal with these three problems?

3. What can each individual student do to deal with these three problems? (Talk about what you specifically feel that you can do.)

When all groups have finished, gather as a class and hear each group's responses. Observe the variety of problems and solutions. Notice whether more than one group came up with one or more of the same problems. If there is time, one person in the class, together with your instructor, could gather these responses into an organized document that you can give to administrators at your school.

personal
IMPROVEMENT *plan*

I commit to three specific communication strategies to improve my interpersonal relationships.
From this chapter, I choose three strategies that I think will help me.

Strategy 1: _____

Strategy 2: _____

Strategy 3: _____

I choose one strategy to focus on (circle this strategy above) and I will:

- describe my goal—what I want to gain by using this strategy.

_____

_____

_____

- describe in detail how I plan to use the strategy.

_____

_____

_____

- describe how I will measure my progress toward the goal this semester.

_____

_____

_____

_____

Activate the Habit of Mind

Here's how I will *question and pose problems* to achieve this goal:

_____

_____

_____

_____

SUGGESTED READINGS

Bertholf, Stephen D. *What Every College Age Woman Should Know About Relationships*. Wichita, KS: Abbey House Books, 1999.

Blank, Rennee and Sandra Slipp. *Voices of Diversity: Real People Talk About Problems and Solutions in a Workplace Where Everyone Is Not Alike*. New York: American Management Association, 1994.

Dublin, Thomas, ed. *Becoming American, Becoming Ethnic: College Students Explore Their Roots*. Philadelphia: Temple University Press, 1996.

Feagin, Joe R., Hernan Vera, and Nikitah O. Imani. *The Agony of Education: Black Students at White Colleges and Universities*. New York: Routledge, 1996.

Gonzales, Juan L., Jr. *The Lives of Ethnic Americans, Second edition*. Dubuque, IA: Kendall/Hunt, 1994.

Hockenberry, John. *Moving Violations*. New York: Hyperion, 1996.

Levey, Marc, Michael Blanco, and W. Terrell Jones. *How to Succeed on a Majority Campus: A Guide for Minority Students*. Belmont, CA: Wadsworth Publishing Co., 1997.

Qubein, Nido R. *How to Be a Great Communicator: In Person, on Paper, and at the Podium*. New York: John Wiley, 1996.

Schuman, David and Dick W. Olufs. *Diversity on Campus*. Boston: Allyn & Bacon, 1994.

Suskind, Ron. *A Hope in the Unseen: An American Odyssey from the Inner City to the Ivy League*. New York: Broadway Books, 1998.

Takaki, Ronald. *A Different Mirror: A History of Multicultural America*. Boston: Little, Brown, and Company, 1994.

Tannen, Deborah. *You Just Don't Understand: Women and Men in Conversation*. New York: Ballantine Books, 1991.

Terkel, Studs. *Race: How Blacks and Whites Think and Feel About the American Obsession*. New York: Free Press, 1995.

Trotter, Tamera and Joycelyn Allen. *Talking Justice: 602 Ways to Build and Promote Racial Harmony*. Saratoga, FL: R & E Publishers, 1993.

INTERNET RESOURCES

Prentice Hall Student Success Supersite (success stories from students from a diversity of backgrounds): www.prenhall.com/success

Asian-American Resources: www.ai.mit.edu/people/irie/aar/

Britannica Guide to Black History: http://blackhistory.eb.com

Latino USA: www.latinousa.org

Latino Website Pathfinder: www.sscnet.ucla.edu.csrc/

The Sociology of Race and Ethnicity: www.trinity.edu/~mkearl/race.html

ENDNOTES

1. "For 7 Million, One Census Race Category Wasn't Enough," *The New York Times*, March 13, 2001, pp. A1 and A14.

2. Jodi Wilgoren, "Swell of Minority Students Is Predicted at Colleges," *The New York Times*, May 24, 2000, p. A16.

3. Sheryl McCarthy, *Why Are the Heroes Always White?* Kansas City, MO: Andrews and McMeel, 1995, p. 188.

4. "Campus Killings Fall, but Some Crimes Rise," *The New York Times*, January 21, 2001, p. A25.

5. Martin Luther King, Jr., from his sermon "A Tough Mind and a Tender Heart," *Strength in Love*. Philadelphia: Fortress Press, 1986, p. 14.

6. Sheryl McCarthy, *Why Are the Heroes Always White?*, p. 137.

7. Adapted by Richard Bucher, Professor of Sociology, Baltimore City Community College, from Paula Rothenberg, William Paterson College of New Jersey.

8. Claude Steele, Ph.D., Professor of Psychology, Stanford University.

9. Much of the information in this section is from Tina Kelley, "On Campuses, Warnings About Violence in Relationships," *The New York Times*, February 13, 2000, p. 40.

10. Ibid.

11. U.S. Department of Justice, Bureau of Justice Statistics, "Sex Offenses and Offenders," 1997, and "Criminal Victimization," 1994.

THINKING IT THROUGH

Check those statements that apply to you right now:

- ☐ Every time I think I've got my life under control, some new stressful situation comes up.

- ☐ I've thought about my attitudes toward drugs, alcohol, and tobacco and am comfortable with my choices.

- ☐ I know what I'm looking for when I date and have other close relationships.

- ☐ I'm unsure of what kind of career I want to have after college.

- ☐ I want to have more control over where my money goes every month.

- ☐ I'm not sure what I want to accomplish in life; I don't have a big-picture mission.

Wellness, Career, and Money

BUILDING SKILLS FOR LIFE SUCCESS

Staying open to continuous learning.

"Intelligent people are in a **continuous learning mode**. Their confidence, in combination with their inquisitiveness, allows them to constantly search for new and better ways. . . . They seize problems, situations, tensions, conflicts, and circumstances as valuable opportunities to learn."

—ART COSTA

*Your wellness, your career, your finances, and your overarching life goals are all subject to constant change. If you **continue to learn and to seek improvement**, you will be better able to stay on top of the changes that happen and to use them to craft the life you dream of.*

IN THIS CHAPTER

In this chapter you explore answers to the following questions:

■ How do you manage stress?

■ How can you make smart decisions about substances and sex?

■ How can you prepare for a successful career?

■ How can you create a budget that works?

■ How can you live your mission?

As you come to the end of your work in this course, you have built up a wealth of knowledge. You are facing important decisions about what direction you want your education to take and how you can find a place at school and in the world.

This chapter rounds out your student success experience by focusing on life skills—managing stress, maintaining wellness, preparing for a career, and budgeting your money. Staying on top of these skills promotes school success, because if you manage your personal needs effectively, you will have energy to devote to academics. You will look at the big picture of these important life skills, seeing how they fit into the framework of your personal mission.

How do you manage stress?

If you are feeling more stress in your everyday life as a student, you are not alone.[1] Stress levels among college students have increased dramatically, according to an annual survey conducted at the University of California at Los Angeles. More than 30 percent of the freshmen polled at 683 two- and four-year colleges and universities nationwide reported that they frequently felt overwhelmed, almost double the rate in 1985. Stress factors for college students include being in a new environment; facing increased work and difficult decisions; and juggling school, work, and personal responsibilities.

Stress refers to the way in which your mind and body react to pressure—that is, increased workloads (a week of final exams), excitement (being a finalist for the lead in a play), change (new school, new courses), time pressure (spending 20 hours a week working and finding the time to study), illness (having a head cold that wipes you out for a week), or happiness (getting an A in a course when you expected a C). Even positive changes can create some level of stress.

At their worst, stress reactions can make you physically ill. But stress can also supply the heightened readiness you need to do well on tests, finish assignments on time, prepare for a class presentation, or meet new people. Your goal is to find a manageable balance. Figure 12.1, based on research conducted by Drs. Robert M. Yerkes and John E. Dodson, shows that stress can be helpful or harmful, depending on how much you experience.

Stress Management Strategies

Stress is a normal part of life. The following strategies will help you avoid overload.

- *Eat right.* A healthy body will help you deal with stress. Work toward eating a balanced, low-fat diet and try to avoid overloading on junk food. Try also to maintain a weight that is healthful for you.

Soccer and other types of exercise provide stress relief along with the workout.

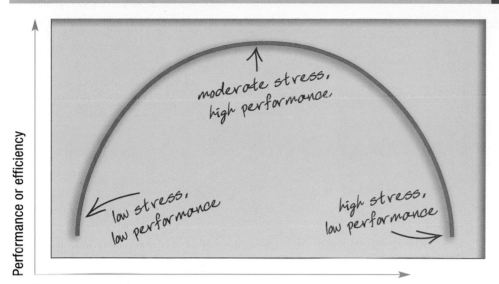

Yerkes-Dodson law: Stress levels affect performance.   FIGURE 12.1

Source: From *Your Maximum Mind* by Herbert Benson, M.D., Copyright © 1987 by Random House, Inc. Used by permission of Time Books, a division of Random House, Inc.

- *Exercise.* Any kind of workout will help you blow off steam. Find a type of exercise you like and make it a regular part of your life.
- *Get sleep.* Avoid the system-wide dysfunction that sleep deprivation can create. Figure out how much sleep you need and do your best to get it.
- *Learn the power of positive thinking.* Try to think of all you have to do as challenges, not problems.
- *Seek balance.* A balanced life includes time by yourself—for your thoughts, hopes, and plans—and time for relaxation, in whatever form you choose.
- *Address issues specifically.* Think through stressful situations and use problem-solving strategies to decide on a specific plan of action.
- *Develop a schedule, and then stick to it.* Use the techniques you learned in Chapter 3 to schedule your tasks effectively and to avoid procrastination.
- *Set reasonable goals.* Goals seem more manageable when approached as a series of small steps.
- *Set boundaries and learn to say no.* Instead of taking responsibility for everyone and everything, try to delegate. Review obligations regularly and consider letting go of activities that have become burdens.
- *Surround yourself with people who are good for you.* Focus on friends who are good listeners and who will support you when things get rough.

Feeling overwhelmed by stress is sometimes related to mental health problems such as depression and eating disorders. It is important to recognize these problems and get help if you need it.

MULTIPLE PATHWAYS TO LEARNING

MULTIPLE INTELLIGENCE STRATEGIES *for* Stress Management

Everyone handles stress differently—the strategies linked to your stronger intelligences can help you improve your coping skills.

INTELLIGENCE	SUGGESTED STRATEGIES	WHAT WORKS FOR YOU? WRITE NEW IDEAS HERE
Verbal–Linguistic	■ Keep a journal of what makes you stressed. ■ Make time to write letters, e-mail friends, or talk with them.	
Logical–Mathematical	■ Think through problems critically using a problem-solving process and devise a plan. ■ Identify possible positive effects that may result from the stress.	
Bodily–Kinesthetic	■ Choose a physical activity that helps you release tension—running, yoga, team sports—and do it regularly. ■ Plan fun physical activities for your free time—go for a hike, take a bike ride, go dancing with friends.	
Visual–Spatial	■ Take as much time as you can to enjoy beautiful things—art, nature, and so forth. Visit an exhibit, see an art film, shoot a roll of film with your camera. ■ Use a visual organizer to plan out a solution to a stressful problem.	
Interpersonal	■ Spend time with people who care about you and are very supportive. ■ Practice being a good listener to others who are stressed.	
Intrapersonal	■ Schedule down time when you can think through what is stressing you. ■ Allow yourself five minutes a day for visualizing a positive way in which you want a stressful situation to evolve.	
Musical	■ Play music that "feeds your soul." ■ Write a song about what stresses you out—or about anything that transports your mind.	
Naturalistic	■ Spend as much time as possible in your most soothing places in nature. ■ Listen to tapes of outdoor sounds to help you relax.	

Beyond Stress: Recognizing Mental Health Problems

Emotional disorders limit the ability to enjoy life and to cope with its ups and downs. They affect people in all walks of life.

Depression. A depressive disorder, an illness that requires a medical evaluation, is treatable. Symptoms include constant sadness or anxiety, loss of interest in activities that you normally like, eating too much or too little, and low self-esteem. Depression can have a genetic, psychological, physiological, or environmental cause, or a combination of causes.

Anorexia nervosa. This condition, occurring mainly in young women, creates an intense desire to be thin. People with anorexia become dangerously thin through restricting food intake, constant exercise, and use of laxatives, all the time believing they are overweight. An estimated 5 to 7 percent of college undergraduates in the United States suffer from anorexia.[2] Effects of anorexia-induced starvation include loss of menstrual periods in women, impotence in men, organ damage, heart failure, and death.

Bulimia. People who binge on excessive amounts of food, usually sweets and fattening foods, and then purge through self-induced vomiting have bulimia. They may also use laxatives or exercise obsessively. Effects of bulimia include damage to the digestive tract and even heart failure due to the loss of important minerals.

reflect

Think about the positive effects of stress. Describe a situation in your life where you benefited from the heightened awareness and energy that often accompany high stress levels. How can you hit that just-right stress level again and use it to your advantage? How can you channel stress into a positive force to help you prepare for tests?

& respond

"To keep the body in good health is a duty. . . . Otherwise we shall not be able to keep our mind strong and clear."

BUDDHA

Binge eating. Like bulimics, people with binge eating disorder eat large amounts of food and have a hard time stopping. However, they do not purge afterward. Binge eaters are often overweight and feel unable to control their eating. Binge eaters may suffer from health problems associated with obesity.

Most student health centers and campus counseling centers can provide both medical and psychological help for students with depression or eating disorders. Treatment may involve psychotherapy, drug therapy, and even hospitalization or residence in a treatment center.

Situations involving substances or sex are sources of stress for many college students. The following will help you make decisions that are right for you.

How can you make smart decisions about substances and sex?

You are responsible for the choices you make regarding alcohol, tobacco, drugs, and sexual practices. Think critically, carefully considering the potential positive and negative effects of your actions.

Alcohol

Binge drinking
Having five or more drinks at one sitting.

Alcohol is a drug as much as it is a beverage. Of all alcohol consumption, **binge drinking** is associated with the greatest problems. Here are statistics from a recent survey of college students:[3]

- Forty-three percent of the students surveyed said they are binge drinkers, and 21 percent said that they binge drink frequently.
- Of surveyed students who do not binge drink, 80 percent reported experiencing one or more secondhand effects of binge drinking (e.g., vandalism, sexual assault or unwanted sexual advances, interrupted sleep or study).[4]
- Students who binge drink are more likely to miss classes, be less able to work, have hangovers, become depressed, engage in unplanned sexual activity, and ignore safe sex practices.[5]

The bottom line is that heavy drinking causes severe problems. The National Institute on Alcohol Abuse and Alcoholism (NIAAA) estimates that alcohol contributes to the deaths of 100,000 people every year through both alcohol-related illnesses and accidents involving drunk drivers.[6] Heavy drinking can damage the liver, the digestive system, and brain and nervous system. Prolonged use also leads to **addiction**, making it seem impossible to quit.

Addiction
Compulsive physiological need for a habit-forming substance.

Tobacco

College students do their share of smoking. The National Institute on Drug Abuse (NIDA) found that 38.8 percent of college students reported smoking at least once in the year before they were surveyed, and 24.5 percent had smoked once within the month before.[7]

When people smoke they inhale nicotine, a highly addictive drug found in all tobacco products. Nicotine's immediate effects may include an increase in blood pressure and heart rate, sweating, and throat irritation. Long-term effects may include high blood pressure, bronchitis, emphysema, stomach ulcers, and heart conditions. Pregnant women who smoke increase their risk of having infants with low birth weight, premature births, or stillbirths.

Quitting smoking is difficult and should be attempted gradually and, if possible, with the support of friends and family. However, the positive effects of quitting—increased life expectancy, greater lung capacity, and more energy—may inspire any smoker to consider making a lifestyle change. Weigh your options and make a responsible choice.

Drugs

The NIDA reports that 31.4 percent of college students had used illicit drugs at least once in the year before being surveyed, and 16 percent in the month before.[8] Drug use can have numerous negative effects, including damage to body and mind, relationships with people who accept you for your drug use and not for who you are, and problems and responsibilities that multiply when you emerge from a high. Furthermore, drug use violates the law; you can jeopardize your reputation, your student status, and your employment possibilities if you are caught using drugs or if drug use impairs your school performance. Table 12.1 shows commonly used drugs and their potential effects.

One drug that doesn't fit cleanly into a particular category is MDMA, better known as Ecstasy. The use of this drug, a combination stimulant and hallucinogenic, is on the rise at college parties, raves, and concerts. Its immediate effects include diminished anxiety and relaxation. When the drug wears off, nausea, hallucinations, shaking, vision problems, anxiety, and depression replace these highs. Long-term users risk permanent brain damage in the form of memory loss, chronic depression, and other disorders.[9]

You are responsible for what you introduce into your body. Read about individual drugs and their effects. Ask yourself: Why do I want to do this? What positive and negative effects might it have? Why do others want me to take drugs? How would drug use affect the people in my life? The more critical analysis you do, the more likely you will make choices that are in your own best interest.

Facing Addiction

If you think you may be addicted to alcohol or drugs, realize that you are the only one who can take the initiative to change. Because substances often cause physical and chemical changes, quitting may involve guiding your body through a painful withdrawal. Many resources can help along the way.

Counseling and medical care. Help is available from school-based, private, government-sponsored, or workplace-sponsored resources. Ask your school's counseling or health center, your personal physician, or a local hospital for a referral.

Detoxification ("detox") centers. If you have a severe addiction, you may need a controlled environment in which to separate yourself completely from drugs or alcohol.

Support groups. You can derive help and comfort from sharing your experiences with others. Alcoholics Anonymous (AA) is the premier support group for alcoholics.

TABLE 12.1 How drugs affect you.

DRUG CATEGORY	DRUG TYPES	HOW THEY MAKE YOU FEEL	PHYSICAL EFFECTS	DANGER OF PHYSICAL DEPENDENCE	DANGER OF PSYCHOLOGICAL DEPENDENCE
Stimulants	Cocaine, amphetamines	Alert, stimulated, excited	Nervousness, mood swings, stroke or convulsions, psychoses, paranoia, coma at large doses	Relatively strong	Strong
Depressants	Alcohol, Valium-type drugs	Sedated, tired, high	Cirrhosis; impaired blood production; greater risk of cancer, heart attack, and stroke; impaired brain function	Strong	Strong
Opiates	Heroin, codeine, other pain pills	Drowsy, floating, without pain	Infection of organs, inflammation of the heart, hepatitis	Yes, with high dosage	Yes, with high dosage
Cannabinols	Marijuana, hashish	Euphoria, mellowness, little sensation of time	Impairment of judgment and coordination, bronchitis and asthma, lung and throat cancers, anxiety, lack of energy and motivation, reduced ability to produce hormones	Moderate	Relatively strong
Hallucinogens	LSD, mushrooms	Heightened sensual perception, hallucinations, confusion	Impairment of brain function, circulatory problems, agitation and confusion, flashbacks	Insubstantial	Insubstantial
Inhalants	Glue, aerosols	Giddiness, lightheadedness	Damage to brain, heart, liver, and kidneys	Insubstantial	Insubstantial

Source: Compiled and adapted from *Educating Yourself About Alcohol and Drugs: A People's Primer* by Marc Alan Schuckit, M.D., Plenum Press, 1995.

TAKE ACTION

Even one "yes" answer may indicate a need to evaluate your substance use. Answering "yes" to three or more questions indicates that you may benefit from discussing your use with a counselor.

WITHIN THE LAST YEAR:

Ⓨ Ⓝ 1. Have you tried to stop drinking or taking drugs but found that you couldn't do so for long?

Ⓨ Ⓝ 2. Do you get tired of people telling you they're concerned about your drinking or drug use?

Ⓨ Ⓝ 3. Have you felt guilty about your drinking or drug use?

Ⓨ Ⓝ 4. Have you felt that you needed a drink or drugs in the morning—as an "eye-opener"—in order to improve a hangover?

Ⓨ Ⓝ 5. Do you drink or use drugs alone?

Ⓨ Ⓝ 6. Do you drink or use drugs every day?

Ⓨ Ⓝ 7. Have you found yourself regularly thinking or saying, "I need" a drink or any type of drug?

Ⓨ Ⓝ 8. Have you lied about or concealed your drinking or drug use?

Ⓨ Ⓝ 9. Do you drink or use drugs to escape worries, problems, mistakes, or shyness?

Ⓨ Ⓝ 10. Do you find you need increasingly larger amounts of drugs or alcohol in order to achieve a desired effect?

Ⓨ Ⓝ 11. Have you forgotten what happened while drinking or using drugs (had a blackout)?

Ⓨ Ⓝ 12. Have you been surprised by how much you were using alcohol or drugs?

Ⓨ Ⓝ 13. Have you spent a lot of time, energy, or money getting alcohol or drugs?

Ⓨ Ⓝ 14. Has your drinking or drug use caused you to neglect friends, your partner, your children, or other family members, or caused other problems at home?

Ⓨ Ⓝ 15. Have you gotten into an argument or a fight that was alcohol- or drug-related?

Ⓨ Ⓝ 16. Has your drinking or drug use caused you to miss class, fail a test, or ignore schoolwork?

Ⓨ Ⓝ 17. Have you rejected planned social events in favor of drinking or using drugs?

Ⓨ Ⓝ 18. Have you been choosing to drink or use drugs instead of performing other activities or hobbies you used to enjoy?

Ⓨ Ⓝ 19. Has your drinking or drug use affected your efficiency on the job or caused you to fail to show up at work?

Ⓨ Ⓝ 20. Have you continued to drink or use drugs despite any physical problems or health risks that your use has caused or made worse?

Ⓨ Ⓝ 21. Have you driven a car or performed any other potentially dangerous tasks while under the influence of alcohol or drugs?

Ⓨ Ⓝ 22. Have you had a drug- or alcohol-related legal problem or arrest (possession, use, disorderly conduct, driving while intoxicated, etc.)?

Source: Compiled and adapted from the Criteria for Substance Dependence and Criteria for Substance Abuse in the *Diagnostic and Statistical Manual of Mental Disorders,* Fourth edition, published by the American Psychiatric Association, Washington, D.C., and from materials entitled "Are You An Alcoholic?" developed by Johns Hopkins University.

Sex and Critical Thinking

What sexuality means to you and the role it plays in your life are your own business. However, individual sexual conduct can have consequences such as unexpected pregnancy and the transmission of sexually transmitted diseases (STDs). These consequences affect everyone involved in the sexual act and, often, their families. Think critically about sexual issues, and make choices that maintain your health and safety as well as that of others involved.

Birth Control

Using birth control is a choice, and it is not for everyone. If you do choose to use it, evaluate cost, ease of use, reliability, comfort, and protection against STDs, and with your partner make a choice that is comfortable for both of you. For more information, check your library or the Internet, talk to your doctor, or ask a counselor.

Table 12.2 describes some of the most established methods and gives effectiveness percentages and STD prevention based on proper and regular use.

Sexually Transmitted Diseases

Sexually transmitted diseases spread through sexual contact (intercourse or other sexual activity that involves contact with the genitals). All are highly contagious. The only birth control methods that offer protection are the male and female condoms (latex or polyurethane only), which prevent skin-to-skin contact. Most STDs can also spread to infants of infected mothers during birth. Have a doctor examine any irregularity or discomfort as soon as you detect it. Table 12.3 describes common STDs.

The most serious of the STDs is AIDS (acquired immune deficiency syndrome), which is caused by the human immunodeficiency virus (HIV). Not everyone who tests positive for HIV will develop AIDS, but AIDS has no cure and results in eventual death. Medical science continues to develop drugs to combat AIDS and its related illnesses. However, the drugs can cause severe side effects, many have not been throughly tested, and none are cures.

HIV is transmitted through two types of bodily fluids: fluids associated with sex (semen and vaginal fluids) and blood. People have acquired HIV through sexual relations, by sharing hypodermic needles for drug use, and by receiving infected blood transfusions. You cannot become infected unless one of those fluids is involved. Therefore, it is unlikely you can contract HIV from toilet seats, hugging, kissing, or sharing a glass. Other than not having sex at all, a latex condom is the best defense against AIDS. Although some people dislike using condoms, it's a small price for preserving your life.

reflect

Describe how you feel about addiction in any form—to alcohol, drugs, food, a person, the Internet, gambling. How has it touched your life, if at all? How did you deal with it? If you have never faced an addiction or been close to someone who did, describe how you think you would face it if it ever happened to you.

Companion Website

& respond

TABLE 12.2		Methods of birth control.	
METHOD	**APPROXIMATE EFFECTIVENESS**	**PREVENTS STDs?**	**DESCRIPTION**
Abstinence	100%	Only if no sexual activity occurs	Just saying no. No intercourse means no risk of pregnancy. However, alternative modes of sexual activity can still spread STDs.
Condom (male)	94%	Yes, if made of latex	A sheath that fits over the penis and prevents sperm from entering the vagina.
Diaphragm or cervical cap	85%	No	A bendable rubber cap that fits over the cervix and pelvic bone inside the vagina (the cervical cap is smaller and fits over the cervix only). Both must be fitted initially by a gynecologist and used with a spermicide.
Oral contraceptives (the pill)	97%	No	A dosage of hormones taken daily by a woman, preventing the ovaries from releasing eggs. Side effects can include headaches, weight gain, and increased chances of blood clotting. Various brands and dosages; must be prescribed by a gynecologist.
Spermicidal foams, jellies, inserts	84% if used alone	No	Usually used with diaphragms or condoms to enhance effectiveness, they have an ingredient that kills sperm cells (but not STDs). They stay effective for a limited period of time after insertion.
Intrauterine device (IUD)	94%	No	A small coil of wire inserted into the uterus by a gynecologist (who must also remove it). Prevents fertilized eggs from implanting in the uterine wall. Possible side effects include bleeding.
Rhythm method	Variable	No	Abstaining from intercourse during the ovulation segment of the woman's menstrual cycle. Can be difficult to time and may not account for cycle irregularities.
Withdrawal	Variable	No	Pulling the penis out of the vagina before ejaculation. Unreliable, because some sperm can escape in the fluid released prior to ejaculation. Dependent on a controlled partner.

To be safe, have an HIV test done at your doctor's office or at a government-sponsored clinic. Your school's health department may also administer HIV tests, and home HIV tests are available over the counter. If you are infected, first inform all sexual partners and seek medical assistance. Then, contact support organizations in your area or call the National AIDS Hotline at 1-800-342-AIDS.

As you consider how to implement the stress management and health strategies in this chapter, remember that one of the primary goals of managing your wellness is to maximize the energy you put toward your education. Being worn down physically makes it hard to focus on your work.

TABLE 12.3　Sexually transmitted diseases.

DISEASE	SYMPTOMS	HEALTH PROBLEMS IF UNTREATED	TREATMENTS
Chlamydia	Discharge, painful urination, swollen or painful joints, change in menstrual periods for women	Can cause pelvic inflammatory disease (PID) in women, which can lead to sterility or ectopic pregnancies; infections; miscarriage or premature birth.	Curable with full course of antibiotics; avoid sex until treatment is complete.
Gonorrhea	Discharge, burning while urinating	Can cause PID, swelling of testicles and penis, arthritis, skin problems, infections.	Usually curable with antibiotics; however, certain strains are becoming resistant to medication.
Genital herpes	Blisterlike itchy sores in the genital area, headache, fever, chills	Symptoms may subside and then reoccur, often in response to high stress levels; carriers can transmit the virus even when it is dormant.	No cure; some medications, such as Acyclovir, reduce and help heal the sores and may shorten recurring outbreaks.
Syphilis	A genital sore lasting one to five weeks, followed by a rash, fatigue, fever, sore throat, headaches, swollen glands	If it lasts over four years, it can cause blindness, destruction of bone, insanity, or heart failure; can cause death or deformity of a child born to an infected woman.	Curable with full course of antibiotics.
Human papilloma virus (HPV, or genital warts)	Genital itching and irritation, small clusters of warts	Can increase risk of cervical cancer in women; virus may remain in body and cause recurrences even when warts are removed.	Treatable with drugs applied to warts or various kinds of wart removal surgery.
Hepatitis B	Fatigue, poor appetite, vomiting, jaundice, hives	Some carriers will have few symptoms; others may develop chronic liver disease that may lead to other diseases of the liver.	No cure; some will recover, others will not. Bed rest may help ease symptoms. Vaccine is available.

Conversely, staying strong and healthy helps power your drive toward success in school and other goals.

As wellness prepares you for successful learning, learning prepares you for a successful career. Because career readiness is one of the most important reasons for getting a college education, you will be wise to spend some time thinking about your career goals and preparing for your future in the workplace.

How can you prepare for a successful career?

Every skill that promotes academic success also contributes to workplace success. For example, critical thinking, teamwork, and writing skills all prepare you to thrive in any career. Use the following strategies to start getting more specific in your preparation for career success.

Investigate Career Paths

The working world changes all the time. You can get a good idea of what's out there—and what you think of it all—by exploring potential careers and building knowledge and experience.

Explore potential careers. A wide array of job possibilities exists for most career fields, and within each job there is a variety of tasks and skills. Brainstorm about career areas. Check your library for books on careers or biographies of people who worked in fields that interest you. Ask instructors, relatives, mentors, and fellow students about careers they are familiar with. Look at Table 12.4 for some of the kinds of questions you might ask as you talk to people or investigate materials.

Build knowledge and experience. Having specific knowledge and experience is valuable on the job hunt. Courses, internships, jobs, and volunteering are four great ways to build both.

- *Courses.* Take a course or two in your areas of interest to see how you react to them. Find out what courses you have to take to major in the field.

TABLE 12.4	Critical-thinking questions for career exploration.
What can I do in this area that I like and do well?	Do I respect the company or the industry? The product or service?
What are the educational requirements (certificates or degrees, courses)?	Does this company or industry accommodate special needs (child care, sick days, flex time)?
What skills are necessary?	Do I have to belong to a union?
What wage or salary and benefits can I expect?	Are there opportunities near where I live (or want to live)?
What kinds of personalities are best suited to this kind of work?	What other expectations exist (travel, overtime, etc.)?
What are the prospects for moving up to higher-level positions?	Do I prefer the service or production end of this industry?

Internship

A temporary work program in which a student can gain supervised practical experience in a particular professional field.

- *Internships.* An **internship** is a great way to gain real-world experience. Your career center may be able to help you explore internship opportunities.
- *Jobs.* No matter what you do to earn money while in college, you may discover career opportunities. Someone who answers phones for a newspaper, for example, might be drawn into journalism.
- *Volunteering.* Offering your services to others in need can introduce you to careers and increase your experience. Many employers look favorably on volunteering.

Know What Employers Want

When you look for a job in a particular career area, your technical skills, work experience, and academic credentials that apply to that career are important. Beyond those basics, though, other skills and qualities make you an excellent job candidate in any career. Table 12.5 describes these skills.

Stay Current

The working world is always in flux. Stay on top of two issues: growing and declining career areas and workplace trends.

Growing and declining career areas. Rapid workplace change means that a growth area today may be declining tomorrow—witness the sudden drop in Internet company jobs and fortunes in 2001. The U.S. Bureau of Labor projects that the five fastest growing occupations from 1998–2008 will be computer engineer, computer support specialist, systems analyst, database administrator, and desktop publishing specialist—all computer-related occupations.[10] You can keep tabs on these statistics by checking the *Occupational Outlook Handbook*, published by the Bureau of Labor every two years. Find it in your library or look up highlights on the Internet at http://stats.bls.gov/ocohome.htm.

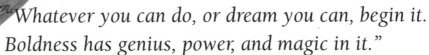

"Whatever you can do, or dream you can, begin it. Boldness has genius, power, and magic in it."

JOHANN WOLFGANG VON GOETHE

Workplace trends. Here are two ways in which companies are responding to workplace change and economic stress:

- *More temporary employment.* The number of temps increased from 800,000 in 1986 to more than 2.5 million in 1997.[11] Temporary jobs offer flexibility and few obligations, but have limited fringe benefits.
- *New variety in benefits.* Companies are offering benefits such as telecommuting (working from home), job sharing (two employees sharing the duties of one full-time job), and on-site child care.

TABLE 12.5	Skills employers seek.

SKILLS	WHY
Communication	Both good listening and effective communicating are keys to workplace success, as is being able to adjust to different communication styles.
Critical thinking	An employee who can assess workplace choices and challenges critically and recommend appropriate actions stands out.
Teamwork	All workers interact with others on the job. Working well with others is essential for achieving work goals.
Goal setting	Teams fail if goals are unclear or unreasonable. Setting realistic, specific goals and achieving them reliably benefits both you and the employer.
Acceptance	The workplace is becoming increasingly diverse. A valuable employee is able to work with and respect all kinds of people.
Leadership	The ability to influence others in a positive way earns you respect and helps advance your career.
Creativity	The ability to come up with new concepts, plans, and products is valuable in the workplace.
Positive attitude	If you show that you have a high level of commitment to all tasks, you may earn the right to tackle more challenging projects.
Integrity	Acting with integrity at work—communicating promptly, being truthful and honest, following rules, giving proper notice, respecting others—enhances your value.
Flexibility	The most valuable employees understand the constancy of change and have developed the skills to adapt to its challenge.
Continual learning	The most valuable employees stay current on changes and trends by reading up-to-the-minute media and taking workshops and seminars.
Emotional intelligence	This includes *personal competence* (self-knowledge, motivation, the ability to control impulses) and *social competence* (social skills plus awareness of the feelings, needs, and concerns of others).[12]

Staying informed about workplace developments will help you handle job change when it happens. If you think creatively about your marketable skills and job possibilities, you will be able to find new ways to achieve when one job or career does not work out.

Consider Your Learning Style

Your Personality Spectrum assessment results from Chapter 2 are significant to career planning because they provide insight on how you work best with others. Succeeding in your search and in your chosen job depends, in large part, on your ability to communicate and function in a team.

Table 12.6 focuses the four dimensions of the Personality Spectrum on career ideas and strategies. Remember to use this information as a guide, not

TABLE 12.6	Personality Spectrum in the working world.

DIMENSION	STRENGTHS ON THE JOB	CHALLENGES ON THE JOB	LOOK FOR JOBS/CAREERS THAT FEATURE . . .
Thinker	■ Problem solving ■ Development of ideas ■ Keen analysis of situations ■ Fairness to others ■ Efficiency in working through tasks ■ Innovation of plans and systems ■ Ability to look strategically at the future	■ A need for private time to think and work ■ A need, at times, to move away from established rules ■ A dislike of sameness—systems that don't change repetitive tasks ■ Not always open to expressing thoughts and feelings to others	■ Some level of solo work/think time ■ Problem solving ■ Opportunity for innovation ■ Freedom to think creatively and to bend the rules ■ Technical work ■ Big-picture strategic planning
Organizer	■ High level of responsibility ■ Enthusiastic support of social structures ■ Order and reliability ■ Loyalty ■ Ability to follow through on tasks according to requirements ■ Detailed planning skills with competent follow-through ■ Neatness and efficiency	■ A need for tasks to be clearly, concretely defined ■ A need for structure and stability ■ A preference for less rapid change ■ A need for frequent feedback ■ A need for tangible appreciation ■ Low tolerance for people who don't conform to rules and regulations	■ Clear, well-laid-out tasks and plans ■ Stable environment with consistent, repeated tasks ■ Organized supervisors ■ Clear structure of how employees interact and report to one another ■ Value of, and reward for, loyalty
Giver	■ Honesty and integrity ■ Commitment to putting energy toward close relationships with others ■ Finding ways to bring out the best in self and others ■ Peacemaking and mediating ■ Ability to listen well, respect opinions, and prioritize the needs of coworkers	■ Difficulty in handling conflict, either personal or between others in the work environment ■ Strong need for appreciation and praise ■ Low tolerance for perceived dishonesty or deception ■ Avoidance of people perceived as hostile, cold, or indifferent	■ Emphasis on teamwork and relationship building ■ Indications of strong and open lines of communication among workers ■ Encouragement of personal expression in the workplace (arrangement of personal space, tolerance of personal celebrations, and so on)
Adventurer	■ Skill in many different areas ■ Willingness to try new things ■ Ability to take action ■ Hands-on problem-solving skills ■ Initiative and energy ■ Ability to negotiate ■ Spontaneity and creativity	■ Intolerance of being kept waiting ■ Lack of detail focus ■ Impulsiveness ■ Dislike of sameness and authority ■ Need for freedom, constant change, and constant action ■ Tendency not to consider consequences of actions	■ A spontaneous atmosphere ■ Less structure, more freedom ■ Adventuresome tasks ■ Situations involving change ■ Encouragement of hands-on problem solving ■ Travel and physical activity ■ Support of creative ideas and endeavors

a label. Take these ideas about your strengths and challenges as a starting point as you consider potential careers.

When you get to the job search, what you know—along with the strategies that follow—will help you along the path to a career that works for you.

Searching for a Job—and a Career

Maximize your opportunities by using the resources available to you and being strategic about the process. The information in this section will help you right away if you are one of the many who want or need to work while in school. In the school year 1995–96, 79 percent of undergraduates—four out of five—reported working while in school.[13] Figure 12.2 shows statistics related to working for both community college and four-year college students.

Use Available Resources

The following resources can help you explore possibilities both for jobs you need right away and for postgraduation career opportunities.

Your school's career planning and placement office. Generally, the career planning and placement office deals with postgraduation job placements, whereas the student employment office, along with the financial aid office, has more information about working while in school. At either location you might find job listings, occupation lists, assessments of skills and personality types, sign-up sheets for interviews, and contact information for companies. The career office may hold frequent informational sessions on different topics. Your school may also sponsor job or career fairs that give you a chance to explore job opportunities. Visit the center early in your college career and work with a counselor there to develop a solid career game plan.

Networking. Networking is one of the most important job-hunting strategies. With each person you get to know, you build your network and tap into someone else's. Networking **contacts**—including friends, instructors, coworkers, employers, alumni, and more—may be willing to answer your questions regarding job hunting, challenges and tasks of their jobs, and salary expectations.

Classified ads. Some of the best job listings are in newspapers. Individual ads describe the kind of position available and give a telephone number or post office box for you to contact. Some ads include additional information such as job requirements, a contact person, and the salary or wages offered.

On-line services. The Internet has exploded into one of the most fruitful sources of job listings. There are many different ways to hunt for a job on the web:

- Look up career-focused and job listing websites such as CareerBuilder.com,

Networking
The exchange of information or services among individuals, groups, or institutions.

Contact
A person who serves as a carrier or source of information.

Using job-hunting resources wisely will help you get to the interview stage—your chance to make a good impression.

FIGURE 12.2   Working students.

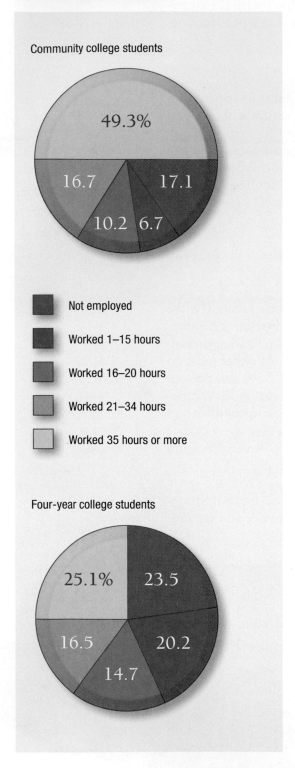

Community college students

49.3%

16.7   17.1

10.2   6.7

- Not employed
- Worked 1–15 hours
- Worked 16–20 hours
- Worked 21–34 hours
- Worked 35 hours or more

Four-year college students

25.1%   23.5

16.5   20.2

14.7

Source: U.S. Department of Education, National Center for Educational Statistics, *Profile of Undergraduates in U.S. Postsecondary Education Institutions: 1995–1996* (NCES 98–084), May, 1998.

CareerMosaic, Monster.com, hotjobs.com, JobsOnline, or futurestep.com.

- Access job search databases such as the Career Placement Registry and U.S. Employment Opportunities.
- Check the web pages of individual associations and companies, many of which post job listings.

Employment agencies. Employment agencies are organizations that help people find full-time, part-time, or temporary work. Most employment agencies put you through a screening process. If you pass the tests and interview well, the agency tries to place you in a job. Most employment agencies specialize in particular careers or skills such as computer operation, child care, or food services.

Be Strategic

After you've gathered enough information to narrow your career goals, plan out how to achieve them.

See the big picture. Make a career time line that illustrates the steps toward your goal, as shown in Figure 12.3. Mark years and half-year points (and months for the first year), and write in the steps when you think they should happen. Using what you know about strategic planning, fill in the details about what you will do throughout your plan. Set goals that establish who you will talk to, what courses you will take, what skills you will work on, and what jobs or internships you will investigate. Your path may change, of course; use your time line as a guide rather than as an inflexible plan.

Keep track of details. After you establish your time frame, make a plan for pursuing particular jobs or careers, organizing your approach according to what you need to do and how much time you have. Do you plan to make three phone calls per day? Will

Career time line.   FIGURE **12.3**

1 month	Enter community college on a part-time schedule
6 months	Meet with advisor to discuss desired major and required courses
1 year	
	Declare major in secondary education
2 years	Switch to full-time class schedule
3 years	Graduate with associate's degree
	Transfer to 4-year college
4 years	Work part-time as a classroom aide
5 years	Student teaching
	Graduate with bachelor's degree and teaching certificate
6 years	Have a job teaching high school

you fill out three job applications a week for a month? Keep a record—on 3 × 5 cards, in a computer file, or in a notebook—of people you contact, companies to which you apply, jobs you rule out, and responses to your communications. Figure 12.4 illustrates a sample file card.

Compile an effective resume. Your resume should always be typed or printed on a computer. Design your resume neatly, using an acceptable format (books or your career office can show you some standard formats). Proofread it for errors, and have someone else proofread it as well. Type or print it on a heavier bond paper than is used for ordinary copies. Use white or off-white paper and black ink.

Interview well. Be clean, neat, and appropriately dressed. Choose a nice pair of shoes—people notice. Bring an extra copy of your resume and any other materials that you want to show the interviewer. Avoid chewing gum

| FIGURE 12.4 | Sample file card. |

Job/company: Child-care worker at Morningside Day Care

Contact: Sally Wheeler, Morningside Day Care,
                    17 Parkside Rd, Silver Spring, MD 20910

Phone/fax/e-mail: (301) 555-3353 phone, (301) 555-3354 fax,
                    no e-mail

Communication: Saw ad in paper, sent résumé & cover letter on Oct. 7

Response: Call from Sally to set up interview
             —Interview on Oct. 15 at 2 p.m., seemed to get a positive
             response, said she would contact me again by end of the week

Follow-up: Sent thank-you note on Oct. 16

or smoking. Offer a confident handshake. Make eye contact. Show your integrity by speaking honestly about yourself. After the interview is over, no matter what the outcome, send a formal but pleasant thank-you note right away as a follow-up.

Examining career goals and readiness leads logically to thinking about money, since one of the primary goals of workplace success is earning what you need to live comfortably. Whether or not you are currently a member of the workplace, budgeting carefully will help you to maximize your financial resources and to keep some options open if you should experience a sudden dip in income.

How can you create a budget that works?

Budgeting

Making a plan for the coordination of resources and expenditures; setting goals regarding money.

Budgeting your money is a process that considers your resources (money flowing in) and expenditures (money flowing out) and adjusts the flow so that you come out even or perhaps even ahead. Being able to budget effectively relieves money-related stress and helps you feel more in control. Your biggest expense right now is probably the cost of your education. However, that expense may not hit you fully until after you graduate and begin to pay back your student loans. For now, include in your budget only the part of the cost of your education you are paying while you are in school.

TAKE ACTION

Think About Careers

Use the sources available to you to develop a "snapshot" of a particular career area. First, name a career area that interests you: _____

Name one or more majors that would suit this career area: *Computer engineering*

_____

Name any friends or family members who could fill you in on the details of this career area:

my father – engineering of electricity.

Name any instructors or administrators who would be good resources for this career area:

_____

Find two help-wanted listings for this career area, from newspapers or the Internet, that look interesting to you. Briefly describe the jobs offered:

1. _____

2. _____

Finally, list any additional helpful contacts at your student employment office or career center:

_____

The Art of Budgeting

Budgeting involves a few basic steps: Determining spendable income (how much money you have after taxes), determining how much money you spend, subtracting what you spend from your after-tax income, evaluating the result, and deciding how to adjust your spending or earning based on that result. Budgeting regularly is easiest—most people budget on a month-by-month basis.

Determine Your Spendable Income

Add up all of the money you receive during the year—the actual after-tax money you have to pay your bills. You may earn some of this money every month—from a part-time or full-time job—while other income may come from summer and holiday employment. You may also receive income from gifts, scholarships, or grants. Divide the total by 12 so that you have an idea of your approximate monthly income.

Figure Out How Much You Spend

Examine your basic spending patterns for a month by recording checks you write for fixed expenses like rent and telephone and noting personal expenditures in a small notebook. Indicate any expenditure over five dollars, making sure to count smaller expenditures if frequent (e.g., daily bus fare). Some expenses, like insurance, are billed only a few times a year. In these cases, convert the expense to monthly by dividing the yearly cost by 12.

Here is a list of expenses to consider:

- rent or mortgage
- tuition (after financial aid is taken into account)
- books, lab fees, and other educational expenses
- regular bills (electric, gas, oil, phone, water)
- food, clothing, toiletries, and household supplies
- child care
- transportation and auto expenses (gas, maintenance)
- credit cards and other payments on credit (car payments)
- insurance (health, auto, homeowner's or renter's, life)
- entertainment and related items (cable television, movies, restaurants, books and magazines)
- computer-related expenses, including the cost of your on-line service
- miscellaneous unplanned expenses

Use the total of all your monthly expenses as a baseline for other months, realizing that your expenditures will vary depending on what is happening in your life.

Determine and Evaluate the Result

Subtract your monthly expenses from your monthly income. Ideally, you have money left over—to save or to spend. If you have a deficit, however, analyze the problem by looking at your budget, spending patterns, and priorities. Use your critical-thinking skills to ask some focused questions.

RISING
TO THE CHALLENGE

Chip Case
Student at Piedmont Virginia Community College, Charlottesville, Virginia

What seems at first like a minor wellness issue can gradually turn into a major problem that makes everything seem hopeless. However, Chip Case found that getting help and looking outside himself to help others can turn a life around and grant newfound perspective.

On the day that I found out I had been awarded the prestigious James R. Gilliam Scholarship from my college, Piedmont Virginia Community College, everything seemed alive. From where I stood in the campus garden, I could see the sun on the bald top of Brown's Mountain above Monticello. Ever since I was a boy I had dreamed of going to the University of Virginia. I've come a long way to be this close to that dream.

As a child, I was an enthusiastic student, but by the time I was a junior in high school, I became a classic underachiever, smoking pot and going to parties instead of studying. I was arrested for possession of marijuana when I was 17 and for being drunk in public when I was 18, and I failed out of Radford University a year later. At 19, I got my first DUI. During the years following, I worked a series of jobs while continuing to drink. In 1994, I came home from a weekend away to find the apartment I shared with my girlfriend empty and abandoned. Deciding it was time to rededicate myself to the dream of attending UVa, I moved to Charlottesville and enrolled at PVCC. However, after two months, I withdrew from all my classes. I was drinking and depressed. I got my second DUI in 1997.

Two years later, after a second girlfriend broke up with me, I started taking Valium and really drinking. I got a medical leave of absence from work and had a nervous breakdown. The night I went to find her, I got my third DUI and ended up in jail. However, something changed in the subsequent two and a half months I spent locked up. As I watched other inmates leaving, I saw that they had nothing and I had the world. I realized I had taken for granted things like a hug from my mom, a phone call, toothpaste.

i started a 12-step program. I decided to admit not only that I was an alcoholic, but that my whole life was out of control. Quitting drinking was easy. It was dealing with the problems inside that was the challenge.

I still visit that empty place within me. When things get rough, I sometimes want to get drunk to escape. I continue reworking the 12 steps; right now I'm on step number two. I know I am always one day away from being where I was. I'm really focusing on not worrying, knowing it's going to be OK. I re-enrolled at PVCC in August 2000, and celebrated my second year of sobriety in February 2001. Currently I am president of PVCC's Phi Theta Kappa chapter and active in community service.

Becoming happy again and finally being able to help myself has made me want to help others. Alcoholism is a selfish disease. Trying to help makes me forget about myself. When I share my experiences, it in turn helps me. It's a circle.

I'm definitely interested in teaching as a career, also in some sort of service. I'm not sure what route I will take. I do plan, however, to major in government and religious studies when I transfer to a four-year college. Recently I applied to UVa. Even if it doesn't go well, faith, family, and friends are the three most important things in my life. All else is a by-product of these.

Take a Moment to Consider . . .

- *What your most difficult personal wellness issue is, and what you plan to do to overcome it.*

- *What you would say are your three most important things in life.*

Question your budget. Did you forget to budget for recurring expenses, or was your budget derailed by an emergency expense that you did not foresee? Is your income sufficient for your needs?

Question your spending patterns and priorities. Did you spend money wisely or did you overspend on luxuries? Are you being hit by high interest payments on your credit card balance?

When you are spending more than you are taking in during a "typical month," you may need to adjust your budget over the long term.

Make Decisions About How to Adjust Spending or Earning

Look carefully at what may cause you to overspend and brainstorm possible solutions that address those causes. Solutions can involve either increasing resources or decreasing spending. To deal with spending, prioritize your expenditures and trim the ones you really don't need to make.

As for resources, investigate ways to take in more money, such as taking a part-time job or hunting down scholarships.

Think critically, too, about the big picture of where your money goes. How does your philosophy about money help or hurt your finances? How can you save now for important purchases you want to make later? Some level of financial sacrifice in the present might be necessary to get you where you want to go in the future. Do whatever you can to "pay yourself" every month—set aside some amount of money in a strategic way to provide for your future needs.

Managing Credit Cards

College students receive dozens of credit card offers. When used properly, credit cards are a handy alternative to cash. They can provide money for emergencies, a record of purchases, and a strong credit history (if you pay your bills on time) that will help you qualify for loans. However, it takes self-control to avoid overspending, and credit cards can plunge you into debt that can take years to erase.

| TABLE 12.7 | Learn to be a smart credit consumer. |

WHAT TO KNOW ABOUT . . .	. . . AND HOW TO USE WHAT YOU KNOW
Account balance—a dollar amount that includes any unpaid balance, new purchases and cash advances, finance charges, and fees. Updated monthly on your card statement.	Charge only what you can afford to pay at the end of the month. Keep track of your balance. Hold onto receipts and call customer service if you have questions about recent purchases.
Annual fee—the yearly cost some companies charge for owning a card.	Look for cards without an annual fee or, if you've paid your bills on time, ask your current company to waive the fee.
Annual percentage rate (APR)—the amount of interest charged on your unpaid balance, meaning the cost of credit if you carry a balance in any given month. The higher the APR, the more you pay in finance charges.	Credit card companies compete by charging different APRs, so shop around. Two websites with competitive APR information are www.studentcredit.com and www.bankrate.com. Also, watch out for low, but temporary, introductory rates that skyrocket after a few months. Look for *fixed* rates.
Available credit—the unused portion of your credit line. Determine available credit by deducting your current card balance from your credit limit.	It is important to have credit available for emergencies, so avoid charging to the limit.
Cash advance—an immediate loan, in the form of cash, from the credit card company. You are charged interest immediately and may also pay a separate transaction fee.	Use a cash advance only in emergencies because the finance charges start as soon as you complete the transaction. It is a very expensive way to borrow money.
Credit limit—the debt ceiling the card company places on your account (e.g., $1,500). The total owed, including purchases, cash advances, finance charges, and fees, cannot exceed this limit.	Credit card companies generally set low credit limits for college students. Many students get around this limit by owning more than one card, which increases the credit available but most likely increases problems as well.
Delinquent account—an account that is not paid on time or for which the minimum payment has not been met.	Avoid having a delinquent account at all costs. Not only will you be charged substantial late fees, but you also risk losing your good credit rating, affecting your ability to borrow in the future. Delinquent accounts remain part of your credit record for many years.
Finance charges—the total cost of credit, including interest and service and transaction fees.	Your goal is to incur no finance charges. The only way to do that is to pay your balance in full by the due date on your monthly statement.
Minimum payment—the smallest amount you can pay by the statement due date. The amount is set by the credit card company.	Making only the minimum payment each month can result in disaster if you charge more than you can afford. When you make a purchase, think in terms of total cost, not monthly payments.
Outstanding balance—the total amount you owe on your card.	If you carry a balance over several months, additional purchases are immediately hit with finance charges. Pay cash instead.
Past due—your account is considered "past due" when you fail to make the minimum required payment on schedule.	Three credit bureaus note past due accounts on your credit history: Experian, Trans Union, and Equifax. You can contact each bureau for a copy of your credit report to make sure there are no errors.

When you make a purchase on credit, the merchant accepts immediate payment from the credit card issuer and you accept the responsibility to pay back the money. *Every time you charge, you are creating a debt that must be repaid.* The credit card issuer earns money by charging interest on your unpaid balance. To avoid unmanageable debt that can lead to a personal financial crisis, learn as much as you can about credit cards, starting with the important concepts in Table 12.7.

The majority of American citizens have some level of debt, and many people go through periods when they have a hard time keeping up with their bills. Falling behind on payments, however, could result in a poor credit rating that makes it difficult for you to make large purchases or take out loans. Particular resources can help you solve credit problems; two are the National Foundation for Credit Counseling (www.nfcc.org) and Consumer Credit Counseling Service (1-800-338-2227).

The most basic way to stay in control is to pay bills regularly and on time. On credit card bills, pay at least the minimum amount due. If you get into trouble, deal with it in three steps. First, admit that you made a mistake, even though you may be embarrassed. Then, address the problem immediately to minimize damages. Call the **creditor** and see if you can pay your debt gradually using a payment plan. Finally, examine what got you into trouble and avoid it in the future if you can. Cut up a credit card or two if you have too many. If you clean up your act, your credit history will gradually clean up as well.

Creditor
A person or company to whom a debt is owed, usually money.

How can you live your mission?

You have explored ways to manage stress, handle personal issues such as substances and sex, think about your career, and manage money. This information, combined with what you have discovered this semester about how to learn and think, is a chapter in the long novel of your career as a learner. With what you know about yourself, you can make important decisions about how you want to continue to learn throughout your life—in school, on the job, and from day to day.

Recall your mission statement from Chapter 3. Now is a good time to revisit it and think about how you might reword or even overhaul it. It should continue to change as you develop, reflecting your goals, values, and strengths.

As you end your work in this course, consider the positive effects of doing your personal best. Your personal best is simply the best you can do, in any situation. It may not be the best you have ever done. It may include mistakes, for nothing significant is ever accomplished without making mistakes and taking risks. It may shift from situation. Whatever the circumstance, doing your best will always invite growth and success.

Aim for your personal best in everything you do. As a lifelong learner, you will always have a new direction in which to grow and a new challenge to

reflect

Describe how you use credit cards. What do you buy? How much do you spend? Do you pay in full each month or run a balance? How does using a credit card make you feel when you charge an item and when you get the bill? Would you like to change how you use credit?

& respond

face. Seek constant improvement in your studies and in your life, knowing that you are capable of such improvement. Enjoy the richness of life by living each day to the fullest, developing your talents and potential into the achievement of your most valued goals.

"And life is what we make it, always has been, always will be."

GRANDMA MOSES

TAKE ACTION

Think 50 Positive Thoughts

Make a list. The first 25 items should be things you like about yourself. You can name anything—things you can do, things you think, things you've accomplished, things you like about your physical self, and so on. The second 25 items should be things you'd like to do in your life. These can be anything from trying Vietnamese food to traveling to the Grand Canyon to keeping your home organized. They can be things you'd like to do tomorrow or things that you plan to do in 20 years. Five to ten items on each list should involve your current and future education. Be creative. Let everything be possible.

I stay open to continuous learning.

Think for a moment: Do you feel more secure when you know something solidly or when you are learning it for the first time? Most people feel more comfortable when they already know something. New learning experiences often provoke fear and avoidance in people, resulting in a retreat from the new and a settling back inside the fortress of what is known and seemingly certain. As comfortable as it seems, the spot inside the fortress can shut you off from growth and knowledge.

Staying open to continuous learning means letting yourself out of the fortress and embracing the unsure, the unanswered, and the new. Even beyond seeking new knowledge, continuous learners welcome problems and situations of conflict because they see the underlying opportunity to learn and grow. Such people are comfortable with *not* knowing—because they realize that the path of resolving what they do not know will lead them to ever-increasing knowledge. Be a continuous learner and you will spend your life improving, growing, learning, and moving ever closer to the person you know you can be.

HABITS OF MIND

REMEMBER!
the important points ∘∘∘

How do you manage stress?

Stress refers to the way your mind and body react to pressure. Although stress can take its toll, it can also provide a heightened awareness that helps you succeed. Stress management strategies include eating right, exercising, getting adequate sleep, using a schedule, and setting reasonable goals. Mental health problems may require professional help. These include depression and eating disorders (anorexia, bulimia, binge eating).

How can you make smart decisions about substances and sex?

Look critically at the facts surrounding substances and sexual activity and make choices that benefit you and others. Alcohol, tobacco, and illicit drugs are substances that, depending on how they are used, can have negative effects on your health and work. You are responsible for what you introduce into your body. If addiction becomes a problem, you can find help through counseling and medical care, detox centers, and support groups.

Consider consequences when you make decisions about sex. Birth control is a choice that some people make. Remember that STDs are diseases spread through sexual contact. The most serious STD is AIDS (acquired immune deficiency synrome), caused by HIV (human immunodeficiency virus). Latex condoms provide the best defense against AIDS.

How can you prepare for a successful career?

Investigating career paths—exploring potential careers and building knowledge and experience—is the first step to preparing for a successful career. Knowing what employers want and staying current about the working world will help you identify opportunities. Considering your learning styles will give you ideas about career areas that may suit you. When searching for a job, use resources such as your school's career planning and placement office, your network of contacts, classifieds, online services, and employment agencies. Finally, be strategic: make a career time line that illustrates the big picture, keep track of who you contact, and make sure your resume and interview are all that they can be.

How can you create a budget that works?

Budgeting involves determining spendable income (how much money you have after taxes), determining how much money you spend, subtracting what you spend from your after-tax income, evaluating the result, and deciding what changes to make in your finances based on that result. When making decisions about how to adjust spending or earning, think critically about the changes that will bring about the best result. Consider, too, how your finances might benefit from "paying yourself" every month even if it involves short-term sacrifice. Finally, think carefully about how you manage your credit cards so that you don't get into debt or bad credit trouble.

How can you live your mission?

Living your mission means knowing what you want out of life, aiming for it, and allowing it to change as your life changes. It also means doing your personal best in any situation. As a lifelong learner, seek continual improvement in your personal, educational, and professional life. Live each day to the fullest.

Name _____   Date _____

CRITICAL THINKING
APPLYING LEARNING TO LIFE

Your Budget

Part One: Where Your Money Goes. Estimate your current expenses in dollars per month, using the table below. This may require tracking expenses for a month, if you don't already keep a record of your spending. The grand total is your total monthly expenses.

EXPENSE	AMOUNT SPENT
Rent/mortgage or room and board payment	$
Utilities (electric, heat, gas, water)	$100
Food (shopping and eating out)	$50
Telephone	$40
Books, lab fees, or other educational expenses	$300
Loan payments (education or bank loans)	$1000
Car (repairs, insurance, monthly payments)	$
Gasoline/public transportation	$40
Clothing/personal items	$80
Entertainment	$
Child care (caregivers, clothing/supplies, etc.)	$
Medical care/insurance	$
Miscellaneous/unexpected	$
Other	$
GRAND TOTAL	$

(handwritten calculations in margin: 80, 60, 140, 300, 440, 50, 490, 100, 590, 1000, 590, 1590, 200, 1790, 1,790)

Part Two: Where Your Money Comes From. Calculate your average monthly income from earnings/grants/other sources. If it's easiest to come up with a yearly figure, divide by 12 to derive the monthly figure.

INCOME SOURCE	AMOUNT EARNED
Regular work salary/wages (full-time or part-time)	$ Full, 300
Grants or work-study payments	$ 1,000
Scholarships	$
Assistance from family members	$
Any independent contracting work	$
Other	$
GRAND TOTAL	$

Now, subtract the grand total of your monthly expenses (Part one) from the grand total of your monthly income (Part two):

Income per month	$ 200
Expenses per month	–$
CASH FLOW	$
Choose one. ○ I have $ + ◉ I have $ – ○ I pretty much break even	

Part Three: Adjusting Your Budget. If you have a negative cash flow, you can increase your income, decrease your spending, or do both. Go back to your list of current expenses to determine where you may be able to save. Look also at your list of income sources to determine what you can increase.

My current expenses	$	per month
I want to spend	$ 100	less per month
My current income	$	per month
I want to earn	$ 300	more per month

Evaluating your situation, describe here what you think are the two most workable ideas about how to adjust your budget. Making smart decisions now will earn you long-term financial gain.

1. _____

2. _____

TEAM BUILDING
COLLABORATIVE SOLUTIONS

Actively Dealing with Stress.

On your own, make a list of stressors—whatever events or factors cause you stress. As a class, discuss the stressors that students listed. Choose the five most common. Divide into five groups according to who would choose what stressor as his or her most important (redistribute some people if the group sizes are unbalanced). Each group should discuss its assigned stressor, brainstorming solutions and strategies. List your best coping strategies and present them to the class. Groups may want to make extra copies of the lists so that every member of the class has five, one for each stressor.

personal IMPROVEMENT *plan*

I commit to three specific career preparation strategies to improve my readiness for the workplace. From this chapter, I choose three strategies that I think will help me.

<u>Strategy 1:</u> _____

<u>Strategy 2:</u> _____

<u>Strategy 3:</u> _____

I choose one strategy to focus on (circle this strategy above) and I will:

■ describe my goal—what I want to gain by using this strategy.

_____
_____
_____

■ describe in detail how I plan to use the strategy.

_____
_____
_____
_____

■ describe how I will measure my progress toward the goal this semester.

_____
_____
_____
_____

Activate the Habit of Mind

Here's how I will *stay open to continuous learning* to achieve this goal:

_____
_____
_____
_____

SUGGESTED READINGS

Adams, Robert Lang, et al. *The Complete Résumé and Job Search Book for College Students*. Holbrook, MA: Adams Publishing, 1999.

Bolles, Richard Nelson. *What Color Is Your Parachute? 2003: A Practical Manual for Job Hunters and Career Changers*. Berkeley, CA: Ten Speed Press, 2002.

Detweiler, Gerri. *The Ultimate Credit Handbook: How to Cut Your Debt and Have a Lifetime of Great Credit*. New York: Plume, 2003.

Goleman, Daniel. *Emotional Intelligence*. New York: Bantam Books, 1997.

Kennedy, Joyce Lain. *Job Interviews for Dummies*. Foster City, CA: IDG Books Worldwide, Inc., 2000.

Mayo Clinic Family Health Book Revised, 2nd ed. New York: William Morrow, 1996.

McMahon, Susanna. *The Portable Problem Solver: Coping with Life's Stressors*. New York: Dell Publishing, 1996.

Schuckit, Marc Alan. *Educating Yourself About Alcohol and Drugs: A People's Primer*. New York: Plenum Press, 1998.

Selkowitz, Ann. *The College Student's Guide to Eating Well on Campus*. Bethesda, MD: Tulip Hill Press, 2000.

Tyson, Eric. *Personal Finance for Dummies*. Foster City, CA: IDG Books Worldwide, Inc., 2000.

INTERNET RESOURCES

Prentice Hall Student Success Supersite (fitness and well-being information): www.prenhall.com/success

Columbia University's Health Education Program: www.alice.columbia.edu

It's Your (Sex) Life: www.itsyoursexlife.com

Monster.com (online job search): www.monster.com

Tripod—Money/Business (financial and career advice, budget counseling): www.tripod.com/money_business

College Grad Job Hunter (advice on resumes, interviews, and a database of entry-level jobs): www.collegegrad.com

JobWeb (career information site for college students): www.jobweb.org

Prentice Hall Student Success Supersite—Money Matters: www.prenhall.com/success/MoneyMat/index.html

Career Path: www.prenhall.com/success/CareerPath/index.html

ENDNOTES

1. The following articles were used as sources in this section: Glenn C. Altschuler, "Adapting to College Life in an Era of Heightened Stress," *The New York Times, Education Life*, Section 4A, August 6, 2000, p. 12; Carol Hymowitz and Rachel Emma Silverman, "Can Workplace Stress Get Worse?" *The Wall Street Journal*, January 16, 2001, p. B1; Robert M. Sapolsky, "Best Ways to Reduce Everyday Levels of Stress . . . Bad Ol' Stress," *Bottom Line Personal*, January 15, 2000, p. 13; Kate Slaboch, "Stress and the College Student: A Debate," www.jour.unr.edu/outpost/voices/voi.slaboch.stress.htm, April 4, 2001; University of South Florida, The Counseling Center for Human Development, "Coping with Stress in College," http://usfweb.usf.edu/counsel/self-hlp/stress.htm, April 4, 2001; Jodi Wilgoren, "Survey Shows High Stress Levels in College Freshmen," *The New York Times*, January 23, 2000, p. NA.

2. Kim Hubbard, Anne-Marie O'Neill, and Christina Cheakalos, "Out of Control," *People*, April 12, 1999, p. 54.

3. H. Wechsler et al., "Changes in Binge Drinking and Related Problems Among American College Students Between 1993 and 1997," *Journal of American College Health*, vol. 47, September 1998, p. 57.

4. Ibid, pp. 63–64.

5. National Institute on Alcohol Abuse and Alcoholism, No. 29 PH 357, July 1995.

6. J. McGinnis and W. Foege, "Actual Causes of Death in the United States," *Journal of the American Medical Association* (JAMA) 270.18, American Medical Association, Nov. 10, 1993, p. 2208.

7. National Institute on Drug Abuse, Capsule Series C-83-08, "Cigarette Smoking," Bethesda, MD: National Institutes of Health, 1994.

8. National Institute on Drug Abuse, "National Survey Results on Drug Abuse from Monitoring the Future Study," Bethesda, MD: National Institutes of Health, 1994.

9. www.usdoj.gov/dea/concern/mdma/mdmaindex.htm; U. S. Department of Justice, Drug Enforcement Administration.

10. U. S. Bureau of Labor. Table 1: Fastest growing occupations covered in the 2000–01 Occupational Outlook Handbook, 1998–2008. Available: http://stats.bls.gov/news.release/ooh.t01.htm. Accessed on-line June 14, 2001.

11. Steven Greenhouse, "Equal Work, Less-Equal Perks," *The New York Times*, March 30, 1998, pp. D1, D6.

12. Daniel Goleman, *Working with Emotional Intelligence*. New York: Bantam Books, 1998, pp. 26–27.

13. U. S. Department of Education, National Center for Education Statistics, *Profile of Undergraduates in U. S. Postsecondary Education Institutions: 1995–96*, NCES 98-084, by Laura J. Horn, Jennifer Berktold, Andrew G. Malizio, Project Officer, and MPR Associates, Inc. Washington, DC: U. S. Government Printing Office, 1998, pp. 4, 31.

Multiple Choice. Circle or highlight the answer that seems to fit best.

1. Prejudiced people judge others before they know them for all of the following reasons *except*

   A They may be afraid of people from different backgrounds.

   B. It is easier to blame others when things go wrong than to look for personal flaws.

   C. They may generalize about all people from a racial or an ethnic group if they had a bad experience with one person from that group.

   D. They want to judge all people against the same standards.

2. Students who experience stereotype vulnerability may

   A. call attention to themselves as members of a minority group.

   B. be self conscious because they see themselves as underachievers.

   C. feel superior to others because of their minority status.

   D. distance themselves from the qualities they think others associate with their group and avoid asking for help because they fear perpetuating a group stereotype.

3. The goal of stress management is to

   A. eliminate all stress from your life.

   B. focus only on school-related stress.

   C. learn to blame all stressful situations on others.

   D. develop strategies for handling the stresses that are an inevitable part of life.

4. AIDS can best be described as a

   A. sexually transmitted disease that can be managed with proper medical treatment.

   B. sexually transmitted disease that will never have a cure.

   C. sexually transmitted disease that only affects certain high-risk groups.

   D. disease that can only be spread through sexual contact.

5. *Networking* can be defined as

   A. visiting your instructor during office hours.

   B. the exchange of information or services among individuals, groups, or institutions.

   C. discovering your ideal career.

   D. making a strategic plan.

6. Annual percentage rate (APR) refers to

   A. the unused portion of your credit card line.

   B. annual credit card fee.

   C. interest charged on your unpaid credit card balance.

   D. the amount of money you are able to pay each year.

Fill-in-the-Blank. Complete the following sentences with the appropriate word(s) or phrase(s) that best reflect what you learned in the chapter. Choose from the items that follow each sentence.

1. _____ factors play an important role in how _____ are interpreted. (Personal/body movements, Biological/verbal cues, Cultural/nonverbal cues)

2. _____ criticism involves goodwill suggestions for improvement. (Nonconstructive, Direct, Constructive)

3. The three most common eating disorders are _____, _____, and _____. (anorexia nervosa/food allergies/binge drinking, anorexia nervosa/bulimia/binge eating, constant dieting/eating too much fat/bulimia)

4. Of all alcohol consumption, _____ (alcoholism, binge drinking, withdrawal), meaning having _____ (5, 7, 3) or more drinks at a sitting, is associated with the greatest problems.

5. Two effective ways to build career knowledge and experience are _____ and _____. (job hunting/networking, internships/volunteering, learning style/critical thinking)

6. The debt ceiling a credit card company places on your account is called a _____. (cash advance, account balance, credit limit)

Essay Questions. The following essay questions will help you organize and communicate your ideas in writing, just as you must do on an essay test. Before you begin answering a question, spend a few minutes planning (brainstorm possible approaches, write a thesis statement, jot down main thoughts in outline or think link form). To prepare yourself for actual test conditions, limit writing time to no more than 20 minutes per question.

1. Discuss the mind–body connection—specifically, the impact of diet, exercise, sleep, and medical care on the development and management of stress. Describe the changes you hope to make in your stress management strategies as a result of the information you have read in this chapter.

2. Choose three important skills you have developed during this course. Explain how they will contribute to your success in the remainder of your college experience and in your life beyond school.

SUCCESS BREAKTHROUGH

Frida Kahlo

Mexican Surrealist Painter

Frida Kahlo turned her biggest setback into a life's work when, following an accident that left her permanently crippled and in constant pain, she found new outlets of artistic expression. Her physical suffering and her tumultuous marriage to world-famous muralist Diego Rivera provided inspiration for her intensely autobiographical paintings.

Born in Mexico City in 1907 to Jewish immigrants, Frida Kahlo was a wild, rebellious child, despite having one leg crippled by polio. Blessed with keen intelligence, Kahlo was one of a handful of girls to attend the prestigious National Preparatory School. It was there that her prankster tendencies blossomed as she joined a pack of other students to torment unsuspecting adults. One of their victims was the famous Mexican muralist Diego Rivera, who had been commissioned to paint a mural in the school auditorium. As she threw water balloons at the artist and soaped the stairs so he would fall, she had no way of knowing that this man—20 years her senior—would one day be her husband.

When Kahlo was 18 years old, her life took a terrible turn when the bus in which she was riding crashed with a streetcar. In the accident, a metal pole impaled her, and she suffered a broken spinal column, collarbone, pelvis, and ribs, and shattered bones in her right leg and foot. Forced to wear a full-body cast for a month, Kahlo was in despair, and expressed her suffering in her letters. She wrote: "Yesterday I was in a lot of pain and very sad; you can't imagine how desperate a person gets with this sickness; I feel a frightful discomfort I can't explain, and there's also a pain that nothing can stop."

Although Kahlo eventually regained her ability to walk, the accident left her permanently crippled. Unable to resume her active lifestyle following the accident, she turned to painting to relieve the boredom of confinement. She endured numerous operations and experienced pain and fatigue for the rest of her life. To cope with the constant pain, she kept up a whirlwind social life. The combination of suffering and vivacity gave her a mystique that attracted Rivera's attention when they met for the second time. They married in 1929.

The accident was not only a catalyst for Kahlo's art, it was also one of her major artistic themes. Many of her deeply autobiographical paintings contain references to mortality and to physical suffering. Sometimes she depicted her suffering as expressions of longing, including the longing to have children. During her marriage, she suffered a number of miscarriages, each of which was a painful reminder of her infertility. She expressed her frustrations in her paintings through the themes of childbirth, blood, and fertility. Her passionate, tumultuous marriage added further inspiration to Kahlo's work. Some of her paintings express their complex relationship and the rejection she felt over Rivera's repeated extramarital affairs.

While Kahlo worked in the artistic shadow of her husband for most of her career, Rivera was one of her greatest admirers. He helped her style herself as an authentic Mexican artist, stressing her indigenous heritage, and encouraging her to wear the colorful traditional clothing that became her trademark. Her distinctive artistic style with its sense of suffering, symbolism, and primitive nationalism distinguished her work from his, and the more than 200 paintings she produced earned her the attention and admiration of the art world.

Eventually Kahlo's physical suffering became too much for her, and she died at the age of 47. By then, she had left an indelible impression on Mexican Art.

Take a Moment to Consider . . .

- *How important a positive attitude is to your success, especially if you are faced with serious personal problems.*

- *When something good in your life emerged from a period of difficulty or hopelessness.*

Source: Information about Frida Kahlo's life from www.brain-juice.com/cgibin/show_bio.cgi?p_id=19 and www.udel.edu/eli/rw4/frida/fridabio.html.

SUCCESS
BREAKTHROUGH

Matthew Alexander Henson
North Pole Explorer

Matthew Henson lived as a free black man at a time when emancipation was still new. Although he encountered racism, he didn't let things get in the way of his sense of adventure. Henson's most significant achievement was being part of the first party to reach the North Pole.

Matthew Henson was born to free black parents in 1866, one year after the emancipation of the slaves. One event made a huge impression on him while he was still very young. Frederick Douglass, a famous black abolitionist, gave a speech at a ceremony honoring Abraham Lincoln. He spoke of overcoming racial prejudice and touted education as a critical component of success. This must have struck a chord with Henson. Combining a daring spirit with a drive to learn, he became such an accomplished adventurer that the color of his skin became secondary to his achievements.

Tragically, he was orphaned at the age of 13. He worked at a restaurant to support himself. A regular of the establishment was a sailor who told tales of his life on the high seas. These stories captivated the already restless young Henson, leading him to seek more adventuresome employment. He traveled the 40 miles from home to Baltimore on foot and went straight to the harbor to try to find work as a cabin boy. Impressed by Henson's self-assured manner, the captain of the *Katie Hines* asked Henson to join the ship. The captain saw the potential in his new cabin boy and made a special effort to educate him. He gave him lessons in reading and writing as well as mechanics, first aid, and other skills important to a well-trained seaman.

Not all of the shipmates were as reasonable as the captain. One white seaman insulted Henson and beat him up. Humiliated, Henson doubted whether any amount of accomplishment would allow him to be judged by something other than his race. Fortunately, the captain was able to convince him that he could use his intelligence to overcome prejudice and gain respect. After five years on the ship, Henson had become a valued crew member. His travels took him to Asia, Africa, Europe, and the seas of the Russian Arctic. When the captain died, Henson left the ship.

Years later, he was hired by Robert Peary as an assistant on a Nicaraguan expedition to chart a course that would join the Pacific and the Atlantic oceans. Although he was initially employed as a servant, he proved that he could learn quickly and became a highly skilled member of the surveying crew. When Peary planned an expedition to the North Pole, he selected Henson as part of the team. At this time, no one had yet managed to get closer than 600 miles from the pole.

The Peary team mounted a total of seven arctic expeditions. As he weathered each expedition, Matthew Henson gradually increased his ability to travel in the inhospitable region. In this part of the world the darkness of his skin was an asset, since it helped him gain acceptance and assistance from the native Inuit people. In addition to teaching him their language, the Inuit taught Henson the intricacies of arctic travel and survival.

To make the voyage the team had to travel at least 18 hours out of each day, travelling during the night and sleeping during the warmest part of the day. It was Henson's job to break trail, and sometimes he would end up as much as five days ahead of Peary. When he mounted a final expedition to the North Pole in 1909, his skills led others to credit him as the most valuable member of Peary's team. This last expedition was successful, and Matthew Henson became one of the first Americans to set foot on the North Pole—an accomplishment that commanded the respect he had earned.

Take a Moment to Consider . . .

- *When someone taught you a lesson, or helped you learn information, that changed your life.*

- *Whether your identity or appearance tends to lead people to an inaccurate impression of you—and what you can do to help them understand who you are.*

Source: From *Matthew Henson: Explorer*, by Michael Gilman. Danbury, CT: Grolier, Inc., 1988.

ANSWER KEY

FOR BECOMING A BETTER TEST TAKER

Part I: Getting Ready To Learn

Multiple Choice

1. D
2. D
3. C
4. A
5. D
6. C

Fill-in-the-Blank

1. academic integrity/respect/responsibility
2. learning preferences/personality traits
3. priorities
4. interests/abilities
5. creativity
6. barrier/resistance to change

Part II: Targeting Success In School

Multiple Choice

1. A
2. B
3. C
4. A
5. B
6. A

Fill-in-the-Blank

1. cue column
2. mnemonic device
3. Freewriting/uncensored/planning
4. Recite
5. Action
6. Pattern

Part III: Creating Success

Multiple Choice

1. D
2. D
3. D
4. A
5. B
6. C

Fill-in-the-blank

1. Cultural/nonverbal cues
2. Constructive
3. anorexia nervosa/bulimia/binge eating
4. binge drinking/5
5. internships/volunteering
6. credit limit

INDEX